Illocutionary Acts and
Sentence Meaning

Also by William P. Alston:

Divine Nature and Human Language:
  Essays in Philosophical Theology

Epistemic Justification:
  Essays in the Theory of Knowledge

Perceiving God:
  The Epistemology of Religious Experience

The Reliability of Sense Perception

Philosophy of Language

A Realist Conception of Truth

Religious Belief and Philosophical Thought:
  Readings in the Philosophy of Religion (editor)

The Problems of Philosophy: Introductory Readings
  (coeditor with Richard B. Brandt)

Readings in Twentieth-Century Philosophy
  (coeditor with George Nakhnikian)

Illocutionary Acts and Sentence Meaning

WILLIAM P. ALSTON

Cornell University Press

Ithaca and London

First published 2000 by Cornell University Press

Printed in the United States of America

Cornell University Press strives to use environmentally responsible suppliers and materials to the fullest extent possible in the publishing of its books. Such materials include vegetable-based, low-VOC inks, and acid-free papers that are recycled, totally chlorine-free, or partly composed of nonwood fibers. Books that bear the logo of the FSC (Forest Stewardship Council) use paper taken from forests that have been inspected and certified as meeting the highest standards for environmental and social responsibility. For further information, visit our website at www.cornellpress.cornell.edu.

Library of Congress Cataloging-in-Publication Data

Alston, William P.
Illocutionary acts and sentence meaning /
William P. Alston
p.   cm.
Includes bibliographical references and index.
ISBN 0-8014-3669-9 (cloth)
1. Speech acts (Linguistics)   2. Semantics.
3. Grammar, Comparative and general—
Sentences.   I. Title.

P95.55.A47 2000
306.44—dc21   99-052786

Cloth printing
10 9 8 7 6 5 4 3 2 1

 FSC Trademark © 1996 Forest Stewardship Council A.C.
SW-COC-098

FOR GEORGE NAKHNIKIAN

FELLOW PILGRIM

Contents

Preface

This book has been a long time in gestation. Or, to be more accurate, a long time has passed since the author had the basic idea of the position developed in this book. During most of that time the book (or incipient beginnings thereof) wasn't receiving much in the way of gestation. The first glimmerings surfaced in the late 1950s. Despite writing a series of articles setting out pieces of the project (see bibliography), and despite giving courses and seminars on the philosophy of language fairly regularly up to the early 1980s, I did not produce anything of a book-length format until the late 1970s. By 1981 I had what I regarded at that time as a more or less complete draft of a book. But it remained gathering dust on my shelf until some two years ago, when I decided it was now or never. As usual, the refurbishing job was more extensive than anticipated, but by now it would appear that I will be only slightly late for the new millennium.

If truth be told, I am more than a little embarrassed over the long delay in publishing this book. But at least I have the consolation of some distinguished precedents. In the preface to his *Frege's Philosophy of Language* (1973) Michael Dummett writes: "This book has been a very long time in the writing". After giving some reasons for this that are internal to the subject matter and his relation thereto, he continues.

In the autumn of 1964, most of the book . . . was in a finished state, and it needed only a few months' work to complete. That I did not finish it early in

1965 was due to a conscious choice. I conceived it my duty to involve myself actively in opposition to the racism which was becoming more and more manifest in English life. For four full years, this work occupied virtually the whole of my spare time. (x)

This distinguished precedent is only partial. Not only was Dummett's delay just half as long as mine, but his chief reason for it was quite different. My "spare time" from 1981 to 1997 was mostly taken up with work on philosophical theology and epistemology, rather than with combating racism, which is certainly at least as manifest in the United States as in England. But whatever the reasons, and however meritorious they may or may not be, I cannot, despite some ingenious philosophical arguments to the contrary, do anything to change the past and alter the course of my philosophical work from 1981 on. Hence I must bite the bullet and present this work to the public in 2000 or forever hold my peace. I am encouraged in this by the reflection that philosophy differs from the more empirical and experimental disciplines, where the phrase "recent discussion" is not applied to anything more than six months old. Perhaps ideas about speech acts and linguistic meaning that originally germinated forty years ago may still have something to contribute to the present philosophical scene.

This is an opportunity for me to express appreciation to the many philosophers of language from whose works I have learned much about the subject. The ones who especially stand out in this connection are C. I. Lewis, J. L. Austin, H. P. Grice, P. F. Strawson, W. V. Quine, Jerry Fodor, Jerry Katz, David Shwayder, John Searle, Stephen Schiffer, David Lewis, Hilary Putnam, Zeno Vendler, Jonathan Bennett, and Saul Kripke. The reader of this book will realize that the list contains a generous selection both of those with whom I am fundamentally in sympathy and of those whom I basically oppose. In philosophy one often learns at least as much from the latter as from the former.

Turning to personal contacts, I have been the fortunate recipient of criticism, stimulation, enlightenment, and suggestion from more people than I could possibly enumerate here. In the 1950s and 1960s I had invaluable discussions with David Shwayder and John Searle, whose work intersected mine more than anyone else's. My Michigan colleagues, Richard Cartwright and the late William Frankena and Paul Henle, were the source of much stimulation and inspiration. During the 1950s and 1960s I had innumerable conversations on this as on many other matters with my dear friend, George Nakhnikian. At the University of Illinois in the late 1970s I profited greatly from interaction with Charles Caton and Hugh Chandler on these matters. While on sabbatical in Oxford in 1974–75 I had a number of sessions with J. O. Urmson that were powerfully illuminating.

From the late 1960s on, but especially since 1980 when we have been colleagues at Syracuse, Jonathan Bennett has been an unfailing resource in this as in many other matters. Despite feeling strongly that this project is fundamentally wrongheaded, he heroically undertook to read the manuscript and provided his usual share of penetrating comments. Others who commented extensively on the manuscript were John Hawthorne, Nicholas Wolterstorff, and a group of graduate students and faculty who met with me weekly in the spring of 1998 to discuss the work, chapter by chapter. All these people helped me to see various aspects of the topic that had eluded me until then.

The students in my courses and seminars in philosophy of language over the years have influenced my thinking about the problems in many more ways than I could pin down at this point. Moreover, they have been responsible for welcome lighter moments. I will never forget one incident. I had asked the students to take the sentence 'Would you give me a hand with this box?' and apply my techniques to the analysis of an illocutionary act for the performance of which this sentence is suited. One imaginative member of the class constructed the following scenario. A plastic surgeon has been constructing a hand for the victim of an accident. When the patient comes in to pick it up, he is handed an old battered shoebox, whereupon he indignantly says "Would you give me a hand with *this* box?!!".

I wish to express heartfelt appreciation for the encouragement and support tendered me in this and other endeavors by John G. Ackerman, director of Cornell University Press, and to the editorial staff there. It is a pleasure to work with them. Many thanks go to the secretarial staff of the Department of Philosophy of Syracuse University—Sue McDougall, Lisa Mowns, and Melissa Linde—for their untiring labors in so many matters and for their unfailing kindness and good cheer that brighten many a gloomy central New York day. And last but certainly not least, my love and gratitude go to my wife, Valerie, for cheerfully putting up with what seemed to be a never-ending series of revisions and for her unfailing love and support.

WILLIAM P. ALSTON

Syracuse, New York

Illocutionary Acts and
Sentence Meaning

Introduction

This book is Janus-faced. On one side it is an account of the nature, variety, and interrelations of illocutionary acts (IA's)—with side glances at other types of speech acts. But in addition to whatever other interest—intrinsic or extrinsic—attaches to that topic, the account of illocutionary acts is used here as the basis for a theory of the nature of sentence meaning, that it consists in *illocutionary act potential*. And this is the other side of the Janus figure.

Illocutionary acts have been called upon to perform many different philosophical tasks. John Searle (1983) has used them as the basis of a general account of the structure and intentionality of propositional attitudes. Nicholas Wolterstorff (1980) has used them as a model for artistic creation. They have figured heavily in the treatment of pragmatics in linguistics (Tsohatzidis 1994, pt. II). It is less common for thinkers to call upon them to provide an account of the semantic side of language. Indeed, J. L. Austin (1962), who first introduced the term 'illocutionary act', thought of such acts as something over and above the "sense and reference" of an utterance. Searle (1969) hints at what I call an "illocutionary act potential" account of sentence meaning, but the idea is not developed there or elsewhere in his writings. In a series of articles and a book I have adumbrated the illocutionary act–based account of sentence meaning developed in this book, but it is not until now that any full statement has been forthcoming.

1

This treatment of illocutionary acts and sentence meaning is based in good part on some familiar themes: the dependence of meaning on use, the crucial role of rules for both illocutionary acts and sentence meaning, the conditions of linguistic fluency as a key to understanding linguistic meaning. And there are some less familiar ones as well: the independence of illocutionary act performance and speaker meaning from hearer responses, the normative character of illocutionary act performance, and the radical underdetermination of reference by meaning. But even the familiar themes are given some new twists. I have been more serious about rules in a distinctive sense of the term than many who brandish the term. And there is a more inclusive conception of "use" than we find in verificationist-minded theorists.

Finally, I have striven to carry the development to the point of providing detailed analyses and analysis-schemata for illocutionary act types, and spelling out in detail samples of rules being governed by which, I claim, gives sentences their meanings. Too many treatments of these issues content themselves with programmatic statements and stop short of the nitty-gritty. I have at least stuck my neck out to provide a clear target for refutation.

Given the long and complex organization of the book, it may be useful to provide a short preview of the highlights.

Part I, dealing with speech acts, comprises five chapters. Chapter 1 deals with types of speech acts, acts performed in speech (where 'speech' is used broadly to cover any use of language or surrogates for language in communication). The taxonomy emerges from a critical discussion of J. L. Austin's path-breaking work, *How to Do Things with Words* (1962). Like Austin I present a trichotomy, though with important differences. Mine looks like this.

1. *Sentential* act—Uttering a sentence or some sentence surrogate.
2. *Illocutionary* act—Uttering a sentence (or sentence surrogate) with a certain *content*, the sort of act paradigmatically reported by "indirect discourse", as in 'Jones asked where the nearest newsstand is'.
3. Perlocutionary acts—Producing an effect on some audience by an utterance.

These acts constitute a hierarchy. One performs an illocutionary act by (in) performing a sentential act. And one (normally) performs a perlocutionary act by (in) performing an illocutionary act. A typical act of speech involves all three.

Chapters 2 and 3 are concerned with the ontology of illocutionary acts—*what it is* to perform an illocutionary act of a certain type. Chapter 2 gives reasons for rejecting a reduction of an illocutionary act to doing something with an intention to produce certain effects on hearers, a view developed in Schiffer 1972. Chapter 3 develops the idea that to perform an illocutionary act of a certain type is to give one's utterance (sentential act) a certain *normative* status. This is initially put in terms of *taking responsibility* for certain conditions holding. So to ask someone to open a certain door is to issue an utterance, taking responsibility for its being the case that, for example, the door in question is closed and that the speaker is interested in its being opened. The relevant notion of *taking responsibility* for the satisfaction of certain conditions is initially explicated in terms of rendering oneself liable to correction, blame, reproach, or sanctions in case the conditions in question are not satisfied. But then it is argued that such liability presupposes *rules* in the background. It is when one's utterance is subject to rules that require satisfaction of certain conditions for correct utterance that one is liable to negative reactions in case the conditions are not satisfied. Thus the final explication of *taking responsibility for the satisfaction of conditions* C is in terms of uttering a sentence as subject to a rule that requires C as a condition of correct utterance. This is all developed in the context of an extended critical discussion of Searle's 1969 analysis of making a promise. A tentative substitute analysis in terms of the above is presented.

Chapters 4 and 5 survey the most general categories of illocutionary acts and settle various issues concerning the analysis of types in each category. Following Austin's lead, but with major modifications, I arrive at the following categories.

1. *Assertives*: merely asserting, acknowledging, concluding, remarking, insisting.
2. *Directives*: ordering, requesting, suggesting, imploring.
3. *Commissives*: promising, contracting, betting, etc.
4. *Exercitives*: adjourning, appointing, nominating, pardoning, etc.
5. *Expressives*: thanking, congratulating, expressing contempt, relief, enthusiasm, delight, etc.

This is only a rough indication of the character and composition of each category. The fully developed view is much more complicated. For example, the illocutionary acts in the exercitive category include not adjourning or pardoning but rather *declaring x to be adjourned* and *purporting to pardon*.

After some false starts a fairly unified pattern of analysis for illocutionary act types in all categories is developed. For acts in all categories except assertives, to perform an illocutionary act of a given type is simply to perform a sentential act, taking responsibility for the holding of certain conditions.[1] Different particular types are distinguished by the detailed content of those conditions, while the major categories are distinguished by the general pattern of the conditions for which one takes responsibility. Thus an exercitive involves, inter alia, taking responsibility for one's having a certain kind of authority, while a commissive involves, inter alia, taking responsibility for one's having a certain intention. As for assertives, though there too what one takes responsibility for is the heart of the matter, it is also required that one's sentential vehicle, if one is not speaking elliptically, presents the propositional content in a fully explicit fashion.

Part II of the book develops an account of the meaning of sentences that builds on the theory of illocutionary acts developed in Part I. Chapter 6 lays out the concept of meaning employed in this investigation, specifies what the account of sentence meaning is and is not designed to do, and sketches the main outlines of the view. As for the concept of meaning involved, it is specified by the use of several axioms, the most important of which are the following.

A2. The fact that an expression has a certain meaning is what enables it to play a distinctive role in communication.

A3. Knowledge of the meaning of the sentence uttered is the linguistic knowledge a hearer needs in order to understand what is being said.

A5. Reference is (only) partly determined by meaning.

As for the kind of theory aimed at, it is ontological in character. I seek to understand *what it is* for a sentence to have a certain meaning. I am concerned with the ontological status of semantic facts, what kind of fact is the fact that a sentence, or other meaningful linguistic unit, means what it does. This is my quarry rather than, for example, an analysis of the concept of linguistic meaning or of the term 'means'. Nor is my quest for a method of discovering the meaning of linguistic expressions, much less a method for describing the semantics of a language.

As indicated at the outset of this introduction, the main thesis to be defended is that sentence meaning is a matter of *illocutionary act potential*. For a sentence to mean so-and-so is for it to be usable (standardly) to perform illocutionary acts of a certain type. This is the basic way in which the semantic aspect of a language, as an abstract system, is a function of what speakers of the language do in their communicative use of it. This thesis is arrived at by a sort of inversion of axiom A2. Sentence meaning enables a sentence to play a certain role in communication just because the sentence's meaning what it does simply consists in its usability to play that role.

---

[1] There is at least one other condition, but it is of a blanket sort that does nothing to distinguish one IA type from another.

Combine that with the demarcation of the semantically crucial role as illocutionary act performance, and we get the result that a sentence's meaning what it does consists in its being (standardly) usable to perform illocutionary acts of a certain type.

In the previous three paragraphs I oscillated between speaking generally of linguistic meaning and speaking more specifically of sentence meaning. That was deliberate. Although I am interested in understanding what it is for any meaningful unit of language to mean what it does, I restrict myself in this book to the meaning of sentences, so far as any detailed treatment is concerned. I can readily explain why I start there. Since my lodestar for semantics is the idea that the meaning of a linguistic unit is a function of what it is *used* by speakers to do (the Use Principle), the appropriate entry point for the elucidation of the nature of meaning has to do with units that can be used to perform complete speech acts, and these are sentences, or lesser units doing duty as elliptical for sentences. (And as I point out in Chapter 6, the priority of the *concept* of sentence meaning to the *concept* of word meaning is quite compatible with the priority of words to sentences in the description of the semantic structure of a language and in the explanation of the fact that a particular sentence means what it does.) But this consideration only explains why I start with sentence meaning. It does nothing to explain, or justify, my stopping there. That is dictated solely by economic and strategic considerations. The book is quite long enough with those limitations. For the meaning of subsentential units I must content myself with indicating the direction in which the book points us, leaving the treatment itself for another occasion.

To return to the Illocutionary Act Potential (IA potential) account of sentence meaning, if it were not further qualified it would be grotesquely inadequate. An unqualified formulation implies that for every difference in IA potential there is a difference in meaning. But it is obvious that a sentence can be used with one and the same meaning to perform illocutionary acts of many different types. The sentence 'The door is open' can be used with one and the same meaning to perform illocutionary acts of the following types and many, many more.

1. Asserting of a certain door that it is open.
2. Asserting that the only kitchen refrigerator door belonging to the speaker is open.
3. Admitting that the only kitchen refrigerator door belonging to the speaker is open.

To avoid this easy refutation the concept of a *matching illocutionary act* for a given sentence meaning is developed. Briefly, an illocutionary act type matches a given sentence meaning *iff* a hearer, just by knowing that the sentence was uttered with that meaning (together with restrictions as to the use the speaker was making of the sentence, roughly that it was a literal, nonderivative use), thereby knows that the speaker intended to be performing an illocutionary act of that type. Thus the matching illocutionary type for the normal meaning of 'The door is open' is 1. from the above list, whereas 3. is the matching illocutionary type for the normal meaning of 'I admit that my kitchen refrigerator door is open'. We can then put the IA potential thesis by saying that for a sentence to have a certain meaning is for it to be (standardly usable) to perform illocutionary acts of the matching type.

In Part I the preferred formulation for the analysis of illocutionary acts was in terms of rule governance. To perform an illocutionary act of a certain type is to utter a sentence (or sentence surrogate) as subject to a rule that requires the satisfaction of certain conditions for permissible utterance. Call such rules *illocutionary rules* (*I-rules*). That result gives us a way of specifying the basis of IA potential. What gives a sentence the potential for being (standardly) usable to perform illocutionary acts of a certain type is its being governed by a certain I-rule. Chapters 7 and 8 contain a detailed investigation of I-rules. A number of thorny problems have to be resolved before we have a satisfactory schema for the formulation of such rules. The obvious first step is simply to list the conditions one takes responsibility for in, for example, reporting that the temperature is rising, and taking an I-rule for 'It's getting hot in here' (the one that constitutes its potential for making that report) to require those conditions for permissible utterance. That won't work. For since the sentence can also be used metaphorically to remark that the argument is becoming acerbic, it is permissible to use it to say that without the conditions associated with *The temperature is rising in here* being satisfied. The rule has to be formulated in such a way as to allow for those and various other possibilitie while, at the same time, rendering the sentence usable to perform the illocutionary act in question. I won't try to spell out the solution here but simply refer the reader to 7.4.[2]

Another complication has to do with singular reference. We want the rule for 'She has the flu' to endow the sentence with the capacity for being used to assert of some particular female that she has the flu, not to assert, unspecifically, that some female or other has the flu. And yet the rule cannot require, for permissible utterance, of any one particular female that she has the flu. For the sentence, by virtue of meaning what it does, can be used to assert of any one of innumerable females that she has the flu. I refer the reader to 7.6 for the solution.

In Chapter 8 I look into the general character and ontological status of I-rules. I have been presenting them as what Searle calls "regulative" rules,

---

[2] When referring to a section of a chapter I will specify number of chapter and number of section, separated by a period.

as contrasted with what he calls "constitutive" rules. I argue against Searle that these are not disjoint classes of rules, but that the same rule can be correctly termed regulative or constitutive, depending on what we think of it as governing. Thus my I-rules *regulate* sentential acts and are *constitutive* of illocutionary acts. They give conditions of the permissible utterance of sentences, and by uttering a sentence as subject to such a regulative rule, the utterance is *thereby* constituted as an illocutionary act of a certain type. Next, since I-rules are seldom formulated, I consider what mode of reality *unformulated* rules have, and what it is for such rules to be in force in a society. Finally, rules like I-rules are contrasted with David Lewis's account of *conventions* (1969), which are taken by various theorists, most notably Jonathan Bennett (1976), as crucial for meaning.

Thus far Part II has been mostly preoccupied with developing, expounding, and applying the IA potential theory of sentence meaning. Relatively little has been done to defend it as superior to its rivals. Chapter 9 is devoted to that task. The scattered remarks earlier in the book concerning the plausibility of the theory, its efficacy in application, and the ways it handles objections are reviewed and expanded. But the bulk of the chapter consists of a critical review of alternative accounts of sentence meaning, and arguments for the superiority of the IA potential theory where its rivals are defective. The one alternative that had been treated earlier is the perlocutionary potential theory, varying forms of which are found in Grice 1989 and Bennett 1976. Most of the attention in Chapter 9 is given to referential theories of varying degrees of sophistication and to truth condition theories. It is argued that all these rivals suffer from disabilities from which the IA potential theory is happily free.

I have assigned numbers consecutively throughout the book to the important principles (Roman numerals), analyses of illocutionary act concepts (I), rules (R), definitions or other explications of terms (D), and axioms of meaning (A). The only exception to this consecutive numbering is a gap in the I-rules in Chapter 7. There are no I-rules numbered 17–22. I did this in order to use the same numbers for correlated I-rules and IA analyses in the list of examples in 7.10. In an appendix I list the definitions, principles, and axioms of meaning, and the schemata for the analysis of IA's of various types to be found in Chapters 4 and 5. Finally, here is a list of the chief abbreviations.

IA—illocutionary act
I-rule—illocutionary rule
U—speaker (utterer)
H—hearer
S—sentence
p—a variable for propositions
U R's that p—U takes responsibility for its being the case that p.

PART 1

THE NATURE OF
ILLOCUTIONARY ACTS

CHAPTER ONE

The Stratification of Linguistic Behavior

My first task in this book is to develop an account of illocutionary acts (IA's). That will involve (a) making explicit what it is to perform an illocutionary act of a certain type and (b) surveying and classifying the variety of such acts. But before addressing myself to that I must indicate the territory I will be examining. 'Illocutionary act' is a technical philosophical term. We cannot enter onto a discussion of illocutionary acts without a preliminary location of such acts, the way we can tackle knowledge or truth or causation on the basis of the working grasp of these concepts every normal human being has. While doing that we will look at the relations of illocutionary acts to speech acts of other sorts.

Since all twentieth-century discussion of speech acts stems from J. L. Austin's seminal work, *How to Do Things with Words*, it would be natural to begin with a look at how Austin, who coined the term 'illocutionary act', identifies that category. But, as will appear shortly, Austin's account is rife with ambiguities and puzzles. Hence I prefer to begin by setting out my way of locating illocutionary acts, then using that as a guide through the twists and turns of Austin's discussion.

i. Types of Speech Acts

I begin with a brief survey of types of speech acts, the variety of things people do in speaking.[1] The types in which I am interested can all be ex-

---

[1] I follow current practice in using terms for speech in a broadened sense to cover any employment of language. Thus 'utterance' is to be taken to range over the production of any

emplified in a single utterance. If a person uttered 'The gate is unlocked' the following might all be correct reports of what she did at that time.

A.

1. U said 'The gate is unlocked'.[2]
2. U asserted that the gate was unlocked.
3. U told Smith that the gate was unlocked.
4. U got it across to Smith that the gate was unlocked.
5. U made me wonder who had been here recently.

In one and the same breath the speaker did all these things and perhaps many more. This phenomenon of performing acts of many different types with the same bodily movements is by no means confined to speech. If a person presses a button at a certain moment, he may thereby do all the following and much more.

B.

1. P pressed a button.
2. P closed a circuit.
3. P started an engine.
4. P followed instructions.

Before I undertake to separate out illocutionary acts from this panoply of linguistic doings, we must deal with the question of how to talk about situations in which a number of nonequivalent specifications can be given of what someone did in a single bodily movement. Should we say that the agent performs a number of different actions, as many as there are nonequivalent specifications, or should we say that the various reports make explicit different aspects of one and the same action? When U said 'The gate is unlocked', told Smith that the gate was unlocked, and made me wonder who had been here recently, did she thereby do three different things, or were these all aspects of one thing she did? This is a question about the individuation of actions. Ordinary speech pulls us in both directions. On the one hand, it seems right to say that "U did all the different things I listed". On the other hand, it seems right that her saying 'The gate is unlocked' *was* a case of telling Smith that the gate was unlocked, thereby suggesting that these are two ways of characterizing the same action.

Both modes of individuation are represented in contemporary action theory, the former by, for example, Goldman 1970, the latter by, for ex-

---

linguistic token, whether by speech, writing, or other means. And 'speaker of a language' is to be understood as 'user of a language'.
[2]   Throughout the book I will use 'U' (for utterer) to designate a speaker.

ample, Davidson 1980. The issues are complex and not to be resolved quickly. Fortunately my enterprise does not require me to do so. I can sidestep the controversy because my central concern is not with actions as concrete events but with act *types, concepts, descriptions, reports,* or *properties.* From this battery of terms, which could be extended, I choose *types, concepts,* and *reports,* between which I will freely oscillate. Thus my concern here is to elucidate illocutionary act types (concepts or reports) and to distinguish them from other speech act types (concepts or reports). However many actions I attributed to Ms. A in the above example, it is clear that I listed a number of different, nonsynonymous *reports,* reporting the carrying out of different act *types* and using different act *concepts* to do so. At the end of the next section I shall offer an apologia for my apparently using the Goldman criterion of act individuation and provide a mechanism for neutralizing its ontological implications.

ii. Illocutionary Acts

In looking over the above list of types of action one might perform in uttering 'The gate is unlocked', we can see that for some of them, in attributing an action of that type to a speaker we make explicit *what* the person said (in a sense of 'what she said' that does *not* mean "what sentence she uttered"). The items of which this is true are 'U asserted that the gate is unlocked' and 'U told Smith that the gate is unlocked'. In other terms these specify the *content* of the utterance. The familiar device of *oratio obliqua* reports ("indirect speech") contains an enormous wealth of resources for doing this. Here is a small sample.

C.

1. U told H that U had left his lights on.
2. U predicted that the strike would be over soon.
3. U suggested to H that they go to a movie.
4. U asked H for a match.
5. U advised H to sell her utilities stock.
6. U promised H to read her paper.
7. U expressed considerable enthusiasm for H's proposal.
8. U reminded H that it was almost nine o'clock.
9. U exhorted H to try to finish before the end of the week.
10. U congratulated H on his performance.
11. U announced that the meeting had been canceled.
12. U admitted that the gate was open.

The list could be continued indefinitely.

Let's think for a moment about the suggestion that all the items on the list make explicit what the speaker *said*, in a sense in which that does not involve direct quotation. The most straightforward way of defending that idea would be to claim that in each case we can restate the report, using 'say' as the main verb. Where the original was not already in the verb + propositional complement form, as in 4., some reshuffling will be necessary. This gives us:

D.

1. U said to H that H had left his lights on.
2. U said that the strike would be over soon.
3. U said to H that they might go to a movie.
4. U said that he would appreciate it if H gave him a match.
5. U said to H that it would be a good idea for H to sell her utilities stock.
6. U said to H that he would read her paper.
7. U said that B's proposal was wonderful.
8. U said that in case H hadn't noticed, it was nine o'clock.
9. U said that H should try to finish before the end of the week.

And so on. It would be very neat if we could maintain that these reformulations simply have the effect of making the main verb less specific while keeping everything else the same. Sometimes this is what happens. Thus 6a is neutral between promising and simply expressing an intention, while 6. makes a definite commitment to the former; otherwise the content is the same. In other cases, however, we have to beef up the propositional content to compensate for the weakening of the main verb if we are to have anything approximating the original; this is the case with 4., 5., 7., 8., and 9. Indeed, as we move through the list, it becomes increasingly implausible to suppose that we can exactly reformulate the *oratio obliqua* report with 'say' as the main verb. We can most felicitously do the job with 'say', where the illocutionary act reported is of an assertive sort—assert, predict, admit, insist, and the like.[3] Otherwise the report is bent out of shape if we try to do it that way. That being the case, I will kick away this ladder, having climbed up it part way. Rather than continue to rely on the formulation in terms of "what the speaker said", I will take as my guiding star the idea that an illocutionary act report is an *oratio obliqua* report that it is plausible to regard as giving the *content* of the utterance.

The identification of illocutionary acts by content specifying *oratio obliqua* reports is a very different way of introducing the term from that employed by Austin. In a bit I will discuss Austin's treatment and consider how

[3] For an extensive discussion of the assertive category of illocutionary acts see Chapter 5.

it is related to mine. The previous few paragraphs spell out the way in which I have identified illocutionary acts since 1963.

Following Searle 1969 I analyze an illocutionary act into a "propositional content" and an "illocutionary force". A full-blown *oratio obliqua* report contains a main verb and an attached "content-specifying" phrase. We may take the former to indicate the *illocutionary force* and the latter to indicate the *propositional content*. Thus in 'A predicted that the strike would soon be over', the illocutionary force is that of predicting and the propositional content is *that the strike will soon be over*. In 'A asked B to give him a match', the illocutionary force is that of requesting and the propositional content is *that B gives A a match*. I do not assume that this technique gives obvious results in all cases. Thus in 'A expressed enthusiasm for B's proposal', we have a choice between taking *expressing* as the illocutionary force and *that A is enthusiastic about B's proposal* as the propositional content, and taking *expressing enthusiasm for* as the illocutionary force and *that B put forward a certain proposal* as the propositional content. But in general the application is clear.

Reactions to this material have made it clear to me that it is common to reserve 'content' for what I have just called 'propositional content'. In that usage admitting that the strike is over, announcing that the strike is over, and denying that the strike is over would have the same content, and the illocutionary force does not belong to the content. That is not the way I am using 'content' in application to utterances. In my usage the content includes anything that U seeks to communicate, anything a hearer (H) must grasp in order to understand what the speaker is saying. And that definitely includes illocutionary force as well as propositional content. If I took you to be announcing that the strike is over rather than denying that the strike is over or admitting that the strike is over, I would have failed to understand you completely.

The distinctive contours of the illocutionary act category can be best appreciated by contrasting it with other sorts of speech acts. Go back to U who uttered the sentence 'The gate is unlocked' at time *t*. Here is a more extended list of what might be a correct report of what she did at *t*.

E.

1. U made vocal sounds.
2. U spoke with a Brooklyn accent.
3. U said 'The gate is unlocked'.
4. U asserted that the gate was unlocked.
5. U told Smith that the gate was unlocked.
6. U explained how the dog got out.
7. U contradicted what Smith had just said.

8. U tried to make conversation.
9. U got it across to Smith that the gate was unlocked.
10. U succeeded in irritating me.
11. U prevented Smith from concentrating on his measurements.

From this list only 4. and 5. would count as *oratio obliqua* reports, at least if we require of such reports that they make explicit the *specific* "content" of the utterance. Other items fail this test for a variety of reasons. Items 1. and 2. are solely concerned with acoustic features of the utterance. Item 3. tells us what sentence was uttered but not what was done with it. On hearing 3. we may assume that U was making the most common standard use of the sentence, but that has not been made explicit. Items 6. and 7. are in the right direction but are insufficiently specific to bring out just what U said to explain that the dog got out or to contradict what Smith had just said. Item 8. specifies U's ultimate goal without making explicit what U said to achieve that goal. And items 9.–11. have to do with consequences of B's utterance rather than with its content.

Of the various types of speech acts reported in this list the ones we shall be most interested in, in addition to illocutionary acts, are *sentential acts*, which like 4. consist in the utterance of a certain sentence, and (again following Austin's terminology), *perlocutionary acts*, those that, like 12.–15., essentially involve an utterance's having a certain effect. As the list indicates, many types of speech act fall outside this trichotomy, but they will not be of concern to us here.

It is worth noting that not all speech act terms are univocal vis-à-vis the categories we have been distinguishing. In particular, illocutionary-perlocutionary ambiguities are not uncommon. A beautiful example is found in Shakespeare's *Henry IV*, part I, act III, scene i. Glendower, the Welsh king, says to Hotspur: "I can call spirits from the vasty deep". To which Hotspur replies, "Why, so can I, or so can any man; but will they come when you do call for them?". Glendower, in his boast, uses 'call' as a perlocutionary verb. In that sense he couldn't correctly be said to call them unless they do come. But Hotspur, in his witty rejoinder, switches to an illocutionary sense, in which one could be said to have called the spirits even if there is no response.

Let this suffice as a preliminary indication of how I identify illocutionary acts, in contrast with the other types of speech acts with which I shall be concerned. I now proceed to a further discussion of these matters in the context of Austin's classic treatment in *How to Do Things with Words*.

The reader will have noted that despite my asseveration that it is IA reports, concepts, or types with which I am concerned, I have been speaking freely of illocutionary acts themselves, and will continue to do so. Moreover, a natural way of understanding talk of a speaker's performing a sentential act, an illocutionary act, and one or more perlocutionary acts in the same breath would imply that these are different acts that are being performed. That would seem to commit me to a Goldmanian principle of individuation for IA's, in which the instantiation of every different act concept is a different act, rather than a Davidsonian principle on which this is not always or necessarily the case. But I don't mean this talk to be understood that way. I prefer the Davidsonian construal for cases like these, but I also want the treatment to be neutral on this ontological question. Then why do I talk this way, and how can I avoid the ontological commitment? First as to why, there are two reasons. (1) Putting everything in terms of act reports, concepts, or types would be intolerably prolix. (2) Formulations using substantive terms like 'illocutionary act' and 'perlocutionary act' are so pervasive and well entrenched in the literature that it would be more difficult for the reader to relate my discussion to that literature if I employed a radically different idiom. As to how I can avoid the unwanted commitment to the Goldmanian (or other) principle of act individuation, I make the time-honored appeal to the ready availability of a translation that can always be used at the cost of awkwardness. Here are few examples of such translations. The first member of each pair is in terms of acts ('a'), and the second is its translation into a concept ('c') formulation.

1a. In performing the act of uttering 'Go home' she performed the act of ordering him to go home.
1c. It is in or by the concept of uttering 'Go home' applying to her that the concept of ordering him to go home applies to her.
2a. Illocutionary acts are acts of performing an utterance with a certain content.
2c. In applying an IA concept to someone we are making explicit the content of an utterance of that person.
3a. Perlocutionary acts consist of producing a certain effect by a certain utterance.
3c. In applying a perlocutionary act concept to someone we make explicit some effect the person produced by an utterance.

iii. Austin's Classification of Speech Acts

Austin presents a trichotomy of *locutionary*, *illocutionary*, and *perlocutionary* acts, with the first category itself including three levels: *phonetic*, *phatic*, and *rhetic*.

The phonetic act is merely the act of uttering certain noises. The phatic act is the uttering of certain vocables or words, i.e., noises of certain types, belonging to and as belonging to, a certain vocabulary, conforming to and as conforming to a certain grammar. The rhetic act is the performance of an act of using those vocables with a certain more-or-less definite sense and reference.[4] (1962, 95)

These are not distinct acts on the same level but are "nested" inside each other, or, in an alternative metaphor, constitute successive strata of a complete locutionary act. The idea is that whereas one can have lower strata alone, the higher strata can be found only as resting on the lower. I can simply make noise without uttering any words or any sentence, but I can't do the latter except by or in doing the former.[5] Again, I can utter words, for example, in practicing pronunciation, without uttering them as meaning something, but I cannot do the latter without uttering words. Austin's "phatic act" is roughly equivalent to my "sentential act".

To continue with Austin, an *illocutionary act* is the act of issuing a locution (upshot of a locutionary act) with a certain "force", for example, the force of a question or a warning or a promise. And to perform a *perlocutionary* act is to produce certain effects on an audience by one's utterance (1962, 98–101). These are still higher strata that again presuppose the lower but are not presupposed by them. I cannot say something with a certain force without saying something, nor can I produce certain effects by my utterance without uttering something.

It should be apparent that the illocutionary act is the weak link in this chain; it is not located nearly as precisely as the others. It is clear that it is supposed to go beyond the locutionary act, but just how? By involving a "force". But what is a force? Austin gives us some examples, but how do these examples differ from other ways in which something richer may be built on the locution, ways that Austin regards as neither illocutionary nor perlocutionary, for example, lying? ("In saying that I had returned the money I was lying.") And are forces absent from locutionary acts? We are faced with two questions. (1) How are illocutionary acts distinguished from other acts in the scheme? (2) How can we make explicit, in a general way, just what it is that is so distinguished? These questions are not unrelated, but neither are they identical. We might characterize illocutionary acts sufficiently to mark them off from locutionary acts on the one side and from perlocutionary acts on the other, and still have only an imper-

---

[4] We must be clear that in specifying a rhetic act we make explicit *the meaning with which the speaker intended to be uttering his words*, the meaning he intended them to have, rather than *the meaning those words have in the language*. This is important both because the words may be ambiguous, in which case we are interested in which of the possible senses the speaker was exploiting, and because the speaker may be, intentionally or unintentionally, giving the words a sense they do not bear in the language.

[5] That is strictly true only if we restrict ourselves to speech in the strict sense of the term. Obviously, I can produce a sentence by writing rather than by making noise. But there too I will have done something on the same semantic level as making noises, viz., making marks. To avoid intolerable circumlocutions I will restrict myself to oral speech, leaving it to the reader to make the application to other modes of linguistic behavior.

fect grasp of their defining features, and hence be unable to say what differentiates them from still other sorts of speech acts, for example, lying and making conversation. Discussion of Austin has focused on the first question, which is obviously crucial. But neglect of the second question has tended to obscure the fact that Austin has done little in the way of giving an explicit characterization of the illocutionary act category that is at all comparable to what he has provided for the others.

Before launching onto a critical discussion of Austin's scheme we will have to resolve an ambiguity in what Austin was after under the rubric "illocutionary act", an ambiguity that can do a lot of damage if unrecognized. Let's recur to the distinction between the propositional content and the illocutionary force of an illocutionary act, a distinction mirrored in the distinction between the main verb and the associated phrase of an illocutionary act report. Did Austin mean by 'illocutionary act' the full package, or was he just talking about the fragmentary "act" of endowing one's utterance with a certain illocutionary force? His initial introduction of the category makes it sound more like the latter.

> . . . it might be perfectly possible, with regard to an utterance, say 'It is going to charge', to make entirely plain 'what we were saying' in issuing the utterance, in all the senses so far distinguished [i.e., the locutionary act], and yet not at all to have cleared up whether or not in issuing the utterance I was performing the act of *warning* or not. It may be perfectly clear what I mean by 'It is going to charge' or 'Shut the door', but not clear whether it is meant as a statement or warning, etc. . . .
>
> To determine what illocutionary act is so performed we must determine in what way we are using the locution:
>
> asking or answering a question,
>
> giving some information or an assurance or a warning,
>
> announcing a verdict or an intention. (1962, 98)

This sounds as if a complete report of an illocutionary act could just be "He issued a warning" or "He asked a question", with the specification of *what warning* or *what question* being cleared up by the specification of the locutionary act.

On the other hand, Austin gives as examples of illocutionary acts such items as "He urged (or advised, ordered, etc.) me to shoot her" (101) and "He protested against my doing it" (102). Here both illocutionary force and propositional content are involved.

We must remember that Austin was striking out in new directions in this work and also that what we have are lecture notes that he was not able to revise for publication before his death. We should not expect terminological exactitude. Although the text does not definitively resolve the ambiguity, I think we can see that the best reading is one that takes the illocutionary act to be the full package: not just warning, but warning someone that something or other. Passages like those first cited are compatible with taking Austin to be implicitly supposing that any particular act of warning or asking a question would also involve a propositional content along with that illocutionary force.

iv. Austin on the Rhetic-Illocutionary Distinction

I begin the critical scrutiny of Austin's scheme by looking at how he distinguishes illocutionary from locutionary acts. Remembering his layered analysis of the locutionary act, we may take the rhetic act—uttering a sentence with a certain sense and reference—as containing the lower levels and so as *being* the complete locutionary act. We can then frame our question as: "How does Austin distinguish illocutionary acts from rhetic acts?".

Austin's main point is that in specifying the rhetic act an utterer, U, performed we have not yet specified the illocutionary force of his utterance, for example, whether it had the force of a warning, a prediction, or a concession. And hence we have not yet fully specified what illocutionary act was performed. Look back at the material quoted above from p. 98 of Austin 1962. When U (utterer) said 'It's going to charge', he performed the rhetic act of uttering that sentence, referring to a certain bull with 'it' and meaning by 'is going to charge' 'is on the verge of rushing at us with aggressive intent' rather than, for example, 'is on the verge of taking out a credit card'. Whereas the illocutionary act he performed was that of, for example, *warning us* that the bull in question is on the verge of rushing at us with aggressive intent. What is *suggested* by this and by other examples in Lecture VIII of 1962 (I don't say that Austin *asserts* this) is that a rhetic act report gives us only the propositional content of the illocutionary act performed, and that when we then add to that the illocutionary force we have a full-blown illocutionary act.

However, as Cohen 1964 and Searle 1968 point out, this will not do. Determination of propositional content but not illocutionary force by the intended meaning and reference of the sentence is an artifact of the choice of examples. In other cases the meaning and reference determines illocutionary force as well, as when I say 'I warn you that it's going to charge' or 'I order you to prepare that form'. In still other cases the rhetic act determines illocutionary force but leaves propositional content wholly or partially undetermined, as when I say 'I order you to', leaving it to the context to indicate what it is I order you to do. And in still other cases both propositional content and illocutionary force are left incompletely determined, as when, in answer to a question, I say 'Tea'. Depending on the context I might have been asking you for some tea, or expressing a preference for tea, or telling that it was tea that the Colonel was drinking when he was shot.[6]

Not only does the rhetic act sometimes precisely determine the illocutionary force. Except when only the shadowiest linguistic devices are employed (as in "Tea"),[7] the rhetic act will limit, more or less severely, the range of possible illocutionary forces. Where I say 'It's going to charge', with my meaning and reference as specified above, my utterance might have the illocutionary force of a warning, prediction, remark, concession, objection, or conclusion; but hardly that of a request, a question (the sentence was not 'It's going to charge?'), or a verdict. Again, to take another of Austin's examples, if I say 'Shoot her', meaning by that the sort of thing one would most usually mean by it, my utterance might have the force of a suggestion or an order, but not that of a promise, prediction, announcement, or question. In these cases the syntactical structure contributes to restricting the range of possible illocutionary forces. Put otherwise, it determines a generic illocutionary force.

This indicates that Austin was misguided in thinking that the rhetic act determines propositional content but leaves open illocutionary force. But that leaves him free to make a broader point about the relationship. The rhetic-illocutionary distinction will significantly parallel the phonetic-phatic and the phatic-rhetic distinction if the following principle holds.

(1) One can perform a rhetic act without thereby performing any illocutionary act at all.

Does it?

Of course, usually when one utters a sentence with a certain sense and reference one is thereby performing a certain illocutionary act. But it looks as if there are exceptions. Suppose someone is reciting poetry with his mind on the meaning and reference of what he is saying.

---

[6] It may be retorted that even though when I say 'I order you to', the intended meaning and reference of my words leave the propositional content undetermined, *what I mean by uttering those words* does not. So "speaker meaning" always fully determines propositional content. Later I will go into different concepts of speaker meaning; pending that discussion I will agree with this point. But then illocutionary force is also always determined by speaker meaning in this rich sense. When I say 'It's going to charge' we can't fully bring out what I meant by uttering that sentence without making it explicit that I was *warning* you that the bull in question was about to charge, rather than *conceding* this or just *remarking* on it. Thus if we are to have any chance of distinguishing the rhetic and illocutionary acts we must interpret the former not in terms of *what U meant by uttering X*, but rather in terms of *the act of uttering X with a certain meaning and reference*.

[7] Cases like this can be construed in different ways. We may say that the rhetic act here is just uttering the word 'tea', meaning by 'tea' the well-known caffeine-containing beverage. But, on the other hand, we might suppose that the speaker uttered 'Tea', meaning by that word, in this instance, 'I would like to have some tea'. In this latter construal the rhetic act already contains a full determination of the illocutionary act performed. It seems clear that Austin had the former interpretation in mind.

> . . . 'tis an unweeded garden,
> That grows to seed; things rank and gross in nature
> possess it merely. . . .

Does he intend to be performing some illocutionary act? Clearly he need not be intending to express the attitude toward the world embodied in the passage. I think it is arguable that no IA concept would apply to him. Again, in telling a (fictional) story I say "Then the brother-in-law ran his car into a ditch". Here there is no doubt but that rhetic acts are being performed. By 'ran his car into a ditch' I meant 'drove his car into a ditch' rather than 'forced his car into a ditch', and by 'his car' I am referring to an automobile owned by the person in question rather than to a railroad car owned by him. It is less clear whether I perform any illocutionary act. Clearly I do not have the primary intentions associated with those sentences. In telling the story I am not reporting that any actual person actually drove a car into a ditch. Perhaps I am performing illocutionary acts of a secondary or derivative sort, each of which is modeled on a primary archetype. Or perhaps it is better to say that I am pretending to perform an IA rather than actually performing one. At least these cases show that it is arguable that one can be performing a rhetic act without performing any illocutionary act, though only in rather special cases. So let's agree with Austin that there is a conceptual distinction between rhetic and illocutionary.

But it must be confessed that certain features of Austin's presentation have provided ammunition for critics like Searle and Cohen, who deny the existence or importance of the distinction. First, he made the following fatal supposition.

> But the rhetic act is the one we report, in the case of assertions, by saying 'He said that the cat was on the mat', 'He said he would go', 'He said I was to go' (his words were 'You are to go'). This is the so-called 'indirect speech' . . . . We cannot, however, always use 'said that' easily: we would say 'told to', 'advise to', etc. if he used the imperative mood, or such equivalent phrases as 'said I was to', 'said I should', etc. (1962, 96–97)

The supposition that the rhetic act is what we report with *oratio obliqua* constructions is reflected in a number of Austin's examples.

> Thus 'He said "The cat is on the mat"' reports a phatic act, whereas 'He said that the cat was on the mat' reports a rhetic act. A similar contrast is illustrated by the pairs:
> 'He said "I shall be there"', 'He said he would be there'.
> 'He said "Get out"', 'He told me to get out'.

'He said "Is it in Oxford or Cambridge?"', 'He asked whether it was in Oxford or Cambridge'. (1962, 95)

Faced with examples like this, Searle and Cohen have little difficulty in arguing that a so-called rhetic act is simply an illocutionary act, perhaps of a less than maximally specific sort. It is clear that what are cited here as reports of rhetic acts all make explicit both an illocutionary force and a propositional content, the illocutionary force ranging from the relatively noncommittal 'say' to the more specific 'ask' and 'tell _____ to _____'. But the moral I draw from this is not that rhetic acts constitute a subclass of illocutionary acts, but that Austin was mistaken in supposing that indirect speech constructions can be used to report rhetic acts, as he defined that term. For reasons made explicit in this section, uttering a sentence with a certain sense and reference does not amount to performing an act with a certain propositional content and a certain illocutionary force. Since both of the latter are made explicit, at some level of specificity, by an indirect speech report, I agree with Cohen and Searle that such reports are to be taken as illocutionary act reports. But since I do not agree with Austin that they are to be construed as rhetic act reports, I do not agree with the critics that rhetic acts collapse into illocutionary acts. It is worthy of note in this connection that when Austin comes to illustrate the difference between rhetic and illocutionary acts he does *not* use the indirect speech form to report rhetic acts, as he did when contrasting the latter with phatic acts.

Act (A) or Locution
He said to me 'Shoot her!' meaning by 'shoot' shoot and referring by 'her' to her.

Act (B) or Illocution
He urged (or advised, ordered, etc.) me to shoot her.

Here the illocutionary act is specified in the way the locutionary (rhetic) act was specified in the earlier passages, while the locutionary act is specified in the way indicated by the definition of the term.

v. Austin on the Illocutionary-Perlocutionary Distinction

Next I turn to what Austin has to say about the distinction between illocutionary and perlocutionary acts. He opined, mistakenly in my opinion, that "it is the distinction between illocutions and perlocutions which seems likeliest to give trouble" (1962, 109). The existence and nature of *that* distinction would seem to be unproblematic, since a perlocutionary act consists in the production of certain effects, whereas, as I will contend throughout, IA's are not so constituted. But Austin thinks that certain kinds of effects might be taken as essential to illocutionary acts, and so he feels constrained to go into the issue. I think the problems can be handled easily.

First, Austin discusses the audience's understanding "of the meaning and of the force of the locution" (1962, 115–116). He wavers between saying that the illocutionary act cannot be "happily, successfully performed" without this "uptake", and suggesting that this is a necessary condition of the mere performance of the act. It is clear that the latter is not the case. Whether I told you that the dean is coming to dinner or asked you to bring me a towel does not hang on whether you heard or understood me. If you didn't, my communicative purpose has been frustrated. But it doesn't follow that I didn't tell you or ask you. In response to a charge that I hadn't told you that the dean was coming I might reply, "I told you all right; perhaps you didn't hear me". Another of Austin's points is that "many illocutionary acts invite by convention a response or sequel" (1962, 116). Thus a request "invites" the response of complying; a question "invites" the response of an appropriate answer. But since Austin does not even suggest that the response must be forthcoming if the illocutionary act is to be performed, this consideration poses no threat to the illocutionary-perlocutionary distinction.

Austin's most substantial worry is that it seems to be necessary for some illocutionary performances that certain "conventional effects" of the utterance be produced.[8] If I really did appoint you ambassador to Nigeria, you have thereby acquired a certain status, have certain obligations and certain rights that you did not possess before. If this is correct, then in making the illocutionary-perlocutionary distinction we must understand a perlocutionary act to consist in producing certain "natural effects" of the utterance, effects that do not obtain in virtue of rules or conventions.

vi. Austin's Characterization of Illocutionary Acts

Thus far we have been dealing with what I called the first question: how illocutionary acts are to be distinguished from other speech acts. But that is not the whole job. We still need to give an intrinsic characterization of illocutionary acts, in addition to relating them to their cousins. In the material so far cited all Austin has done along this line is to (a) provide a number of examples and (b) employ the unexplained term 'force'. Does he go beyond that?

---

[8] In Chapter 4 I will consider whether this is so. There I will argue that any act that has as a necessary condition the production of such effects is not a "pure" illocutionary act.

In a number of passages Austin alludes to conventionality as a distinguishing feature of illocutionary acts. "We must notice that the illocutionary act is a conventional act: an act done as conforming to a convention" (1962, 105. Cf. 108, 114, 120, 127). It is plausible to say that what makes a certain utterance a case of promising to read your paper is something on the order of a social convention or rule. And this distinguishes illocutionary from perlocutionary acts. If I surprise you by what I say, this is *not* by virtue of any social rule or convention. But it is equally clear that this does not mark a distinction between illocutionary and rhetic acts. If I say 'It's going to charge' with a certain sense and reference, this is due, at least in part, to the relevant linguistic rules and conventions. To be sure, the locutionary act is not fully determined by such rules; they do not uniquely determine to what I am referring with 'it', nor do they determine in which sense I am using 'charge'. The speaker's intentions come in also. But likewise the illocutionary act is, in general, not wholly determined by the operative conventions, apart from the speaker's intentions. The latter are what make an utterance of 'It's going to charge' a warning rather than a prediction, a remark, or a concession. If we are to distinguish illocution from locution by its conventionality, we will have to find a sort of convention that is involved in the former but not in the latter. Thus Austin fails to show that conventionality will even differentiate illocutionary acts from other types of acts in the scheme. Much less does he show how to give an account of their nature in these terms.

Finally, Austin suggests, rather halfheartedly, that it is distinctive of illocutionary acts that they can be done by means of the "performative formula", that is, by uttering a sentence that begins with an illocutionary act verb in the first-person simple present tense (1962, 103, 130). I can warn you that p by saying 'I warn you that p', but I cannot surprise you by saying 'I surprise you'. That might in fact surprise you, but uttering that sentence is in no sense a "standard" way of doing that. But Austin confesses that this is at best a "very slippery test". In Chapter 4 I will present reasons for denying that all illocutionary acts can be done with the "performative formula".

I conclude that Austin has done little more, on the question of the nature of IA's, than present us with an intuitive list of illocutionary verbs. I suggest that my appeal to the *oratio obliqua* construction, together with the suggestion that such constructions make explicit the "content" of an utterance, does as much as we can reasonably expect by way of identifying illocutionary act concepts, prior to developing a theory.

My own trichotomy, to which I now turn, will feature an illocutionary and a perlocutionary level that are roughly coextensive with Austin's though differently characterized, especially for the illocutionary. But for the lowest stratum it will suffice to use Austin's "phatic act", rebaptized as a "sentential act", the act of uttering a sentence.

vii. Interrelations of Sentential and Illocutionary Acts

I now turn to a more thorough presentation of my trichotomy.

D1. *Sentential act concept*—a concept the application of which to a person makes explicit what sentence he uttered.

D2. *Illocutionary act concept*—a concept the application of which to a person makes explicit the "content" of her utterance. Alternatively, it is a concept the application of which to a person constitutes an *oratio obliqua* report.

D3. *Perlocutionary act concept*—a concept the application of which to a person makes explicit some effect his utterance had on his audience.

Thus different sentential act concepts (types) are distinguished by differences in the sentences uttered. Different illocutionary act concepts are distinguished by differences in the "content" of the utterance. Different perlocutionary act concepts are distinguished by differences in effects produced by the utterance. This formulation makes explicit the point brought out earlier that my distinctions are between act *concepts* or *types*, rather than between the acts themselves.

My scheme, like Austin's, is stratified. A higher act needs lower acts as substrata, but the lower do not require the higher. Let's characterize the "higher than" relation more formally.

Act type C is higher than act type D—An agent, A, cannot perform a token of C without, in the same bodily movement, performing a token of D.

In such a case we can also speak of C as "presupposing" some D, and of D as "underlying" C; and we may speak of doing C *by* or *in* doing D.

Now let's consider the principle:

I. *Illocutionary acts presuppose sentential acts, but not vice versa.*

The idea here is that in order to, for example, request someone to open a door, one must do so by uttering a sentence. Making a request is something we do only *by* or *in* doing something else. One can't present a content without presenting it in something. But one can utter a sentence without communicating any content, as when one is practicing pronunciation in solitude.

This thesis that one can perform a sentential act without thereby performing any illocutionary act can stand in this simple form. But if the dependence of illocutionary on sentential acts is to be acceptable, we must enrich our concept of the latter. For it is clear that one can a perform an illocutionary act without uttering any sentence. First, there are the cases already canvassed in which one utters some subsentential unit as elliptical for a sentence, leaving it to the context to fill out the rest of the content. Upon being asked whether the museum is to the right or the left, I may say 'Left', thereby performing the illocutionary act of informing my interlocutor that the museum is to the left. Second, it is possible to perform illocutionary acts with nonlinguistic devices. I can tell my wife that it is time to leave the party by making a prearranged signal, for example, scratching my head; and I can agree with you that Smith has gone too far by nodding assent.

The first kind of counterexample involving ellipticity can be handled by enlarging the concept of a sentential act to include the utterance of some smaller unit as elliptical for a sentence. This does not mark any change of principle. The elliptical case is parasitic on the full-blown case. We couldn't take the utterance of a word as elliptical for a sentence without the possibility of a complete expression of one's illocutionary intent by a full sentence. This modification simply recognizes the existence of derivative cases.

How we handle the second point depends on what kinds of cases we acknowledge as genuine illocutionary acts. In the above examples the nonlinguistic vehicle is parasitic on the use of sentences to do the same illocutionary job, just as is the elliptical use of words and phrases. My wife and I wouldn't have been able to arrange our signal for "saying" that it is time to leave the party unless we had the capacity to say that explicitly with a sentence. Let's term such nonlinguistic devices "sentence surrogates". We can then allow the production of sentence surrogates to count as sentential acts.

But it may be claimed that our illocutionary act concepts are too closely tied to their typical linguistic embodiments to be happily applied outside that area. In the case under discussion one cannot felicitously report what I did by saying that I "told (reminded, pointed out to . . .) my wife that it was time to leave the party". I can't *tell* anyone anything, or *point out* anything to anyone, by scratching my head. We have to use some special term like 'signal' to say what I did. I *signaled* her that it is time to leave the party. However, I am going to rule against this contention. Any strain one feels in using illocutionary verbs here can be explained by the fact that the linguistic doing of these things bulks so large in our lives. It is like the strain one would have felt at one time in saying of a doctor that *she* told me that I was in good shape. It seems to me no more part of the *meaning* of 'told her it was time to go' that it must be performed by a linguistic device than it was ever part of the *meaning* of 'doctor' that doctors are males. But even if

I am mistaken about this, the restriction to strictly linguistic underlying acts is a relatively superficial feature of IA concepts, one that can be sheared off without disturbing the core of the concept.

So far I have ruled that sentential acts can be performed by the use of derivative sentence surrogates. But why the restriction to derivative ones? To be sure, it is an important fact about human life that language has been the primary form of communication. All other human systems of communication, at least within historical times, have been based on language. Smoke signals as well as conventionally significant gestures have arisen as substitutes for speech, ones that are more convenient in certain situations.[9] But this is a contingent fact about the way things have developed. It is conceivable that human beings, or other intelligent agents, might develop some nonlinguistic system as their basic, underived conventional means of communication. If so, shouldn't we say that for those folk the production of nonlinguistic vehicles would underlie illocutionary acts in an underivative way? I cannot see why we shouldn't. But then the category of *sentence surrogate* will have to be enlarged to include any perceptible device that has the kind of communicative role that some sentence in a language might be given, whether any sentence in any language has that role or not. In the light of all this we can reformulate our definition of 'sentential act concept' as follows.

D4. Sentential act concept—a concept the application of which to a person makes explicit what sentence he uttered, or what subsentential unit he uttered as elliptical for a sentence, or what sentence surrogate he produced.

In parallel fashion we will widen the notion of an utterance. 'Utterance' will extend over both any production of a sentence token or of other linguistic tokens as elliptical for a sentence, and any production of a sentence surrogate.

It may be thought that our notion of a sentence surrogate has become so wide as to make it trivially true that every illocutionary act presupposes a sentential act on which it is based. But it is not so. Our widened notion is still restricted to devices that are fitted by a rule or convention[10] to have the same communicative function as some sentence might. The rule or convention need not be widely dispersed or long-lived. In a limiting case they can be restricted to a tiny subcommunity, as in the signaling arrange-

---

[9] At least this is true of systems that are based on convention or social rules; there may be natural systems of communication by look or gesture, but we are not concerned with them for the moment. See the discussion of nonconventional "expressions" in Chapter 4.
[10] These terms will be extensively discussed in the sequel, especially in 8.4.

ment with my wife. Indeed if, as we must, we allow illocutionary act concepts to apply to talking to oneself, the convention can apply to only one person. But whatever the scope of the convention, nothing is a sentence surrogate in the intended sense unless its illocutionary act potential accrues to it by convention or rule.

Because of this our identification of sentential and illocutionary acts does still have a cutting edge. It implies that illocutionary acts cannot be performed save by "conventional devices". This contradicts the position taken by Schiffer 1972 (91). On his account of illocutionary acts, which I will discuss in the next chapter, to perform an illocutionary act of a certain type is to do something with a certain kind of intention of affecting the beliefs or behavior of one's auditor(s). So long as one does what one does with the right kind of perlocutionary intention, one has performed a certain illocutionary act, whatever the character of the more basic act. On his view it is no part of the concept of, for example, asking someone for a match, that one employs a device that is conventionally tagged for that job.

It will help to consider this issue between Schiffer and myself to think about situations he and I would categorize differently. Consider cases in which persons who share no common language, or other conventional symbol system, attempt to communicate with each other. Suppose that Christopher Columbus, on landing in the West Indies, was short on drinking water and wanted to obtain some from the natives. He might attempt to look and act very thirsty, following by going through the motions of drinking and then making imploring gestures to the natives. He has exploited no conventions, even of the temporary ad hoc sort. Or, to use Schiffer's favorite example, in the absence of a common language I might utter 'Grr' to convey to someone that I am angry. Here I imitate a natural expression of the state I want my audience to realize I am in.

Now consider whether we would use illocutionary act terms to report these doings. Suppose that Columbus, when giving his report of the voyage to Queen Isabella, said at this point in his narrative, "And then I asked them for some water", or "I told them that we were very thirsty", or "I expressed a desire for water". The Queen might well have cried out in surprise "You mean that they could speak Spanish!". This indicates that when an illocutionary act term is used we take it that the user is reporting the activity as involving the use of language, or at least the use of some conventional surrogate for language. What Columbus should have said is that "he tried to get across to the natives that he and his men were thirsty", or that he "put on a pantomime in the attempt to bring them to realize . . .", or that he "attempted to communicate to them that . . .". In the absence of conventional devices what went on is describable as an attempt at a certain effect, rather than as an illocutionary act. I would make the same negative judgment about the claim that the person who went "Grr!" was "telling his companion that he was angry". These attempts to get some idea across to someone by natural, nonconventional means are much further removed from natural characterization in IA terms than the conventional use of gestures in a special code illustrated above.

viii. Perlocutionary Acts and Other Speech Acts

The analogue to I. for perlocutionary acts is:

II. Perlocutionary acts presuppose sentential acts, but not vice versa.

I cannot produce effects on an audience by an utterance without issuing an utterance, but I can issue an utterance without producing effects on an audience.

The terms we naturally use to specify particular perlocutionary acts are not restricted in their application to utterances, even in the enlarged sense we have developed.

got H to realize that Susie was across the street
got H to take a drink of water.

These are what we might call "pure effect-production terms". They specify the act purely in terms of the effect produced, without any restrictions on how it was produced. Though these are effects that one can bring about by an utterance, they can be brought about in other ways as well. I can get you to realize that Susie is across the street by pointing her out to you. I can get you take a drink of water by feeding you a lot of salted peanuts. When we use terms like this to report perlocutionary acts, we do so with the presupposition that the effects in question were produced by an utterance. It is only on this understanding that perlocutionary acts necessarily supervene on sentential acts.

What about the other direction—that one can perform a sentential act without thereby performing any perlocutionary acts? The possibility of uttering sentences in solitude is sufficient to ensure this possibility. When I am practicing pronunciation or testing a microphone with no one within hearing distance, I produce no effects on any audience. Even when I am speaking to someone there is the possibility that I will not be heard.[11] But when my addressee hears me, I produce at least auditory effects and so perform some perlocutionary act.

Principles I. and II. make explicit the fact that both illocutionary and

---

[11]   If the perlocutionary act category ranged over the production of *any* effect by an utterance, then it would be impossible to perform a sentential act without a perlocutionary act. For any production of anything is going to have some effects, at least on the immediate physical environment. Even if I utter a sentence in solitude, I will thereby have affected the surrounding air in certain physically describable ways, not to mention hearing my own speech. But the category is explicitly restricted to the production of effects on an *audience*.

perlocutionary acts are based on sentential acts, though they build on them in different ways. But what about their relation to each other? Do the three categories stand in a linear hierarchy, with illocutionary acts in the middle? In that case perlocutionary acts would be based directly on illocutionary acts and only indirectly on sentential acts. Or do illocutionary and perlocutionary acts simply branch off in different directions from sentential acts, standing in no particular hierarchical relationship to each other?

There are linguistic indications of an asymmetrical dependence of perlocutionary on illocutionary acts, particularly the "by" construction. I can get you to realize that Joe is at the door or frighten you (perlocutionary) *by* telling you that Joe is at the door (illocutionary). But what would it mean to tell you that Joe is at the door *by* getting you to realize that Joe is at the door? I can induce you to bring me a towel (perlocutionary) by asking you to bring me a towel (illocutionary). But what would it be to ask you to bring me a towel *by* inducing you to bring me a towel? The illocutionary can be a means to the performance of the perlocutionary, but not vice versa. This strongly suggests that perlocutionary acts can be based on illocutionary acts, but not vice versa. The issuing of an utterance with a certain content can itself have effects, and so the production of those effects can supervene on that content presentation. But a content cannot attach to the production of an effect by an utterance, so as to make that effect production to be what carries that content. Presumably the deep reason for this last point is that we do not want the significance of our utterances to be at the mercy of the external contingencies that determine the ways in which the audience is affected. Whether a hearer, H, believes what I say, or whether H is moved to action in the intended fashion, depends on, among other things, whether H understands what I say and how H is disposed toward me. These matters are not wholly in the control of the speaker. But for good and sufficient reason we want the speaker to be able to determine what message he is issuing. And if illocutionary acts were based on perlocutionary acts, then whether I perform a given illocutionary act would not be wholly up to me. Hence the illocution supervenes on something that is up to me, namely, what sentence or sentence surrogate I issue and what rule I issue it as subject to.

Though these considerations show that perlocutionary acts can be based on illocutionary acts and that the reverse is not possible, they do not show that perlocutionary acts are never generated directly by sentential acts. And it is clear that they are. Where an utterance produces its effect by virtue of the content it carries, the perlocutionary supervenes on the illocutionary. But in other cases the effect is due rather to the sentential content or sheer physical qualities of the utterance. I might frighten you by speaking loudly, regardless of what I am saying. Or the mere sound of the words, or some of the associations they arouse in the hearer, may produce effects, whatever the illocutionary act, if any, that is being performed. Consider the lulling effect produced by the lines:

> In Xanadu did Kubla Khan
> A stately pleasure-dome decree
> Where Alph, the sacred river, ran
> Through caverns measureless to man
> Down to a sunless sea.

In these cases the perlocutionary act is based directly on a sentential act. And, of course, perlocutionary acts will always be based directly on a sentential act in cases where no illocutionary act is in the cards.

Thus the principle for the illocutionary-perlocutionary relationship will have to be weaker than the principles for the other pairs.

III. *Perlocutionary acts may be based on illocutionary acts, but not vice versa.*

One further point about the illocutionary-perlocutionary relationship. A perlocutionary act *consists* in the production of some effect, whereas an illocutionary act does not. But that is not to say that an illocutionary act does not *produce* effects or does not *have* consequences. Just by virtue of being an act it will have consequences. We must distinguish between certain effects of a lower-level act being part of given act *concept*, and a given act's having effects. It is part of the *concept* of the act of *irritating H* that the something the agent did resulted in H's being irritated. Whereas my *reminding H that he had promised to read my paper* can have as a result his being irritated without its being part of the concept of *reminding someone that he promised to read my paper* that the addressee becomes irritated. We should also note that where an act type is defined by some lower-level act having results of a certain sort, for example, frightening someone, a particular token of that type can also *have* further consequences. It may be a further consequence of my frightening you that you have a heart attack.[12]

---

[12] G. H. von Wright (1971) uses the terms 'result' and 'consequence' for what I have been calling the consequences conceptually constitutive of an action and those further consequences the action produces.

CHAPTER TWO

Perlocutionary Intention Theories
of Illocutionary Acts

i. Explicating Illocutionary Act Concepts

Having made a pretheoretical survey of the territory for which a theory is to be given, we can now turn to the task of spelling out what it is for a speaker to perform an illocutionary act of a certain type. I begin by recalling the identifying features of illocutionary act concepts, as set out in the previous chapter.

> **Illocutionary act concept**— a concept the application of which to a person makes explicit the "content" of his utterance. Alternatively, it is a concept the application of which to a person constitutes an *oratio obliqua* report.

Thus the question of what makes an utterance an illocutionary act of a certain type can be rephrased as "What endows an utterance with a certain content?".

In working toward an answer to that question, and in critically evaluating answers that have been given, it will help to have a sense of the total illocutionary act field, including the main categories into which it is divided. In Chapters 4 and 5 I will be exploring this variety in detail. Here is a preliminary sketch of the field.

Assertives	Directives	Commissives	Expressives	Exercitives
allege	ask	promise	thank	adjourn
report	request	bet	apologize	appoint
insist	beseech	guarantee	commiserate	pardon
claim	implore	invite	compliment	name
maintain	tell	offer	congratulate	nominate
answer	command		express:	bequeath
agree	enjoin		enthusiasm	sentence
concede	order		contempt	hire, fire
remark	forbid		interest	approve
mention	advise		relief	
announce	recommend		desire	
testify	suggest		willingness	
remind	propose		intention	
admit			opinion	
disclose			opposition	
deny			agreement	
complain			determination	
predict			unhappiness	
			delight	

This is just a small sample of what falls under each category. As for the categories: roughly speaking, *assertives* are ways of asserting a proposition, ways of putting it forward as true. *Directives* are concerned with guiding the behavior of others. *Commissives* commit the speaker to a certain line of action. *Expressives* express some psychological state of the speaker. *Exercitives* are verbal exercises of authority, verbal ways of altering the "social status" of something, an act that is made possible by one's social or institutional role or status. The reader will find no difficulty in putting the illocutionary verbs in the above list with appropriate content-specifying phrases so as to make up complete illocutionary act reports.

Now for the question of what sort of condition will convert a sentential act into an illocutionary act of a certain type. What features must a condition have in order to do the job?

First, the proposition that *p*, where that is the propositional content of the act, will have to figure in the condition. Otherwise why would it make the utterance into an illocutionary act with that propositional content rather than some other? If the condition is going to make the utterance a case of advising Steve to take organic chemistry next year, it will somehow have to involve the proposition *Steve takes organic chemistry next year*. But that proposition does not figure in the most obvious way, namely, by its truth or falsity being required. Obviously, I can have advised Steve to take organic chemistry next year whether or not he actually does so, that is, whether or not the proposition in question is true. I can have remarked that the weather is warming up whether or not it is; I can have promised to meet you for lunch whether or not I actually show up.

The truth value of the propositional content is not sufficient as well as not necessary. If some state of affairs is going to convert my sentential act into my remarking that the weather is warming up, it must not only involve that proposition. It must also involve my being related to that proposition in some way. And a proposition can be true or false regardless of how I am related to it.

The most obvious way of satisfying this last constraint would be to make the condition require some attitude of the speaker to the proposition—belief, wanting it to be true, undertaking to make it true, or whatever. All the views I shall be discussing, including my own, could be thought of in this way, provided we understand 'propositional attitude' in a sufficiently broad sense. But at this stage I want to point out that a requirement of certain familiar propositional attitudes of the speaker—belief, doubt, desire, approval—will not do the job. I can illustrate this with illocutionary acts that are plausibly thought of as expressing propositional attitudes of these sorts. Thus in asserting that p I am expressing the belief that p; in requesting you to do A I am expressing a wish or desire for you to do A, or an interest in your doing A. But even in these cases it is not a necessary condition of illocutionary act performance that the speaker actually have the propositional attitude expressed. I could be lying when I assert that p, thus lacking the belief that p. It is possible to request you to do A when I have no interest in your doing so; perhaps I made that request just to distract your attention for a moment. If asserting that p essentially involves expressing the belief that p, as I believe it does, we will have to understand 'express' in such a way that it is possible to express an attitude one does not have. (See 4.6 for a discussion of this.)

This disposes of the idea that the possession of one or another familiar propositional attitude is *necessary* for illocutionary act performance. We can see two reasons why it is not *sufficient* either. (1) A sufficient condition would have to connect the attitude with the sentential act in some more intimate way than just temporal coincidence. Even if belief that p were required for asserting that p, the mere fact that I utter a sentence, S, while believing that p, could not possibly make my utterance a case of asserting that p. If it could, then I would simultaneously be asserting everything I believe when I utter any sentence. Even if it is further required that the belief be one I am conscious of at the moment, the same conclusion follows. I can consciously believe that Susie loves me while telling H that the colloquium begins at four o'clock. Some more intimate relation is required. (2) The condition must be something that the speaker can realize at will, in a way that I cannot believe or desire something at will. Let me explain. I am not suggesting that for any speaker, U, and for any proposition, p, U can assert that p at will. One cannot assert propositions that involve concepts outside one's repertoire. Nor am I saying that for a given p that is within my repertoire I can assert it by using any sentence whatever. That issue will be taken up later. What I mean is this. Take some p that I am capable of asserting and a sentence, S, that is usable to assert it. Then in uttering S it is wholly up to me whether I am thereby asserting that p rather than, for example, practicing pronunciation or giving an example. Whatever it takes to make my utterance of S the former rather than the latter is something I can institute at will. This rules out belief, desire, and other standard examples of propositional attitudes, as well as ruling out the truth value of p.

Let's bring together the constraints we have uncovered for the condition, C, that will turn a case of uttering S into a case of $F(p)$ (where 'F' denotes the illocutionary force and 'p' the propositional content).

1. C must involve p.
2. C must involve the speaker, U's, being related in some way to p.
3. This relation of U to p must itself be related to U's underlying sentential act in some more intimate way than temporal coincidence.
4. C must be institutable by U at will.

So what can U do at will to relate his sentential act to p in such a way as to make that act into a case of $F(p)$? A plausible answer is: U can intend her sentential act to produce a certain propositional attitude toward p in her auditor, H. A (much too simple) version would hold that, for example:

U asserts that p in uttering S *iff* U utters S with the intention of getting H to believe that p.
U orders A to do D in uttering S *iff* U utters S with the intention of getting H to form the intention to do D.

This suggestion would seem to satisfy all the constraints just listed. It is a matter of U's relating his sentential act to an attitude of his toward p in some more intimate way than just temporal coincidence. U's attitude to p that is involved here cannot be stated without bringing in the underlying sentential act; the attitude *is* the intention to produce in H a propositional attitude toward p *by means of uttering S*.[1] And it is up to me whether,

---

[1] I will not delay mentioning a possible objection to this approach. When I say something in order to get my auditor to believe or do something, isn't it my *illocutionary* act I am performing to bring this about rather than my sentential act? When I tell my wife that I was invited to a conference in Cedar Rapids, intending to get her to realize that this is the case, wouldn't I think that I aim to bring about this effect by *telling* her this (illocutionary act) rather than by uttering the sentence I uttered? And doesn't that pose a fatal difficulty for this approach? For if my intention to produce a propositional attitude to p in A is an intention to do this by performing a certain illocutionary act, that intention *presupposes* the illocutionary act concept rather than serving to analyze it. Hence the intention could hardly

when I utter S, I do so in order to achieve one goal rather than another, at least among those goals that I think the utterance has some chance of achieving.

The act of affecting H in some way—getting H to believe that p or to form the intention to do D—is a perlocutionary act. And so the intention to affect A in some way can be termed a 'perlocutionary intention'. The approach currently under consideration can, then, be called a "perlocutionary intention" (PI) account of illocutionary acts. Please be clear that this approach does *not* identify illocutionary and perlocutionary acts. What it presents as a necessary and sufficient condition of performing an illocutionary act of a certain type is not that one succeed in producing a certain effect in the addressee (actually perform an perlocutionary act), but only that one *have the intention* to produce that effect (to perform the correlated perlocutionary act).

ii. Grice on Speaker Meaning

In Schiffer 1972 the author develops an impressive PI theory of illocutionary acts. In my judgment it constitutes a near miss. By seeing where it falls short I will be in a better position to develop my own view.

Schiffer gives his account of illocutionary acts in the course of developing his version of the Griceian program in semantics, first adumbrated in Grice's seminal paper, "Meaning" (Grice 1957). Here is a condensed version of that program.

I. Explain what it is for a speaker to mean something by an utterance on a given occasion ("speaker meaning") [2] in terms of the speaker's intending to produce, in a certain way, effects of a certain sort in his audience.

   A. It will be expected that *what* U meant by his utterance will be a function of what kind of effect he intended to produce in his audience.

II. Explain what it is for a sentence to have a certain meaning in terms of a regular practice of its being used by speakers to mean

---

be *constitutive* of the illocutionary act. I consider this to be a cogent objection to this account of illocutionary acts. But in order to bring out other difficulties in the approach, I will ignore this objection for this discussion.

[2] In Chapter 1 I distinguished two kinds of speaker meaning: (1) what U meant by uttering x and (2) what U meant by x. As Schiffer points out (1972, 2), this distinction is secured by the fact that if one is speaking ironically in saying 'I'm in hock', what he means by uttering that sentence is that he is in excellent financial shape; but what he means by the sentence is that he is in debt rather than that, e.g., he is in white Rhine wine. I said in Chapter 1 that Austin's rhetic act is to be understood in terms of meaning something by a sentence (sense 2). But throughout this discussion of the Griceian theory of speaker meaning it will be sense 1 that is under consideration—what U means by uttering x.

so-and-so, or in terms of a convention for its being used by speakers to mean so-and-so.[3] Note three important features of this program.

A. It is a form of "semantic nominalism",[4] in the sense that the basic semantic concept—speaker meaning[5]—is one that applies to particulars rather than to universals, to tokens rather than types. It is a concept of what a speaker means by what he says on a particular occasion. The concept of the meaning of linguistic types is then derived from that. My theory, by contrast, will be a form of "semantic realism", in which the most basic semantic concepts apply to linguistic *types*.

B. The basic concept of speaker meaning is not restricted to the use of language, or even to the use of conventional devices for effecting one's purposes. These concepts range over any occasions on which an agent means something by what he does, including meaning something by (nonconventional) gestures, posture, demeanor, displaying pictures, or simply striding out of the room. Hence terms like 'utterance' and 'speaker' are given an even wider sense than in my approach.

C. Thus in this program one aspires to exhibit linguistic communication and linguistic meaning as special cases of more general phenomena. And since speaker meaning is itself to be understood in terms of propositional attitudes like belief and intention, these psychological concepts cannot be explicated in terms of semantic notions, on pain of circularity.

Grice's procedure was to go directly from speaker meaning to linguistic meaning via social practice or convention, and Bennett follows him in this.[6] But Schiffer puts in an additional step via illocutionary acts, and that is why we are discussing his views at this point. Having given an account of illocutionary acts in terms of speaker meaning, he says, in effect, that a sentence has a meaning in a language iff it is a conventional means for performing illocutionary acts of a certain type.[7]

But whether one takes the detour through illocutionary acts or not,

---

[3] Carrying out II. would involve developing a "perlocutionary act potential" theory of sentence meaning, which I will be discussing in 6.5. For now my interest lies in the nature of illocutionary acts.

[4] Cf. Bennett 1976, chap. 1.3.

[5] Actually in Grice's "Meaning" the basic concept was that of "token meaning", the meaning of what it is that the speaker produced. Speaker meaning was then derived from that. We may safely neglect that extra step in this brief sketch. Taking token meaning as basic does not alter the character of the enterprise.

[6] This route will be critically discussed in 6.4.

[7] He does not put it in these terms, but it is easy to see that this what his account on pp. 157–159 amounts to.

the account of speaker meaning in terms of perlocutionary intentions is the foundation of the edifice. I will take a brief look at this, only a brief look because my objections to the perlocutionary intention account of illocutionary acts do not depend on objections to this account of speaker meaning.

In "Meaning" (1957) Grice arrives at his formulation by the following steps.

A first shot would be to suggest that "x meant$_{NN}$ something"[8] would be true if x was intended by its utterer to induce a belief in some "audience" and that to say what the belief was would be to say what x meant$_{NN}$. This will not do. I might leave B's handkerchief near the scene of a murder in order to induce the detective to believe that B was the murderer, but we should not want to say that the handkerchief (or my leaving it there) meant$_{NN}$ anything or that I had meant$_{NN}$ by leaving it that B was the murderer. Clearly we must at least add that, for x to have meant$_{NN}$ anything, not merely must it have been "uttered" with the intention of inducing a certain belief but also the utterer must have intended an "audience" to recognize the intention behind the utterance.

This, though perhaps better, is not good enough. . . . Compare the following two cases.

(1) I show Mr. X a photograph of Mr. Y displaying undue familiarity to Mrs. X.

(2) I draw a picture of Mr. Y behaving in this manner and show it to Mr. X.

I find that I want to deny that in (1) the photograph (or my showing it to Mr. X) meant$_{NN}$ anything at all; while I want to assert that in (2) the picture (or my drawing and showing it) meant$_{NN}$ something (that Mr. Y had been unduly familiar), or at least that I had meant$_{NN}$ by it that Mr. Y had been unduly familiar. What is the difference between the two cases? Surely that in case (1) Mr. X's recognition of my intention to make him believe that there is something between Mr. Y and Mrs. X is (more or less) irrelevant to the production of this effect by the photograph. Mr. X would be led by the photograph to at least suspect Mrs. X even if instead of showing it to him I had left it in his room by accident; and I (the photograph shower) would not be unaware of this. But it will make a difference to the effect of my picture of Mr. X whether or not he takes me to be intending to inform him (make him believe something) about Mrs. X, and not to be just doodling or trying to produce a work of art. (Grice 1989, 217–218)

---

[8] Grice is here speaking of token meaning; x is a token. He brings in speaker meaning as the discussion proceeds. The subscript "$_{NN}$" stands for 'non-natural'. It serves to distinguish non-natural meaning from natural meaning, where the latter, roughly speaking, consists in one item's being a reliable indication of another item. Grice doesn't do much to provide a pretheoretical concept of non-natural meaning.

These considerations lead to the ingenious and fruitful suggestion (restricting ourselves for the moment to the cases in which U seeks to get A to believe something) that it is essential to the agent's meaning$_{NN}$ something by what he does or produces that it be part of his intention that the audience, A, take as part of its reason for believing that p (the belief that U was seeking to produce in A) *that U produces his utterance with the intention of getting H to believe that p.* Thus, after broadening things to include other effects on audiences, Grice produces the following formulation.

"A meant$_{NN}$ something by x" is (roughly) equivalent to "A intended the utterance of x to produce some effect in an audience by means of the recognition of this intention"; and we may add that to ask what A meant is to ask for a specification of the intended effect. . . . (220)

In the subsequent literature this formulation has been subjected to numerous qualifications and refinements. It has been found necessary to ensure that at no point does U intend that H do or undergo something, at the same time intending that H shall not realize that U intends this. Everything must be out in the open, or intended by U to be out in the open, if we are to have a genuine case of speaker meaning. Again, Schiffer has shown that the restriction to U's intending that A believe that p because U uttered x intending to produce that belief, leaves out many clear cases. And so on. In Schiffer 1972 he proffers what cannot fail to stand for all time as the most complicated formulation of necessary and sufficient conditions for speaker meaning, or for anything else for that matter. If I were to go into all these labyrinthine complexities, I would never get to my main concerns in this book. Fortunately, it is not necessary. My criticism of Schiffer's account of illocutionary acts will be based on the following points. (1) The account is based on the notion of speaker meaning. (2) Speaker meaning is so analyzed that it is a necessary condition of U's meaning something by x that U utter x with the intention of producing a certain psychological effect in his audience. By virtue of resting on these claims the view fails to give an adequate account of illocutionary act concepts, whatever the details of the most adequate perlocutionary intention account of speaker meaning.

iii. Schiffer's Account of Illocutionary Acts

A cardinal feature of Schiffer's account of speaker meaning is that he holds that all cases fall into one or the other of two categories:

(A) U means that p by uttering x.
(B) U means that H is to do D by uttering x.

'p' is a dummy for propositional phrases. 'D' is a dummy for act specifications. In (A) cases, what U intends to produce in H is the "activated"[9] belief that p. In (B) cases what U intends to bring about is A's doing D.

Schiffer then claims that "U performed an illocutionary act in uttering x iff U meant something by uttering x" (103), that is, iff U either meant that p by uttering x, or meant that H was to do D by uttering x. The various types of illocutionary acts are distinguished as follows. First, some distinctions can be made in terms of the two main forms of speaker meaning. Thus predicting involves meaning that p for some p, while requesting involves meaning that H is to do D, for some D. Inside each main division illocutionary act types are distinguished both in terms of the p or D involved and in terms of the reasons U meant H to have for believing p or for doing D. Using 'R' for *reasons U intended H to have for his response*, this means that the "assertive" illocutionary act types divide up into those that are:

A1. Identifiable by the kind of p involved.
A2. Identifiable by the kind of R involved.
A3. Identifiable by both the kind of p and the kind of R involved.

Similarly the "directives" divide up into those that are:

B1. identifiable by the kind of D involved.
B2. identifiable by the kind of R involved.
B3. identifiable by both the kind of D and the kind of R involved.

Schiffer's examples of these categories are (99):[10]

A.			B.	
I.	2.	3.	2.	3.
affirming	assuring	apologizing	advising	asking
answering	inferring	estimating	commanding	interrogating
correcting	reporting	permitting	entreating	questioning
denying	suggesting	predicting	ordering	
describing	telling	promising	prescribing	
explaining		thanking	requesting	
illustrating			telling (to)	
objecting				
replying				

For example, (A1.) U was *objecting* to A's claim that q (and objecting to it that p) iff U meant by uttering x that the fact that p constitutes a good rea-

---

[9] This qualification is introduced to handle cases in which U knows or believes that H already believes that p, but wants to "activate" that belief, to make H consciously aware of it. Reminding A that p would be such a case.
[10] Schiffer suggests that category B1. is empty.

son for thinking that A's claim that q is false.[11] (A2.) When U means that p by uttering x, U *reports* that p iff U intended that (part of) A's reason for believing that p is that U uttered x intending A to think that, on the basis of U's observations or investigations, U believed (or knew) that p. (A3.) When one means that p by uttering x, one *estimates* the value of something y only if what one meant by uttering x is that the value of y is such-and-such (kind of p involved), and only if he intended part of A's reason for believing that p to be that U uttered x intending A to think that, as a result of having examined y and of having applied to his findings certain general knowledge of his concerning the value of things of that type, U believed (or knew) that p. (B2.) In meaning that A was to do D by uttering x, U was *ordering* A to do D only if U intended part of A's reason for doing D to be: there is a certain legal or conventional or institutional relation, R, between U and A, such that by virtue of their being related in way R, U has the right to expect A to do an act of such-and-such a sort if in circumstances of such-and-such a sort U means that A is to do an act of that sort; that D is an act of the relevant sort; and that the circumstances in which U uttered x were of the relevant sort.

iv. Criticism of Schiffer's Account

My critical reactions to this account will fall under two headings. (1) Can illocutionary acts of all types be construed as so many ways of meaning that p or meaning that H is to do D? (2) Does every illocutionary act involve intending to produce a distinctive sort of effect on an audience?

Beginning with (1), let's first note that Schiffer's account is tailor-made for assertives and, to a lesser degree, for directives. When I assert that p in one way or another, I mean that p. The garment doesn't fit directives nearly so well. As Schiffer notes (60), when I request, implore, or advise H to do D, it is not true, in any ordinary sense of the terms, that I meant that H *is to* do D. That is much too peremptory for these illocutionary forces, though not for ordering. Schiffer needs something that is neutral between different directive forces, but it is clear that he doesn't have it. But let's suppose that we have given a suitable sense to 'H is to do D' and pass on. The point still remains that he needs something to distinguish between different directive types—ordering, requesting, advising, suggesting, and so on. If what is meant is the same for all these (where the propositional content is the same), then the only principle of distinction Schiffer has left is the reasons U meant H to have for doing D. Schiffer makes no suggestion as to how this can do the job, and I can't see how it could.

[11] This example contradicts the impression one might have formed that in the A. cases the p that is meant is confined to the propositional content of the illocutionary act, leaving out the illocutionary force.

Once we get beyond the assertive and directive groups, the problem becomes much more acute. On p. 93 Schiffer says: "such speech acts as belong to highly conventionalized institutions are, from the point of view of the theory of language and communication, of marginal interest only". And he does not include any exercitives in the table quoted above. But even if Schiffer is right in this judgment of centrality, it is still of interest to see whether his account can handle exercitives and if so how. He does include one commissive, promising, in his table, but he does not spell out how it would be treated. Does his approach provide sufficient resources for handling commissives and exercitives?

Suppose I promise to read your paper by Friday, by uttering 'I promise to read your paper by Friday'.[12] What do I mean by uttering that? One answer would be: I meant that I would read your paper by Friday. This would neatly fit the "means that p" model. But that fails to distinguish *promising* that p (I will read your paper by Friday) from *expressing an intention to bring it about that p* or *predicting* that p. Thus, just as with the various directive illocutionary forces, the distinction will have to be made in terms of the reasons U intended H to have for his response. And, again, Schiffer makes no suggestion as to how this might be done. Nor do I see any way out along these lines.

I now move to the second question, whether all illocutionary acts involve the intention to produce a certain distinctive type of effect on an audience. It is here that we will find fatal difficulties in Schiffer's account. To focus the question, let's recall that Schiffer's theory involves the following central claims.

1. U performs an illocutionary act in uttering x iff in uttering x U means that p or means that H is to do D.
2. U means that p in uttering x only if U uttered x with the intention of producing in H the activated belief that p; and U means that H is to do D only if U uttered x with the intention of getting H to do D.
3. Therefore U performed an illocutionary act in uttering x only if U uttered x either with the intention of producing in H the activated belief that p or with the intention of getting H to do D.
4. What illocutionary act U performed in uttering x depends on what belief or action of H U uttered x in order to bring about, and/or on what reasons U intended H to have for that belief or action.

[12] It doesn't matter for this example whether or not the illocutionary force, or any other part of the illocutionary act, is explicitly spelled out in the sentence uttered. The sentence could just as well have been 'I'll read your paper by Friday' or 'I'll do it by Friday'. Remember that what we are about is *what U means by uttering x*, not *what U means by X*.

Thus it is crucial for Schiffer's theory that to each illocutionary act type there is correlated a type of belief or action, such that the illocutionary act type is made the type it is, at least in part, by the fact that one issues one's utterance with the intention of producing a belief or action of the correlated type in H. Let's consider whether this is the case.

We may profitably divide the question. (1) Does each illocutionary act type have a correlated type of perlocutionary intention such that speakers *normally* perform illocutionary acts of that type with a perlocutionary intention of that type? (2) Is it the case that *whenever* U performs an illocutionary act of type I, U utters *x* with a perlocutionary intention of the type associated with I? If Schiffer's theory is to stand, both questions must be answered in the affirmative.

I believe that it is (2) that most obviously fails to hold. I do not want to contest an affirmative answer to (1). I will admit for the sake of argument that for every illocutionary act type there is some type of belief or action such that the intention to elicit a belief or action of that type in A normally accompanies illocutionary acts of that type. One typically requests A to do D in order to get A to do D; one typically tells A that *p* in order to bring A to realize that *p*.[13] Even with commissives and exercitives it may well be true that such acts are normally performed with the intention, inter alia, of getting the audience to realize that the appropriate conventional effect is engendered. Beliefs to that effect are not of the sort Schiffer seems to have had in mind, and they may well give rise to various difficulties. But I will not pursue these issues further, conceding for the sake of discussion that subquestion (1) can be answered in the affirmative.

Turning to (2) I shall first look at assertives and directives, for which Schiffer's account is specially designed. I shall argue that it is possible to perform illocutionary acts of a certain assertive or directive type *without* the perlocutionary intentions that Schiffer takes to be constitutive of that type. I shall then make similar remarks about illocutionary acts of other categories. But the heart of the argument is the claim that Griceian perlocutionary intentions are not necessary for the performance of even those types of illocutionary acts that Schiffer places in the center of the picture. Even for those types illocutionary act performance does not consist in uttering a sentence with a certain kind of perlocutionary intention.[14]

The most obvious difficulties concern illocutionary acts one directs to oneself. I often raise objections to what I have just said, remind myself that *p*, reply to myself that *p*, predict that *p*, all in the absence of any auditor

[13] Note that I have put this, idiomatically, in terms of a perlocutionary intention with which we perform the illocutionary act, rather than a perlocutionary intention with which we perform the sentential act. That means that we remain saddled with the difficulty mentioned in n. 1.

[14] When discussing assertives I shall simplify matters by restricting attention to types, like telling H that *p*, in which (at least part of) the perlocutionary intention said to be necessary is the intention to produce the activated belief that *p*, rather than more complicated types,

other than myself. The mere fact that one is talking to oneself does not pose a difficulty. Such cases will still conform to Schiffer's analysis provided I utter *x* with the intention of producing in myself the activated belief that *p* or with the intention of getting myself to do D (and provided the rest of Schiffer's conditions are satisfied). In some cases of monologue I do have such intentions. I sometimes tell myself, in a stern tone of voice, that I must turn off the lights when leaving the car, thereby trying to get myself to do so. Examples of self-belief-production are harder to come by. If I flatly and sincerely assert that *p*, I already believe that *p* (actively) and realize that I do so. Here I cannot be trying to get myself to actively believe that *p*. But by broadening the concept of the effect we may bring some cases of monologial assertion into conformity with the account—those in which one seeks to "talk oneself into something". But even if the account fits these cases, there are many types of monologue it cannot accommodate. Sometimes I simply *express*, give voice to, my beliefs or attitudes. When engaged in doing something I may comment to myself on various stages of the endeavor as I go along. I may say "That is coming along quite well", or "That line is a little crooked"; or if listening to music I may remark to myself that the third movement is being taken too fast or that the oboe has a particularly beautiful tone. It would be absurd to suggest in these cases that I am trying to produce or enliven any of my beliefs.

But I don't want to rest my case against Schiffer on monologue alone. For one thing, as I have just been intimating, it is notoriously difficult to determine the psychological fine structure of such proceedings. And it might be claimed that monologue is a logically secondary case of illocutionary act performance, and that the only sensible aspiration is to give an adequate account of the logically primary cases of interpersonal discourse. Hence it would be much more significant to show that Schiffer's theory is not adequate for other-directed illocutionary acts.

v. Counterexamples to Schiffer's Account

First I will consider some possible counterexamples discussed by Schiffer.

1. *Countersuggestible cases.* "The Berkeley police, thinking that the campus would be the best place to contain a riot, announce to the Berkeley radicals that under no circumstances are they, the radicals, to hold their rally on the campus. It is the intention of the police that this announcement should cause the rally to be held on campus." (69)

---

like objecting that *p*, where the perlocutionary intention is said to be the intention to produce a more complicated belief.

2. *Examination cases.* Teacher: "Tell me, if you can, when the Battle of Hastings was fought." Student: "1066." (70)
3. *Confession cases.* Police: "O.K., Capone, the jig's up. We know you stole the bubble-gum, so you'd better confess." Capone: "I confess, I stole the bubble-gum." (70)
4. *Accusation cases.* Mr. Smith: "I was working at the office all evening." Mrs. Smith: "You're lying." (71)

These are all putative counterexamples. In each assertive case (2–4), where what is asserted is p and where U means that p, U does not issue the utterance in order to get H to believe that p. This is because in each case U is quite sure that H already actively believes that p. In 1., a directive case, U directs H not to do D, meaning that H is not to do D, but he does this not to get H *not* to do D, but, on the contrary, to get H to do D.

Schiffer's general line is to hold that in all these cases "the sense in which it may be said of S [speaker] in these examples that he meant that p or meant that A [hearer] was to do D is an extended or attenuated sense, one derived from and dependent upon the primary sense captured in the definitions" (71). But his arguments for this are extremely weak. In the countersuggestible case he does make the relevant point that "the very possibility of this type of deception is dependent upon its being *at least* generally the case that one who means that A is to do D intends A to do D" (71). This seems correct, but it does not follow that it is in a different or "attenuated" sense of 'mean' that the police meant that the radicals were not to hold their rally on campus. It seems equally true that the possibility of lying depends on its being generally the case that people assert what they believe to be the case. But surely when I lie in asserting that p it is not in some different sense of 'mean' that I mean that p, nor is it in some different sense of 'assert' that I assert that p. Later in his discussion Schiffer says: "Whatever one's intuitions about *meaning*, it seems more difficult to deny that in uttering x S *ordered* A to do D only if S uttered x with the intention of getting A to do D" (71–72). But I cannot see the difference Schiffer claims here. Provided that the police issued their order in the appropriate way, with full knowledge of what they were doing, and with the intention of taking appropriate steps to enforce it (though it is not clear that this last condition is essential), we have a clear case both of ordering the radicals not to do D and of meaning that the radicals are not to do D, whatever the ultimate intentions of the police.

In the other cases Schiffer's arguments are even weaker. His treatment of the examination case simply amounts to claiming that the student does not, in the primary sense, "tell" the teacher that the Battle of Hastings was fought in 1066. This may or may not be, but even if it is, that takes care of only one illocutionary verb; there are others that have a "primary" application here. Surely one can unproblematically say that the student *replied* that the Battle Hastings was fought in 1066, or *expressed the belief* that the Battle of Hastings was fought in 1066. And we still need an account of those illocutionary acts.

As for the confession case, Schiffer points out, correctly, that some confessions are intended to provide others with evidence that *p*. Of those that are not, like George Washington's confessing to having cut down the cherry tree, he writes:

> My inclination is to say that here, too, our willingness to say that S "meant" that *p* derives from the fact that in this type of case . . . S utters *x* as if he were informing (telling) A that *p*. (72)

Again the arbitrary selection of *telling* or *informing* as the paradigmatic acts of the assertive category, to the neglect of their numerous kindred. For my part I would have no compunction in saying that little George *told* his father that he had cut down the cherry tree (*inform* is a different story). And even if Schiffer were right about 'tell', there is still 'confess'. What account is to be given of the illocutionary act report 'George Washington *confessed* that he cut down the cherry tree'?

On the accusation case Schiffer says flatly that:

> While it is true that Mrs. Smith meant that she knew (or believed) that her husband was lying, it is, strictly speaking, false that she meant that he was lying. (73)

I am staggered by this. Surely it is only by looking at the case through his theory that Schiffer can so blithely deny that Mrs. Smith meant that her husband was lying. Perhaps she did *also* mean that she knew that he was lying; but does that prevent it from being the case that she meant that he was lying? But "whatever one's intuitions about meaning", there will be clear, unproblematic illocutionary act reports that are appropriate here. Mrs. Smith surely *alleged, claimed* that her husband was lying, and *accused* him of lying. And we need a way of handling those.

Moreover, even if it were possible to treat cases like the above as "secondary" or "derivative" in some significant respect, it would clearly be preferable to have an account that applied in the same way to these cases and to the ones that Schiffer's analysis fits. For, whatever is to be said about "primary" and "secondary", it is at least obvious that these are clear, uncontroversial cases of I'ing that *p* (where 'I' is some illocutionary act verb). And it would be desirable to have an account that applies in the same way to all clear cases. I shall seek to provide such an account.

Grice's version of perlocutionary intentions does not run into difficulties with these cases. He substitutes for "getting H to believe that *p*", "getting H to believe that U believes that *p*", and for "getting H to do D", "getting H to believe that U intends (wants) H to do D". This nicely handles all the above examples. The police certainly intend to get the radicals to believe that they (the police) want the radicals not to hold the rally on campus; Mrs. Smith wants her husband to believe that she believes (knows) that he is lying; and so on. However, Grice's version does not fare any better than Schiffer's in the more stubborn cases to which we now turn.

First, consider situations in which one makes a report or announcement, gives advice or information, or testifies to something, because it is one's job to do so or because one is under obligation to do so, but where one doesn't care in the least about H's reaction. This description often applies to persons in charge of information booths in railway stations, those announcing flights in airports, academic advisers, and persons who are subpoenaed to testify before congressional committees. In such cases one is clearly performing an illocutionary act of informing A that p, announcing that p, advising someone to do D, or testifying that p. But sometimes one is not uttering one's sentence in order to get any H actively to believe that p, or actively to believe that one oneself believes that p. One doesn't care whether one's audience believes this or not. One is simply performing the illocutionary act because one is committed to do so. Perhaps it is a presupposition of the institution that gives rise to this obligation that, by and large, such announcements and information-givings will lead to corresponding beliefs in their recipients; and perhaps if this were not the case there would be no such jobs as flight announcing. But this does not imply that in each individual case of I'ing that p such results are produced or that the speaker has the intention of producing them.

Schiffer does consider "don't care" cases like these and responds as follows.

> Customer: "Where is lingerie?"
> Clerk: "Lingerie is on the fifth floor."
> No doubt the clerk, in saying that lingerie is on the fifth floor, intends to be complying with the customer's request; i.e., the clerk intends to be supplying the customer with the information requested. But it may also be that the clerk is completely indifferent as to whether or not the customer accepts this information and that the clerk would not be at all disturbed were the customer to refuse to believe that lingerie is on the fifth floor. (68)

In this passage Schiffer seems to be conceding that this is a counterexample to his theory. I take "intends to be supplying the customer with the information requested" to be a particular kind of "illocutionary intention", an intention to perform an illocutionary act of a certain type, namely, informing A that p. He admits that one can intend to perform this act (and succeed in doing so) without having the perlocutionary intention (to get H to believe that p) that his theory takes to be a necessary condition of that illocutionary act.

There are also cases in which the speaker does care how the hearer reacts but has no hope of producing the standard response. I may feel certain that my wife won't believe me when I tell her why I have come home so late, but still I feel obliged to tell her the truth when she asks me. Again, I may be quite sure that my son will not respond to my exhortations to get his homework done on time; but nevertheless I consider it my duty to remind him that this is what he ought to do. Here, as in the "don't care" cases, the illocutionary act is performed because the agent takes it to be his duty to do so. They differ with respect to what inhibits the usual perlocutionary intention.

Schiffer tries to handle these "hopeless" cases as follows.

> In general, one cannot do an act X with the intention of bringing about a certain result if one knows or believes that one will not thereby bring about that result. But while this is generally the case, it is not necessarily the case. A person trapped in a burning building might leap from a seventh floor window with the intention of saving his life. Somewhat analogously, it is not uncommon to try to convince someone that p despite its being virtually certain that one will fail. (69)

To be sure, there might be such cases. But this is in no way incompatible with the existence of cases like the ones I have just described in which one carries on "just for the record" *without* the normal perlocutionary intentions, and where one lacks those intentions just because one has no hope of achieving the standard result.

Another kind of illocutionary activity that falls outside Schiffer's net is "making conversation". We are thrown together at a party. I open with "Beastly weather lately, isn't it?". You reply "Oh I don't know, it's not as bad as it might be". "Well, at least we aren't having freezing rain". And so on, with more of the same. It is clear to both of us that we both already know that the weather is beastly, but not as bad as it might be, and so on. Although it is conceivable that a person in this situation has the aim of activating these beliefs in her interlocutor, it is clear to both of us that neither of us has any such aim. We are simply responding to the social imperative not to keep silence and are saying the sorts of things it is conventional to say in such a context. We are performing illocutionary acts of the assertive type. I *remark* that the weather is beastly; you *reply* that it could be worse. And yet we are completely innocent of any Schifferian intentions.

Nor would Grice's version fare better in these last three kinds of cases. If our flight announcer does not aim at getting his addressees to believe that p, he may be equally indifferent to whether H believes that U believes that *p*. And my aim in making conversation at the party may be equally well served, whether or not my companion believes that I believe that the weather is beastly.

Thus, not even in the areas for which it was specifically designed does Schiffer's account provide necessary conditions for illocutionary act performance. I conclude that perlocutionary intentions of the sort featured in the Grice program are not necessary for illocutionary act performance, and hence that uttering sentences with such intentions cannot be what it is to perform an illocutionary act.

CHAPTER THREE

The Nature of Illocutionary Acts

i. Searle's "Non-Defective" Promising

If illocutionary acts cannot be construed as sentential acts with perlocutionary intentions, how are they to be construed? By virtue of what is an utterance turned into an illocutionary act of a certain type? In this chapter I will work toward my answer by way of a critical analysis of the account given by John Searle in *Speech Acts* (1969).

In chapter 3 of 1969 Searle presents an analysis of a sample illocutionary act concept—promising.

Given that a speaker S utters a sentence T in the presence of a hearer H, then, in the literal utterance of T, S sincerely and non-defectively promises that *p* to H if and only if the following conditions 1–9 obtain:

1. Normal input and output conditions obtain.
2. S expressed the proposition that *p* in the utterance of T.
3. In expressing that *p*, S predicates a future act A of S.
4. H would prefer S's doing A to his not doing A, and S believes H would prefer his doing A to his not doing A.
5. It is not obvious to both S and H that S will do A in the normal course of events.
6. S intends to do A.
7. S intends that the utterance of T will place him under an obligation to do A.

8. S intends (i-1) to produce in H the knowledge (K) that the utterance of T is to count as placing S under an obligation to do A. S intends to produce K by means of the recognition of i-1, and he intends i-1 to be recognized in virtue of (by means of) H's knowledge of the meaning of T.
9. The semantical rules of the dialect spoken by S and H are such that T is correctly and sincerely uttered if and only if conditions 1–8 obtain. (57–61)

Some of these conditions need explication, which will be provided as the discussion proceeds.

Searle alleges that each of the listed conditions is necessary for "sincerely and non-defectively" promising that p to H and that their conjunction is sufficient. The first point to note is that some of the conditions are not necessary for promising *tout court*. For example, there are clear cases of promising where (4) is not satisfied. I might say to you, "I promise to take you to the meeting tomorrow", where, unbeknownst to me, you would prefer not being taken by me, but, for fear of offending me, you do not make this explicit. Despite this I could still be promising to take you to the meeting tomorrow. I could have assumed an obligation to do so and could justly be blamed for failing to do so. Even the second part of (4) could be violated without preventing a promise from being made. Thus I might realize, or believe incorrectly, that you would prefer not to go to the meeting with me, but utter the above sentence anyway. Perhaps I want to make you uncomfortable. In such a case, at least so long as I do not make explicit that I believe you would rather not be taken by me to the meeting and you do not make your preference explicit, I could still be promising to do so. Similar points can be made about conditions (5) and (6).

Condition (1) is not necessary for promising either. Look at how Searle explains this condition.

> I use the terms "input" and "output" to cover the large and indefinite range of conditions under which any kind of serious and literal linguistic communication is possible. "Output" covers the conditions for intelligible speaking and "input" covers the conditions of understanding. Together they include such things as that the speaker and hearer both know how to speak the language; both are conscious of what they are doing; they have no physical impediments to communication, such as deafness, aphasia, or laryngitis; and they are not acting in a play or telling jokes, etc. It should be noted that this condition excludes both impediments to communication such as deafness and also parasitic forms of communication such as telling jokes or acting in a play. (57)

Searle also says: "I am construing condition 1. broadly enough so that together with the other conditions it guarantees that H understands the utterance. . . ."

Now clearly it is not necessary for promising H that I will do A that H not be deaf or that I do not have laryngitis! More seriously, it is not necessary that H understand what I said. To be sure, if H did not understand me, she didn't *realize* that I made that promise, but I could still have done it. Suppose that I mistakenly think that H heard and understood me. I show up to take H to the meeting, and H is surprised at this. I might well say, "Didn't you hear me when I promised to take you?", thereby presupposing that I did promise this even if H didn't realize it.

Searle will respond by pointing out that these conditions were presented as necessary, not for promising *tout court*, but for "sincere and non-defective" promising. Condition 6. is necessary for that because even though I might promise to read your paper without intending to do so, I cannot, by definition, *sincerely* promise to read your paper without intending to do so. Cases in which the other conditions fail will be branded "defective" in one way or another.

Searle is, of course, free to pick any analysandum he chooses. But the difficulty with focusing on "non-defective promising" is that there are too many ways in which promises can be defective, vis-à-vis their standard social function. I might promise to do something it would be very foolish for me to do. The promisee might not take me seriously. The consequences of my keeping the promise might be disastrous, as it would be if I were president of the United States and had promised Senator Helms to drop the H-bomb on Teheran. The promiser might be an unreliable person, though always sincere at the moment. And so on. Thus even if we leave out defects that are not distinctive of promises, such as conceptual confusions and bad pronunciation, the absences of which Searle may have meant to ensure by his catchall condition 1., there are a large number of ways in which promises can be defective. The absence of all of them would be necessary for completely "non-defective" promising. And yet I doubt very much that Searle would want to include "A is a good thing for S to do" as a necessary condition. Searle apparently has a sense that some possible defects are such that the absence of the defect is, so to say, "intrinsic to the notion" of promising (54), and it is these that he wants his conditions to rule out. But the trouble is that the term 'non-defective' and Austin's term 'infelicitous' simply fail to make that distinction. For this reason I feel that Searle's analysandum is too indeterminate, too hazy, to present a useful target. I agree that S's intending to do A, and H's preferring S's doing A to S's not doing A, are *somehow* involved in the notion of promising, even though they are not necessary conditions thereof. In a bit I will bring out how this is.

ii. Taking Responsibility

Suppose, then, we set out to say what it is to promise H to do A, whether "defectively" or not. I want an account that will cover all clear cases of promising—sincere or insincere, well-advised or misguided, explicit or elliptical. I also recognize that conditions 4. and 6. are somehow involved in important ways, although their satisfaction is not necessary for promising. How, then, can they be brought into the account? Fortunately, Searle himself has shown the way.

> A promise involves an expression of intention, whether sincere or insincere. So to allow for insincere promises, we need only to revise our conditions to state that the speaker takes responsibility for having the intention rather than stating that he actually has it. A clue that the speaker does take such responsibility is the fact that he could not say without absurdity, e.g., "I promise to do A but I do not intend to do A". (62)

The notion of taking responsibility for the satisfaction of a condition is one that I have repeatedly used in previous publications (1964a, 1964b, 1977, 1980b, 1994) as a way of bringing conditions like 4. and 6. into the analysis of illocutionary act concepts. We may save both these conditions for an account of promising by prefacing each with "S takes responsibility for its being the case that . . .".

At this point it is necessary to take a detour from Searle's analysis in order to go further into this concept of taking responsibility for something's being the case. In section vi I will return to the traversal of Searle's conditions.

'Take responsibility' must be understood in a special way. The idea is not that U (utterer, speaker) [1] took responsibility for state of affairs C in the sense that he was prepared to acknowledge that he *brought C into existence*. It is, rather, like the way in which, when I become the head of a department or agency, I take responsibility for the efficient and orderly conduct of its affairs, including the work done by my subordinates. I am responsible for all that work, not in the sense that I have done it all myself, but in the sense that I am rightly held to blame if the work is not done properly. I am the one who must "respond" to complaints about that work. It is in this sense that U takes responsibility for 4. and 6. being satisfied in promising H to do A. U, in uttering S, knowingly lays herself open to complaints, objections, correction, blame, or the like in case 4. or 6. is not satisfied. She utters S, recognizing that there is just ground for complaint, in case 4. or

---

[1] In accordance with my practice throughout the book, I will, when speaking in my own person, use 'U' for speaker, while leaving the abbreviation for speaker as 'S' when quoting from Searle and any other writers who follow that practice. I trust that this will not cause confusion. I myself will use 'S' as a dummy term for sentences.

6. is not satisfied. We may take the following as explanations of "In uttering S, U took responsibility for (its being the case that) p". (From now on, I will abbreviate 'U took responsibility for (its being the case that) p' as 'U R'd that p'.)

D5. In uttering S, U R'd that p—In uttering S, U knowingly took on a liability to (laid herself open to) blame (censure, reproach, being taken to task, being called to account), in case of not-p.

D6. In uttering S, U R'd that p—U recognized herself to be rightfully subject to blame, etc., in case of not-p.[2]

I take D5. to be superior to D6. in that it brings out that taking responsibility for p is something that U *does*. It involves U's *instituting* a state of affairs, rather than just being a matter of U's *recognizing* an already existing state of affairs, as might be suggested by D6. The state of affairs in question is a *normative* one. It consists of U's utterance being subject to just complaint or censure in case of not-p. And it is not that U's utterance of S automatically becomes subject to a requirement that p just by virtue of being an utterance of S. Not all utterances of S are subject, willy-nilly, to this requirement. I noted earlier that whatever it is that makes an utterance of S into, for example, a case of promising H to do A is something that is within U's voluntary control. For it is up to U, at least within certain limits, whether U is using S on a given occasion to promise H to do A, rather than to practice pronunciation or to test a microphone. Hence if part of what makes the utterance into a case of promising to do A is that it becomes subject to blame if not-p, then its becoming subject to this must itself be under U's voluntary control. Initially I shall rely on D5. as the canonical explanation of the notion of taking responsibility. I have stated D5. in terms of *knowingly* taking on a liability because I am restricting myself to *intentional* illocutionary act performances.[3]

"Renders oneself liable to blame . . ." is not to be understood as "creates the logical, causal, or psychological possibility of someone's blaming one . . .". It is not that as a result of something U does, H acquires the ability to lodge a complaint against U's utterance. H would have that ability, whatever U does. It is rather that by doing what she does U introduces the possibility of someone's *appropriately*, *rightfully*, *relevantly* objecting to her utterance on the grounds of not-p. It is a *normative* possibility that U has

---

[2] These formulations do not require U to be consciously or explicitly thinking of the liability. All this may be implicit, below the level of explicit notice or conscious awareness, just as the intentions involved in habitual action typically are.

[3] In 5.9 I consider the possibility that someone who did not mean to be promising to do A might nevertheless be correctly taken to do so, provided she uttered the right kind of sentence in the right kind of context.

created. Certain grounds for censure that otherwise would not have been relevant now become relevant.

iii. Epistemological Complexities

There is another problem about D5. We may approach it by considering whether the falsity of the relevant p is by itself necessary and sufficient for U's being subject to blame. Let's say that U intends to be promising H to do A in uttering some appropriate sentence, and it is not the case that H prefers U's doing A to U's not doing A. Is that *sufficient* for U's being liable to blame for uttering that sentence with that intention? Clearly not. Suppose that U had every reason for supposing that H does have that preference, even though H doesn't. Surely that would render U blameless; surely it would excuse her issuing that utterance, since her ignorance of the real facts of the matter was excusable. We can't require anyone to do better than to proceed on the basis of what they are amply justified in believing. By the same token H's lack of this preference is not *necessary* for blameworthiness either. If U had every reason to suppose H not to have that preference, even though H did, U would still be blameworthy for speaking as she did. Justifiably believing condition 4. to be false, even though it isn't, will render blame in order, just as justifiably believing it to be true, though it isn't, will inhibit blameworthiness. With the sincerity condition, 6., this complexity is masked, because we assume that U will know that she intends to do A if and only if she does so intend. In this case there is, ordinarily, no room for discrepancy between what U justifiably believes and what is the case. But with most relevant conditions there is room for such discrepancies; and there it is what U justifiably believes rather than what is actually the case that would seem to determine blameworthiness.

This discussion has all been carried on in terms of justified belief. Why not do it, more naturally, in terms of knowledge? Why not say that one is blameworthy just in case one doesn't know that p, and free of blame in case one does? The trouble with this is that an adequately justified belief that p may not qualify as knowledge. Apart from Gettier problems, it may not so qualify because it is not true that p. That, indeed, was what started us on the idea that it is U's epistemic status vis-à-vis p, rather than whether it is the case that p is what is crucial for blameworthiness. If U is adequately justified in believing that p, then she cannot be faulted for issuing the utterance, whether it is true that p or not, and hence whether she knows that p.

We must realize that when one is *blameworthy*, that is, *liable to blame* or *subject to blame*, one does not necessarily get blamed, even if there are other people who are aware of the situation. There are two reasons for this. First, the blameworthiness of which we have been speaking is only prima facie;

whether one is actually justified in blaming the speaker depends on various other factors. If the transgression for which I am subject to blame is very minor, or if being blamed for it would upset me in such a way as to endanger my health or my life, one would not be justified on the whole in blaming me.[4] Second, even if blame would be justified on the whole, whether anyone actually levels it depends on a variety of factors. The matter may not be important enough to warrant anyone's taking the trouble. There may be no one who is both apprised of the situation and sufficiently involved to care. Considerations of decorum or social rank may preclude any knowledgeable auditor's calling me to account.

iv. Blameworthiness and Incorrectness

The above discussion raises questions as to how we should formulate what U is taking responsibility for in promising H to do A. Prior to introducing the epistemological complications, we were supposing that U takes responsibility for various "objective" facts, such as those concerning H's preferences. But, in the light of the recent discussion, shouldn't we put an epistemological gloss on this? Shouldn't we say that what U takes responsibility for is not, for example, that H prefers S's doing A to S's not doing A, but rather that U is adequately justified in believing that H prefers U's doing A to U's not doing A?

Well, this depends on a further issue. I will introduce it by noting that where one of the conditions like Searle's 4. or 6. is not satisfied, the utterance is *wrong, incorrect*, or *out of order*, even if the epistemological conditions for blameworthiness are not satisfied. Even if U was adequately justified in believing that 4. is satisfied but in fact it wasn't, his (seriously) uttering 'I promise you to do A' was *out of order*, though his doing so was excusable. Although U's being subject to blame, censure, or sanctions of various sorts depends on U's epistemic situation vis-à-vis 4., the *correctness* of the utterance does not. If 4. is not satisfied, it was the *wrong* thing to say, whatever the correct judgment as to U's fault. This suggests that we could give an account of what it is for U to take responsibility for a condition's holding in terms of *incorrectness* or *being out of order*, rather than in terms of being subject to blame, censure, or reproach.

D7. In uttering S, U R'd that *p*—In uttering S, U knowingly took on a liability to being incorrect (wrong, out of order) in case of not-*p*.

This alternative is clearly relevant to the question of what it is for which U takes responsibility in, for example, making a promise. Since correctness

---

[4]   Note that I am thinking of blaming as an overt act, not simply the recognition that the subject is to blame. It is only the former the justifiability of which would be affected by factors like those just mentioned.

of utterance, unlike liability to blame, is a function of whether the conditions in question are actually satisfied, if we adopt D7. as our explication of choice, we can stick with the simpler account according to which what U R's in making a promise is, for example, a condition like 4., rather than that she is adequately justified in supposing 4. to be satisfied.

But which account should we choose, D5. or D7.? To answer this question we need to bring out another aspect of the situation.

v. The Crucial Role of Rules

I have been speaking in terms of U's instituting a certain normative state of affairs in uttering S. In the earlier version (D5.) what U does in R'ing certain conditions is to bring it about that certain states of affairs are grounds for *blame* or *censure*, whereas previously they were not. In the later formulation (D7.), U brings it about that the utterance is incorrect under certain conditions. But how is either of these possible? What *can* one do to change one's liabilities in this way? And what does it take for whatever one is doing to have this effect?

To answer these questions we need to consider more generally what is required for the existence of a normative state of affairs, like blameworthiness or incorrectness or the opposites. The suggestions I am about to make will not receive a full development until Chapters 7 and 8, but a preliminary exposition is needed to further explicate the notion of R'ing.

What is it for an action to *be* blameworthy or the opposite, or to be incorrect, out of order, or the reverse? Isn't it a matter of whether certain rules, regulations, norms, or principles are being conformed to or violated? Since the detailed development of this idea in Chapters 7 and 8 will be in terms of 'rule', that will be the term of choice here. Where U is blameworthy he has violated some relevant rule, and where he is not, he has not done so. Where an utterance is out of order it is because the utterance is not in conformity with what is required for an utterance of that sentence in that kind of context by some applicable rule; and when it is in order it is in conformity with those requirements. Thus the possibility of a normative state of affairs being initiated by U's R'ing that C depends on the existence of a system of rules that is in force within a community that includes U.

The claim that *socially* entrenched rules are required can be supported as follows. When U R's that C in performing an illocutionary act, that is not a purely private performance that could be what it is regardless of how it engages the surrounding community.[5] For R'ing consists in making certain kinds of reactions by *others* appropriate. That is, to R that *p* is to give one's

[5] The insistence on a system of *social* rules will shortly be qualified to allow for cases that involve idiosyncratic rules. But we must first delineate the primary interpersonal case before we can understand private variations on that.

utterance a certain normative status in a community. Thus (except for the atypical case, to be discussed shortly, of the speaker who is making up rules as he goes along), in R'ing one is subjecting one's utterance to social rules. Apart from such rules I can no more bring it about that my utterance is wrong in case of not-C than I can bring it about that my firing Jones is wrong in case certain procedures were not observed.

Now for the derivative idiosyncratic case. A person who exists in a society that is structured by social rules, as we all do, thereby acquires the concept of a rule, at least a working concept. Having come to understand what it is for a rule to be in force, what it is to obey or flout a rule, and what it is for one's behavior to be subject to a rule, he can then *institute* rules to govern his behavior and/or those of others. A linguistic realization of this possibility is the creation of a special code for communication with oneself or with a few chosen associates. Such cases can still be construed as conforming to the general description but with a drastic limitation of the society within which the rules are in force.

Before proceeding further I had better clear up an ambiguity in this talk of a speaker's being subject to reproach or blame in case condition C is not satisfied, or of an utterance's being incorrect or out of order. The ambiguity is between a *spectator* and a *participant* standpoint from which one is speaking. When I, as a philosopher of language, make judgments of these sorts I am (or can be) speaking as a spectator rather than as a participant. In saying that U brought it about that his utterance would be wrong in case of not-C, I am not necessarily committing myself to the con-attitudes that are involved in a full-blooded, participant use of these terms. I need not have any disposition myself to reproach or blame U, or to judge the utterance out of order, in case of not-C or U's not being justified in believing that C. My statement should be taken in the same spirit as that of an anthropologist who, in describing a culture, tells us what actions are taboo under what conditions. In informing us that among the Maui it is taboo to touch a woman during her menstrual period, the anthropologist is not expressing any reluctance to do this herself, or any sense that such behavior is wrong. She is simply making a statement about the status such an action has within a certain society. My remarks about what is brought about by R'ing are of the same sort. When I say that in asserting that *p* U lays himself open to *just* reproach in case of his not being justified in believing that *p*, I am not expressing my own normative commitments (though I may in fact have such commitments), but rather saying something about how U's behavior fits into the system of rules in U's linguistic community.

I have suggested that one cannot, in uttering S, take on a liability to blame in case he is not adequately justified in believing that C, or take on a liability to one's utterance being incorrect in case of not-C, except by putting one's utterance under subjection to a rule that requires C. This gives us still another way of defining 'R'.

D8. U R'd that _p_ in uttering S—In uttering S, U subjects his utterance to a rule that, in application to this case, implies that it is permissible for U to utter S only if _p_.[6]

This construal in terms of rules enables us to give a more satisfactory treatment of the variety of possible reactions to the utterance of one who R's that _p_. We have already noted that whether the speaker is subject to blame or reproach will depend not on whether _p_ is actually the case but rather on U's epistemic position vis-à-vis that issue. U can rightfully be blamed only if she was not adequately justified in believing that _p_. But we have spoken of one who R's that _p_ as prepared to recognize that "something will be wrong" with her utterance, that it will be "out of order", if it is not the case that _p_, whatever U's epistemic position. Thus if U asks H to close the kitchen door, U is prepared to recognize that something is wrong with his utterance, that it can be "objected to" or "corrected", just on the grounds that the kitchen door is already closed. If U had adequate reason for supposing it to be open, then she will not incur censure or blame for having spoken as she did; but even so there was something fundamentally amiss with the utterance. The formulation in terms of rules enables us to put all this together into a systematic treatment.

First, note that, according to D8., what the presupposed rule lays down as a necessary condition of the permissibility of uttering S is _p_ ("The kitchen door is open") itself. One might think that if the rule, in application to this case, implies that S is to blame only in case S does not firmly believe that _p_ with adequate justification, that is what the rule should require for permissible utterance. But if we take that line, we will not be able to understand why the utterance is amiss provided that not-_p_, regardless of U's epistemic position. On the other hand, if we think of the rule as requiring _p_ itself, then we can understand this last point and the conditions of blame as well.

The first point is obviously taken care of; the utterance is out of order in case of not-_p_ just because the rule says that the utterance is permissible only if _p_. But the point about the epistemic conditions of blame is accommodated as well. To see this we have only to note a distinction that applies to practical principles of any kind. Consider a rule that lays down a condition, C, as necessary for permissibly doing D, and consider a person, P, who is subject to the rule. Relative to this rule we can distinguish between the person's "objective" and "subjective" obligations, with a parallel distinction for the terms 'right' and 'wrong' and other normative terms. P's objective obligation is to do D only if C. If P does D when C is satisfied or refrains from D when C is not satisfied, then he is objectively in the right, so far as

---

[6] The reason for the qualification 'in this context' will be made clear in 7.6.

this rule is concerned.[7] Whereas if he does D when C is not satisfied, he is doing the wrong thing objectively. But, as we have noted for the illocutionary act case, if he does D where C is not satisfied but where he has adequate reason for feeling sure that it is, then he is not to blame. Although he is objectively in the wrong, he is not subjectively in the wrong. He is not in the wrong from his perspective; he is doing what, according to his best lights, constitutes conformity to the rule. Likewise, if C is satisfied but P has every reason to suppose it isn't, and he does D anyway, then though he is objectively in the right he is subjectively in the wrong; he did what, according to his best judgment, was the wrong thing to do. Consider a rule to the effect that questions are to be raised from the audience only after the end of the lecture. If I raise a question before the end of the lecture, where I have every right to suppose that the lecture is over, I am objectively in the wrong but subjectively in the right. Whereas if I raise a question, thinking the lecture has not ended though it has, I am objectively in the right but subjectively in the wrong. And it is clear that blameworthiness goes with subjective, rather than with objective, wrongness.

I didn't really need all this machinery to make the point that a rule that lays down p as a necessary condition for uttering S would imply that S is to blame only if S fails to justifiably believe that p. That point follows just from general considerations about blame. But the machinery gives us a useful framework for interrelating the reactions that are appropriate to not-p and to U's failure to be adequately justified in believing that p. The mere failure of p will imply that the utterance is not what it should be, but S is not necessarily subject to blame. Whereas S's failure to believe that p with adequate justification will put him subjectively in the wrong, leave him subject to blame, but the utterance is not necessarily "defective", and U is not necessarily objectively in the wrong.

I originally introduced the concept of 'R'ing' by reference to conditions of blame, that is, of subjective wrongness (D5.), because we seem to have firmer intuitions as to when an agent is subject to blame than we do concerning when an utterance or other action is "out of order" or "not as it should be" (D7.). But the present discussion shows that once we explain R'ing in terms of subjecting an utterance to a rule (D8.), we can move equally well to both these other formulations—to conditions of objective wrongness as well as to conditions of subjective wrongness.[8]

---

[7] We need this last qualification because even if his doing D does not violate this rule it might violate some other rule to which he is subject, in which case he would not be doing the right thing overall.

[8] In view of the philosophical obsession with morality, it will not be amiss to note explicitly that these formulations are *not* in terms of moral wrongness. One does not fall afoul of morality by violating rules for the utterance of a sentence. If I *deliberately* violate a rule that requires C as a condition of permissibly uttering S (e.g., by lying) I may *also* be morally at fault, but that will be something extra involving the violation of a moral rule and does not follow just

I should say a word about the apparent tension between my saying that one can bring about a normative state of affairs only if one's action is subject to rules that hold in a society to which one belongs, and my speaking, in D8., of S's *subjecting* his utterance to a certain rule. The latter implies that S has a choice as to whether the utterance is subject to the rule in question. That would seem to contradict the earlier claim that some rule holding in the society applies to the utterance whatever the speaker chooses to do. And while we are worrying about how it all fits together, let's also remember that one of the four constraints I laid down near the beginning of Chapter 2 for the condition that turns a sentential act into an illocutionary act of a certain type was that "the condition must be institutable by the speaker at will". This constraint obviously fits nicely with D8. and just as obviously seems to conflict with the idea that the utterance *is* subject to a certain social rule whatever the speaker does about it.

To answer this puzzle I must say something about the kinds of rules that are in question here. The rules alluded to in D8. are more like rules of games than like traffic regulations. Traffic regulations apply to one's driving willy-nilly, whatever one might choose. If one is stopped by a policeman for speeding, it will cut no ice to say, "I didn't choose to subject my driving to that regulation". But rules of games are, or can be, different. One has the latitude, within limits, to decide *when* one is playing a game and, hence, to decide when the rules of the game apply to him. Think of the rule in tennis that requires that in serving one's feet must be back of the baseline before one's racket touches the ball. This rule applies only when one is playing a point for score-keeping purposes. It does not apply when one is warming up. Consider a situation in which it is up to the players when they are playing for points and when they are just hitting the ball. Here it is up to the players when the foot-faulting rule applies to what they are doing. *Illocutionary rules*, as I will call them, have that kind of status. In formulating the rules we will have to stipulate that the conditions they lay down are necessary for permissible utterance only within a certain sphere of activity, only when U is playing the appropriate "language-game". And it will be up to U whether she is doing that at a given moment. For example, no matter what the "standard" illocutionary act potential of a sentence, it is always possible for a speaker to use the sentence to practice pronunciation or test a microphone. Moreover, many sentences have more than one standard illocutionary act potential. 'He got a good hand' can be used to report that he received a lot of applause or that he hired a good worker. Thus it depends on the intentions of the speaker just what rules

from the violation of the illocutionary rule governing sentence utterance. It is worthy of note that in this case the moral rule supervenes on and presupposes the illocutionary rule, which is itself constitutive of the concept of lying, a concept employed in the moral rule that forbids lying.

apply to a particular utterance of the sentence. This point is developed more fully in Part II.[9]

Since R'ing that p involves subjecting one's utterance to a rule that requires p as a condition of permissible utterance, we can make use of another aspect of rule recognition to bring out another aspect of R'ing. When I do something *as subject to a rule that requires p*, I thereby, as we might say, *"represent" p as being the case*. I display my commitment to p's being the case by doing D as subject to that rule. As since I can hardly do D as subject to the rule without "purporting" to follow the rule and thereby purporting to know that I am doing so, we could just as well say that in R'ing that C, I *purport to know that C*. This gives us two more ways of explaining R'ing.

D9.   U R's that p in uttering S—In uttering S, U purports to know that p.

D10. U R's that p in uttering S—In uttering S, U represents p as being the case.

But through all these variations D8. is the most fundamental formulation, the one in terms of which we can understand the others. We will, from now on, think of R'ing as essentially a matter of placing one's utterance under the jurisdiction of a certain rule, at the same time keeping in mind the other formulations as bringing out various implications of the rule subjection made explicit in D8. And since R'ing is central to illocutionary act performance, illocutionary acts are essentially what we may call *rule-subjection acts*, acts that essentially consist in subjecting a lower-level act to a certain rule.[10]

Another consequence of taking rule subjection as the heart of R'ing is that we can think of what we can call "rule-violation-perception" as the fundamental response to the relevance of which one is committed in R'ing that. When one places one's utterance under the jurisdiction of a rule that requires p as a necessary condition of permissible utterance, one thereby commits oneself to recognizing that one's utterance is correctly seen as a rule violation in case of not-p.

[9]   In Part II I will develop the thesis that it is being governed by illocutionary rules that gives a sentence its illocutionary act potentials, and hence, on my account of sentence meaning, gives the sentence its meanings.
[10]   This is in contrast to thinking of an illocutionary act, with Searle, as a "rule-conformity" act, one that consists essentially in making one's lower-level act conform to a rule. This difference reflects the point that while Searle restricts himself to "non-defective" illocutionary acts, I range more widely over all clear cases. Since I admit "defective" acts into the account, I have to allow that one can be performing the act while violating the rule to which one has subjected one's utterance. I must acknowledge, however, that the contrast with Searle on this point is not as sharp as I have just represented it. In Chapter 7 it will come out that some IA types require at least partial rule conformity. But even there rule subjection is most fundamental.

vi. Further Modifications of Searle's Analysis

It is time to return to the traversal of Searle's conditions for promising. In section i I made the points that Searle's conditions 1., 4., and 6. are not necessary conditions of making a promise, but that 4. and 6. could still figure in the account, provided we preface each with 'S R's that . . . '. I will now nail down the point that U's R'ing 4. and 6. are necessary conditions of (intentionally) promising, even though 4. and 6. themselves are not. Suppose U says "I'll write those letters tomorrow" and H says "You know you don't have any intention of writing those letters tomorrow" or "What makes you think I care whether you write them or not?". U then replies "What does that have to do with it?", thereby indicating that he does not take the failure of condition 4. or 6. to be just grounds for complaint about his utterance. If he is sincere in denying the complaints to be relevant, we must conclude that U did not promise to write the letters, or least did not mean to do so. He may have been practicing pronunciation or *predicting* that he would write the letters, or it may have been a slip of the tongue. But whatever he was doing, it was not intentionally promising to write them.

Further support can be provided by considering cases in which a sentential act can underlie two or more illocutionary acts. I say to you, "You're not going out this evening". Using that sentence I might be *ordering* you not to go out or *predicting* that you will not go out. I suggest that which I am doing is a function of the conditions I am R'ing, which is shown by what complaints I am prepared to recognize as relevant. When U orders H to do D he takes responsibility for, inter alia, his being in a position of authority vis-à-vis H. And when U predicts that H will do D, U takes responsibility for its being the case that H will do D. When I say "You're not going out this evening", H, supposing me to be issuing an order, retorts indignantly "You have no right to order me around". If I am issuing an order I will recognize his objection as relevant and will either admit my order was out of order or defend my claim to authority. If, on the other hand, I was making a prediction I will reply in some such ways as "That's beside the point." or "What does that have to do with it?", possibly followed by a clearer exhibition of my intent. On the other hand, if H responds with "How do you know what I'm going to do?" or "You're wrong, I wouldn't miss that show for a million dollars.", these would be relevant if I were making a prediction, irrelevant if I were issuing an order.

I have not included Searle's condition 5. among those a promiser is R'ing. That is because I doubt that it has the same status as 4. and 6. I can't see that it is necessary for promising that U even take responsibility for its being the case that it is not already obvious both to U and to H that U will do A. It's true that a standard function of promising is to assure the addressee that the promiser will do what is promised. But, so far as I can see, it is *possible* for someone to "seal" the matter with a promise even if it is completely on the table for both parties that U is going to do A. And so I am loath to include 5. among the conditions U is R'ing in promising. But I am moved to include another condition that Searle omits, namely, *that it be possible for U to do A*. It seems clear that in promising to do A I am representing it as something that I can do. If I promise to do A I cannot avoid recognizing the allegation this is impossible as a relevant complaint.[11] Hence I will replace Searle's 5. with:

5. It is possible for S to do A.

I do not anticipate complete agreement with my judgments as to what conditions one does or does not R in performing an illocutionary act of a certain type. Nor am I particularly disturbed by this. I doubt that our illocutionary act concepts are precise or determinate enough to permit us to draw a sharp line in every case between what a speaker must be committing himself to and what he need not commit himself to. When I list conditions for various illocutionary act types, I put them forward as plausible suggestions for how such a list should go. The general theses I defend would be unaffected if these lists were altered in their details.

Now look at Searle's 7., which runs as follows:

7. S intends that the utterance of T will place him under an obligation to do A.

Searle calls this the "*essential condition*". I agree with this to a certain extent.[12] The basic point of promising to do A, as contrasted with predicting that one will do A or expressing an intention to do A, is that one places oneself under a prima facie obligation to do A.[13] But this makes it surprising that Searle made the condition to require only that S *intend* his utterance to place him under the obligation, rather than flatly requiring that the utterance *does* place him under the obligation. Searle does say that "further conditions will make clear how that intention is realized" (60). But I cannot see that all Searle's conditions together imply that S *is* put under an obligation to do A. Therefore I will reformulate 7. so that it explicitly requires this.

---

[11] I hope it goes without saying that to recognize a complaint as relevant is not, necessarily, to recognize it as justified. It is only to recognize that *if* things are as the complainer alleges then there is just ground for complaint.

[12] Only up to a point because in 4.4 it will turn out that promising necessarily involves only *purporting* to put oneself under a certain prima facie obligation. In this chapter I do not question the claim that to promise to do A is to lay on oneself a prima facie obligation to do A.

[13] This obligation is only prima facie because it is subject to being overridden by stronger incompatible obligations. Even though I promised to give you a ride to the meeting, that obligation will be overridden if it turns out that I need to take my daughter to the emergency room at the hospital at that time.

7. In uttering S, U places himself under an obligation to do A.

It is clear that something along the lines of this "essential condition" is indeed essential for promising. Searle's 4.–6. alone, what Searle felicitously calls "preparatory conditions", cannot by themselves make the utterance a case of promising. They are *presupposed* as a background for doing what is at the heart of promising, namely, laying an obligation on oneself. But once we realize this, we may suspect that 7. can do the whole job by itself. Is anything else required to make the utterance a case of promising to do A? I think the answer depends on how narrowly we take 'promise'. If it is used narrowly, in contrast to *vowing, contracting*, and other ways of verbally taking on an obligation, then 7. is not enough to make the utterance a promise. If, on the other hand, we use 'promise' in such a way that it covers all linguistic ways of assuming obligations, then 7. is sufficient by itself. Since I take *promising* to contrast with, for example, *vowing* and *contracting*, I will not regard 7. as doing the whole job.[14]

Next consider Searle's 8., which reads:

8. S intends (i-1) to produce in H the knowledge (K) that the utterance of T is to count as placing S under an obligation to do A. S intends to produce K by means of the recognition of i-1, and he intends i-1 to be recognized in virtue of (by means of) H's knowledge of the meaning of T.

Searle's 8. imports a Griceian element into the analysis. But there are crucial differences between the way Griceian intentions enter this account and the way they come into Schiffer's account. First and most important, they are not in the center of the picture here. In Schiffer's theory Griceian intentions (or Schiffer's version thereof) bear the whole burden of making the illocutionary act the kind of act it is, with respect to both propositional content and illocutionary force. Here, by contrast, Griceian intentions are relegated to the periphery. The specific character of the act has been set by other conditions before they come onto the scene. Second, the knowledge that according to 8., S intends to produce in H concerns S's speech act rather than the propositional content thereof.[15]

The last clause of 8. embodies another difference from Griceians. Since Searle restricts himself to linguistic communication, he can lay it down

---

[14] I do not suppose that the above completes the discussion of just what is required for promising. For one thing, R'ing that 5. and 6. would seem to be required as much for contracting as for promising. For another, as foreshadowed above, I will argue in 4.4 that the actual engendering of an obligation is not required for promising.

[15] Don't forget that Schiffer did not explicitly discuss commissives, like promising, and exercitives. If Schiffer had addressed himself to acts of these sorts he might well have been driven to the sort of intended effect Searle brings in.

that S expects H to divine his intentions through H's knowledge of the language.[16]

If the identity of the act has already been determined by other conditions, why is 8. needed? Searle says of 8.: "This captures our amended Griceian analysis of what it is for the speaker to mean the utterance as a promise." This suggests that without 8. S might not intend to be promising to do A. But that is strange, given the fact that Searle's 7. ensures that "S intends that the utterance of T will place him under an obligation to do A". This implies that S means the utterance as a promise, or at least as some sort of commissive. And 8. doesn't do any more than 7. to make the utterance a promise rather than a vow or entering into a contract. I can't see that 8. is needed for this purpose.

Nevertheless, I am not averse to including some such condition as 8., so long as we restrict ourselves to interpersonal communication. It does seem that if one is seriously making a promise or a request or an announcement *to* someone, then one ipso facto intends to get the addressee to realize what illocutionary act one is performing, even where one doesn't also have the further intentions featured by Schiffer. Including such a condition will ensure that the utterance is addressed to someone else. I have argued that Austin's "uptake"—H's actually hearing and understanding what one says—is not a necessary condition of illocutionary act performance. But if I make a request *of* H or make a promise *to* H or make a remark *to* H, my utterance must at least be *addressed* to H. And the present condition provides a way of making that explicit.

If I am to include something like Searle's 8., how shall it be formulated? I have been speaking in terms of the aim at getting one's addressee to realize what illocutionary act one is performing. But, of course, we don't want *one* of several conditions for doing I to be "S intends H to realize that S is doing I".[17] But we can achieve the same result by the following formulation: "S intends that H realizes that the previous conditions are all satisfied".[18]

There is also the question of whether we need to specify that S intends to produce this knowledge by the Griceian mechanism, that is, by means of the recognition of that intention. Since in Chapter 6 I will argue that in

---

[16] Even if U is speaking as explicitly as possible, he would, in general, be ill advised to expect H to figure out his intention from H's knowledge of the language alone. For where an illocutionary act concerns one or more particular individuals, H will have to take contextual features to figure out to what individuals U is referring. This aspect of the matter will receive detailed discussion from Chapter 6 on.

[17] This is both because of circularity problems and because this formulation presupposes that S *is* doing I, and so it would be sufficient by itself for S's doing I.

[18] Searle, let's remember, formulates the intended effect as H's realizing that one of the conditions, 7. (or rather the fulfillment of the intention specified in 7.), is satisfied. That is very puzzling. Why should we require U to aim at H's realizing that only part of the conditions for U's promising to do A are satisfied?

a linguistic community speakers do not generally rely on the Griceian mechanism for communication, I will not add this requirement. Thus my replacement for Searle's 8. runs as follows.

8. U intends to produce in H the knowledge that the previous conditions have been satisfied.

Now for a brief glance at Searle's 9. An adequate treatment would require an exploration of the relation between what it takes to perform an illocutionary act of a certain type and what gives a sentence a certain illocutionary act potential, and that is a task for Part II. Searle's 9. embodies the assumption that a sentence is usable to perform illocutionary acts of a given type by virtue of being subject to a rule that requires, as a condition of correct and sincere utterance, the satisfaction of the necessary conditions for the performance of illocutionary acts of that type. Thus Searle and I are very much in the same ball park in (1) taking sentence meaning to consist in illocutionary act potential and (2) supposing that illocutionary act potential consists in being governed by rules of a certain sort. But, as will become clear in Part II, this program is carried out in quite different ways by Searle and myself. I have already pointed out one way in which the relationship between illocutionary act performance and sentence meaning envisaged by 9. is too simple: a given sentence can be used to do various different things, and what rule(s) is applicable to that utterance depends on which of these things the speaker intends to be doing. In the last section of this chapter, and much more fully in Chapter 7, I will point out more ways in which Searle's 9. is oversimplified. In any event, I cannot see that we need any restriction on the sentential vehicle employed in order to get sufficient conditions for performing an illocutionary act of a certain sort. Hence I will not include an analogue of Searle's 9.

Items 2. and 3. are the only remaining conditions from Searle's list. Together they require that in uttering S U expresses a proposition that predicates a future act, A, of U. But in my analysis this does not require separate statement. If U takes responsibility for the satisfaction of 4.–6. in uttering S, he has thereby expressed the proposition that U does A at some future time. U could not take responsibility for, for example, intending to do A (represent it as being the case that he intends to do A) without expressing the proposition that he will do A. This is what expressing that proposition amounts to. Each of conditions 4.–6., in one way or another, has to do with U's doing A in the future.[19]

[19] Searle's 1969 account of promising, which I have subjected to minute analysis, by no means represents the totality of his contributions to the topic. In 1969 he builds on this to give brief indications of how analyses of other types of illocutionary acts would go. In 1979 and 1983 he introduces a variety of additional concepts, primarily *illocutionary point, direction of fit*, and *conditions of satisfaction*. If I were primarily concerned with Searlean exegesis and

Before exiting the critical analysis of Searle, let's note the fact that after his detailed account of promising, he takes that as a model for a brief discussion of other kinds of illocutionary acts. He suggests that the analysis of any illocutionary act concepts will involve the following elements.

1. Restrictions on the propositional content. With requests it has to do with a future act of H. With thanks it has to do with a past act of H. With assertions there is no restriction.
2. Preparatory conditions, analogous to 4. and 5. in the analysis of promising. For requesting H to do A, for example, we have the condition that H is able to do A.
3. The essential condition, analogous to 7. in the analysis of promising.
4. The sincerity condition, specifying the psychological state expressed. For assertions this is a belief, for requests a desire, and so on.

It will come as no surprise that I have objections to this general program that are analogous to the ones I lodged against the account of promising. Here too the "preparatory conditions" come in, at most, only in the form of what U R's. What I take to be the most serious difficulty concerns the "essential condition". Searle says "In general, the essential condition determines the others" (69). That is plausible with respect to the laying of an obligation on oneself in promising. But there isn't anything in, for example, requesting or asserting that plays a closely analogous role. Searle takes the essential condition of a request to be that "it counts as an attempt to get H to do A" (66). But the discussion of Schiffer in Chapter 2 revealed that so far from being "essential" for requests, attempting to get H to do A is not even always involved in requests. For assertion he suggests "Counts as an undertaking to the effect that p represents an actual state of affairs" (66). But this is, so to speak, too essential. It is the whole package, rather than one piece of the structure that determines the rest. What is called the essential condition here just *is* to assert that p.

vii. A New Analysis of Promising

More could be said about Searle's theory, but this will suffice both to bring out the basic difficulties in his account and to pave the way for a presentation of my view. Let's see what picture of promising has emerged from the criticism of Searle.

---

criticism, as I was in Alston 1991, I would have to bring all this into the picture. But my concern here is to lay out and defend my own theory. I have found Searle's 1969 account of promising a useful way of introducing my own approach, both by way of agreement and by way of contrast. I will give a brief discussion of Searle's later approaches in 9.11.

I₁. U promised H to do A in uttering S iff:
   A. In uttering S U took responsibility for:
      1. It is possible for U to do A.
      2. H would prefer U's doing A to U's not doing A.
      3. U intends to do A.
   B. In uttering S U placed himself under an obligation to do A.
   C. In uttering S U intended that H realize that conditions 1. and
      2. are satisfied.

This account will be modified somewhat in the next chapter, but for now I present it as a first approximation.

I₁. represents promising as consisting of the speaker's taking responsibility for the satisfaction of certain "preparatory conditions", the truth of which she is "presupposing" in performing the act, plus the engendering of a certain conventional effect, in this case the acquisition of an obligation by the speaker.[20] It is the latter that is the basic point of the act, that for the sake of which the presuppositions are made. Both the propositional content and the illocutionary force of the act are determined by these conditions, though in somewhat different ways. The propositional content, *U's doing A in the future*, is an ingredient as a whole in all the conditions and subconditions; any one of them by itself suffices to carry it. Whereas it takes all of them together to determine the illocutionary force. Each might be presupposed in an act with some other force. I presuppose that it is possible for me to do A when I ask you whether you want me to do A. I presuppose that I intend to do A when I warn you not to stop me from doing A. And so on. The sum of the preparatory conditions is presupposed by my asking you whether you realize that A1., A2., and A3. are satisfied.

I₁. embodies a view of the nature of illocutionary acts that is radically different from Schiffer's position and, to a lesser degree, from Searle's. To be sure, it agrees with Searle, and differs from the others, in emphasizing the place of the production of conventional effects.[21] A more fundamental difference from perlocutionary intention theories lies in the way I bring Searle's condition 4. and my replacement for his 5. into the picture. They come in by U's taking responsibility for their being satisfied. This is what endows the utterance with "content". The utterance is made the illocutionary act it is, apart from any conventional effect production that is essentially involved, not by any "natural" facts about the speaker—his beliefs, perlocutionary intentions, or whatever—but by a "normative" fact

---

[20]   I take C. to be less central. I include it only because it is plausible to think that it is typically involved in interpersonal illocutionary acts. Moreover, except for the reference to conditions 1. and 2., it is in no way distinctive of promising.
[21]   Though there will be important alterations in this part of my theory, the notion of conventional effects will continue to play a prominent role.

about the speaker—the fact that he has changed his normative position in a certain way by laying himself open to the possibility of censure, correction, or the like in case the conditions in question are not satisfied.[22] What the speaker does, again apart from conventional effect production, to make his utterance a token of a certain illocutionary act type, is to "stick his neck out" in this way, making himself the one who is to "respond" if the conditions in question are not satisfied. This is the way in which these conditions enter into the illocutionary act. Though the account of promising given in I1. will undergo substantial changes before it assumes its final form, the point just made will continue to be my key to the understanding of illocutionary acts. An utterance is most basically made into an illocutionary act of a certain type by virtue of a normative stance on the part of the speaker.[23]

viii. Extension to Other Illocutionary Acts

I have elicited the key concepts of my theory of illocutionary acts from a critical analysis of Searle's account. Before using those concepts to assemble the full theory, I want, in the remainder of this chapter, to show how *taking responsibility* for the holding of various conditions comes into illocutionary acts other than promising, and to make some other preliminary points.

Here are some other types of illocutionary acts together with some of the conditions in each case that the speaker is R'ing.

I2. Asking Jones to lend me his copy of *Individuals*.
   A. Jones has exactly one copy of *Individuals*.
   B. It is possible for Jones to lend me that copy.
   C. I have some interest in Jones's lending me that copy.
I3. Telling (ordering) my daughter to help wash the dishes.
   A. There is dishwashing under way or imminent.
   B. It is possible for her to participate in this activity.
   C. I have the authority to lay on her an obligation to do so.
I4. Thanking Jones for recommending me for a fellowship.
   A. Jones has recommended me for a fellowship.
   B. I feel grateful to Jones for having done so.
I5. Adjourning the fall meeting of the University Senate.
   A. The fall meeting of the University Senate is currently in session.

---

[22] And, of course, to knowingly lay an obligation on oneself to do A, or to knowingly produce some other conventional effect by one's utterance, is also to assume a certain normative stance.

[23] This kind of point is central, in a different way, to the treatment of the content of propositional attitudes and the meaning of linguistic items in Brandom 1994.

B. I have the authority to terminate that meeting.

C. Conditions are appropriate for the exercise of that authority.

Next let's look at assertion,[24] which in our account will be a case of limiting simplicity. In all the cases considered so far, except for thanking (which, along with other expressives, we will finally see to be much closer to assertions than is generally supposed), the conditions for which one takes responsibility are preparatory conditions, conditions one presupposes as a background for the main show—laying an obligation on oneself, terminating the meeting, or whatever. But in the case of my asserting that my car is in the garage, if we ask what condition(s) it is that I take responsibility for holding, what I represent myself as knowing to be the case, the best answer is: *my car being in the garage*. Of course, I also take responsibility for anything presupposed by that, for example, that I have a car. But that does not require separate notice, though it may be useful to underline it. Just by virtue of taking responsibility for my car's being in the garage I thereby take responsibility for anything necessarily presupposed by that, for example, my having a car. Thus in an assertion what I take responsibility for coincides with what I am asserting. The condition I am R'ing is out front, in the center of the picture. I am explicitly saying what it is I represent myself as knowing, whereas in the other cases the conditions that have that status are in the background. Thus we may add to our list of conditions R'd:

16. Asserting that my car is in the garage.
    A. My car is in the garage.

I have not provided a complete account of what it is to assert that p, any more than I have provided a complete account of any of the other illocutionary acts on the list. That is a task for the next two chapters. It is clear that asserting that p cannot just amount to R'ing that p. If it did, then for each of the conditions one R's in making promises, requests, and so on, one would be asserting that condition to hold. Nevertheless, R'ing certain conditions will be a central feature of our final account.

I am *not* claiming in these cases any more than in the promising case that the conditions listed have themselves the status of necessary condi-

---

[24] Before launching onto this I should remind the reader how I am using the term 'assert'. I intend it to range over all illocutionary acts that involve an "explicit truth-claim", acts in which a certain proposition is put forward as true. This is one of the wide senses in which the term is used in philosophy. Thus I am not using 'assert that p' in contrast to 'admit that p', 'report that p', 'agree that p', etc., though it certainly can be used in that way. I use 'assert' as a generic term, construing 'admit', 'report', etc., as denoting specific forms that it can take. On the other hand, I distinguish assertions from illocutionary acts in which one does not make a flat truth claim, but rather, e.g., surmises that p, or expresses the opinion that p.

tions for the application of the illocutionary act concept in question. Just as it is possible for me to assert that p without its being the case that p, it is possible for me to ask Jones to lend me his copy of *Individuals* even though it is impossible for him to do so, and even though I realize this. (He might respond, "Why did you ask me to lend you that book when you knew perfectly well that I had just lent it to Smith?".) It may be that some of the conditions listed are necessary conditions for the correlated illocutionary act performance. Exercitives like I5. seem to be cases in point. It does seem that I cannot (actually) adjourn the fall meeting of the University Senate unless that meeting is actually in session, I have the authority to do so, and conditions are appropriate for the exercise of that authority. If any of those conditions fails to be satisfied, I did not succeed in adjourning that meeting.[25] Be that as it may, I do not claim in general that the conditions R'd in performing illocutionary act I are necessary for (intentionally) doing I, but only that U's R'ing that those conditions hold is necessary.

ix. De Re and De Dicto

There is another issue concerning the necessity of some of our conditions. How about the "referential success" conditions like I2A.? Can I ask Jones to lend me *his copy of Individuals* if Jones has no copy of that work, that is, if the italicized phrase fails to refer to anything? Can I assert that your son is in my introductory course if you have no son? More generally, can I have performed a token of an illocutionary act type involving reference to x if I fail to refer to x, either because there is no such entity or because even though there is I fail to connect with it in such a way as to enable me to say something about it?

Our ordinary ways of thinking pull us in both directions. On the one hand, it is very plausible to say that I can't have asserted that your son is in my course unless I succeeded in picking out your son as someone to say something about. But, on the other hand, if I seriously uttered the sentence 'Your son is in my course', realizing what it means and intending to exploit that meaning for the purpose of communication, didn't I assert that your son is in my course, whether I succeeded in picking out anyone with the phrase 'your son' or not? If that isn't what I asserted, then what did I assert?

To resolve this dilemma we must make a distinction (what else!) between two ways of reading an illocutionary act description. I will call these *de re* and *de dicto*. I am far from having invented this distinction. It is widely used and discussed in the philosophical literature, though not often in

[25] In Chapter 4 I will suggest a treatment of exercitives that is somewhat different from this, but the above points hold when we are using exercitive terms in their customary senses.

application to illocutionary acts. By far the most common application to items with propositional contents is to beliefs. Since I will be putting the distinction to a relatively unfamiliar use, some of the things I say will be novel. But the main lines will be familiar.

Consider the illocutionary act report:

M. U asserted that H's son is tall.

On a *de re* reading this asserts a relation between a certain object, in this case H's son, and U. To use a common way of expressing the *de re* construal, it asserts that:

MR. U asserted, *of H's son*, that he was tall.

That is, MR. represents U as picking out H's son as an object of thought and speech and applying the predicate 'tall' to him. One crucial point for present purposes is that MR. represents U as *succeeding* in referring to H's son, not only as intending to do so. And this means that MR. entails not only that H has a son (and if H has more than one, that something in the context singles out one of them as the one under discussion), but also that U is *connected* with that person in such a way as to be able to "have him in mind", to *refer* to him. The question of just what it takes for this kind of connection between subject and object is the most fundamental question in the theory of reference, something I will not be able to go into in this book.[26] If U doesn't succeed in referring to a particular son of H, either because there is none or because he is not properly connected with any, no *de re* assertion has been made. Note, too, that the MR. reading presupposes that the reporter of the IA also succeeds in referring to H's son. Otherwise he would not have specified the object he says that U is related to in this way.

On a *de dicto* reading of M. there are no such entailments. M. could still be true even if H has no son, or if there is but U failed to pick him out. And hence there is no requirement that the reporter refer to any son of H either. Let's take

MD. U asserted that [H's son was tall]

as the canonical *de dicto* reading. The brackets are meant to indicate that if we are to read M. as a relation between U and something, the something is a *proposition* rather than an object. This explains why it is not required

---

[26] One of the chief issues in contemporary discussion of this matter is whether some kind of causal connection between subject and object is required, and if so, just what kind.

for the truth of MD. that either the reporter or the agent of the IA succeed in referring to a certain object. Indeed, though this is controversial, we might suppose that no proposition is involved in MR. There the constituents are U, H's son, and the property of being tall. We have, so to say, only the materials for a proposition.

Another important difference between MR. and MD. is that the latter, but not the former, carries implications as to how U refers, or intends to refer, to what U is talking about. That isn't implied by MR. just because it is enough for the truth of MR. that U have *that object* in mind, and ascribe tallness to it, however the object is picked out—whether as H's son, with some other definite description, a proper name, a pronoun, or whatever. But it is implied by MD. because the proposition that figures essentially there contains the referring expression, 'H's son', as a component. Hence, U wouldn't be making an assertion with *that* propositional content unless U referred to the subject of the assertion as U's son. A deeper reason for this difference is that since MD. doesn't imply that U succeeded in referring to a son of H's, some putative instrument of reference must be included in *what is asserted*, or we don't have a singular assertion at all.

Is this a distinction between two kinds of IA's, or between two ways of reporting or conceptualizing IA's? Both are involved. It is at least the latter. That is how I introduced it. And clearly many particular IA's can be truly reported in either way. If U succeeded in referring to a particular son of H's by saying to H 'Your son is tall', then the IA could be correctly reported either as *de re* or as *de dicto*. But not every singular IA is susceptible of both specifications. If H has no son or if U failed to refer to any son of H, then U's IA could be truly reported by MD but not by MR. Singular IA's with successful reference can be specified in either way, but those with an unsuccessful attempt at reference only as *de dicto*.

How widely does the *de re–de dicto* distinction extend? I have been illustrating it with assertions, but, though this is often neglected, it applies to any IA's that involve singular reference. Thus if I ask you to hand me the magazine on the kitchen table, this might be construed as my asking you, with respect to the magazine on the kitchen table, that you hand it to me (*de re*), or as my asking you to make true the proposition [you have handed me the magazine on the kitchen table]. Moreover, singular reference is involved in the vast majority of requests, promises, and other nonassertive IA's. In the list at the beginning of section viii, we have *asking Jones to lend me his copy of Individuals*, which involves singular reference to a certain book, the example that launched the present discussion. And *adjourning the fall meeting of the University Senate* involves referring both to a certain University Senate and to the fall meeting thereof. General propositional content is found more frequently in assertions, but there too singular reference is very common. But does the distinction also apply to general statements, where there is no putative reference to any individual? Some theorists think so.[27] It is clear that it does apply some way beyond strictly singular reference. Another example at the beginning of viii is *telling my daughter to help wash the dishes*. The reference to "the dishes" is not strictly singular, but here too we can distinguish between *asking, with respect to the dishes, that my daughter help wash them* and *asking my daughter to make it true that [she helps wash the dishes]*. But, of course, this is reference to a limited, local group of particulars. What about unqualifiedly general reference, as in the assertion that lemons are yellow? Here too one might claim that there is a distinction between *asserting of lemons that they are yellow* (*de re*, involving a real connection between the speaker and lemons) and *asserting that [lemons are yellow]* (*de dicto*). Twentieth-century logic favors the latter, since it construes 'lemons are yellow' as 'for all x if x is a lemon then x is yellow'; if this involves reference to anything it is to all entities in the relevant universe of discourse. Whereas Aristotelian logic is more congenial to the former. To simplify the discussion, I will adopt the modern logical construal of general propositions and use the *de re–de dicto* distinction only for propositions that involve singular reference.

Is it *de re* or *de dicto* IA's that we should concentrate on for purposes of the present account? If a choice were required, I would have difficulty, for both have their attractions. The *de dicto* construal seems crucial because, as my initial criteria for picking out IA concepts indicated, I am interested in IA reports insofar as they make explicit the "content" of an utterance, what the speaker seeks to communicate to her audience. And what U seeks to communicate is the same whether or not her references are successful. What U *said* (asserted, asked, requested, etc.) is the same when she uttered 'Your son is tall', 'Is your son at home?', or 'Please introduce me to your son', whether or not H has a son.[28] That content is unaffected by the failure of reference, just as it is by the falsity of the assertion. Moreover, the way in which U refers to an object, x, is part of the content of what U says, and it is the *de dicto* specification that makes this explicit.

On the other hand, there are reasons for being concerned with *de re* IA types. Where an assertion involves singular reference, it is arguable that it has a truth value only if the references come off. As Strawson and others have contended, if H has no son, the question of whether it is true that H's son is at home does not arise. There are also considerations internal to the development of my theory of sentence meaning that require us to attend to *de re* IA's. These will emerge in Chapters 6 and 7.

So there are strong reasons for bringing both *de dicto* and *de re* IA types

<hr />

[27] See, e.g., Dennett 1982.
[28] This would be denied by an advocate of what are often called "Russellian" construals of singular propositions, in which an *object* is a part of the proposition. I shall work with the more customary "Fregean" construal, in which the constituents of a proposition are concepts (plus connectives of various sorts).

into the picture. Fortunately, nothing constrains us to limit ourselves to only one. We can use our approach to develop analyses of IA concepts of both sorts. I will illustrate this with a simple singular assertion—U asserting that his computer is on. Remember that I am still restricting myself to the R'ing involved in IA's.

In its *de re* form the R'ing involved can be specified as:

IR. U R'ed, with respect to his computer, that it is on.

The *de re* character of the IA is captured by specifying the R'ing itself as *de re* in character. U has to have that object, his computer, in mind (satisfying one of the sufficient conditions for that) and attribute being on to that object. And since the R'ing itself involves a relation to the object, it is not necessary for the *de re* IA that U referred to the object in any particular way.

In its *de dicto* form the R'ing involved can be specified as:

ID. U R'd (the truth of the proposition that) [his computer is on].

Here an (at least attempted) reference to his computer *as his computer* is required, since that is part of the proposition involved. And, unlike the *de re* analysis, the success of reference to his computer is not required, for there is no requirement of U's being related to *that object*.

This way of distinguishing between *de re* and *de dicto* IA's throws light on the puzzling question: "How is it possible to have a genuinely singular assertion (question, request . . .) if the speaker's referential attempt fails?". If U failed to refer to her Mercedes, either because she doesn't have one or because she fails to have it in mind, how could she make an assertion that is in any sense *about* her Mercedes, for example, that her Mercedes is in the shop? I don't claim to have given an ideally satisfactory answer to this question. In the most obvious and straightforward sense of 'about', this is not possible. Only a *de re* assertion satisfies that demand. But the idea that the IA can involve a relation of U to a *proposition* that involves an attempted singular reference to a Mercedes owned by the speaker gives us a weaker sense of 'about' in which the speaker could be said to have made an assertion "about" her Mercedes. For she did assert that [her Mercedes is in the shop].

x. How to Identify Conditions for Illocutionary Acts

One may wonder how I compiled my lists of conditions for each illocutionary act type. I could answer by saying that I exploit my familiarity with illocutionary act concepts and determine by reflection what conditions one is R'ing in performing illocutionary acts of a certain type. But the unfamiliarity of my R-concept may make this answer less than wholly satisfactory. As a supplement I offer the following. Where one is R'ing that p in I'ing (performing an illocutionary act of type I) it would obviously be self-defeating for one to conjoin the I'ing with denying that p or even disclaiming knowledge that p. If requesting Jones to do D necessarily involves representing oneself as knowing that Jones can do D, it would be self-defeating to make that request and then in the same breath deny that one knows whether Jones can do D. We may put the same point in terms of the rule-subjection construal of R'ing. It is self-defeating to do something as subject to a certain rule, while simultaneously admitting that what the rule requires is not satisfied. It would be like a tennis player saying in the midst of his serve "My feet are not back of the baseline".

Here, then, is a rule of thumb for deciding whether a given condition, p, is such that R'ing that p is a necessary condition of performing illocutionary acts of a certain type:

Consider a case in which U utters a sentence, S, that would normally be used in that context to I, conjoined with a denial that p or that U knows that p. Would that conjoined denial inhibit us from taking U to be I'ing in uttering S? If so, the condition should be included. If not, not.

Thus I3B. passes the test. If I were to say to my daughter, "I realize that it is impossible for you to help wash the dishes, but I order you to help wash the dishes", this is not a clear case of ordering her to help wash the dishes. But the condition that she wants to help wash the dishes does not pass the test. If I said "I realize that you don't want to help wash the dishes, but I'm telling you to do it anyway", this could be a clear case of ordering her to help wash the dishes.

xi. Illocutionary Rules

The D8. account of R'ing, as subjecting one's utterance to a rule governing the sentence uttered, is only a rough sketch and leaves many questions dangling. What sorts of rules are we envisaging? How are they to be formulated? In what sense do they "exist" in the community antecedently to a given speaker's bringing an utterance under one of them? What place do they have in the structure of a language? These questions will not be dealt with until Part II. But rather than leave things completely mysterious until then, and in order to give a bit more of an idea of how D8. is to be applied to particular cases, I will say just a word at this point.

First a bit of terminology. Since a given rule of this sort fits a sentence for the performance of IA's of a certain type, I will call them *illocutionary rules* ('I-rules'). And, though this is not pertinent at this point, I will hold that what it is for a sentence to have a certain meaning is that it is governed by a certain I-rule and thereby has a certain *IA potential*. In a word, sentence meaning = IA potential = I-rule governance. So in seeking I-rules we are at the same time seeking rules being governed by which gives a sentence its meaning, and hence gives it an IA potential, including the usability for whatever R'ings are involved in performing IA's of the type in question.

The simplest way of relating R'ing to semantic rules would be the way indicated by (9) of Searle's analysis of promising:

(9) The semantical rules of the dialect spoken by S and H are such that T [the sentence S utters to make a promise] is correctly and sincerely uttered if and only if conditions 1–8 obtain.

For Searle a sentence is rendered suitable for use in promising to do A by being governed by such a rule. There is a coincidence between what it takes to promise to do A and what it takes to correctly use a sentence that has that illocutionary act potential. To translate this idea into my approach I have to recognize that some of the conditions that Searle takes as necessary for nondefective promising enter my account only by way of its being necessary for promising that U R them. With respect to such conditions our closest approach to Searle's (9) would be this. In promising to do A in uttering S, U R's that these conditions hold, by virtue of the fact that in the language S is subject to a rule that requires these conditions for permissible utterance. Thus if in uttering a sentence, S, I promise to leave H alone, then in doing so I R that:

1. It is possible for me to leave H alone.
2. H would prefer my leaving H alone to my not doing so.
3. I intend to leave H alone.

And I do so by virtue of the fact that S is subject to the following rule:

R1. S may be uttered only if: [29]
   1. It is possible for U to leave H alone.
   2. H would prefer U's leaving H alone to U's not doing so.
   3. U intends to leave H alone.

However, for several reasons that will be explored in Chapter 7, this is too simple a picture. First, there is ellipticity. I may promise to leave you alone by saying "Yes." in answer to the question "Do you promise to leave

[29] This is merely 'only if' because these are clearly not the only conditions required for permissible utterance. Most important, the taking on of an obligation is left out here for simplicity of illustration. I will provide tighter formulations in Chapter 7.

me alone?". And "Yes" is not permissibly uttered only if the above conditions are satisfied. Second, many sentences are multivocal (have more than one meaning), in which case permissible utterance does not depend on one unique set of conditions being satisfied. Third, any sentence can be uttered for non-IA purposes, such as testing a microphone. Fourth, where singular reference by the usual devices is involved, as with 'The door is open' when that is used to assert that a particular door, D, is open, one R's that D is open, but obviously that sentence is not permissibly uttered only when that particular door, D, is open.

In Part II, especially Chapter 7, I will find ways to construe I-rules so as to accommodate all these complexities.

CHAPTER FOUR

Types of Illocutionary Acts: Commissives, Exercitives, Directives, and Expressives

i. Prelude: Conventional and Normative Facts

In Chapter 3 I put forward a tentative account of what it is to make a promise.

I1. U promised H to do A in uttering S *iff*:
    A. In uttering S, U R'd that:
        1. It is possible for U to do A.
        2. H would prefer U's doing A to U's not doing A.
        3. U intends to do A.
    B. In uttering S, U placed himself under an obligation to do A.
    C. In uttering S, U intended that H realize that conditions A. and B. are satisfied.

If we leave aside C., which is simply a "communicative intention" condition that is common to all illocutionary acts that are addressed to someone(s), I1. represents making a promise as a combination of R'ing certain conditions and intentionally producing a "normative effect" of a certain kind, in this case an obligation on the part of the speaker. Asserting that *p*, on the other hand, was tentatively presented as simply a matter of R'ing that *p*, the proposition asserted. We also noted some conditions that are R'd in other types of illocutionary acts.

These preliminary results suggest the following picture. Asserting that *p* is simply a matter of R'ing, and indeed R'ing just what is asserted, giving us a case of limiting simplicity. Other categories are more complex; they all involve producing some distinctive sort of normative or conventional effect, as well as R'ing various conditions. These nonassertive types can be individuated both by the kinds of conditions R'd and by the kind of normative or conventional effect produced. This pattern would seem to fit exercitives like adjourning a meeting. Here is a parallel account of that illocutionary act type.

I7. U adjourned the fall meeting of the University Senate, in uttering S *iff*:
   A. In uttering S, U R'd that:
      1. The fall meeting of the University Senate is currently in session.
      2. U has the authority to terminate that meeting.
      3. Conditions are appropriate for the exercise of that authority.
   B. In uttering S, U brought it about that the meeting is no longer in session.
   C. U uttered S with the intention that U's audience should realize that conditions A. and B. are satisfied.

Unfortunately, this picture is much too simple. First, asserting that *p* in uttering S cannot just be a matter of U's R'ing that *p* in uttering S. If it were, then U would be asserting all the propositions she R's in making a promise or adjourning a meeting. Furthermore, the various specific forms of assertion—admitting, reporting, replying, etc.—must involve some further features by virtue of which they differ from each other. And in the course of the discussion we will uncover inadequacies in the above accounts of promising and adjourning.

In this and the following chapter I will work toward a more adequate account by developing a schema of analysis for act types in each major category. I begin by considering J. L. Austin's well-known fivefold classification in Lecture XII of *How to Do Things with Words* (1962). But before proceeding further I had better say something about the disjunction between "normative" and "conventional" effects mentioned two paragraphs back.

I turn first to *conventional effect*. The more basic notion here is that of a "conventional fact". A conventional effect is such a fact brought about by something, in the cases in point by an utterance. So what is meant by a "conventional fact"?

First, let's enumerate some facts we want to include under this rubric.

Having a certain job
Holding a certain office

Being married or divorced
A meeting being in session
Being convicted of a crime
Being under a sentence of imprisonment
Owing a certain amount of money to a bank
Owning a house or a car
Being a member of a club

What do these facts have in common? I will suggest two different answers and then relate them.

(1) A "conventional fact" is one that holds by virtue of certain conventions, rules, or regulations.[1] It is because rules or conventions are in force in the relevant society, and apply in a certain way to the case at hand, that the fact in question obtains. One is married or divorced when certain laws and customs apply to one's relations to other persons, especially but not exclusively to one's present or former spouse. One has committed a crime when one has violated certain laws; and one is convicted of a crime when a duly constituted court has rendered a verdict of guilty. One owes money to a bank when one has entered into certain undertakings in accordance with certain rules and regulations. And so on. A conventional fact is a rule-constituted fact, one that would not and could not hold if certain rules did not exist. Thus conventional facts are "soft" facts, malleable by social agreement, consensus, the force of custom and usage. Though not all rules and conventions come into force by the agreement of a solemn assembly, any rule or convention can be altered or abolished by social consensus. And they will fall into limbo if pervasively enough ignored.

By virtue of this dependence on rule or convention, conventional facts differ from what we may call "natural facts". Two persons can live together and engage in sexual intercourse whatever rules apply to them; but they can be married or divorced only by virtue of certain laws or customs. I can occupy a house whatever the social fabric; but I can own a house only in a society that "recognizes" private property and regulates it in some way. The fact that three of us are sailing a ship is a "natural fact"; but we can be members of a sailing club only if there is such an organization with its rules and regulations.

(2) As these last examples indicate, we could also have brought out the common character of the above list by saying that the items are all *social* facts. Each consists in a person or group having a certain "social status" or "social position", occupying a certain place in society, or playing a certain role therein. Thus they all depend on the relevant society's having a certain constitution. This notion of "social status" has an obvious application

[1] For the present I will use the terms 'rule' and 'convention' interchangeably for the whole family of terms that also includes such terms as 'law', 'regulation', and 'custom'. In 8.4 I will pry apart 'rule' and 'convention'.

to holding a job, being married, being under a sentence of imprisonment, and being a member of a club.

How are these two explanations of the term related? Since rules and conventions, at least those under consideration here, require social establishment if they are to be in force, we may take it that any state of affairs that is dependent on convention is ipso facto a social state of affairs.[2] The converse implication is not so clear. I think it is plausible to suppose that all distinctively social facts are dependent on the operation of social conventions and rules. But I will not try here and now to argue for that. Hence I will rely primarily on the first explanation of 'conventional fact', remembering the social character of such facts.

Now for the concept of *normative status* and its relation to *conventional fact*. We might be tempted to identify the two. But there is a significant distinction to be drawn. I have pointed out that conventional facts are "soft", alterable by social consensus or the lack thereof. But what about such normative statuses as obligation and blameworthiness? Some thinkers treat them in the same way. But it is more traditional to think of them as objective statuses, not subject to social agreement. "Let justice be done, though the heavens fall!" For present purposes I need not take a stand on this issue. But I acknowledge it as a reason for stepping back from a flat identification of conventional facts and (some) normative statuses. To be sure, any conventional facts could be thought of as (involving) normative statuses of a sort. But the question remains as to whether there are other, more objective sorts.

This issue has a bearing on the analysis of illocutionary act types. I have been distinguishing the production of conventional effects like someone's being appointed to a position or a meeting's being adjourned from what the speaker R's in uttering a sentence. But I have explained R'ing itself in terms of instituting a normative status—being under the governance of a rule or being liable to reproach in the absence of certain conditions. It may look as if we can nail down the distinction between R'ing and conventional effect production in terms of the distinction between normative status and conventional fact. But what I have called the conventional effect of commissives is an *obligation*, and later I will say the same of directives. And if we are to distinguish between normative statuses and conventional facts, obligations certainly belong with the former. As a terminological matter, I will use the term 'conventional effect' to range over everything in the conventional-normative territory that is produced by illocutionary act performance, *other than what is produced by the speaker's R'ings*.

---

[2] As I not infrequently have had occasion to point out in this book, there are limiting cases of a rule being instituted by a single individual for his or her exclusive use. But such cases are derivative from more basic, full-blooded social rules.

ii. Commissives, Exercitives, and Verdictives: Preliminary

Austin's classification of illocutionary acts was a first sketch, and he would undoubtedly have modified it had he lived. It is unsatisfactory as it stands, both by reason of including verbs that do not denote illocutionary acts at all ('plan', 'contemplate', 'resent') and by reason of the fact that some of the categories are very much mixed bags. Nevertheless, I find it an insightful first approximation.

1. *Verdictives.* "Verdictives consist in the delivering of a finding, official or unofficial, upon evidence or reasons as to value or fact, so far as these are distinguishable." (152)
   acquit
   assess
   diagnose
2. *Exercitives.* "An exercitive is the giving of a decision in favor of or against a certain course of action, or advocacy of it. It is a decision that something is to be so. . . ." (154)
   appoint
   pardon
   name
   nominate
   bequeath
3. *Commissives.* "The whole point of a commissive is to commit the speaker to a certain course of action." (156)
   promise
   contract
   bet
4. *Behabitives.* "Behabitives include the notion of reaction to other people's behavior and fortunes and of attitudes and expressions of attitudes to someone else's past conduct or imminent conduct." (159)
   apologize
   thank
   congratulate
   blame
5. *Expositives.* "Expositives are used in acts of exposition involving the expounding of views, the conducting of arguments, and the clarifying of usages and of references." (160)
   affirm
   report
   remark
   agree

It is clear that the explanations of these categories fail to specify clear principles of differentiation.[3] I will deal rather freely with Austin's scheme, using his discussion as a springboard from which to arrive at my own taxonomy.

To begin with, of the two examples presented in section i., promising belongs to Commissives and adjourning to Exercitives. Austin's characterization of commissives is clear enough. To perform a commissive is to "commit" oneself to a certain course of action; that is, to take on an obligation to do so-and-so. That differentiates it from other nonassertive illocutionary acts. This category is more tightly unified than its cousins. In fact, one might think of all commissives as simply varieties of promises. What we call (mere) promises are relatively informal ways of obligating oneself to do A, for any sort of A. For certain kinds of A's we have special terms ('bet'), and we have other special terms for promises entered onto in some special institutional setting—'contract', 'guarantee', 'vow'.

But for Exercitives Austin's characterization does not do the job. "Giving of a decision in favor of " or "advocacy of " fails to bring out what (most of) Austin's examples have in common. These phrases do not fit appointing or bequeathing, for example. His next sentence is better. "It is a decision that something is to be so, as distinct from a judgment that it is so" (154). This captures the "executive" character of an exercitive, that it is the bringing into being of a certain state of affairs, rather than the "recording" of a preexisting state of affairs. But *this* formula applies equally to all illocutionary acts that involve conventional effect production; in particular, it applies to commissives. So what is distinctive of exercitives as over against commissives?

Note that while the category of commissives is defined by a sharply restricted category of conventional effects, exercitives range over a wide variety of social statuses that can be taken on by persons, groups, or things. These include:

1. *Hiring* and *firing*—someone's having or not having a certain job.
2. *Naming*—someone's or something's having a certain name.
3. *Nominating*—someone's being a candidate for a certain office.
4. *Sentencing, pardoning*—someone's being subject to imprisonment or not.
5. *Marrying, divorcing*—someone's being married or unmarried.
6. *Opening* or *adjourning* a meeting—a meeting's being or not being in session.[4]

[3] Austin has much more to say about these distinctions than the fragmentary remarks just quoted, as well as providing lengthy lists of verbs for each category. Nevertheless, the above judgment stands.

[4] I assume that conventional effects can be characterized in terms of what actions are or are not appropriate by a certain person toward certain persons or objects, perhaps in certain circumstances. Thus the difference between being married and being unmarried is a matter of

This suggests that *Exercitive* is a "wastebasket" category. We define commissives and other more restricted categories in terms of a specific kind of conventional effect, leaving all the remaining conventional effect-types to the exercitive category.

But whether this is the whole story about exercitives depends on what we say about another distinctive feature of paradigmatic examples—namely, that the production of the conventional effect depends on S's having some special position, status, or role, as defined by nonlinguistic rules, conventions, or institutions. Not every speaker of English can hire or fire a secretary in Syracuse University; it is not any user of the language that can open or adjourn a meeting of the local Audubon Society. One must be empowered to do these things by the relevant institution. Anyone can promise to do anything, whatever her position or status. To be sure, one's social status puts limits on what one can sensibly or honestly promise. It would be grossly dishonest of me to promise to get you the number-two job in the Defense Department. But I can make the promise. I can represent myself as having the power to dispose of that job, and I can, by what I say, lay on myself a prima facie obligation to get you that job.[5] No particular status is required for me to ask you to give me a match. If I am a bum on skid row and you are the president of General Motors, it may be futile or presumptuous of me to do so; but if I address the right sentence to that person with the right intentions, I have asked him to give me a match. By contrast consider *vetoing a bill passed by Congress*. It is not that it would be presumptuous, ill-advised, or silly for me to do this. I cannot do it. It is strictly impossible. No matter what sentence I uttered with no matter what intentions, it would not count as vetoing a bill of Congress.

If this is correct, exercitives do not constitute a purely wastebasket category. If there are conventional effects that do not fall within any of the more restricted categories, but which can be produced by anyone whatever her official position, their linguistic production will not count as exercitives. In the interest of a sharper delineation of categories I am going to include this restriction. We will take exercitives to involve the production of some conventional effect that does not fall within the range of one of the other nonassertive categories, where this production is contingent on S's having a special institutional position or status.

---

what actions by the other partner and by other people are socially allowed or required vis-à-vis a particular person. Similarly for a person's having or not having a certain job, and being or not being a member of a certain organization. This assumption will be exploited at a later stage.

[5] It is not hard to see why commissives do not require an official position while exercitives do. In the former I am binding only myself; I am not imposing obligations on others. But when I sentence or fire someone I alter that person's obligations, opportunities, etc. It is not surprising that there should be social controls over affecting the social status of others but not over merely affecting one's own.

I turn next to what Austin calls "verdictives", "the delivering of a finding, official or unofficial, upon evidence or reasons as to value or fact . . .". On examination I find that Austin's disjunction "official or unofficial" determines two groups that should be treated differently. I do not pretend to know just what Austin meant by 'official', but I shall distinguish official from unofficial verdictives in terms of whether the "delivering of the finding" gives its object a certain social or official status. Thus when an umpire calls a batter out, a judge finds a defendant guilty, or a tax assessor assesses a piece of property as a basis for taxation, the batter, the defendant, or the property has thereby changed its social status in a certain way. The batter may no longer continue batting (at that stage of the game), the defendant is liable to sentencing, and so on. Whereas we have an "unofficial" verdict when a doctor diagnoses my illness, an expert estimates the market value of my property (for my information), or an art critic pronounces on the merit of a new painting. The targets of these judgments have not thereby received any new official status; there is no alteration in what behavior toward them is permitted, forbidden, or required.

Thus an "official" verdict is like an exercitive in the kind of conventional effect involved and what it takes to bring it about. Whereas an "unofficial" verdictive is like an assertion. In fact it *is* an assertion, being distinguished from others only by its propositional content. Just what sort of proposition is it the assertion of which counts as a verdictive? The closest Austin comes to a general specification is to say that a verdictive is "giving a finding as to something—fact, or value—which is for different reasons hard to be certain about" (150). Matters may be "hard to be certain about" for a variety of reasons—indeterminacy of concepts or lack of conclusive evidence, for example. Evaluations of works of art, people, and intellectual products qualify on the first count and often on the second. Diagnoses of pathological conditions and interpretations of conduct, literary or philosophical works, and dreams often qualify on the second count. However, "difficulty of being certain about it" is obviously a matter of degree and could hardly be taken to mark out a natural kind. I do not see that there is a fundamental distinction between "unofficial verdictives" and other assertions.

As for "official verdictives", we are faced with the problem of distinguishing them from exercitives. So far I have said only what they have in common. Austin brings out the difference as follows.

> Verdictives have obvious connections with truth and falsity as regards soundness and unsoundness or fairness and unfairness. That the content of a verdict is true or false is shown, for example, in a dispute over an umpire's calling 'Out', 'Three strikes', or 'Four balls'. (152)[6]

---

[6] Austin may be excused, on grounds of Englishness, for distorting baseball umpires' calls, more correctly reported (in the second and third cases) as "Strike three!" and "Ball four!".

In a verdictive the "exercitive" act of endowing something with a new social status is based on a judgment as to the way things are. Hence it is challengeable as to the truth or falsity, soundness or unsoundness, of that judgment, as well as challengeable in ways it shares with exercitives—the authority of the speaker or the conditions in which that authority is exercised. When the umpire calls "Strike two!", we can contest this on the grounds that the pitch was not in the strike zone, as well as on the grounds that the person is not authorized to act as an umpire or that the inning is over. When my property is assessed, I can challenge the truth, soundness, or grounds of the claim that the present market value of my property is so-and-so, as well as claim that the period of reassessment has passed. Thus we can treat an official verdictive as a combination of an assertion and an exercitive that is based on that assertion. I will not recognize *official verdictives* as a separate category.

We encounter somewhat different questions in connection with Austin's other categories—behabitives and expositives. But before getting to that I want to point out some features of the categories already discussed that put the lie to the relatively simple model we have been working with.

iii. The Final Model for Exercitives

I have been suggesting that a nonassertive IA can be construed as the R'ing of various conditions, plus the production of a certain kind of conventional effect. This sounded plausible for commissives and exercitives. But now we must confront the possibility that what we have been calling exercitives are not IA's at all in my sense of that term.

One can see how Austin was led into counting hiring and adjourning as illocutionary acts. His approach was to look for "forces" an utterance might have over and above the "sense and reference" of the words. The focus is on the notion of illocutionary *force*. Hence it is natural to think that just as when I say 'The gate is open' with a certain sense and reference my utterance may have the force of *admitting* or *insisting* or *concluding* that a certain gate is open, so when I say "The meeting is adjourned" my utterance may have the force of *reporting* that the meeting is adjourned or of *adjourning* the meeting. And when I say "You're hired" my utterance may have the force of *remarking* that you've been hired or of *hiring* you.

But on my way of construing illocutionary acts things turn out differently. My initial criterion was that we make explicit the illocutionary act U has performed when we use the indirect discourse form to make explicit the "content" of his utterance. Now is that precisely what we are doing when we report that U adjourned the meeting, hired A, nominated Jones to be vice-president, or bequeathed his fortune to the Huntington Library? There are reasons for a negative answer.

1. The above test leads us to expect that illocutionary act reports can

serve as answers to questions like "What did he say?". As we saw earlier, that doesn't mean that all illocutionary reports can be made in the form "He said that . . .". It is rather that indirect discourse forms, with a variety of illocutionary verbs, can be used to make explicit what someone said. It is natural to answer the question "What did she say?" with "She admitted that the gate was open", "She asked me to move over", or "She promised to meet me for lunch". But "She adjourned the meeting" or "She hired a new secretary" are decidedly off color as answers to that question. I have *not* told you what she said when I tell you that she hired a new secretary. No doubt, she said various things in the course of doing that, but I haven't told you what any of them was. I have given you a different sort of information, namely, the conventional upshot of her performance. Even if at some point in the proceedings she said to the job-seeker, "O.K., you're hired", and that was the final stroke that ensured the hiring, still in telling you that she hired a new secretary I don't thereby tell you just what illocutionary act(s) she performed in doing so; and that for two reasons. First, hiring a new secretary is an activity that normally involves a considerable range of activities, not just the final clincher. In the second place, U herself, the one who is said to have hired H, may have produced no such final clincher. The matter may be have been settled by an official letter from some other official. So although it may follow from the fact that U hired H that U performed a number of illocutionary acts, still in telling you that U hired H I have not reported any particular illocutionary act that she performed.

2. The reasons why adjourning doesn't count as an illocutionary act by my lights are rather different. Here, unlike the case of hiring, the deed is normally done by the utterance of a single sentence. Hence we don't have the above difficulty. Adjourning is not too large and varied a behavioral unit to be an illocutionary act. Nevertheless, when I tell you that he adjourned the meeting, where I mean this in the full sense that implies that meeting was in fact terminated, I have told you too much for a "pure" illocutionary act report. My report may include a specification of what he said (that the meeting is hereby adjourned), but it is not confined to that. Compare cases in which I do and in which I do not have the authority to terminate the meeting, but where in each case I utter the appropriate formula, 'I declare this meeting adjourned', intending to terminate the meeting. It would seem that in both cases what I said, the "content" of my utterance, was the same; and yet in one case I did adjourn the meeting and in the other I did not. So even if adjourning *includes* a certain distinctive illocutionary act, it includes more as well.

3. This last point is reinforced by the fact that with exercitives, unlike other putative illocutionary acts, to perform an act of this sort one must not only R certain p's, but in addition those p's must be *true*. In asserting that p I R that p; in asking H to move over I R that it is possible for H to

move over; in promising H to meet him for lunch I R that it is possible for me to do so. But, as we have seen, the truth of these propositions is *not* a necessary condition for the performance of the illocutionary act. I can assert what is not the case; I can ask people to do what they are incapable of doing; I can promise to do what I am incapable of doing. But with adjourning and hiring what I R must in fact be the case, at least the R'd conditions we have been considering. Recall the conditions R'd in adjourning a meeting. Unless the meeting in question is actually in session and unless I have the authority to terminate it at that point, it can't be true that I adjourned that meeting. This reinforces the idea that adjourning is more than an illocutionary act.[7]

The double-barreled point we have made about adjourning suggests a way out of the problem. So long as we stick to conditions requiring U to R various *p*'s, we are confining ourselves to what U says, the content of U's message. It is only when we go beyond that and require both the truth of what U R's and the actual production of the conventional effect, that we enlarge the act concept beyond illocutionary bounds. So why shouldn't we say that the illocutionary act involved in adjourning consists simply in R'ing the *p*'s in question? This is common to the case in which I actually brought off the termination of the meeting and the case in which I did not. We might call the speech act so constituted "purporting to adjourn the meeting", as distinguished from the full-blooded "adjourning the meet-

---

[7]   These points are connected with a linguistic point, though we will not be able fully to appreciate the connection until we come to the discussion of illocutionary act potential and semantic rules in Chapter 7. (I owe my appreciation of this point to discussions with J. O. Urmson.) It seems clear that the rules or conventions by virtue of which the social status of objects is altered by exercitives are not linguistic rules or conventions and hence, ipso facto, are not constitutive of the meanings of sentences. We can see this most clearly where explicit legislation or institutional rules are involved. The question of what sort of formula the presiding officer must utter to adjourn a meting is a matter to be decided, if at all, by the rules of the organization. An organization could include in its constitution a provision that what the presiding officer must utter to terminate the meeting is 'This meeting stands adjourned'. Saying 'I declare the meeting adjourned' or 'The meeting is adjourned' or 'That's it for today' wouldn't do the job. If the organization did so legislate it would *not* have thereby enriched the English language or changed the meaning of 'adjourn' or any other English words, phrases, or sentences. Similarly, if the words required for a valid contract of marriage are different in Montana and in Indiana, this does not imply any difference in the dialects of English spoken in those states, nor does it imply that any English sentences have different meanings in the two localities. The conventions that enable a given sentence to be used to alter the social status of something are extralinguistic conventions, conventions of some extralinguistic institution or other.

This point is connected with the above discussion of exercitives just because I want my concept of an illocutionary act to be such that what makes a sentence usable for performing an illocutionary act is the meaning of that sentence. And to use a sentence with a certain meaning (and certain references) is, normally, to be performing an illocutionary act of a certain type. Hence the fact that what fits sentences for altering social status is not rules of language fits in nicely, from my point of view, with the fact that alterations of social status do not count as illocutionary acts on my intuitive criterion for illocutionary acts.

ing", which does require the actual truth of the conditions R'd, as well as the actual production of the conventional effect.

Although this suggestion does meet the points about adjourning, it does not meet the one concerning hiring, namely, that the act concept is "too large" to be an illocutionary act concept. Since hiring someone can involve a number of different illocutionary acts, the exact nature of which will vary over different instances, there isn't any one set of conditions the R'ing of which could be said to constitute the illocutionary act associated with hiring. The same is true of a number of other exercitives, for example, *appointing, sentencing, pardoning,* and *resigning.* However, a given instance of sentencing or appointing *may* include a final "clincher" utterance, the full content of which is simply that U is purporting to bring about the conventional effect in question. That is, whatever the judge may say about the convict, his crime, the course of the trial, and so on, in the course of pronouncing sentence, there will undoubtedly be a point in the proceedings at which he does just purport to sentence the convict to six years in prison by saying 'I sentence you to six years in prison' or the like. Wherever this is true an illocutionary act has been performed that can be felicitously denominated *purporting to sentence.* Assuming that this is true for all exercitives, we can specify pure illocutionary act concepts for all exercitive act types.

Let's continue by determining just what *p*'s it is the R'ing of which is constitutive of purporting to adjourn a certain meeting, M. The *p*'s listed earlier were:

1. M is currently in session.
2. U has the authority to terminate M.
3. At the time of utterance conditions are appropriate for the exercise of that authority.

Now clearly R'ing just these conditions is not sufficient even for purporting to adjourn M. For U might be *asserting* that these conditions are satisfied, rather than purporting to adjourn any meeting. This could happen where the parliamentarian, realizing that I am about to declare the meeting adjourned, challenges my right to do so. In response to this challenge I might say, if I were extremely pedantic or given to heavy irony, "Look, the meeting is in session, I have the authority to terminate it, and the present circumstances are appropriate for the exercise of that authority". Here I would be R'ing (just) the conditions in question but *not,* just then, purporting to adjourn the meeting.

This formulation of the problem points to its own solution. What is lacking in the above list is any reference to the crucial conventional effect. So long as we were working with the full-blooded concept of adjourning the meeting, that lack was supplied by adding the production of the conventional effect as another necessary condition. But now that we have shifted to the thinner concept of purporting to adjourn M, we need only stipulate that U does so purport. He must take responsibility not only for the holding of the preconditions for adjourning, but also for actually bringing it about that the meeting is terminated. Thus we must add to the list of conditions R'd the following:

4. In uttering S, U brings it about that M is terminated.

This ensures that U *purports* to terminate the meeting, without making the actual termination of the meeting a necessary condition for the application of the illocutionary act concept.

We can take the above to yield a general model for the analysis of exercitive illocutionary acts, including the exercitive component of verdictives. Each such act is tied to a certain kind of conventional effect. The model can be formulated as follows.

EXER. U O'd in uttering S (where 'O' is a term for purporting to be producing a particular conventional effect, E) = df. In uttering S, U R'd that:

1. Conceptually necessary conditions for E.[8]
2. U has the authority to produce E.
3. Conditions are appropriate for the exercise of that authority.
4. By uttering S, U is bringing about E.

At the risk of being tedious let me repeat that this model does *not* present the four conditions, 1.–4., as necessary for the performance of illocutionary acts of type O. What is presented as necessary is that U subject his utterance to a rule that requires that these conditions hold. And that, of course, is logically compatible with some or all of the conditions not being satisfied.

Note that the analysans does not spell out what it takes for one to have the authority to bring about the relevant conventional effect; nor does it spell out what it takes for the context to be appropriate for the exercise of that authority. It merely unspecifically lays it down that U R's that these conditions are satisfied, whatever they are. This is connected with the point

---

[8] These are conditions without which E could not exist, whether brought about by this utterance of U's or not. For adjourning a meeting this would include the meeting's being in session. For appointing H to a position this would include the existence of the position, its not already being filled, and H's eligibility. For divorcing a couple this includes their being married and their having satisfied whatever requirements there are for the marriage's being dissolved at this time. These are general requirements for E's being produced by anyone at this time. They have no special reference to U's ability to do so or to the circumstances of his utterance.

made in note 7 that it is *extralinguistic* conventions that determine what sentences can be used to engender a certain conventional effect and (I now add) the conditions under which the sentence can do so. I take these extralinguistic conditions not to be constitutive of the *concept* of a given conventional effect. This is reflected in my separation of conditions 2. and 3. from condition 1. I take it that one can understand what it is to be married or divorced, to be hired or fired, to have a meeting in or out of session, without knowing what it takes to bring these about in one or another jurisdiction. The concept of the relevant conventional effect is what is at the heart of an exercitive illocutionary act concept. Conditions that are necessary, in a certain social milieu, for its production but not conceptually necessary for its existence form no part of the exercitive act concept. What does get included is the unspecific requirement that all such conditions are satisfied.[9]

In 3.6 I said that for IA's directed to other people, the usual case, it is necessary that U utter S with the intention of getting the hearer(s), H, to realize that the other conditions are satisfied. But the above schema contains no such additional necessary condition. The reason for that is twofold.

First, with many illocutionary act types, including assertions, requests, and expressions of attitudes, a given type as identified by the other conditions (primarily if not exclusively what is R'd) can be performed either in interpersonal communication or in soliloquy. Hence we would not want the specifically interpersonal condition to be required across the board. Second, this requirement of getting H to realize that the other conditions are satisfied is a blanket one for (interpersonal) IA's of all types. It does nothing to bring out what distinguishes one type of IA from others. Hence it would be unnecessarily cumbersome to add it to the analysis of every IA concept. Instead I will just issue a general announcement that analyses of IA concepts are to be understood as including this intention to get H to realize that other conditions are satisfied, for cases in which the particular IA performance is other-directed. Doing it this way not only saves us from repeating the condition verbatim for each concept. It also saves us from deciding which IA types can be realized in soliloquy and which cannot. For the general ruling is that the condition in question is operative when and only when the type in question is addressed to other persons.

A rather neat picture of exercitives is emerging. One performs the illocutionary act by R'ing certain conditions in uttering S. This illocutionary act type is essentially related to the relevant conventional effect, even though the production of that effect is not required; performing an act of that type is *purporting* to produce such a conventional effect. Although in

---

[9] That is, not only are these extralinguistic conditions not required for the performance of the illocutionary act. It is not even required that S R *them*.

some cases we have a special term for the illocutionary act (*declaring* the meeting adjourned, as contrasted with adjourning the meeting),[10] in many cases we have no better way of specifying the illocutionary act than as "purporting to _____", where what fills the blank is the specification of some alteration of social status. The actual conventional effect production can be represented by the same model. We only need add the further requirement that the conditions R'd are also satisfied.

To be sure, we are still faced with the problem of accounting for the assertion-nonassertion distinction. Presumably it is possible to assert the conjunction of the enriched list of conditions that go into the definition of 'purport to adjourn M'. In that case R'ing those conditions will be equally involved in asserting that set of conditions and in purporting to adjourn M. So what distinguishes the two? So long as exercitive illocutionary acts were thought of as containing a conventional effect production condition over and above the R'ing that is involved, they could be distinguished from any assertion by that. But now that we think of exercitive illocutionary acts as consisting only of R'ing, the distinction will have to be made by finding something in asserting that *p* other than merely R'ing that *p*. That will be done in 5.2.

iv. The Final Model for Commissives

Now that we have decided that exercitive illocutionary acts do not require the actual production of conventional effects, what are we to say of commissives? Remember that it was the consideration of promises that led to the now abandoned view that what distinguishes nonassertive illocutionary acts from the "corresponding" assertions was that the former essentially involve the production of a distinctive kind of conventional effect. And commissives do not present the difficulties for that view that we encountered with exercitives. Unlike adjourning and hiring, promising does seem to qualify fully as an illocutionary act. To say that U promised H to do D would be a quite acceptable way of specifying *what U said*. It does not seem to go beyond a specification of the content of the message to a report of something U does *in* or *by* saying what he says. Try the "understanding what is said" test. I could understand just what you are saying when you utter 'You're hired', intending to hire U, but not know that you are hiring U. I may doubt that you are in a position to determine who gets the job; or I may know that the job is already filled. On the contrary, I couldn't understand what you are saying without knowing that you are *purporting to hire U*. That is our basic reason for taking *purporting to produce e* rather than *producing e* as the illocutionary act type in such cases. By contrast, when you say 'I promise to meet you for lunch tomorrow', meaning it in the usual

---

[10] Searle (1979) uses the term 'declarations' for what we are terming 'exercitives'.

way, I couldn't understand what you said without realizing that you did promise to meet H for lunch on the following day.[11] Thus promising to do D counts as an illocutionary act type. But it also involves the production of a conventional effect, namely, obligating oneself prima facie to do D. Here it would seem that just by saying something one produces the conventional effect.

So how are to we to fit commissives into our scheme? Considerations of symmetry push us in the direction of going against the appearances and looking for some hidden gap between the illocutionary act performance and the obligating.

As pointed out above, it is not difficult to see why commissives should differ from exercitives in the way just specified. In a commissive the conventional effect production consists in the *speaker's* taking on a certain obligation; while in the latter it consists in the engendering of obligations, rights, permissions, or other normative statuses for other people or for the society at large. It is understandable that society should hedge in the latter with restrictions not applicable to the former. If a person chooses to obligate *herself* in a certain way, she should have carte blanche to do so. Therefore society "allows" a speaker to take on an obligation *just by saying something*. But with exercitives society is not so permissive. We can't allow people to alter the social status of other people at will. Hence, further conditions will be required before the relevant conventional effect is forthcoming.

But recognition of this difference is compatible with applying the exercitive model to commissives, that is, with taking the illocutionary act involved in promising to be *purporting to obligate oneself*, rather than *actually obligating oneself*. Even if issuing the appropriate message is sufficient for obligating oneself, it does not follow that the latter is identical with or part of the former. The sufficiency of a whole for itself or for its parts is not the only sort of sufficient condition. It is consistent with the previous paragraph to hold that taking on a prima facie obligation to do D goes beyond the illocutionary act involved in promising to do D, even though, given the conventions of our society, the latter invariably generates the former. The difference from exercitives we have been noting is to be explained by the fact that our social conventions are such that *purporting to place a prima facie obligation on oneself by an utterance* engenders the obligation with no further conditions required, whereas *purporting to obligate others* achieves that effect only where further conditions are satisfied. The difference is an extrasemantic one. And so, on the principles I have been following, it should not enter into illocutionary act constitution. I set up the account

[11]   This is on the assumption that any referential attempts are successful. In presupposing that reference has been successfully carried out we are restricting ourselves to *de re* IA types. In Chapter 5 I will go into this issue and explain how to give analyses of both *de re* and *de dicto* IA types.

of illocutionary act concepts so as to preserve the intuition that sentence *meaning* is tied to illocutionary act potential. And so if, in a society with different extrasemantic conventions, one can utter a sentence of the form 'I promise to do A' with the same meaning it would have in our society, without succeeding in taking on a prima facie obligation to do A, we should not take the actual engendering of the obligation to be part of the illocutionary act a potential for which is constitutive of that sentence meaning. If nonlinguistic rules or conventions, as well as linguistic ones, are needed to generate S's obligation to do D that he takes on in promising, that is a reason for denying that the actual obligation production counts as an illocutionary act.[12]

Therefore we will treat commissives and exercitives in the same way. The ordinary act terms from which we start—'promise', 'adjourn', 'hire', etc.— are used for the total package that includes both the pure illocutionary act and the conventional effect production that is typically thereby engendered. The illocutionary act in each case can then be specified as *purporting to——*, where the blank is filled in with either act terms like the above or 'produce an e', where 'e' is one or another conventional effect. Thus I will adopt the following model of commissives.

CO: U C'd in uttering T (where 'C' is a term for a commissive illocutionary act type, a purporting to produce an obligation on U to do D) iff in uttering S, U R'd that:

1. Conceptually necessary conditions for U's being obliged to do D are satisfied.
2. H has some interest in U's doing D.
3. U intends to do D.
4. By uttering S, U places herself under an obligation to do D.

v. Directives

Next I want to discuss a category not given separate attention by Austin, but treated by later theorists, including Searle and Schiffer—what we may call "directives". These are illocutionary acts that, in a sense to be explained, are typically intended to "direct", or "influence", the behavior of the addressee. Familiar directive types include *ordering, commanding, requesting, suggesting, imploring, entreating,* and *interrogating.*

It would greatly simplify the general account if we could treat directives in the same way as exercitives and commissives. The idea suggests itself of taking a directive to be like a commissive, except that where the com-

---

[12] This intimate connection of illocutionary act constitution and sentence meaning will be spelled out in detail in Chapters 7 and 8.

missive involves R'ing that one is laying an obligation on oneself, a directive involves R'ing that one is laying an obligation on the addressee. This would, again, be combined with R'ing suitable presuppositions. I shall eventually come out with something like this, but not before wrestling with difficulties.

First, note that institutional[13] orders unproblematically fit this model. When I promise to do D I lay on myself an obligation to do D. When I issue a valid order to an employee or a military subordinate, I lay on my addressee, H, an obligation to do D.[14] Indeed, the ordinary concept of an order fits the model more smoothly than our ordinary exercitive or commissive concepts. In those cases, to get to what we take as the pure illocutionary act concept we had to add a "purport to" rider to the verb— 'appoint', 'promise', or whatever. But the terms 'order' and 'command', as ordinarily employed, are already in that form. It is *not* a necessary condition of my having ordered you to do D that you have acquired even a prima facie obligation to do D. There are clear cases of ordering without the conventional effect being engendered. This happens whenever U lacks authority to give such orders, either altogether or in these circumstances. You, an army lieutenant, order a private to shine your shoes, but army regulations give you no authority to issue any such order. You have not obligated H to do D, but we would *not* deny that you ordered H to do D. On the contrary, we would say that you shouldn't have issued that order. This reproach presupposes that you *did* order H to shine your shoes. Thus all that is required for me to order you to do D is that I *R* that I am laying on you an obligation to do D, along with R'ing appropriate background conditions. In Chapter 3 I presented a list of such background conditions for ordering my daughter to help wash the dishes. Adding now the obligation production to that list, we get the following schema for orders.

I8. U ordered H to D, in uttering S, iff in uttering S, U R'd that:
1. Conceptually necessary conditions for H's doing D are satisfied.
2. It is possible for H to do D.[15]
3. U has the authority to lay on H an obligation to do D.
4. By uttering S, U lays on H an obligation to do D.

But not all directives fit this model unproblematically. Consider *requesting* and its cousins, *entreating*, *imploring*, and *beseeching*. When I request you

---

[13] This qualification is designed to exclude, for example, a thief "ordering" me to hand over my wallet.
[14] As with promises this will have to be construed as a prima facie obligation. When my employer orders me to finish work on this contract before going home for the day, my obligation to do so can be overridden by my learning that my child is seriously ill.
[15] It is not necessary to add 2. to 1., but it is as well to make it explicit.

to do D, it seems that I do not even purport to *obligate* you to do D. Isn't it just because I am in no position to put you under an obligation that I have recourse to requesting, entreating, or imploring you to do so? To be sure, even if I do not *obligate* you to D, I may be altering your normative status in some other way. But if so, in what way?

Recall the preparatory conditions for requesting. In Chapter 3 we listed the following conditions as relevant to asking H to lend me his copy of *Individuals*.

1. H has a copy of *Individuals*.
2. It is possible for H to lend me that copy.
3. I have some interest in H's lending me that copy.

To generalize over *requesting H to do D*, U requests H to do D in uttering S only if U in uttering S R's that:

1. Conceptually necessary conditions of H's doing D are satisfied.
2. It is possible for H to do D.
3. U has some interest in H's doing D.

At least this much is clear. Requesting you to do D involves something over and above R'ing the above conditions. I can combine the expression of a desire that you give me a ride home with the claim that it is possible for you to do so, thereby R'ing all those conditions without thereby requesting you to do so. If I were to conjoin those two acts it might be taken as an indirect way of making the request, but it need not be so taken, and it need not be so intended. I might just be laying certain facts before you as a prelude to discussing our relationship, or I might be suggesting that it would be nice for you to take me home without actually requesting you to do so. What changes when I move from laying those facts before you to coming right out and *asking* you to give me a ride home? I have in some sense moved to "putting you on the spot". I have put you in a position where you are faced with a practical decision with which you were not otherwise faced—to comply with my request or to refuse to comply. Some theorists have tried to bring out what is special about the request in just those terms, saying that a request is something with respect to which the addressee has a choice between compliance and noncompliance. That is surely correct. But the trouble with using it as an explanation of requesting is that the compliance invoked here has to be explained in terms of a request or other directive. Compliance with what? With the request (order, entreaty . . .) to do so-and-so. That is too small a circle.

Let's go back to the idea that coming right out and *requesting* you to give me a ride "puts you on the spot", "puts it up to you" in some important sense. If we could show that this being put on the spot is a matter of your *normative status* being altered in some way, that would enable us to represent the distinctive character of requests in terms of the model for exercitives and commissives. And if we can distinguish the kind of normative status engendered by requests from that engendered by institutional orders, that will give us a neat way of distinguishing those two stretches of the directive territory.[16]

Something like this is involved in at least "appropriate" requests, such as my asking a friend for a ride home where this will not take him significantly out of his way, as contrasted with asking this of a perfect stranger where I am in no special need. The recipient of an appropriate request will be subject to censure if he rejects or ignores it without having an acceptable reason. Here I have altered your normative status in such a way that you are subject to blame for doing something (just going about your business and ignoring how I get home) for which you would not have been subject to blame otherwise. How can we describe in a more concise way the conventional effect I produced by my utterance, the new status I conferred on you by asking you to give me a ride home? At the risk of overworking the term 'obligation', and in the absence of a more finely articulated normative vocabulary, we might say that whenever you are subject to blame for doing or not doing something, what lies behind this is some obligation on your part you failed to carry out. If that is right, then in making my request I laid a certain obligation on you. This obligation is different from the one laid on you by a valid institutional order. When I request you to do D, it is "up to you" whether or not you do D, in a way it is not up to you when someone validly orders you to do D. Even the most appropriate request does not bind the addressee in the way a valid order does. But it does not follow that a request engenders no obligation.

I have said that the recipient of an appropriate request will be subject to blame if he fails to comply without being prepared to give an acceptable reason for noncompliance. We can build this point into the specification of the obligation engendered by saying that when I request you to do D, I thereby oblige you to either do D or be prepared to give an acceptable reason for not doing so. This captures the idea that the target of a request "has a choice" in a sense in which the target of an order does not. We can think of the request-generated obligation as disjunctive, the order-generated obligation as categorical.

This may seem to make the order-generated obligation too categorical. After all, even a valid order does not bind unconditionally. If I suddenly become critically ill, I will be excused for not carrying out a valid order. But we can see that the categorical-disjunctive distinction still holds by distinguishing between a prima facie and a disjunctive obligation. The reminder just issued concerning orders involves the former. Since the obli-

---

[16] In what follows I am indebted to Charles Caton.

gation laid on the addressee by a valid order is only prima facie, it is subject to being overridden by more pressing contrary obligations. *But the disjunctive obligation engendered by a request is also prima facie.* It too can be overridden by more pressing obligations the carrying out of which would prevent the addressee from either complying with the request or giving (or even being prepared to give) an adequate reason for not doing so. In the case of the "asking for a ride" example, suffering a heart attack would play this role. Thus orders and requests share the prima facie status of obligations engendered, while they differ in the character of those obligations in terms of their categorical or disjunctive character.

So far we have been speaking only of appropriate requests. And inappropriate requests are still requests. If I ask a perfect stranger at a party to lend me his record collection, I have not engendered even the relevant disjunctive obligation on his part to do so, but I did make the request. Fortunately, this complexity is nicely handled by the fact that our general model of nonassertives construes them not as the actual production of conventional effects, but merely as the purporting to do so. When I issue an invalid order I purport to be obligating you to do D, even where I fail to carry this through. And so with inappropriate requests.

Let's sum up the picture of requesting that has emerged. The institution of requesting presupposes a background of social rules, expectations, and discriminations. First, there are largely implicit, context-dependent, and imprecise principles for determining the appropriateness of requests. These have to do with such factors as the social relation of requester and requestee, the content of the request, the situation of each party, and so on. If I am in dire distress it is appropriate for me to ask things of strangers I would not otherwise be justified in asking. If you are obviously involved in matters of considerable importance, it will be inappropriate for me to ask you to do things I could ask you to do in other circumstances. There will be disputes and uncertainty over many cases, but it is undeniable that the making of such discriminations is essential for social intercourse as we know it. In addition there is a complex set of largely implicit principles concerning the conditions under which a request-generated obligation can be overridden. When I make a request I tap into this social network by way of R'ing that I engender such a weak obligation on the part of the addressee. This carries with it the implicit claim that my request is an appropriate one, just as an order carries with it the implicit claim that it is valid.[17]

Other treatments of directives have heavily featured the standard per-

---

[17] What about a hitchhiker? Let's assume that he has no claim whatever on the passing motorist. But does he even purport to have such a claim? And if not, how does this account accommodate the obvious fact that he is requesting the motorist to give him a ride? I am not sure that this is a genuine difficulty, for I am not sure that the appropriate social norms are such as to render this request inappropriate. But if they are, and if the hitchhiker does not purport otherwise, I would handle the case by taking the hitchhiker to be, in effect, asking

locutionary intention to get H to do D. Schiffer, as we have seen, treats illocutionary acts generally in terms of perlocutionary intentions, but even Searle gives as the "essential" condition for a request that it "counts as an attempt to get A to do D" (1969, 66).[18] And it must be confessed that the standard perlocutionary aim seems more prominent here than elsewhere. I myself introduced the category by reference to that aim. For reasons given in Chapter 2 I am convinced that the intention to get H to do D cannot be constitutive of a directive; any directive *can* be performed in the absence of such an intention. But the introduction of the concept of R'ing opens up new possibilities for bringing the standard perlocutionary intention into the analysis. We could add 'U utters S with the intention of getting H to D' to the list of conditions U R's. And our rule of thumb would seem to support such a move. It seems self-defeating to conjoin a purported request or order with the explicit assertion that one is not issuing the utterance in order to get H to do D. If I were to say, "I'm not saying this in order to get you to leave, but I order you to leave", this would hardly count as a clear case of issuing an order. Likewise with "I'm not saying this in order to get you to give me a ride home, but would you please give me a ride home?". Thus I am inclined to add the standard perlocutionary intention condition to the list of those R'd by U.

Against this background I suggest the following model for the analysis of directive illocutionary act concepts.

DI: U D'd in uttering S (where 'D' is a term for some directive illocutionary act type, a purporting to be producing a certain kind of obligation on H to do D) iff in uttering S, U R'd that:

1. Conceptually necessary conditions for the existence of the obligation are satisfied. (These include such things as that it is possible for H to do D, that D has not already been done, etc.)
2. Circumstances of the utterance of S are appropriate for the production of the obligation in question. (This includes the appropriate authority for orders, the right kind of interpersonal relationship for requests, etc.)

---

the motorist to treat the case as if the request were appropriate. That would be thinking of it as a higher-level request, one that presupposes the machinery of first-level requests. We may assume that such a higher-level request is always in order.

[18] Searle does not explain this puzzling phrase, which looks like an incoherent mixture of the rule-constituted ("counts as") and the perlocutionary intention ("attempt to get A to do D"). What my utterance was an attempt to do is a psychological fact about my motivation, and no rule could make the utterance "count as" an attempt at one thing rather than another. But my present point is that Searle felt constrained to bring a perlocutionary element into his account of directives in a way he does not bring it into his account of other kinds of illocutionary acts.

3. By uttering S, U lays on H a (stronger or weaker) obligation to do D.
4. U utters S in order to get H to do D.

vi. Expressives

Two of Austin's categories remain to be discussed—behabitives and expositives. The remainder of this chapter will be devoted to the first, and the next chapter to the second.

Austin admits that behabitives constitute "a very miscellaneous group" (151). The canonical description reads:

> Behabitives include the notion of reaction to other people's behavior and fortunes and of attitudes and expressions of attitudes to someone else's past conduct or imminent conduct. There are obvious connections with both stating or describing what our feelings are and expressing, in the sense of venting our feelings, though behabitives are distinct from both of these.
> Examples are:
> 1. For apologies we have 'apologize'.
> 2. For thanks we have 'thank'.
> 3. For sympathy we have 'deplore', 'commiserate', 'compliment', 'condole', 'congratulate', 'commiserate', 'sympathize'.
> 4. For attitudes we have 'resent', 'don't mind', 'pay tribute', 'criticize, 'grumble about', 'complain of', 'applaud', 'overlook', 'commend', deprecate', and the nonexercitive uses of 'blame', 'approve', and 'favour'.
> 5. For greetings we have 'welcome', 'bid you farewell'.
> 6. For wishes we have 'bless', 'curse', 'toast', 'drink to', and 'wish' (in its strict performative use).
> 7. For challenges we have 'dare', 'defy' 'protest', 'challenge'. (159)

I do not profess to see exactly what Austin had in mind here. The general statement is of little help. Clearly, many assertions, which he wishes to exclude, "have to do" with attitudes and social behavior. And the examples are such a mixed bag that one despairs of finding anything interesting in common. In making my own way from Austin's list toward a fundamental illocutionary act category, I shall take as my cue Austin's suggestion that "expressions of attitudes" are involved in important ways.

Let's extract from Austin's list of examples some verbs that can be used to report the expression of feelings and attitudes.

apologize	congratulate
thank	criticize
commiserate	sympathize
compliment	

The first job is to widen this list.

Austin restricted himself to ways of reporting the expression of attitudes by use of a one-word illocutionary term ('A thanked B', 'A commiserated with B'). This means that he ignores locutions that pair the verb 'express' with a specification of the attitude in question ('A expressed appreciation for B's help', 'A expressed enthusiasm for B's proposal'). But the latter count as reports of expressions of attitudes as much as the former. Moreover the one-word devices cover only part of the territory. There is no one word that can replace 'express disgust', 'express contempt', or 'express enthusiasm'. My category will range over all attitude-expressings, however reported.

What is it to express some attitude in the utterance of some sentence or sentence surrogate? If we approach this question in the spirit of our general approach to illocutionary acts, a very simple answer suggests itself.

U expressed attitude T_1 in uttering S iff in uttering S U R'd that:

I. U has T_1.

In other words, the illocutionary act of expressing an attitude simply consists in linguistically purporting to have that attitude. It is a matter of linguistically making it public, getting it out into the open.

This answer will undoubtedly seem too simple. Indeed, it constitutes a radical departure from virtually the entire literature on the subject.[19] Let's see how it stands up against objections and against more common views.

First, we are confronted with a particularly virulent form of our old problem of distinguishing a nonassertive illocutionary act from the parallel assertion. If expressing one's disgust at Jones's behavior *is* just R'ing that one is disgusted at Jones's behavior, how does it differ from asserting that one is disgusted at Jones's behavior? The problem is aggravated by the fact that illocutionary acts of the behabitive category, unlike other nonassertive categories, are regularly and unproblematically performed by the use of declarative, nonperformative sentences that look for all the world as if they are usable for asserting. I can express enthusiasm for your plan just as well by saying 'I'm terribly enthusiastic about that' as by saying 'Bully!'. I can express disgust at your behavior at least as well by saying 'That's disgusting' as by saying 'Ugh!'. What is the difference between expressing enthusiasm for your plan by uttering 'I'm terribly enthusiastic about it' and *asserting* that I'm enthusiastic about your plan by uttering the same sentence? Are we always doing the one whenever we do the other? If so, how can we differentiate between the expressive and assertive aspects of the performance? This problem will be best considered in connection with the general discussion of assertion in 5.4. For now I want to confront the above

[19] An exception, unsurprisingly, is Alston 1965.

account of expressing with the radically different accounts prevalent in the literature.

The dominant view is that the sense in which I express, for example, disgust in an utterance is the same sense as that in which my voluntary and involuntary nonverbal behavior may express disgust. And that sense is simply this. For behavior *b* to express mental state *m* is simply for *b* and *m* to be of types B and M, such that B's are regularly correlated with M's, thereby making it possible to take a B as a reliable indication of an M.

> Almost all the conscious and unconscious movements of a person, including his linguistic utterances, express something of his feelings, his present mood, his temporary or permanent dispositions to reaction, and the like. Therefore we may take almost all his movements and words as symptoms from which we can infer something about his feelings or his character. That is the expressive function of movements and words. (Carnap 1935, 27)

> If A's behavior B is an *expression* of X, then there is a warrantable inference from B to an intentional state of A, such that it would be true to say that A has (or is in state) S; where S and X are identical. (Tormey 1971, 43)

I have no wish to deny that, in general, when U expresses some attitude as an illocutionary act, his utterance is a reliable sign of that attitude. But I do wish to deny that this is what *makes* his utterance an illocutionary act of that sort. This is because the reliable sign account leaves out the *normative, rule-governed* character that is essential to illocutionary acts. When what U is doing, illocution-wise, is to express his enthusiasm for X or his disgust at X, what gives his utterance that content? We can run through the unsatisfactory answers we considered for illocutionary acts generally in Chapter 2. The mere fact that U is enthusiastic about X, or that she knows or believes that she is, is not sufficient for its being the case that she is expressing enthusiasm. Obviously, these conditions might be satisfied while she is remarking that the weather is cold. If we took Schiffer's line that what is crucial is that U utter S with the intention of getting H to believe that U is enthusiastic about X, we would run into the same stubborn counterexamples we encountered in discussing Schiffer's view of assertion. For example, I might just be "going through the motions" in expressing enthusiasm for X, not caring whether you believe I am enthusiastic about it or not. Nor does the reliable sign view fare any better, since it fails to provide a sufficient condition. I may ask H why he did D, in a tone of voice that functions as a reliable sign of disgust at H's behavior. In this case I did not *express* disgust at his behavior (using 'express' as an illocutionary act term). To generalize the point, one may verbally produce a reliable sign of a certain attitude by saying something with a content far removed from one's having the attitude in question. In such cases it is the *way* one says what one says, rather than *what* one says, that functions as the reliable sign. In these cases one does *not* perform the illocutionary act of expressing one's attitude.

So my general point about IA's holds for the expressing of attitudes, namely, that we cannot bring out what makes an utterance an expression of enthusiasm about X without bringing out the way in which the utterance alters one's normative status, brings it about that one is liable to correction and the like under certain conditions, in this case one's not being enthusiastic about X. And again, this is possible only if there is a rule in force that implies that her utterance is in order only if she is enthusiastic about X. All this holds for an interjection like 'Bully!' just as much as for a declarative sentence like 'I'm terribly enthusiastic about that'. Expressing one's enthusiasm for X by saying 'Bully!' or 'Splendid!' is just as essentially a matter of putting one's utterance under a rule requiring one to be enthusiastic about X as is expressing enthusiasm by uttering a declarative sentence.

I am far from supposing that there is no sense of 'express' that is captured by the reliable sign view. Consider locutions like 'Her face expressed great determination' or 'His every movement expressed his indignation at the proceedings'. Here the expression of the attitude does not involve one's putting one's behavior or demeanor under a rule requiring that one have the attitude in question, or under any other rule. And the reliable sign view captures at least a large part of what is involved in such cases. But note that these are cases of one's *face* or one's *movements* expressing something, not a case of the *person* expressing something, and hence not a case of *the person's* expressing something linguistically. This can be brought out by the following example. I say to you: "When I approached Jones on the matter, he expressed real enthusiasm for my plan". You ask "What did he say exactly?". I reply, "Oh, he didn't say anything, but there was a definite glow in his eyes while I was talking". It is clear that I misrepresented the situation when I said that *Jones* expressed enthusiasm for my plan. One does not express enthusiasm for something by throwing one's hat in the air, dancing a jig, emitting squeals of delight, or "lighting up" one's eyes. If the only reaction is of one of these sorts, one may be said to have *shown*, *demonstrated*, *evinced*, or *betrayed* enthusiasm, but not to have *expressed* it. Though, as just pointed out, my facial "expression" or my movements can be said to have expressed it. Likewise, if my only response to your helping me carry a heavy box was a gracious smile, I would not be said to have expressed appreciation for your help. Indeed, I might be taken to task for not having expressed appreciation. Thus the idiom 'U expressed his a for X' is restricted to *illocutionary acts* of expressing one's a for X. This leaves us a wealth of idioms for reporting that U issued some reliable sign of his a for X.

One may still maintain that expressing fails to qualify as a "pure" illocutionary act in our sense, since it is also necessary for expressing that the condition R'd be satisfied. The argument for this is that one cannot be said to express something that isn't "there". It makes no sense to say "U expressed *his enthusiasm for B's plan,* but he is not enthusiastic about it". The underlined referring expression, like all such expressions, carries a presupposition of the existence of that to which it purports to refer. It is, therefore, self-defeating to conjoin a use of that expression with an admission that the putative referent does not exist.[20]

I admit that there is a locution containing 'express' that carries this implication. It is, in fact, the one exploited in the above paragraph. It is the locution that refers to a particular attitude as belonging to the speaker, as in:

U expressed *his* annoyance at the interruption.
U expressed *her* contempt for A.
U expressed *her* admiration for A.

But there is also the form that omits the possessive pronoun.

U expressed satisfaction at the outcome.
U expressed appreciation for her contribution.
U expressed contempt for A.

The actual possession of an attitude of the sort specified is not a necessary condition for the truth of the latter three statements. Provided I say the right things (realizing what I am saying) I have *expressed contempt* for A, whether or not I am actually contemptuous. If it turns out that I did not feel contempt for A, I can be upbraided for expressing contempt when I didn't actually feel that way. That would be a natural way to charge insincerity, and it presupposes that I *did* express contempt. Hence I will take the forms without the possessive pronoun as pure illocutionary act reports. The forms with the possessive pronoun will be taken as reports of illocutionary acts + the claim that a condition R'd is actually satisfied, parallel to reports employing ordinary exercitive verbs.

It may still be felt that my account fails to do justice to the "emotional warmth" of expressing, to the fact that it is, after all, a species of "expressive behavior". Can one be said to be *expressing* annoyance (indignation, disgust, delight . . .) if his utterance is not colored by the state expressed, unless he is saying whatever he is saying in a *tone* of annoyance? The suggestion is that a necessary condition for expressing M is that one's utter-

---

[20] For an extended defense of this claim see Tormey 1971, esp. chap. 2.

ance count as acting in an M-ish manner; or, more strongly, that one's utterance count as one of the things that go to make up *being* M.[21]

The seas of language run high at this point, and I can imagine reasonable theorists taking different positions on this issue. I am convinced, though, that the phenomena can be handled without this extra condition. From the standpoint of my leaner account, any temptation to say what is said in the last paragraph reflects a certain leakage from the sense of 'express' in which facial "expressions" and tones of voice express something. If I express annoyance or indignation or admiration in a flat tone of voice, then my tone of voice is not expressive of such feelings; *it* does not express them. But *I* express annoyance, nonetheless, by virtue of *what* I said. The illocutionary act of expressing annoyance depends on *what* he says, not on *how* he says it.

I take this position to receive support from several quarters. First, we have to give some account of the sense of 'express' in which I did express admiration for A, even though my admiration did not show itself in my tone of voice, look, or gestures. My account does this. And are we not forced to admit that when I say 'He's a wonderful guy' in an awestruck tone, I am still expressing admiration for him in the same sense of the term in which I did so in a flat tone of voice, even though more is going on in the former case? Second, there are many attitudes that do not show themselves in tones of voice the way annoyance, indignation, and delight do, for example, approval, satisfaction, and interest.

A third reason for this position appears when we broaden the behabitive category. There are many kinds of psychological states expressed by speech other than "attitudes to someone else's past conduct or imminent conduct". These include beliefs, doubts, agreement, intentions, willingnesses, and desires. We can often specify the content of U's utterance by saying that U expressed the belief that *p* or a desire for X, or an intention to do A. Expressing such things are illocutionary acts, just as much as expressing admiration or disgust. Again, it seems that what performing such an illocutionary act consists in is R'ing that one has the psychological state in question. But then it is exactly the same concept of expressing that is involved across these distinctions. Even though there are important psychological differences between beliefs, desires, and interpersonal attitudes, this is no basis for separating out the expression of attitudes as one of our fundamental illocutionary act categories. Expressing disgust, as an illocutionary act, differs from expressing a belief in terms of subject matter, not in terms of the structure of the act. *Expression of attitude* no more constitutes a fundamental illocutionary act category than does *assertion about ge-*

---

[21] This requirement may seem to reinstate the claim that one cannot express M without being M, but it is not so. I can speak in an annoyed tone of voice without actually being annoyed.

ology. Thus we may give a unified account of all illocutionary acts that consist in the expression of some psychological state.

EXP: U expressed a P (some psychological state) in uttering S iff in uttering S, U R'd that U has a P.

In recognition of this wider scope, let's rechristen the category *Expressives*.

Now for the third reason for my "lean" treatment of expressions of attitudes and feelings. It is clear that beliefs, intentions, and desires are even less susceptible to manifestation in tones of voice than satisfaction or appreciation; and so there is little or no expectation that one who expresses these states in what he says will simultaneously be manifesting them in how one says it. Hence if our illocutionary act concept of expressing is to capture what is common to the whole category, it will not include any requirement of "emotional warmth".

This broadening of the category does introduce one fresh problem. As our analyses of commissives and directives make clear, a great variety of illocutionary acts involve R'ing that one has some psychological state or other. Promising to do D involves R'ing that one *intends* to do D, and requesting H to do D involves R'ing that one has some *interest* in H's doing D. But then whenever one makes a promise or a request, or performs some other commissive or directive, one expresses an intention to do something or an interest in something's coming about, or some other psychological state. So it seems that we must regard commissives and directives as, at least in part, expressives. How, then, can we regard Expressives as an illocutionary act category coordinate with Commissives and Directives? Should we say that a Commissive, for example, is an Expressive plus something else?

This is not a serious difficulty. We can still separate out a coordinate category of Expressives, provided the requirement for membership is that expressing is all that is involved, including whatever is conceptually required for expressing whatever is being expressed. To merely express one's intention to do D is an Expressive, for the expression of that intention exhausts the illocutionary act performance. But to promise to do D, though it essentially involves expressing that intention, also involves other R'ings; hence it will not be classified as an Expressive. In this way we can construe Expressives as a category coordinate with Commissives and Directives.

But isn't the problem more extensive than this? It would seem that every R'ing whatever involves expressing a belief. Whenever I R any *p* whatever, including those extra ones in promising and requesting just mentioned, I represent myself as believing that *p*. Hence for any such *p* it would seem that I express the belief that *p*. But then if all illocutionary acts are constituted wholly by R'ings, as I have been suggesting, it would seem to follow that every illocutionary act is an Expressive through and through. For whatever R'ings constitute a given commissive, exercitive, or whatever, they seem to turn into a set of expressings. And so the Expressive category threatens to swallow up all the others.

But the threat is hollow. It rests on a misconstrual of my account of expressing. According to that account, expressing a certain psychological state is a matter of R'ing *that one has that psychological state.* But the R'ings involved in illocutionary acts, according to my account, are generally not R'ings to the effect that U has a certain kind of psychological state. In some cases they are. As just pointed out, in a commissive one R's that one has a certain intention and in a directive one R's that one has an interest in H's doing something or other. For the most part, illocutionary performance, including exercitives and most assertives, involves R'ing facts about shoes and ships and sealing wax, about cabbages and kings. Hence it is just not true that on my theory every R'ing involves expressing a belief.

Nevertheless, it does seem plausible to suppose that if, as I have contended, R'ing that p involves representing oneself as believing that p, there is some sense in which R'ing that p involves expressing a belief that p. In the case of assertion this impression can be reinforced by G. E. Moore's point that there is something self-defeating about conjoining a flat assertion that p with a denial that one believes that p. Indeed, this has become a paradigm of a "pragmatic contradiction".

I believe that we can resolve this dilemma by distinguishing senses of 'express'. I have already distinguished expressing as an illocutionary act from the kind of expressing carried out by one's facial expression, demeanor, and the like. The present problem indicates the need to distinguish expressing as an illocutionary act from a nearer relation, a different kind of speech act of expressing. In terms of the present theory, as developed to this point, we can explain expressing$_1$ that P (some psychological state) as R'ing that one has P, and expressing$_2$ that P (a belief that p) as R'ing that p (not that one has P). It is in the second sense, but not the first, that one expresses a belief whenever one R's anything whatever. Since the *illocutionary act* of expressing is defined in terms of the first sense, we can continue to maintain that only a small proportion of R'ings involve expressing anything, while at the same time recognizing a sense in which any R'ing involves expressing a belief. And this nicely accommodates Moore's paradox. If, in asserting that p, I R that p, then it is indeed self-defeating to conjoin this with a denial that I believe that p. For R'ing that p is to express a belief that p in the second sense.

Here is an example. I assert that the weather has turned cooler. In doing so I R that the weather has turned cooler. But I have not thereby performed an illocutionary act of expressing a belief that the weather has turned cooler unless I also R *that I believe that the weather has turned cooler.* And why suppose that I have done that? According to my canonical formulation of what it is to R that p, I R whatever is required by the linguistic rule to which I subject my utterance. As I have set things up, the relevant rule here requires that *the weather has turned cooler*. Should we say that the rule also requires that I believe that the weather has turned cooler? I have refrained from claiming this,[22] and a good reason for doing so is that it is unnecessary. Just by virtue of the requirement I have recognized, I am subject to blame for uttering my sentence without believing that the weather has turned cooler. For in that case I have deliberately produced the utterance without supposing (much less knowing or supposing with good reason) that the requirements of the rule are met. The rule is best construed as making an "objective" requirement. It will then automatically lay on the speaker the requirement of seeing to it that the rule is followed, which means that the speaker at least justifiably believes that the original requirement is met.

If one were to hold that whenever one R's that p one also R's that one believes that p, one would be launched on an infinite regress. Call 'that one believes that p' 'q'. By the same principle if one R's that q, one also R's that one believes that q (call that latter proposition 'r'). But then, by the same principle, one also R's that one believes that r. And so on ad infinitum. To avoid the regress we had better block it at the source, denying that R'ing that p implies that one R's that one believes that p.

Nothing that I have said should be taken as implying that one cannot perform the illocutionary act of expressing a belief, for example, by making a standard use of 'In my opinion, p', or 'I am inclined to believe that p' or 'It is my belief that p'. But in these cases what one R's is *that one believes that p*, not, as in a flat assertion that p, that p.

It is time to return to the point that the part of Austin's lists of behabitive verbs that overlaps our Expressive category is restricted to one-word phrases like 'thank' and 'apologize' and lacks any phrases involving the verb 'express'.[23] I have been assuming that Austin's one-word examples constitute just a small subclass of the total range of Expressives, all of which can be reported by the 'He expressed a for X' formula. 'He thanked H for X' reports just the same illocutionary act as 'He expressed appreciation to H for X', and this common illocutionary act is adequately treated by my simple schema. But perhaps I have been too hasty in making this as-

[22] In 3.4.
[23] Perhaps the omission of 'express' is due to the fact that it cannot be used in performative formulas. While I can express appreciation by saying to H 'I thank you for . . .', I can't do it by saying 'I express appreciation to you for . . .'. Since most treatments of illocutionary acts have relied on the explicit performative formula to identify illocutionary verbs, this may account for the neglect of expressing in those treatments. This is one point at which our approach to the subject in terms of illocutionary act *reports* demonstrates its superiority. For though the expresser can't do it by saying 'I express appreciation for . . .', one reporting her illocutionary act can do it by saying 'She expressed appreciation for . . .'. And surely the latter reports an illocutionary act just as much as 'She thanked H for . . .'.
  It is also worthy of note that 'express appreciation' can figure in performative formulae like 'Let me express my appreciation for . . .' and 'I would like to express my appreciation for . . .'.

sumption. May it not be that apologizing is a somewhat different illocutionary act from expressing contrition, thanking from expressing appreciation, and so on?

I will approach this problem by considering why we have "behabitive verbs" for some expressings and not others. For expressing appreciation we have the verb 'thank'; for expressing a favorable evaluation of some performance we have the verb 'compliment'; for expressing contrition we have 'apologize'; for expressing sympathy we have 'commiserate'. But there is no analogous verb for expressing disgust, enthusiasm, or indignation. Why is this? It would seem that we have the single verb where the expression is definitely called for, expected, or mandated in certain social circumstances. There are contexts in which one is expected to express contrition, appreciation, or sympathy, and in which one will be unfavorably evaluated if one does not. When I am given something I am expected to express appreciation; when I have offended someone I am expected to express contrition. But though the verbal act of expression can be socially mandated, the attitude expressed cannot. I can't take on an attitude of appreciation or contrition at will, though I can take steps to encourage the development of such attitudes in myself over the long haul. Hence society is, so to say, prepared for these performances being more or less perfunctory. One is expected to do the expressing even when one doesn't have the correlated attitude. Hence it is useful to have special terms for such expressings. This sets them apart from the usual run of expressings, which are normally sincere and spontaneous and expected to be such. By using the pat formula 'I apologize for ___', instead of reporting feelings of contrition or expatiating on the reprehensible character of his deed, it is easier for U to satisfy the social imperative without actually feeling contrite; it also signals to the addressee that he is conforming to a social expectation and that he does not necessarily have the attitude being expressed.

If this is the way the land lies, we may be tempted to suppose that apologizing differs from expressing contrition as an illocutionary act, that is, in terms of what is R'd. For if one who apologizes for having done D is not expected to feel contrition for doing it, we can't suppose that her apologizing consists in her R'ing that she is contrite for having done D. The relevant social conventions would not be such that one who apologizes issues her utterance as subject to a rule that requires feeling contrite as necessary for permissible utterance. But this would be to push the difference too far. Even though one is unsurprised to learn that a thanker does not really feel appreciation, still one who thanks is *purporting* to feel appreciation. This is shown by the usual tests. We get the familiar pragmatic contradiction from "I don't feel any appreciation for the gift, but thanks a lot", or "I apologize. Of course, I feel absolutely no contrition for what I did". Such utterances, meant literally and straightforwardly, are self-canceling. I can't overtly admit that I don't have the attitude in question while performing the socially required act. But if the social ritual had been effectively disengaged from the spontaneous expressing, this would be possible. Hence we must hold that thanking or apologizing by saying 'I thank . . .' or 'I apologize . . .' still essentially involves R'ing that one has the attitude in question, and hence is the same illocutionary act as what could also be called "expressing appreciation or contrition".

The identity of thanking H for X and expressing appreciation to H for X is further underlined by the fact that these terms can be used interchangeably in illocutionary act reports. No matter how perfunctory and socially constrained my illocutionary act, it can perfectly well be reported as 'He expressed appreciation for X' as well as 'He thanked H for X'.[24] And the heartfelt outpouring of appreciation without social constraint can be reported as U's thanking H for what she did.

Of course, there is a difference between a socially unconstrained expression of contrition and one that is socially mandated. We have failed in our attempt to build this difference into the constitution of the illocutionary act by omitting from the latter what is contained in the former. But we might try to add something to the latter, for example, R'ing that the social situation requires an expression of M. But our working criterion will not support this. Is there anything self-defeating about saying 'I realize that I am not socially required to express appreciation, but I do want to thank you for ___'? Even if this is a situation in which I *am* socially required to express appreciation, my (mistaken) allegation that I am not would not prevent my utterance from counting as a case of thanking. Hence it seems that the difference does not lie in what is R'd, does not lie in the content of what is said, but rather lies in how saying it fits into the social situation. There are many differences of that sort. Of two cases of remarking that the election will be close, one may be relevant to the ongoing conversation and the other not. Of two tellings of the same joke, one may be suited to the audience and the other not. The difference between mandated and unmandated expressings is another example of the same phenomenon. What is said is the same, but the difference in the social situation leads to its being received in different ways.

[24] Those who take the position rejected earlier, that one expresses A only if one actually has A, will be, misguidedly, led by that view to deny that ritualistic thankings, in the absence of any real appreciation, can be termed an expression of appreciation.

CHAPTER FIVE

Assertions and Other Assertives: Completing the Account

i. The Problem of Assertion

now turn to the task of completing the account of assertion. In Chapter 3 I suggested that asserting that *p* essentially involves R'ing that *p*. However, if this were the whole story, we would not be able to make several important distinctions between assertions and other speech acts. We must keep all these distinctions in mind, for it may turn out that an effective way of dealing with one will not work with another.

First, there is the distinction that initially gave rise to the problem, that between presupposing or implying that *p* in a commissive, directive, or exercitive, and asserting that *p*. If asserting that *p* simply consists in R'ing that *p*, then what are we to say about the fact that in promising H to do D, I R that it is possible for me to do D? On this account of assertion I assert that it is possible for me to do D whenever I promise to do D. But when I make a promise I make no such assertion. One might try the move of putting closure on the analysis of assertion, as we did with expressing in the last chapter. To assert that *p* is to R that *p* and to do nothing more in the illocutionary line. That would handle this particular difficulty, for when I promise to do D my illocutionary act involves much more than R'ing that it is possible for me to do D. But that merely postpones the day of reckoning. There is still the problem of distinguishing, to change the example, declaring the meeting adjourned from the assertion of the conjunction of *all* the propositions the R'ing of which constitutes that exercitive act. If asserting that *p* is constituted wholly by R'ing that *p*, then in R'ing all those propositions I am both declaring the meeting adjourned *and* asserting those propositions. But clearly when I declare the meeting adjourned I am *not* asserting those propositions or any others. And even if I were, we would still be faced with the problem of distinguishing the assertion from the purporting to adjourn.

The second distinction we have not yet accommodated is that between expressing a certain attitude or other psychological state and asserting that one has that attitude or that psychological state. On the account as thus far developed, expressing contempt for H and asserting that I have contempt for H both consist of R'ing that I have contempt for H. Then what is the difference?

Third, within an assertion there is the problem of discriminating between what is asserted and what is presupposed. In asserting that (p1) *the chair in the corner is broken*, I am presupposing but not asserting that (p2) *there is a chair in the corner*. The problem stems from the fact that in asserting that *p* I R what is presupposed by that assertion as much as I R what is asserted. For when I assert that (p1) I subject my utterance to a rule that requires that there be a chair in the corner just as much as it requires that the chair in the corner be broken. But clearly when I assert that the chair in the corner is broken I do not, ipso facto, also assert that there is a chair in the corner. To be sure, although (p2) is R'd it is only R'd for the sake of setting up a further R'd proposition, p1, which is what is asserted. But this will do the trick only if we already have a stipulation as to what is asserted in a given utterance. It gives us no basis for making that discrimination. Contrast the following two cases.

1. U makes a normal use of the sentence 'The chair in the corner is broken'.
2. U makes a normal use of the sentence 'There is a chair in the corner and it is broken'.

In 1. U asserts (only) p1, while in 2. U asserts both p1 and p2. But the analysis, as so far developed, gives us no basis for making that distinction. For what U is R'ing is exactly the same in the two cases.

In presenting this last problem I side with Strawson against Russell on to how to handle referring expressions other than Russellian proper names. On Russell's account of a sentence like p1, when we use the sentence to make an assertion we are asserting both that there is a chair in the corner and that it is broken. At least this is a natural way of extending Russell's theory of definite descriptions[1] to the topic of assertion. On that theory

---

[1]   See Russell 1919, chap. 16.

'the chair in the corner is broken' is to be understood as 'there is exactly one chair in the corner, and whatever is a chair in the corner is broken'. Given this interpretation our problem does not arise. We *are* asserting both p1 and p2 when we say that the chair in the corner is broken. Whereas on Strawson's account,[2] when we say that the chair in the corner is broken, we assert only that the chair in question is broken, and we *presuppose*, but do not assert, that there is a chair in the corner. This is the construal that gives rise to the present difficulty. I have no stake here in the outcome of this dispute. If Russell is correct, then my account faces one less difficulty. I assume Strawson's account, which I take to be correct, thereby making things maximally difficult for myself.

In the ensuing discussion we should keep before our minds the necessity of providing a basis for all these discriminations.

ii. Assertion as Explicitly Presenting a Proposition

The nature of assertion has received a surprisingly small amount of attention. The most prominent failings of such suggestions as have been made are the following. (1) They rely on unexplicated semantic concepts like *refer*, *designate*, or *extension*.[3] (2) They are in terms of conditions of truth, thereby presupposing that we have a way of determining which illocutionary acts, namely, assertions, can be assessed in terms of truth value, as well as failing to distinguish what is asserted and what is presupposed.[4] (3) Like Schiffer's account in terms of intentions to produce beliefs in addressees they fail, as was brought out in Chapter 2, to apply to all clear cases of assertion. (4) Like Searle's account in 1979 that is just in terms of something like R'ing that *p* ("commit the speaker to something's being the case, to the truth of the expressed proposition" [12]), they apply to other types of illocutionary acts as well, in addition to being subject to objection (2) above. (5) A recent attempt that is worthy of more serious attention is that in Brandom 1994, an important and far-ranging book that intersects the present work in emphasizing the normative character of illocutionary act performance (Brandom does not use the term 'illocutionary act') and of linguistic meaning. The general idea for assertion is that it amounts to undertaking a certain kind of commitment, one that has the dual role of something for which reasons can be asked and something that can be offered as a reason. This is then equated to the idea that "assertions are fundamentally fodder for inferences" (167–168). For giving reasons is thought of as the fundamental case of inference. My main criticisms of this are two. (1) It leaves us with the job of distinguishing assertions from the R'ings in other types of illocutionary acts (something not undertaken in

---

[2] Strawson 1950.
[3] For criticism of theories of meaning that exhibit this fault see Chapter 9.
[4] See Dummett 1973, 354; Moore 1962, 180.

Brandom's book). (2) I take both reason giving and inference to be more sophisticated performances than what is minimally required for assertion.

An adequate criticism of the above suggestions, particularly Brandom's, would require much more space than I can allot to it here. Instead I turn to the question of whether I can do better than the above. I suggest that we look to a clue that has been strangely neglected. Think back on the contrasts we have been drawing. Begin with the one between presupposing that it is possible for me to do D in promising to do D, and asserting that it is possible for me to do D. A natural way of formulating the latter side of this contrast is to say that we assert that p when we "come right out and say that p *in so many words*", when "we *explicitly* say that p". This suggests that the difference between asserting that p and R'ing that p without asserting it lies in the character of the verbal means employed in the utterance, rather than in the psychological attitudes expressed or in any other inner factor. Furthermore, it suggests that the crucial feature of the sentential vehicle is the "explicitness" with which it "presents" the p in question. Where the p R'd is "explicitly presented", it is asserted; where not, not.

There are two directions in which this suggestion might be developed. The most obvious one involves a doctrine of propositions as bearers of truth values and as "expressed" or "presented" by sentences. Each proposition is made up of certain constituents and displays a certain structure. Consider the proposition *that the door is open*. (When we take the underlined phrase to specify a particular proposition, we are using it in a context that, we suppose, makes clear what door it is to which we are referring.) The proposition in question can be thought of as made up of the door (alternatively, an individual concept of that door) and the property of being open, bound together in a structure by the "predicative tie". Whether U, who was R'ing *that the door is open* in uttering sentence S, was asserting that the door is open depends on whether S "explicitly presents" that proposition. That is a matter of whether S is isomorphic with the proposition— whether there is a semantic element of S corresponding to each element of the proposition, and whether these elements are put together in the sentence and the proposition in corresponding ways. If S is 'The door is open' or 'That door is open' or 'It's open', then this isomorphism obtains. The sentence contains a referring expression that picks out the door in question (assuming reference comes off all right), a predicate term for being open, and in the sentence the latter is attached predicatively to the former. If S, on the other hand, is 'Please close the door', although U, in uttering S, is R'ing that the door is open, the sentence does not explicitly present that proposition. There is no term for *being open*, for example.

Note that a sentence fails to explicitly present a proposition not only when, as in the case just mentioned, something is lacking, but also when too much is present, when the sentence as a whole fails to fit the proposition even though a part of it does so. This would be the case if the sentence had been 'Jones knows that the door is open'. Here the subordinate clause is isomorphic in the specified way with the proposition *that the door is open.* But because the sentence as a whole is not isomorphic with that proposition, the sentence will not be said to "explicitly present" the proposition, as I have explained that term; and hence one is not asserting that the door is open in uttering this sentence, even though one is R'ing this in a normal use of the sentence.[5] If it is correct to say that the proposition that the door is open *is* explicitly presented in this case, we can use the term 'exactly express' for the concept of what is required for asserting. The sentence 'Jones knows that the door is open' clearly does not *exactly express* the proposition *that the door is open.*

This approach in terms of sentence-proposition isomorphism has a long and, in the opinion of many, a tragic history. Partisans of Ockham's razor and other lovers of desert landscapes have felt that propositions clutter the ontological scene. More seriously, propositionalists have encountered a variety of difficulties in working out the theory in a way that is neither circular, vacuous, nor fatally obscure, especially with respect to what "ties" the elements together in a proposition. These difficulties have led to attempts to show that more undeniable and less troublesome entities can do the work of propositions. Instead of holding that the same assertion is made in different utterances only if the same proposition is expressed, we may try to show that certain relations between the sentences uttered, or between the utterances themselves, will do the trick. My second way is of this sort. When we specify what it is that U may or may not have asserted, we do so by using a declarative sentence, for example, 'There is a chair in the corner'. Our first way involved taking that sentence to specify a proposition and then asking whether S's sentence was related in a certain way to that proposition. But instead of taking this detour through the proposition, why not go directly from the sentence used to specify the assertion to U's sentence and ask whether they stand in the appropriate equivalence relation, R? We can then say that U has asserted that p only if S1 (S's sentence) is related by R to S2 (the sentence used to specify what was putatively asserted).

This sounds promising until we ask just what relation R is. It is clearly not identity. S1 and S2 might be in different languages. Nor is it synonymy. You may assert that *you are hungry* by uttering the nonsynonymous sentence 'I am hungry'. Nor is it intentional isomorphism.[6] The last example

---

[5] What about a conjunction? If I assert something of the former 'p and q', have I have not thereby asserted that p, despite the fact that my sentence does not exactly express the proposition that p (and only that proposition)? It is not clearly mistaken to say this. Nevertheless, it is also acceptable to hold that what I have asserted is p *and* q, not p alone, even though what I asserted entails that p. And I will adopt this latter position.

[6] See Carnap 1947, sec. 14. Intentional isomorphism requires a synonymy relation between each semantic element of the one sentence and some semantic element of the other, as well as these elements being bound together in the same way.

shows this as well. Intentional isomorphism requires synonymy between corresponding semantic elements of the two sentences; and 'you' is not synonymous with 'I'. Furthermore, the fact that a given sentence under a given interpretation ('I am hungry') can be used to make many different assertions, depending on contextual determination of referents and other matters, indicates that the crucial equivalence relation will have to hold not between the two sentence types but either between two sentence utterances (tokens) or between the two sentences as used in whatever the relevant context is in each case. So what we are shooting for is a relation, R, such that S_1 stands in that relation to S_2 *iff* the assertion normally made by S_1 in the context in which U utters it is the same as the assertion normally made by S_2 in the context in which it was used to specify the proposition. The relation we want is such that an S_1 and an S_2 that stand in that relation would be normally used, in contexts of the types in question, to make the same assertion. But to specify the relation in this way is blatantly circular, leaning heavily on the notion of *what assertion is made*. What we need is a way of specifying R that does not make use of the notion of what assertion is made. We could, of course, bring in the notion of proposition to do this. S_1 and S_2 stand in the appropriate relation when the proposition explicitly presented by S_1 in its context is the same as the proposition explicitly presented by S_2 in its context. But if we are going to appeal to propositions anyway, we may as well go back to the first way.

I lack the space to carry this discussion further. To bring it to a close, let me say that we can use the propositionalist approach without getting into ontological difficulties by the following maneuver. Given that we have the mastery of that-clauses that is possessed by any fluent speaker of a language that includes them, we have a practical, know-how mastery of the concept of a proposition. If what I asserted was *that it is raining*, the proposition *that it is raining* is the one that I asserted. And so on.[7] No doubt, this leaves various fine-grained questions about propositional identity unanswered, but we may take the concept of a proposition to be usable without an ability to answer all such questions, just as many other concepts are. I will proceed to employ the propositional approach in developing the present account of assertion.[8]

I had best spell out a point that has been just under the surface in the above. A sentence explicitly presents a proposition in the simplest way when its semantic constituents correspond to the elements of the proposition just by virtue of the meanings of the former. This is the case with general sentences like 'Lemons are sour'. But where singular reference is involved, the underdetermination of reference by meaning prevents anything this simple. Here contextual parameters and referential intentions

---

[7] For a bit more on this maneuver see Alston 1996a, chap. 1.
[8] For a spirited and (to my mind) convincing defense of the attribution of structure to propositions see Bealer 1982.

of speakers must come into the picture. An utterance of 'I am hungry' explicitly presents the proposition that *I, W. P. Alston, am hungry at time t* not just by virtue of the meaning of the constituents of the sentence, but also by virtue of the time of utterance and the identity of the utterer. Part of what enables an utterance of 'The chair is broken' to present a proposition about a particular chair is that there are certain features of the context of utterance and/or the speaker's referential intentions that pick out a particular chair as the referent of 'the chair'. This is an application to the present topic of the pervasive phenomenon of the underdetermination of reference by meaning that is emphasized in several sections of this book.

The above is, at best, an account of what we may call *"explicitly* asserting that *p"*. Recalling the earlier discussion of ellipsis, we must recognize the possibility of asserting that *p* without uttering a sentence that itself explicitly presents the proposition that *p*. Surely when I assert that I had soup for lunch by saying 'Soup', in answer to the question 'What did you have for lunch today?', my sentence does not explicitly present the proposition that I had soup for lunch today. Hence we must allow for derivative cases of assertion in which what one utters is used elliptically for a sentence that does explicitly present the proposition in question. This does not rob the account of its teeth. When, for example, I make a normal utterance of 'Please open the window' I have *not* uttered my sentence as elliptical for 'The window is closed', and hence the account gives the correct judgment that I did not assert that the window is closed.

Thus the analysis schema for assertion is:

AS: U asserted that *p* in uttering S *iff*:

1. U R'd that *p*.
2. S explicitly presents the proposition that *p*, or S is uttered as elliptical for a sentence that explicitly presents the proposition that *p*.[9]

iii. How This Account Deals with Problems

This analysis was suggested by the third problem, that of distinguishing between asserting that *p* and presupposing whatever is presupposed by that assertion. Unsurprisingly, it handles that distinction well. Our reluctance to say that one asserts that there is a chair in the corner when making a normal use of 'The chair in the corner is broken' is nicely explained by the fact that the sentence does not explicitly present the proposition that there is a chair in the corner. It is equally clear that the analysis ex-

---

[9] The second disjunct will be tacitly understood in future mentions or applications of this second condition.

plains our unwillingness to say that one asserts what is R'd in commissives, exercitives, and directives. I request you to open the door by saying things like "Please open the door" or "Would you please open the door?". If these sentences explicitly present any proposition it is that *the door is open* or *you are opening the door*, but neither of these is R'd in making the request. Instead what one R's here is, for example, that *I am interested in your opening the door* and that *it is possible for you do so*. If I were representing myself as knowing that the door is open or that you are opening it, I wouldn't be requesting you to open it. And the propositions I am R'ing are obviously not explicitly presented by these sentences. The same point can be made about the other cases, as one can quickly verify by looking at the lists of what one R's in various IA's that were presented in 3.8.

What about the remaining problem of how to distinguish expressing one's enthusiasm for G from asserting that one is enthusiastic about G? Where one expresses enthusiasm by an interjection or an expletive like 'Wow!' or 'Splendid!', my analysis of assertion straightforwardly implies that one is not asserting that one is enthusiastic. But what about the case in which one expresses one's enthusiasm by saying 'I'm very enthusiastic about that'? Here one's sentence does explicitly present the proposition R'd. But, as I see it, the analyses of asserting and expressing give the correct result. In this case one is both expressing one's enthusiasm for G *and* asserting that one is enthusiastic about G. The illocutionary act types, *expressing enthusiasm for G* and *asserting that one is enthusiastic about G*, are still quite distinct, since the conditions for their exemplification are not entirely the same. The two sets of conditions coincide in the propositions R'd, but the assertive type carries an additional requirement on the nature of the sentence. Hence it is the reverse of surprising that the same utterance can exemplify both types. That happens whenever the sentence used to express M happens to be one that satisfies the second condition for asserting that one has M, as well as the condition that is common to the two illocutionary acts.

iv. Assertive-Nonassertive Overlaps

This expressive-assertive overlap could in principle be paralleled for commissives, directives, and exercitives. To do so one need only use a sentence that explicitly presents the conjunction of the conditions R'd in performing the nonassertive act in question. I could, perhaps, purport to promise H to do D by saying "It is possible for me to do D, you would prefer my doing so to my not doing so, I intend to do D, and by this utterance I take on an obligation to do D". This is a very unusual way to make a promise, but if anyone should make a serious literal use of that sentence, she would presumably both purport to promise to do D *and* assert that the relevant conditions are satisfied. I could conceivably purport to declare a meeting adjourned by saying "This meeting is in session, I have the authority to terminate it, conditions are appropriate for the exercise of this authority, and by this utterance I am bringing it about that this meeting is no longer in session". Again, this would be a very unusual way of doing the deed, but if anyone should make a serious literal use of that sentence, he would presumably be purporting to adjourn a meeting *and* asserting that the relevant conditions are satisfied.[10]

At least with exercitives we can get some insight into why it is so outlandish to perform the act by way of asserting that the R'd conditions hold. Since the first three conditions are presupposed by the fourth, I can confine myself to the latter without losing any content. Why then is it so unusual to purport to adjourn a meeting by asserting that by one's utterance one is bringing it about that the meeting is terminated? Consider the fact that with exercitives, unlike expressives, an essential role is played by extralinguistic conventions that specify conditions for the actual production of the conventional effect, including constraints on the linguistic devices employed. Constraints of the latter sort vary from nonexistence to complete rigidity. Legally binding contracts often require pat formulae. Adjourning a meeting is usually a more flexible affair. There are standard locutions for doing it, like 'I declare the meeting adjourned', and marked departures from them are apt to be puzzling and to sound odd. However, if the chairman said at the appropriate moment 'By this utterance I am terminating this meeting', I doubt that anyone would claim that the meeting had not been adjourned, though one might wonder why he had chosen such a strange way of doing so. But the fact that there are sometimes extralinguistic constraints on the linguistic devices that are required (permissible, standard) for engendering the conventional effect explains the rarity and oddity of purporting to, for example, terminate a meeting by asserting condition D. Indeed, where there are rigid specifications for the sentential device, specifications that exclude any that explicitly presents D., to purport to produce the conventional effect by asserting that D. is not only odd but self-defeating. But even here if anyone is foolish enough to do so, it would still be true that he is both asserting that D. and *purporting* to terminate the meeting, however self-defeatingly.[11]

I have been illustrating the possibility of one and the same utterance exemplifying both an assertive and a nonassertive illocutionary act. Let's look

[10] Whether I would thereby *succeed* in terminating the meeting depends on whether the relevant nonlinguistic conventions allow this formula for an official adjournment. But, as we have seen, this matter lies beyond the boundaries of the pure illocutionary act.

[11] I am *not* suggesting that there is anything problematic about asserting that one is currently engaged in producing a certain conventional effect so long as one does not attempt to make that assertion in the very utterance in which one purports to produce that conventional effect. I might have occasion to interrupt myself in the middle of adjourning the meeting to explain to someone what I am doing.

at this phenomenon from a broader perspective. My analysis of assertion combines two quite different principles of classification. By virtue of the constraint on the sentential vehicle, asserting that p is distinguished from nonassertive ways of R'ing that p. That is the side of the matter on which I have been concentrating. But it is also true that by virtue of the first requirement (that U R's that p) the assertion is distinguished from utterances that explicitly present p without R'ing that p. In general, nonassertive illocutionary acts are performed by uttering a sentence that explicitly presents a proposition that is not among those R'd in the utterance. Thus when I request you to open the door by saying 'Please open the door', I explicitly present the proposition *the door is open*,[12] but clearly I don't R it; I don't represent myself as knowing that proposition to be true, or subject my utterance to a rule that requires its truth. The point of my asking you to open it is to get you to make it true.

If this is the way the land lies, it is understandable that there should be utterances that are correctly classifiable both as an assertion and as an illocutionary act of some other type. Nonassertive illocutionary act categories are defined with reference to the type of p's R'd. We get promising when what is R'd is that the speaker intends to perform D, that the speaker is taking on an obligation to D, etc. We get purporting to adjourn a meeting when what the speaker is R'ing is that a certain meeting is in session, that the speaker is bringing it about that that meeting is terminated, and so on. But no limit can be placed on what can be asserted, that is, on the kinds of p's R'd in asserting. Hence the generic character of assertion cannot lie in the kinds of p's one R's. Instead it lies in the relation of the sentence uttered to the p's R'd. This is a quite different principle of classification, and it naturally crosscuts the first one. Whenever one R's p's that satisfy the requirements for a commissive or an expressive, *and* does so by uttering a sentence related to those p's in the way required for asserting, then one's performance will be categorizable both as a commissive (or whatever) and as an assertion. Now think back on the case in which I express admiration for T by saying 'I admire T very much'. In Chapter 3 we noted that this also seems to be a case of *asserting* that I admire T, and we were puzzled as to how these two descriptions of the performance were interrelated. But now we see that this is just a particular example of the phenomenon presently under consideration. So far from being paradoxical, it is a natural outgrowth of our principles of classification. Since the requirements for asserting and for performing an illocutionary act of one

---

[12] Perhaps our notion of *explicitly presenting a proposition* is not determinate enough to make it completely clear that this is so. If no proposition is explicitly presented in these cases, that suffices to prevent S's asserting any proposition. If, as I am assuming in the text, a certain proposition is explicitly presented, S doesn't assert the proposition for the reason given there. Either way I win.

of the nonassertive categories belong to different orders of classification, it is not at all surprising that requirements from both orders should sometimes be satisfied by one and the same utterance.

The neatest way of accommodating all these considerations would be to exclude assertion from our list of illocutionary act categories. We would then divide up the field on a single principle—character of p's R'd. That would give us an exhaustive and mutually exclusive classification. We could then have a different classification of ways of performing illocutionary acts. But though the taxonomy could be set up in this way, it would fail to reflect adequately the facts of linguistic communication, facts that are embodied in our, admittedly sloppier, scheme. If we should proceed as just suggested, once we had filtered out expressives, commissives, directives, and exercitives, we would left with a miscellaneous grab-bag of "other sets of p's". There seem to be no interesting common features of this group. Nor does it divide up in ways that reflect important differences in communication. To organize it would be to redo Roget's *Thesaurus*. Moreover, these "leftover" sets of p's are always R'd in ways characteristic of assertion. And although it is *possible* to assert the sets of p's characteristic of illocutionary acts of the nonassertive categories other than expressing, it is unusual to do so, though it is quite common to assert particular constituents of those sets. So for all practical purposes, assertion roughly divides up the field with the other categories. The only interesting way of categorizing what falls outside commissives, expressives, directives, and exercitives is in terms of the kind of sentence employed. But since we cannot rule out the possibility of asserting sets of p's characteristic of nonassertive categories, we do not get a neat scheme of mutually exclusive categories, even though for all practical purposes we may think of assertive and nonassertive acts as excluding each other. In those cases where they coincide, for example, the expression-assertion case, we just have to recognize that duality of category does not carry with it a difference in illocutionary act content.

A controversial case of a possible assertive-nonassertive overlap, and one that has excited considerable debate, is posed by the use of "explicit performatives", sentences that consist of an illocutionary verb in the first-person present indicative followed by some content-specifying phrase, where the former specifies the kind of illocutionary act standardly performable by uttering the sentence. Familiar examples are 'I promise to do D', 'I command you to do D', 'I suggest that we do D', 'I declare this meeting adjourned', 'I nominate Jones'. These sentences are paradigmatically usable to promise, to command, to nominate, and so on. And it has been alleged by some theorists (Warnock, D. Lewis) and stoutly denied by others (Austin, Schiffer) that they are also, or instead, standardly usable to assert that the speaker is performing the illocutionary act in question. If that is the case, we have a device that can be used simultaneously to adjourn a meeting and to assert that one is doing so.

Though much ink has been spilt over this question, I cannot see that it is of any considerable importance for my enterprise. We have already encountered much less questionable examples of sentences usable both to make an assertion and simultaneously to do something of a nonassertive variety. And whatever we say about explicit performatives, there clearly are sentences that are usable for asserting that one is currently performing a certain illocutionary act, namely, the progressive present-tense variant of the explicit performative, 'I am adjourning this meeting', 'I am requesting H to do D'. Since this kind of assertion is possible anyway, it is of no great importance whether the explicit performative form also has this assertive use. To me it seems most plausible that the language reserves the present progressive form for asserting that one is performing the illocutionary act. But I shall not go into the pros and cons of the matter.[13]

v. Kinds of Assertives

The only Austinian category left for discussion is *expositives*. This is even more of a mixed bag than the others, including such nonillocutionary act terms as 'mean', 'refer', 'understand', and 'neglect',[14] as well as a miscellany of illocutionary act terms. As usual, I shall take suggestions from Austin, shaping the category in my own way.

Austin says: "Expositives are used in acts of exposition involving the expounding of views, the conducting of arguments, and the clarifying of usages and of references". My transformation of this is to take as our defining feature the fact that to perform an expositive is to make an assertion in one way or another. Thus I use the term *Assertive* for the category. To perform any assertive is to make an assertion. Where the verb is other than 'assert' there will be one or more extra conditions beyond those required for assertion. The Austinian examples that fit this criterion are:

affirm	report	tell	concede
deny	remark	answer	agree
describe	mention	rejoin	object
class	appraise	accept	explain

[13] But I do not take the same neutral stance toward Lewis's attempt to exploit the assertive potential of explicit performatives to handle all sentence meaning in terms of truth conditions. See the discussion of this in 9.10.

[14] It was probably a concentration on the explicit performative formula that led Austin to include such items. One might say in the course of an argument 'I neglect the numerous infelicities in this passage', or 'I meant by that _____'. These may superficially look like 'I promise _____' or 'I admit that _____'. But a correlative look at illocutionary act reports would have saved Austin from putting them on the list. For in these cases we would not report his linguistic performance by saying 'He neglected to _____', or 'He meant that _____'. If we are saying what he did in uttering his sentence, we would say 'He said he was neglecting _____' or 'He said he meant _____'. It is to Austin's credit that he affixed question marks to 'doubt', 'know', and 'believe'.

To these we may add

reply	admit	insist	remind
respond	disclose	claim	
acknowledge	complain	maintain	
conclude	warn	announce	

The general picture here is that my asserting that p counts as an example of one of these more special modes of assertion when certain additional conditions are satisfied and (normally) when U R's that these conditions are satisfied. I am not confident that I have found the best way of classifying these conditions; and in addition the distinctions between illocutionary act types seem wobblier here than elsewhere. With these disclaimers I offer the following classification.

I. How the assertion fits into the discourse or conversation
answer, reply, respond, rejoin
agree, concede, acknowledge, object
conclude, premise
remark, mention
explain

For example, one *replies* that p when his assertion that p is, and is designed as, an answer to a question that had been raised. One *concedes* that p when, in an argument, one's opponent maintained, or would be prepared to maintain, that p, while the fact that p is, or might be thought to be, damaging to the speaker's position.[15]

II. Opposition from the audience
insist, claim, maintain

Roughly, to maintain that p is to assert that p in the face of actual or likely opposition.

III. Position of the speaker vis-à-vis some institution
announce, testify

Roughly, to announce that p is to perform one's official function of informing some group of people that p. To testify that p is to assert that p as a participant in some sort of hearing.

---

[15] In laying out these conditions I will not say explicitly each time that the condition must be R'd by S, as well as actually hold. I assume that this is generally so, and possible exceptions will be discussed later.

IV. How the speaker came to know it
    report

To report that p is to assert that p, where p is something of which one has firsthand knowledge.

V. Position of the addressee
   inform, warn, remind

To inform H that p is to assert that p to H, where H was not previously cognizant of the fact that p, or was believed by U not to be previously cognizant of it. (It also, perhaps, requires the truth of p; see below.) To warn H that p is to assert that p to H, where the fact that p is something that might be dangerous to H.

VI. Position of the speaker [16]
    admit, disclose, complain

To admit that p is to assert that p, where the fact that p is something that is, or might be thought to be, discreditable or unfavorable to the speaker. To disclose that p is to assert that p, where the fact that p is something that U has not publicly asserted heretofore and that U might well be thought to have reasons for concealing.

VII. Relation of the utterance to the propositional content
     affirm, deny
VIII. Character of the propositional content
      describe, identify

I have said that in general these terms require both the actual satisfaction of the relevant conditions and U's R'ing the conditions. The former is essential in almost all cases. I can't be truly said to have replied that p unless my utterance does hook onto a preceding question in the right way. Otherwise I may suppose I have replied to something, but I haven't actually done so. Again, I haven't disclosed that p unless something like the condition mentioned above actually holds. If I have told everyone in my social circle that I will be married soon, I *can't* then *disclose* to someone in that circle that I will be married soon, however much I may suppose that is what I'm doing. I can't be said to have concluded that p unless my assertion that p did come as a conclusion of an argument. But this requirement does not hold universally. For example, it seems that U could be said to *report* that the gunman went off in a northerly direction, even if U did not

---

[16] Admittedly V. and VI. have something of the nature of wastebasket categories.

see the gunman leave, provided he purports to have done so. I can certainly be said to *warn* you that the postman is coming, even if the advent of the postman poses no danger to you at all, provided that I purport that there is such a danger. Likewise I can be said, in a perfectly straightforward sense, to *complain* that there is garlic in the soup, even if there being garlic in the soup is in no way harmful or distasteful to me, again provided I purport that it affects me adversely in some way. And questions may be raised about this requirement in other cases, especially where the speaker makes it explicit that he is producing his utterance as a case of R'ing, perhaps by the use of an explicit performative formula. Suppose I say 'Let me inform you that _____', and you were already aware of this. Did I inform you of it? I am inclined to say so, provided we are using 'inform' as an illocutionary rather than as a perlocutionary verb. Or I say 'I admit that _____', where what I admit fails to satisfy the above condition or anything like it. Did I admit that p, nonetheless? Here my intuition goes the other way. I am not inclined to take this as a genuine case of admitting.

I will not try to decide these fine points concerning the ordinary use of all these verbs. It will be sufficient to rule that whenever conditions are required for their application over and above what U R's in uttering S, the term is not, by our lights, a pure illocutionary act term. It does not merely specify the content of the utterance. Where the truth of some or all of the p's R'd are required, I will use the familiar device of taking the pure illocutionary act term to be '*purporting* to conclude that p', '*purporting* to disclose that p', and so on.

What about the requirement that U R these conditions? Is that strictly required? It would seem not to be required for, for example, 'disclose' or 'admit'. One can disclose or admit something inadvertently. One discloses something inadvertently when he asserts it, not realizing that it was something he was supposed to keep concealed. One admits something inadvertently when he asserts it, not realizing that it will weaken his position in some way. But the actual satisfaction of the condition is required to make it a case of (inadvertently) disclosing or admitting. Moreover, if we restrict ourselves to intentional illocutionary acts, as we have been doing, R'ing the condition is required in these cases as well. Inadvertently disclosing is not intentionally disclosing.[17] And apart from these two types we don't get full-blooded cases without R'ing. Even if my utterance does answer your question, it would not be a clear case of my *replying* that p unless I intended my utterance to be an answer to your question. If someone happens to overhear me while I am practicing an announcement I am about to make, this would not amount to my announcing that p to that person. In these cases the auditors might take my utterance as an answer or an announcement. And we might even say that the *question got answered* or that the *event*

---

[17] See Section viii of this chapter for a discussion of unintentional illocutionary acts.

was announced. But we would not say that the *speaker* answered the question or announced the event.

Another interesting case is *remind.* If I say something which reminds you that *p*, you may say "He reminded me that *p*", regardless of whether I had issued the utterance as a reminder that *p*. But this is just an illocutionary-perlocutionary ambiguity in 'remind'. Here what you say is that as a *result* of hearing what I said you were reminded that *p*, that is, the fact that *p*, previously known to you, was recalled to your attention. Your report specifies a nonconventional effect of my utterance and so counts as a perlocutionary report. It doesn't follow from this that I reminded you that *p* in an illocutionary sense of that verb, in which it could have been true that I did that regardless of what effects my utterance had on you.

Thus for at least most assertives, U's R'ing the relevant conditions is a necessary condition for clear cases. And where it is not required for the ordinary language term, it will come to be required when we move from, for example, 'disclose' to 'purport to disclose'. Whatever is true of the former, it is clear that one cannot *purport* to disclose that *p* without R'ing whatever conditions go toward making it a case of disclosing in the ordinary sense.

Another significant point of detail is the question of whether the truth of the proposition asserted is required for the application of one or another assertive verb. 'Inform', 'admit', and 'disclose' tend in that direction. If I suppose that it is not the case that *p* I will say 'He informed me that *p*' only in an inverted-commas way. It is significant that 'disclose' is perhaps most felicitously used with 'the fact that *p*' rather than just '*p*'. But for most assertive verbs no such condition would be plausible. I can be said in a perfectly straightforward sense to reply, agree, conclude, remark, maintain, announce, or testify that *p*, regardless of whether it is the case that *p*.

I shall handle all this by adopting the following model of analysis for Assertives.

ASSER: U E's that *p* (where 'E' is a term for a mode of asserting that *p*) in uttering S *iff*:

A. U R's that:
 1. *p*[18]
 2. One or more further conditions as indicated above, these conditions differing for different E's.

Since we take each act in this category to be a particular way of asserting that *p*, we must add the restriction on the sentential vehicle that is required to make the act a case of assertion.

[18] This "truth of the proposition" condition will undergo considerable expansion for many cases when we grapple with problems of reference in Chapters 6 and 7.

B. S explicitly presents the proposition that p, or S is uttered as elliptical for a sentence that does explicitly present the proposition
that p.

Where the actual satisfaction of one or more of the conditions R'd is required for the ordinary language term, or where R'ing that p is not required, we may take the illocutionary act term to be, for example, 'purport
to reply that p' rather than 'reply that p'.

The relation between one of these special assertives and merely asserting is similar in some ways and dissimilar in others to the relations between
illocutionary acts of other categories and asserting. With respect to the
other categories, when one performs an illocutionary act of that category
he usually is not asserting any of the p's he R's in performing that act. But
sometimes, especially though not exclusively with expressives, he may do
so. When that happens the utterance counts both as an assertion that p
and as, for example, a promise. But this is, so to say, *per accidens*. It is in no
way essential to the nonassertive category that this should be possible. But
in the case of assertives it is essential to that category that every assertive
involves asserting that p, where p is not only one of the propositions R'd in
performing that act but the very proposition that is specified in reporting
the act. So there is a close connection between admitting and asserting that
we don't find between asserting and the acts in the various nonassertive
categories.

However, with respect to the additional propositions one R's in an assertive that goes beyond mere asserting, the situation is analogous to the
nonassertive categories. When I reply that p, I R that what I am asserting
constitutes an answer to some question that has been asked, but I do not
assert that. When I announce that p, I R that I am performing a duly constituted function of bringing it to the attention of certain people that p, but
I do not assert that. For these extra conditions the reason for saying that I
do not assert them is exactly the same as that for the conditions R'd in a
normal case of promising, requesting, or adjourning a meeting, namely,
that the sentence uttered is not in the right form to assert *that*. We could,
of course, assert these extra conditions along with asserting that p. But in
that case I doubt that we would take the whole conjunctive utterance as a
replying that p or as an announcing that p. It would seem better to take the
utterance of the original sentence, 'p', as the replying or the announcing,
even when it is accompanied by an explicit assertion of what one R's in using it to reply or announce.

vi. Analysis Patterns for Illocutionary Act Types

I will sum up the results of Chapters 4 and 5 by presenting a number
of sample analyses of illocutionary act types of various categories. Remem-

ber the stipulation in 4.3 regarding the blanket condition for IA performance in interpersonal discourse, that U intends to get H to realize that the other conditions hold. There I said that rather than try to determine which IA types could be realized only in interpersonal discourse, I would understand all analyses of IA types to carry the tacit rider that this additional condition is required wherever the IA is directed to another person.

Assertives

I9. In uttering S, U *asserted* that lemons are yellow.
   A. In uttering S, U R'd that lemons are yellow.
   B. Either S explicitly presents the proposition that lemon are yellow or S was uttered as elliptical for a sentence that explicitly presents that proposition.
I10. In uttering S, U *purported to reply* that lemons are yellow.
   A. In uttering S, U R'd that:
     1. Lemons are yellow.
     2. A question had just been asked to which the assertion that lemons is yellow is a relevant answer.
   B. Either S explicitly presents the proposition that lemons are yellow, or S was uttered as elliptical for a sentence that explicitly presents that proposition.
I11. In uttering S, U *asserted* that the typewriter in his office is broken.
   A. In uttering S, U R'd that the typewriter in his office is broken.[19]
   B. Either S explicitly presents the proposition that the typewriter in U's office is broken, or S is uttered as elliptical for a sentence that explicitly presents that proposition.

Expressives

I12. In uttering S, U *expressed* his contempt for Jones.
   A. In uttering S, U R'd that he was contemptuous of Jones.

Directives

I13. In uttering S, U *requested* H to close the front door.
   A. In uttering S, U R'd that:
     1. It is possible for H to close the front door.
     2. U has some interest in H's closing the front door.

---

[19] In 7.10, after developing an account of the form of I-rules, I will be using a more complex mode of analysis for IA's that involve singular reference. But the account there will entail the R'ing of singular propositions like this (for *de re* IA's).

3. By uttering S, U lays on H a weak obligation to close the front door.
4. U uttered S in order to get H to close the front door.

I14. In uttering S, U ordered H to close the front door.
   A. In uttering S, U R'd that:
     1. It is possible for H to close the front door.
     2. U's position gives her the authority to lay on H an obligation to close the front door.
     3. By uttering S, U lays on H an obligation to close the front door.
     4. U uttered S in order to get H to close the front door.

Commissives

I15. In uttering S, U purported to promise H to contact Smith.
   A. In uttering S, U R'd that:
     1. It is possible for U to contact Smith.
     2. H would prefer U's contacting Smith to U's not doing so.
     3. U intends to contact Smith.
     4. By uttering S, U lays on herself an obligation to contact Smith.

Exercitives

I16. In uttering S, U purported to adjourn a certain meeting, M.
   A. In uttering S, U R'd that:
     1. M is currently in session.
     2. U has the authority to terminate M.
     3. Conditions are currently appropriate for the exercise of that authority.
     4. By uttering S, U brings it about that M is terminated.

With respect to the IA's on this list the specification of which involves singular referring expressions other than the dummy expressions 'S' and 'H' (I11–I16), the analyses are ambiguous between a *de re* and a *de dicto* reading. It all depends on whether the R'ing of the conditions is to be understood as *de re* or as *de dicto*. Look at I13. Among the conditions U must R in order to perform this IA are *It is possible for H to close the front door*, and *By uttering S, U lays on H an obligation to close the front door*. In doing so U attempts to pick out some unique item with the phrase 'the front door', the same one picked out by that phrase in the specification of the IA type to be analyzed. But that R'ing can be understood either as *de re* or as *de dicto*. In a *de dicto* sense U could be said to have R'd that first condition even if

U failed to pick out any unique item with 'the front door', provided he used that phrase with its standard meaning, and intended thereby to pick out a particular door. But in a *de re* sense U R'd that only if U succeeded in that referential endeavor. The specification of the condition does not carry its interpretation on its face with respect to this contrast.

I could adopt a notation for the specification of IA's and of conditions R'd that would distinguish between the two readings. Perhaps the best way to do this would be to take the "propositional" notation used above as canonical for *de dicto* IA's and R'ings, and the 'of x' or 'with respect to x' form as canonical for *de re* IA's and R'ings. Following that convention, the above examples would count as *de dicto*. To change I13, for example, to *de re* the IA would have to be specified as follows. *With respect to the front door, U ordered H to close it*. And the first condition R'd would be formulated as *With respect to the front door, it is possible for H to close it*. But since in Chapter 7 I will develop a more analytical way of marking the distinction, I will not bother to develop and utilize such a canonical notation here, leaving the above formulations ambiguous between *de re* and *de dicto*.

Here are some of the interrelations of the major IA categories. The most fundamental dividing line would seem to be between assertives and expressives, which do not involve S's R'ing that a certain conventional effect is produced by her utterance, and the other categories, which do. If we can inhibit ourselves from attaching inappropriate connotations to the terms, we might call the first group "Constatives" and the second group "Performatives", thereby suggesting that this distinction constitutes one way of developing Austin's constative-performative distinction into something tenable and important.

Within the performative category commissives and directives are distinguished in terms of the conventional effect—whether an obligation is laid on U or on H. But exercitives involve a wide range of conventional effects, the only unifying thread of which is negative—that they don't consist just[20] in either U's or H's taking on an obligation. On the positive side exercitives are distinguished by the fact that U purports to have a certain official position by virtue of which the conventional effect gets produced. (These points were made in more detail in 4.4.) This feature attaches also to (institutional) orders, which means that they might have been classified as exercitives rather than as directives. I chose the latter alternative, thereby giving the type of conventional effect priority over the position of the speaker.

Contrary to what one might suppose, "performative" illocutionary acts cannot be adequately analyzed just in terms of the final purporting to bring

[20] That qualification is needed, for the conventional effect of an exercitive may involve such obligations inter alia. When the priest pronounces the couple man and wife he lays various obligations on them. But that by no means exhausts the conventional effect produced.

about a certain conventional effect by the utterance. The conventional effect production is the heart of the matter. Nevertheless, that doesn't exhaust the distinctive character of a given type of performative illocutionary act. We cannot identify promising to do D with any and every linguistic production of an obligation on U. I may vow or undertake to do D, where there is no one in the position of a promisee; I haven't vowed this to anyone. Here I have undertaken an obligation to do D, but it is not a promise. We need condition B. of the above analysis of promising to make the engendering of an obligation on U a *promise*. To promise H to do D is to lay on oneself an obligation to do D in such a way that one is also purporting that H, the promisee, would prefer one's doing so to one's not doing so.

Assertives differ from other illocutionary acts in putting restrictions on the S uttered, as well as requiring that certain p's be R'd. And expressives differ from other constatives in the character of the p's R'd.

It is clear from this survey that our categories are not generated by the operation of any single principle of distinction. Except for assertions we could claim that the categories are distinguished in terms of the pattern of p's R'd. In requests U R's that it is possible for H to perform a certain act, that U has an interest in H's doing so, and so on. Whereas with exercitives the pattern involves conditions concerning U's position or authority and what is brought about by the exercise of that authority. But, as we have seen, assertions do not fit this pattern. Since no limit can be placed on what one can assert, there is no distinctive feature to what is R'd in assertions. Hence the simplest summary of the taxonomy is this. Apart from assertions, each category of illocutionary acts is distinguished by a distinctive pattern of conditions R'd. Assertions are distinguished by a certain constraint on the sentence uttered.

vii. Restrictions on Sentential Vehicles

There are two problems that remain to be dealt with before this account of illocutionary acts can lay claim to completeness. First, except for assertions, my analyses put no restriction on the sentential vehicle. Indeed, since we have to recognize the possibility of using something nonlinguistic as a surrogate for a sentence, the analyses allow for performing a given type of illocutionary act with any perceptible device whatever. But is this realistic? Do we enjoy this degree of license? Can I suggest that we go to the movies by uttering any sentence whatever or making any gesture whatever?

There are restrictions, but there is no point in going into them until we give our treatment of illocutionary rules and sentence meaning in Part II. Roughly speaking, in order to perform an illocutionary act of type I, one must either:

(1)   Utter a sentence the meaning of which fits it to be used to
      I, or
(2)   Utter a sentence, word, or phrase, as elliptical for a sentence
      that satisfies (1), or
(3)   Utter a sentence or other linguistic unit to which one has
      given that illocutionary act potential for some special pur-
      pose, as in a private code, or
(4)   Utilize some nonlinguistic device as a surrogate for a sentence
      that satisfies (1).

If this is the way the land lies, then, although any perceptible device whatever *can* be used to perform an illocutionary act of any type, there are constraints on its being used to do so. The constraints just mentioned have to
do with the speaker's intentions. Either he must be knowingly exploiting
the meaning of a sentence in the language, or he must be presenting his
device as a substitute for such a sentence.

There is also the question as to whether there are constraints from the
side of the hearer on using device D to perform illocutionary act I. It's clear
that we can't go all the way along this line and hold that one can I with D
only if one's intended audience realizes that one intends to be I'ing with
D. Surely there are cases in which I ask you where you are going or express
the opinion that the country is in bad shape, without your realizing what I
am saying. (Your mind may be elsewhere or you may not know the language very well.) But there is some plausibility in requiring that the audience is provided with sufficient clues to the speaker's intentions.[21] Consider cases like the following. I work at an information booth in a railway
station. I say to an inquirer 'The next train for Rahway leaves at 4:15',
knowing that the person understands no English. Did I tell that person
that the next train for Rahway leaves at 4:15? I can hardly be said to have
carried out my responsibility to have done so, especially if I either could
speak the language of the inquirer or could have pointed out someone
else who does. On the other hand, where duty and obligation do not come
in as they do in this case, it is not so clear what to say. Suppose that in
the midst of a philosophical discussion of counterfactuals I, emulating
Humpty Dumpty, say "Hurrah for the stars and stripes". When my interloc-

[21]   This should be construed as "clues that U was justified in supposing to be sufficient for
the intended audience". One can be providing sufficient clues in this sense even if the audience doesn't get it. The addressee may not be paying sufficient attention or may be hard of
hearing. Of course, if U knows of this or should have known of this, then U has not provided
sufficient clues in the above sense unless he takes account of these obstacles. (Though even
if he does, this by no means guarantees success.) But U may not have had any way of knowing of these problems. In that case he could have been providing what he was justified in supposing to be sufficient clues even though they were not in fact sufficient for that particular
addressee.

utors express consternation at this irrelevant outburst, I say "By saying 'Hurrah for the stars and stripes', I was evaluating what she said as a nice knockdown argument". What should we say about this? Should we say that I *couldn't* have been using that sentence to perform that act of evaluation in that company, without giving my auditors some advance notice of my idiosyncratic choice of words? Or should we say that I was indeed saying that it was a nice knockdown argument, but that, owing to my perversity, I refrained from getting it across that that was what I was doing? I suspect that there is no clear answer to these questions. Either this is an area in which it is indeterminate how illocutionary act concepts apply, or in order to decide the question we have to take into account a variety of different factors without having any rules for weighting them—the practical or moral importance of whether the illocutionary act was performed, the extent of the speaker's grasp of the interpersonal context, the speaker's motivation for using the unorthodox device, and so on. Despite these complexities I shall take it as a necessary condition for a clear case of I'ing that U shall have seen to it that the addressee is given sufficient clues, in the sense explained above, as to how to understand the utterance. This requirement hooks onto the one discussed in 3.6, the requirement, for interpersonal discourse, that one intend one's addressee to know what illocutionary act one is performing. The present discussion adds a specification of the means by which one seeks to bring that about—providing the addressee with what one is justified in supposing to be sufficient clues to the identity of the illocutionary act. But the two parts play a different role in interpersonal illocutionary acts. The intention is itself a necessary condition for the performance of an illocutionary act addressed to someone other than the speaker. It is not sufficient that the speaker R that he has such an intention. But as for the provision of sufficient clues it is required only that the speaker R this. Even if I fail to provide H with a sufficient indication that I am asking her to close *that* door, it could still be the case that I did ask her to do that. If, puzzled in the absence of sufficient indication as to which door I mean, she were to ask, "Which door?", I wouldn't respond by admitting that I hadn't asked her to do anything. I would rather provide the clues lacking in the original request. On the other hand, it is plausible to suppose that unless I at least take responsibility for providing sufficient clues to my illocutionary intent, I cannot be said to have made the request of her. If I were to respond to her "Which door?" with "What difference does that make?" or "Why should I identify the door for you?", and I am sincere in so saying, that would decisively count against this being a clear case of asking her to open a certain door.

I will treat this *R'ing that sufficient clues are provided* requirement just as I do the *intend to get H to realize that the other conditions are satisfied* requirement. That is, in neither case will I include the condition in the analysis of particular IA types. Instead I will understand such analyses as carrying the tacit rider that both these conditions hold for IA's that are addressed to other persons.

viii. Unintentional Illocutionary Acts

The second problem that remains to be considered is this. Can there be unintentional illocutionary acts? This is, in a way, the reverse of the issues we have just been discussing. We were considering the extent to which the speaker's intentions are sovereign, the extent to which they can ride roughshod over the established meanings of the linguistic devices she uses. In asking whether there can be unintentional illocutionary acts we will be considering the possibility of sovereignty on the other side, the possibility that the established illocutionary act potential of one's sentential vehicle determines what illocutionary act one is performing, regardless of one's intentions. For the only reason one could have for supposing that U was I'ing though U did not intend to be I'ing is that U uttered a sentence, S, that, in the context of utterance, would standardly be used only to I. This issue is of crucial importance for my account because, since the account rests on the notion of U's subjecting her utterance to a certain rule, it applies only to intentional illocutionary acts. If U asked for a beer without having intended to do so, then she did *not* issue her utterance *as subject to* the relevant rule, and it will not count as asking for a beer on the present account.

Look at some cases in which it is plausible to impute an unintentional illocutionary act. First, slips of the tongue. A noted war correspondent, relating in a lecture his first meeting with a famous general, said "And then the bottle-scarred veteran strode into the room". (According to another version of the story, what he said was "battle-scared".) One could report this incident by saying that the correspondent had reported a meeting with a bottle-scarred general. Second, inadequate grasp of the language. A friend who had spent a sabbatical in Florence reported going into a grocery and asking for a dozen "oggi" (todays), intending to have been asking for a dozen eggs ("uovi"). One can imagine the grocer gleefully telling his friends about the stupid American who came into his shop and asked for a dozen todays!

On the other side are cases in which we would *not* allow the meaning of the sentence in the language to determine what illocutionary act was performed. Sometimes the speaker provides or exploits indications that he either is making no illocutionary use of the sentence or is using the sentence in some idiosyncratic way. Perhaps the social situation is appropriate for nonillocutionary activities like practicing pronunciation or testing a microphone. Or U is speaking figuratively and there is some significant chance of his being understood. Or the addressee is au courant with some private code. In these cases no one would be tempted to use the literal meaning of the sentence as a basis for illocutionary act attribution. If I say 'I'm going to become a hermit', where it is clear that I am testing a microphone, no one would take me to be expressing an intention to embrace the eremitic life. Or if I say of a remark someone else has made, "That's off the wall", I wouldn't be (properly) taken as having said of something that it is not clinging to a wall of the room. Here speaker intentions clearly prevail. Even if it's not perfectly clear antecedently that I am speaking figuratively or doing something nonillocutionary, provided these activities are not grossly inappropriate to the situation, it would still be allowed that my illocutionary act, or nonillocutionary act, was the one I intended to be performing. Here speaker intentions override sentence meaning.

What general formula will distinguish these two groups? The most obvious difference is that in the second group U was deliberately making some use of the sentence that is at variance with the standard IA potential it has by virtue of its meaning; *and* U provides indications of this, or at least the intention is not widely different from what would be suggested by the situation of utterance. Whereas in the first group U did not intend to make a nonstandard use of the sentence. It is rather that, either because of an inadvertent slip or inadequate grasp of the language, U unintentionally fails to use a sentence with the right IA potential for his illocutionary intention. I will build this distinction into the fourth item in the following list of conditions for justified attribution of an unintentional illocutionary act. The earlier conditions are satisfied by both groups, at least whenever an illocutionary act was intentionally performed or attempted.

1. The sentence or sentence surrogate was produced voluntarily, and in order to perform a certain illocutionary act. When one utters a sentence by virtue of some kind of automatism, in a fit or in one's sleep, one will not be credited with any illocutionary act at all.
2. There is a divergence between U's illocutionary (or nonillocutionary) intentions and the standard illocutionary act potential of that sentence in that context. If there is no such divergence, the only plausible illocutionary act attribution is the one indicated by both the intention and the sentence-in-context.
   a. When we speak of the illocutionary act potential of the sentence in the *context*, we are taking into account not only any features of the context that will fill out that potential (such as indications of the identity of referents), but also contextual features that indicate nonstandard uses of the sentence as appropriate— microphone testing, figurative uses, and the like. Thus the case in which U utters a sentence to test a microphone, and where it is appropriate to do so, is *not* a case of divergence between the speaker's intentions and the illocutionary act potential of the sentence *in that context*.

3. The sentence-in-context is standardly used to perform illocutionary acts of only one type. If the sentence has more than one standard use in that context, and U doesn't intend to be performing any of those, we have no basis for any particular unintentional illocutionary act attribution.[22]
4. The speaker did not *knowingly* use the sentence uttered to perform some illocutionary act other than the one indicated by the meaning of the sentence.

Condition 4. nicely distinguishes between our two groups. The utterances we saw to be plausibly counted as unintentional illocutionary act performance definitely satisfy 4. Whereas the speakers in our second group deliberately did something other than exploit the standard IA potential of the sentences uttered. But there are other sorts of cases that fail to satisfy 4., cases in which U does attempt to deviate from standard IA potential, but which one may want to classify as involving the unintentional production of an illocutionary act that does conform to the standard IA potential. These are cases in which, unlike our second group, U is neither producing nor relying on clues to the nature of his intentions. Here are two examples.

A. After having said 'I do' in the marriage ceremony, the groom alleges that he was using a private code in which 'I do' means 'It's too hot in here'. There was nothing in the situation, nor did he do anything, to indicate that he was making anything other than the normal illocutionary use of those words.
B. In the course of a philosophical argument I say to my opponent "You're a bare-faced liar". When he rounds on me, I allege that what I said in this curious fashion was that he had just produced a brilliant argument. Again, when I spoke there was nothing to indicate anything other than a normal use of my sentence.

It is often alleged that in such cases, whatever my intentions may have been, I am stuck with the ordinary force of my utterance. I did agree to marry the woman, whatever I supposed I was doing, and therefore I find myself married by virtue of having said the right words at the right time. In the other case it will be alleged that I did call the other chap a bare-faced liar, whatever my protestations. But on the account just laid out I can't be credited with these unintentional illocutionary acts because I do not satisfy condition 4. I did intend to be performing an illocutionary act that is radically nonstandard for my sentential vehicle.

[22] This is subject to qualification with respect to referential aspects of illocutionary acts. See the discussion of this in Chapter 7.

Before squarely confronting these examples I want to make two preliminary remarks.

(1) We must not confuse the question of whether the groom purported to marry the bride, *whatever his intentions,* with the question of what illocutionary act would normally be attributed to him by those who witnessed the proceedings. *Of course,* everyone present would unhesitatingly take it that he had undertaken to marry the woman. But then they would have equally unhesitatingly taken it that he had *intended* to marry her. No one not privy to his secret intentions would have had the slightest doubt on either of these points until his later protestations. Since the confidence about what he is doing goes hand in hand with a confidence about his intentions, we can't infer that the former is independent of the latter. Thus we can't infer that the spectators suppose him to have been undertaking to marry the bride, whatever his intentions.

(2) We must also not identify the question of what illocutionary act, if any, he performed with the question of what conventional effect was generated. It is conceivable that the law should be such that when certain words are uttered (in the absence of certain kinds of defeaters such as coercion or mental incapacity) the utterer has taken on certain obligations and this consequence might hold regardless of what is the correct illocutionary description of his activity.

With these preliminaries out of the way I will concentrate on the first case. We must be clear that it does *not* involve the following features. (1) The groom cracks under the strain and temporarily loses contact with his surroundings, thereby failing to realize that he was participating in a marriage ceremony and fancying that he was alone in the room, free to utter any sentence whatever, just for the sheer joy of vocalizing. If that were the case, he was performing no illocutionary act at all, intentional or unintentional. (2) The groom mistakenly supposes himself to have called "time out", to have suspended the proceedings so that he could practice saying the fatal words, roll them over on his tongue, get the feel of them, before he actually did the deed. In that case we would all agree that he had not yet undertaken the marriage contract. If he had supposed himself to have called time out but had not gotten this across to the other participants, then the fact that he had made a stupid but honest mistake would shield him from any imputation of undertaking the marriage.

Thus in order for this to be a serious candidate for unintentionally promising the marry the woman, we need a different picture. The groom is perfectly cognizant of what is going on. He has lost neither his grip on the current situation nor his grasp of the language. He is speaking voluntarily in full knowledge of what he is saying. It just so happens that at that moment he decided, without notice to anyone, to opt out of the current proceedings and start using a private code. And, it is suggested, even if we recognized this to be the case, we would still hold him to have undertaken to marry the woman.

At this point I lose my grip on the case. We are asked to envisage a person who realizes that in this situation if he utters 'I do' without any indication of a nonstandard use, he will be taken to have undertaken to marry the prospective bride. Realizing this, he says 'I do' without giving any indication of a nonstandard use, even though his intention is not to make the marital promise. I find this incoherent as a description of a person in possession of his senses. I can make no sense of the idea that a person in full possession of his faculties, realizing that uttering S will place him in a certain position, proceeds to utter S in full awareness of what he is doing but without intending to place himself in that position. I would say that such a person has *intentionally* entered into the contract, whatever he may say later. With the constraints specified I don't know how to give a coherent description of the case except in those terms. To say 'I do' in full knowledge of what that means in this context but not intend to enter the marital state is rather like jumping out of a seventieth-story window in full knowledge of what that means, but not be intending to kill oneself. Thus I don't take such cases to involve *unintentional* illocutionary acts that we cannot handle by our account, since they don't involve unintentional illocutionary acts at all. (I forego a detailed discussion of the second case, which I take, in all essentials, to parallel the one just presented.) Since cases like this do not involve unintentional illocutionary acts, they do not pose any difficulty for the above list of conditions.

Despite my position on these cases, I have tentatively acknowledged that there are cases of unintentional illocutionary acts. If this conclusion holds up, my pattern of analysis for illocutionary act concepts is not completely adequate, for it puts R'ing at the heart of what makes an utterance an illocutionary act of a certain type; and R'ing is, by definition, something one does intentionally. 'R'ing that *p*' has been defined as 'subjecting one's utterance to a rule requiring that *p*', which is equated with 'issuing the utterance *as subject to* a rule that requires that *p*'. Presumably, to do something *as subject to a certain rule* entails that one meant to subject one's action to that rule. And so if unintentional IA's are possible, we are faced with the question of what to do about them.

First let's consider whether we can make the problem go away by showing the nonexistence, or at least the non-full-bloodedness, of unintentional illocutionary acts. Go back to our initial examples, the slip-of-the-tongue and partial-ignorance-of-the-language cases. It cannot be denied that we naturally use illocutionary act lingo there. The correspondent *related* a meeting with a bottle-scarred general. My friend *asked* for a dozen todays. But it is not clear that we are wholly serious with these attributions. I have already pointed out that the correspondent would not be held to the usual normative consequences of the illocutionary act as soon as it was clear that it was a slip of the tongue, and the same can be said of my temporary Florentine. There is a strong temptation to put the unintentional parts of these propositional contents in scare quotes. The correspondent reported meeting a "bottle-scarred" veteran; my friend asked for a dozen "todays". This would indicate that all we are really committing ourselves to is the words the speaker used.

But if we do recognize unintentional illocutionary acts, how could they be treated in my theory? They don't involve R'ing the relevant conditions. Nevertheless, a simple modification will accommodate them. In such cases one's utterance *becomes* (prima facie) subject to incorrectness in case of not-*p*, even though one doesn't deliberately make it so. In terms of rules, it falls under a certain rule because of the character of the sentence and the nature of the context, even though the speaker hasn't knowingly *put* it under that rule. Hence we can bring out what makes an unintentional illocutionary act the act it is by specifying that the utterance has the normative status that the speaker would have intentionally given it had the act been intentional. We can define a variant of 'R'; call it 'R-U' ('U' for 'unintentional'). If R'ing that *p* is *deliberately* putting oneself in such a position that one is subject to correction in case of not-*p*, then R-U'ing that *p* is *being* in such a position by virtue of one's utterance, though not by deliberately putting oneself in that position. By substituting 'R-U' for 'R' throughout we can transform any analysis of an illocutionary act concept into an analysis of a concept that applies indifferently to intentional and unintentional performances. The concept of being in the relevant normative position by virtue of uttering S will be the concept of, for example, promising to do D, whether intentionally or unintentionally. If the act is intentional, U has deliberately *put* himself in that position.

I could rewrite all the analysis schemata in this form, and if I felt that unintentional illocutionary acts were of sufficient importance I would do so. But since they are at worst nonexistent and at best of marginal importance, I do not choose to proceed in this way. I will stick with concepts of intentional illocutionary act types, remembering that the analyses can be easily modified to fit unintentional variants should there be occasion to do so.

ix. Comparison with Perlocutionary Intention Accounts

Finally, I will make explicit how my analysis of IA concepts enables us to take account of the cases excluded by Schiffer's perlocutionary intention analysis. In 2.5 I pointed out that one might be telling someone that *p* or remarking that *p* or testifying that *p*, even though one was not trying to produce in anyone the activated belief that *p* or the activated belief that the speaker believes that *p* or the activated belief that the speaker intends to get the hearer to believe that p, or . . . We get this phenomenon in what we called the "don't care" cases, the "hopeless" cases, and the "making conversation" cases. When I have absolutely no hope that my addressee will believe what I say, or even believe that I believe it, or even believe that I am trying to get him to believe any of these things, but I feel that it is my duty to testify to the fact anyway, we have a case of *testifying* that p where the normal perlocutionary intentions are lacking. My analysis isolates something that is common to both normal cases and these more unusual cases, something by virtue of which the same illocutionary act concepts apply. Whether I have any hope of H's believing me or not, whether I have any interest in H's believing me or not, in either case in uttering my sentence I render myself subject to blame in case I do not have adequate reason for a firm belief that p. The jaded flight announcer who couldn't care less whether anyone believes what he says about the flights is, as much as someone with more normal perlocutionary intentions, taking on a liability to blame in case he doesn't know what he is talking about. And so for the other cases. The analysis in terms of R'ing, in addition to its other virtues, vindicates the intuition that ordinary illocutionary act concepts apply across the line separating utterances with normal perlocutionary intentions from those without such intentions. It brings out the common element by virtue of which speakers on both sides of the line are, for example, telling someone that p; and so it explains why standard perlocutionary intentions are not necessary for illocutionary act performance.

PART II

AN ACCOUNT OF THE MEANING OF SENTENCES

CHAPTER SIX

The Problem of Linguistic Meaning

i. Meaning: Preliminary

Now that the account of illocutionary acts is in place, it is time to turn to the theory of linguistic meaning. Although the nature of illocutionary acts is an interesting and important topic in its own right, and although a theory of illocutionary acts has various other applications, my extrinsic reason for pursuing the topic in this book is that, as I take it, it enables us to give an account of what it is for a linguistic expression to have a certain meaning, an account that, I shall be arguing, is superior to its alternatives.

The first order of business here is the clarification of the question, "What is it for a certain linguistic expression to have a certain meaning?". Two points require attention. (1) What concept of meaning is under discussion? (2) How is the question to be understood, that is, what is meant by "What is it for . . ."? I shall address these in turn.

A. The Concept of Meaning

The word 'mean' and its cognates sprawl over a considerable stretch of semantic territory.[1] But a lot of that is excluded by the fact that our question concerns the meanings of linguistic expressions. A linguistic ex-

---

[1] For surveys of this territory see Alston 1964a and Stampe 1968.

pression is a constituent of a language; hence it is something of an abstract order, something that can have many "realizations" of different sorts. 'Favorable' can be spoken on many occasions, pronounced in different ways, and written in different orthographies. What I am calling an 'expression' is a *type*, not a *token*. Thus an expression's having a meaning is distinguishable from a speaker's meaning so-and-so by what he said and from the meaning of an utterance, as well as from the meaning (in various senses) of dark clouds, the increased budget, or the fact that Arafat didn't show up at the meeting.

Depending on how one counts senses, it may be that there is only one sense of 'means' in which linguistic expressions can be said to mean something. If so I have already sufficiently marked out the concept I am employing. But since I am far from certain that this is the case, I will provide a more explicit indication of my intended target, something that commends itself on three further grounds. (1) Confusions between meaning and reference and between linguistic meaning and speaker meaning have tended to obscure the concept in learned and semilearned circles. (2) Under the influence of Quine and others skepticism about the concept of linguistic meaning and about the whole enterprise of the semantic description of language has acquired a certain currency. Hence there is a need to exhibit the concept as viable. (3) A preliminary delineation of the concept will provide criteria for the evaluation of theories of meaning.

As a rough indication we could say that the concept in question is the lexicographer's concept or, in more up-to-date terms, the concept one is using when one gives a semantic description of a language. But we can be more explicit than that by listing a number of "axioms" of meaning, on the basis of which we can delimit the concept in question as one that makes all these axioms true. I preface the list of axioms with a few comments.

1. At the outset of Chapter 1 I pointed out that I use terms for speech in a broadened sense to cover any employment of language. Thus 'utterance' ranges over the production of any linguistic token, whether by speech, writing, or other means.[2] And 'speaker of a language' is to be understood as 'user of a language'.

2. I avoid any suggestion that each expression has only one meaning. That is why I ask what it is for an expression to have *a certain meaning*. From time to time I employ phrases like 'the meaning of E' or 'the fact that E means what it does', but only for the sake of concision. I devote much effort to complicating formulations so as to take account of multiple meanings.

3. I do not assume that all linguistic meanings are completely precise or determinate. Quite the contrary. Various forms of vagueness and indeter-

---

[2] Later I will broaden it still further to include production of nonlinguistic tokens that are playing a communicative role that might be played by linguistic tokens.

minacy are the rule rather than the exception in natural languages.[3] But that does not imply that there are no objective facts as to what a given linguistic expression means. It only implies that such facts are often not completely precise and determinate.

Axioms of Meaning

A1. *A fluent speaker of a language ipso facto knows the meanings of many of the expressions of that language.*

This is practical, *know-how* knowledge. It does not necessarily involve being able to say what various expressions mean, though speakers will have this ability to one degree or another.

A2. *The fact that an expression has a certain meaning is what enables it to play a distinctive role (enables it to be used in a distinctive way) in communication.*

This seems obvious enough. Surely it is the fact that the sentence 'The lawyers are here' means what it does that renders it usable to tell someone that certain lawyers are at the place in question. If it meant something different it would not be (standardly) usable to tell someone that. And it is because 'lawyers' has one of the meanings it does that when placed in the frame 'The _____ are here' the resultant sentence is usable to tell someone that, rather than, for example, to tell someone that the police have arrived. This axiom will play a crucial role in the development of my theory of meaning.

A3. *Knowledge of the meaning of the sentence uttered is the linguistic knowledge a hearer needs in order to understand what is being said.*

This is the other side of the coin from A2. If the meaning of a sentence is what fits it to be used to say one thing rather than another in communication, then this is what the hearer needs to know about the sentence in order to determine what is being said. Normally she will need to supplement that knowledge with other information. If the sentence uttered was 'I'm hungry', she will have to know the identity of the speaker and the time of utterance, as well as the meaning of the sentence, in order to know who it is that is being said to be hungry when. But it is the meaning of the sentence that determines what supplementary information is required. And this supplementary information does not concern the language; the meaning of the sentence is all that the hearer need know *about the language* in order to interpret the utterance.

---

[3] See Alston 1964a, chap. 5.

A4. *The meaning of a sentence is a function of the meanings of its constituents plus relevant facts about its structure.*

This is a fundamental principle of linguistics. Indeed, all of the description of a language may be thought of as ultimately directed to bringing out how the meaning of a sentence is determined by the way in which it is built up out of constituents with certain meanings.

A5. *Reference is, usually, only partly determined by meaning.*

To know to whom a speaker is referring with a particular expression—'I', 'he', 'the tree', . . .—it is necessary but not sufficient to know the meaning of that expression. By knowing the meaning of 'he' I know that the speaker, if she is using language in a standard fashion, is referring to some male or to something treated as being male. Extralinguistic clues are needed to tip me off as to what that something is. This is the usual situation with referring expressions.

A6. *The truth conditions of a statement are at least partly determined by the meaning(s) of the sentence used to make that statement.*

Where knowing the meaning of the sentence is all that is necessary for determining what statement is made, the determination of truth conditions by meaning is complete. This may be the case with general statements like 'Hexagons have six sides'. But where we have such factors as (most cases of) reference and verb tenses ('He's hungry') or multivocality ('He got a good hand') the meaning of the sentence in the language does not suffice to determine the conditions of truth for the statement. In 'He's hungry', for example, in order to determine what it takes for a statement made with that sentence to be true, we have to know who is being referred to by 'He' and the time of the utterance, as well as the meaning of the sentence. But even in these cases sentence meaning plays a crucial role.

A5. and A3. are intimately related. Where what a speaker says is about one or more entities to which he is referring, then knowing to what the speaker is referring is essential to fully understanding what he said. And so if understanding the meaning of his referring expressions is only partly sufficient for knowing to what he is referring, then knowing the meaning of the sentence he utters, which involves knowing the meaning of its constituents, will be only partly sufficient for understanding what he is saying.[4] And both are intimately related to A3. Where what the speaker is doing is making a statement, knowing the truth conditions of his statement consti-

---

[4]   Unless knowing the meaning of the rest of the sentence serves to complete the determination of the referents, a possibility that is not often realized.

tutes understanding what he is saying; and so if knowing the meaning of his sentence is only partly determinative of the latter it will also be only partly determinative of the former. A5. and A6. spell out particular ways in which knowing the meaning of the sentence uttered may go (only) part way toward understanding what the speaker said.

Thus my preliminary demarcation of the relevant concept of meaning is that it is meaning in this sense that satisfies the above axioms. It is having a certain meaning in this sense that renders a sentence usable to communicate one "message" rather than another, that must be known by a hearer in order to understand the speaker, and so on. I take it that it is in this sense of 'meaning' that a linguist who seeks to give a semantic description of a language aims to provide one or more meanings for each meaningful expression of the language. In determining what meaning should be assigned to a given sentence he is trying to determine what a fluent speaker of the language knows about the sentence that is requisite to his understanding what someone who is making a standard use of the sentence is saying, what it is that is a function of the meanings of the constituents and the structure of the sentence, and so on.

A further contribution to locating the concept is made by considering nontechnical semantic judgments ("intuitions") made by fluent speakers of the language. These include:

A. What various expressions mean. We often have occasion to tell someone unfamiliar with a word what it means.
B. Synonymy or near-synonymy of two expressions.
C. Possession by an expression of two or more meanings.
D. Whether a phrase or sentence makes sense (has a meaning).

Thus we can further specify what we are after by saying that it is what a person tells another person about the word 'tweeter' when he says that it means *high-frequency speaker*, what one is saying the words 'cemetery' and 'graveyard' have in common when he says they mean the same, and so on. But it must admitted that nontechnical discourse sometimes brings in matters I should not wish to identify as meaning in the sense under consideration, as when one says of a highly improbable account that "it makes no sense". Hence I give the axioms priority and use them to determine when nontechnical talk about the meanings of expressions employs the relevant concept.

I will use the above axioms to test accounts of the nature of linguistic meaning, as well as to locate the relevant sense of 'meaning'. In order for an account of sentence meaning to be acceptable, that account will have to be such that what, according to this account, constitutes having a certain meaning is what gives a sentence the capacity for being used to communicate a certain message, such that knowing this of the sentence goes part way toward understanding what someone using the sentence (in a standard way) is saying, and so on. Likewise, the account should allow for most of the semantic judgments of fluent speakers of the language to be at least roughly correct.[5]

B. What I'm Looking for in a Theory of Meaning

In asking *"What is it* for an expression to have a certain meaning?", we are trying to determine what having a certain meaning *consists in*, what sort of *fact* it is by virtue of which a certain expression can be said to mean so-and-so. There will undoubtedly be many correct answers to this question, many of which fail to advance our understanding. Unilluminating answers include the following.

1. The expression means something.
2. The expression has a semantic rule attached to it.
3. An adequate semantic description of the language provides at least one entry for the expression in question.

(1) is unilluminating because it is a simple syntactical transformation of the question, (2) and (3) because they don't tell us (a) what makes something a "semantic rule" or an "entry" and (b) under what conditions an expression has a semantic rule attached to it. We want our answer to differ from these by virtue of providing interesting answers to questions like the following.

A. How does an expression's meaning fit it to play its distinctive role in communication?
B. What is it to know (learn) the meaning of an expression?
C. How is an expression's having a certain meaning related to what a speaker means by the expression on a certain occasion?
D. What is it to understand what a speaker has said?
E. What is the relation of meaning and reference?

It would be surprising if an account that throws light on these issues were other than long and complex.

It may save the reader from some false scents if I make explicit some of the ways in which my question is not to be understood.

1. I am not seeking a "reductionist" analysis in a way that would forbid the use of any semantic terms in the answer. I am not trying to escape from the "circle" of semantic terms. My objection to the unilluminating answers

---

[5] We have to allow for some errors in intuitive judgments, and we have to allow for those judgments to be relatively unrefined. Moreover, we are not assuming that expressions in a natural language typically have completely precise and determinate meanings.

cited above is not that they include semantic terms. It remains true, nonetheless, that answers formulated in terms too close to those used in the question, like (1), will thereby be unilluminating.

2. An analysis or interpretation of ordinary meaning specifications would not be enough. This is one of the benefits to be expected from the account, but it will not carry the whole load. It will not, for example, bring out what it is to know or learn the meaning of an expression. One can know what an expression means (in the know-how sense) without being able to specify its meanings.

3. We are not seeking a characterization of the ordinary meaning(s) or use(s) of 'means' in the style of "ordinary language philosophy". Our ordinary concept of meaning is too implicit and undeveloped to make this kind of investigation sufficiently rewarding. Even if we could get a maximally accurate and comprehensive characterization of the ordinary concept, it would not yield all the answers we seek. This is not to say that the ordinary concept plays no role in the investigation. On the contrary, it sets our direction. What we are after is an explicit account of that aspect of language that is roughly indicated in our ordinary talk about the meaning of expressions. I have already said that ordinary semantic judgments constitute one of the devices for demarcating the concept of meaning in which we are interested. And our axioms might be said to be implicit in commonsense thought. Some may take the account I finally develop to be simply a description of the ordinary concept. But I make no such claim. Rather than become enmeshed in fruitless controversies over what is and is not "part of " the ordinary concept, I choose to rely on ordinary semantic talk only to partly identify the kind of meaning under discussion, leaving me free to strike out on my own in providing a detailed account of its nature.

4. We are not looking for a criterion or discovery procedure that will enable us to determine the meaning of a given expression. An accurate account of linguistic meaning will have a bearing on this. If we are trying to discover something it helps to know what we are looking for. But the account will not necessarily provide a discovery procedure. In particular, it cannot be relied on to provide a discovery procedure that falls within the behavioristic or physicalistic or extensionalistic limitations often imposed by those who seek reductive accounts of meaning.

Thus far I have had much more to say about what I am not looking for than about what I am looking for. Indeed, I prefer to let the latter show itself in the finding. However, the reader may find it useful to think of the enterprise as a quest for an adequate theoretical characterization of a certain "phenomenon", rather than a search for an "analysis" of a concept or a term. We are looking for a fruitful account of the kind of fact that constitutes an expression's meaning something or other.

One last remark of a general methodological sort. Our question has often been stated as: "What is a meaning?". And the answer has often taken the form of specifying the kind of entity a meaning is—an idea, S-R connection, property, function, or whatever—and how an entity of that sort must be related to an expression to be the meaning of that expression. I deliberately avoid couching my question and its answer in that way. In previous publications (1963b, 1964a) I have alleged that this "entitative" construal of the problem rests on a misinterpretation of ordinary meaning specifications. Since I no longer think of my task as the elucidation of such specifications, this argument does not loom large in my present thinking. Although I remain convinced that ordinary meaning talk does not envisage meanings as entities, I don't take that to rule out theories of meaning couched in these terms. But I prefer to avoid postulating meanings unless required to do so. And since, so far as I can see, the most illuminating account of what it is for an expression to have a certain meaning does not require that we specify some entity that is its meaning, I shall avoid the entitative style of formulation.

ii. Use as the Key to Meaning

My main clue to the nature of meaning is to be found in A2., which, you will remember, goes as follows:

A2. The fact that an expression has a certain meaning is what enables it to play a distinctive role (be used in a certain way) in communication.

I have already suggested that this principle is inescapable. How can we deny that it is by virtue of what 'The house is on fire' means that it is usable to report that a given house is on fire, or that it is by virtue of what 'Thanks very much' means that it is usable to express gratitude? But then the idea suggests itself of taking this as the main clue to the nature of meaning. Why not say that the meaning of an expression *is* just whatever fits it for a certain communicative role? Following that line of thought we can inflate A2. into a statement of the nature of linguistic meaning, which I will dub the "Use Principle".

IV. An expression's having a certain meaning consists in its being usable to play a certain role (to do certain things) in communication.

If this principle is to have a chance of being correct, we must find some appropriate subclass of what could be called "communicative roles" or linguistic "doings", for clearly there are roles and doings for which it does not hold. We could hardly suppose that the meaning of 'You've been putting on weight lately' consists in its usability to offend or irritate someone. I have already hinted more than once that the appropriate subclass of linguistic doings (speech acts) is the class of illocutionary acts, as that has been explained in Part I. I will shortly be working out this suggestion.

I won't argue for the Use Principle at this point. Here, as elsewhere in philosophy, the proof of the batter is in the cooking. Such recommendation as I will offer for it, in addition to exhibiting its working out, will mostly consist of contrasting it with alternatives in Chapter 9. But I will say a few words in further elucidation of the principle.

In affirming the Use Principle I am committed to the thesis that it is essential to language to be a vehicle of communication,[6] in the sense that a system is not a language unless it *could* be used as a vehicle of communication. But I do not understand this thesis to have certain further consequences that are often embraced by those who stress communication as the key to the nature of meaning.

1. Interpersonal communication is the primary function of language; its other functions, for example, its use in the articulation of thought, are derivative from that.

I accept this priority in a developmental sense, both ontogenetically and phylogenetically. As for conceptual priority, I do not know what to say; that is difficult to make out. But no sort of priority is *required* by the Use Principle. That principle requires only that every difference in meaning be mirrored in a difference in communicative usability and vice versa. That is compatible with the view that communicative usability depends on usability for other purposes.

2. Every language is actually used in communication.

That is not required, because there can be usability without actual use. Not every capacity is exploited.

3. To be a language a system must consist of perceptible elements—sounds, marks, or the like.

It is true that to be actually used in interpersonal communication a language must at least be realizable in perceptible items. But whether we take a system of phonetic or orthographic types to be part of a language depends on how we individuate languages. If, as seems reasonable, we allow that the same language can have alternative physical realizations—in different dialects, or in speaking and writing—we do not count any particu-

---

[6] As I use 'language', a system is not a language unless meanings are attached to its constituents. An uninterpreted syntactical system can be viewed as the skeleton of various possible languages, but it is not itself a language.

lar realization as part of the language. In that case 3. follows from the Use Principle, at most, only in the form:

3A. To be a language a system must be capable of a physical realization in a system of perceptible elements.

This allows a purely abstract system to be a language.

4. There cannot be a private language in the Wittgensteinian sense, that is, a language that is used by only one person and that is such that it is in principle impossible for any other person to learn to use it.

Clearly the Use Principle does not rule out a de facto private language, one that only one person in fact understands; for such a language is not necessarily incapable of use in interpersonal communication. But a Wittgensteinian private language is ruled out provided we understand the Use Principle to restrict communication to interpersonal communication. But I do not so understand it. I have been treating communication with oneself as a limiting case of communication. With this proviso a Wittgensteinian private language is not ruled out by the Use Principle.

With this understanding of 'communication', 3A. does not follow either. If a language can satisfy the requirements of usability for communication just by being used to communicate with oneself, then it can pass the requirement even if it is realizable only in a system of private design types, for example, mental images, and is not realizable in publicly perceptible elements.

To develop a theory of meaning[7] on the basis of the Use Principle, we must (1) separate out the kind of communicative job usability to perform which is constitutive of meaning, a task the groundwork for which has been laid by the theory of illocutionary acts in Part I, and (2) make explicit what it is by virtue of which a particular expression is usable to perform a job of that sort. That too has received a preliminary sketch in Part I in the delineation of the notion of illocutionary rules, rules being subject to which gives a sentence a certain illocutionary act potential. But much work remains to be done to develop in detail both parts of this program.

It should be noted that in basing this account of meaning on the Use Principle, I ally myself with what might generally be termed "Use Theories

[7] Unlike many of my contemporaries, I use 'theory of meaning' not for the semantic description of a particular language, or for a general theory of how such descriptions should be constructed, but in the more traditionally philosophical sense of an account of the nature of linguistic meaning, an attempt to say what it is for a linguistic expression to have a certain meaning.

of Meaning", in contrast to what I will call "Hypostatic Theories of Meaning". I will say more about the variety of meaning theories in Chapter 9.

iii. Sentence Meaning as Primary

Along with most recent philosophy of language, I will take sentence meaning as my initial point of attack. I shall first determine what it is for a sentence to have a certain meaning and then construe word meaning as a matter of the word's making a distinctive contribution to the meanings of sentences in which it occurs.[8] From the standpoint of the Use Principle the reason for this procedure is that we understand the meaning of an expression in terms of what it is usable to do in communication. But the sentence is the minimum linguistic vehicle for a complete autonomous act of communication; a word, or other subsentential unit, can be used only to make some partial contribution to complete sentential acts.[9] (This is not to deny that there are one-word sentences.) To be sure, with suitable contextual support a word can be used as elliptical for a sentence; in answer to the question "Would you like red or white wine?", I can express a preference for red wine just by saying "Red". But here as elsewhere the elliptical is to be understood in terms of the fully explicit. A sentence is the minimum linguistic unit that is fitted by its linguistic features to be the vehicle of a complete nonelliptical act of communication. Hence our first task is to understand what complete communicative jobs are such that usability to perform them constitutes sentence meaning.

This order of priority is reflected in our resources for characterizing communicative jobs done by sentences and by subsentential units. While, as has been brought out in the account of illocutionary acts in Part I, we possess a rich repertoire of concepts for specifying what a speaker does with sentences, our language makes comparatively meager provision for saying what is done with sentence constituents. I say to you, "Would you bring me that book with the red cover?". We are well equipped to say what was done with the whole sentence, namely, request the hearer to bring a certain book with a red cover to the speaker. But what task did I perform by uttering the word 'would' or 'bring' or 'with' or 'red'? We can, of course, make explicit the syntactical role of each of these expressions in the sen-

---

[8] The treatment of meaning in this book is almost entirely confined to sentence meaning. Only a sketchy indication is given as to how an account of word meaning could be developed on that basis.

[9] This is the crucial difference between language and simpler systems of communication, like smoke signals, in which the minimum meaningful units are themselves vehicles of complete messages. It is distinctive of language that the minimum message-bearing units are themselves semantically complex, formed by recursive rules of composition out of a relatively small stock of minimal meaningful units. It is because of this that no limit can be put on the number of distinct messages that can be conveyed in a language.

tence. And we can, somewhat artificially, convert these role specifications in act reports. (The speaker was using 'red' to modify 'cover'.) But this is all purely intralinguistic. With some of these constituents we have terms that can be used for act specifications that do reflect semantic content. Thus we can say that I was using 'book' to denote published linguistic productions, rather than, for example, the action of charging someone with a crime. But when we try to think of denotation as something a speaker does, we are forced to do it in terms of how this contributes to the illocutionary act performed by uttering the whole sentence. What is it to use 'book' to denote published linguistic productions? It is to bring the concept of such productions into the semantic content of sentences in which the word occurs, the exact mode of introduction of the concept varying with the place of the word in a given sentence frame. Again, it might be said that 'with the red cover' is being used to *specify* the kind of book an instance of which the addressee is asked to bring to the speaker And if our sentence were declarative instead of imperative ('That book has a red cover'), we could say that 'has a red cover' is used to predicate a certain property of the book. But these "subsentential acts", as much as denoting, are ancillary to the illocutionary act to which they contribute. The former has to be construed in terms of the latter, and not vice versa. To say that the speaker specified (as having a red cover) the kind of book he was requesting the addressee to bring him is just a backhanded way of saying that he was requesting the addressee to bring him a book with a red cover. The illocutionary act is conceptually prior.

Even where we do have a more robust way of saying what is done with a certain subsentential unit, as we do with referring expressions, the action is clearly ancillary to the more complete sort of action done with the whole sentence. The former cannot be done except in the context of the latter. In the above example we can say that the phrase 'that book with the red cover' is being used to refer to a certain book. And reference, as I have been assuming throughout, is something that speakers do, not something that linguistic expressions do. But it is clear that referring is ancillary to the more complete sort of act exemplified by requesting. One cannot burst into a room, just refer to a certain book, and then leave. Referring is something that is done in the course of performing a complete illocutionary act.

It must be admitted that a semantic description of a language does not proceed by assigning meanings to sentences one by one, a fact reflected by the already noted fact that in nontechnical discourse we speak much of the meanings of words and little of the meanings of sentences. This has led some thinkers to view the very concept of sentence meaning with suspicion (Ryle 1961), or at least to question the idea that the concept of sentence meaning occupies a fundamental place in a theory of meaning. But the facts noted at the outset of this paragraph are adequately explained by the point made earlier about the distinctive character of language—that sentences are semantically complex in such fashion that an indefinitely large number can be produced from a finite stock of minimal meaningful units. Because of this it would be quixotic to attempt a semantic description of a language by assigning meanings to sentences, one by one. And it is also because of this that our ordinary talk of linguistic meaning is conducted in terms of word-sized units. But none of this implies that sentences do not have meanings, or that understanding what it is for a sentence to have a meaning is not crucial for understanding linguistic meaning generally. On the contrary, it suggests just the opposite. For although the semantic description of a language must proceed by assigning meanings to individual morphemes, and formulating principles that give the meanings of larger units as a function of meanings of constituent morphemes plus the structure of the larger unit, the whole point of all this is to generate a meaning for any given *sentence* of the language. Its success in doing that is the crucial test of its adequacy. In that way the concept of sentence meaning plays a crucial role in our understanding of the semantic side of language.

However, in what I have just said I have appealed to the fundamental principle (our A4.) that the meanings of complexes, including sentences, are a function of the meanings of their constituents. And doesn't that amount to taking morpheme meaning to be prior to sentence meaning? And if so how can we both accept A4. and take sentence meaning to be prior to morpheme meaning? Can we have it both ways?

Yes, we can, provided the orders of priority are different, or, more precisely, provided the terms of the opposite priority relations are not the same. And that is the case here. It is *the fact that a given sentence has a certain meaning* that is derivative from *facts about the meanings of its constituent words*; whereas it is the *general concept of word meaning* that is derivative from the *general concept of sentence meaning*. It is in the order of derivation (or explanation) of particular semantic facts that word meaning is prior, while it is in the order of derivation (or analysis) of semantic concepts (or *ontological constitution* of semantic facts) that sentence meaning is prior. It is not part of my position that the same kind of derivation can be carried out in both directions. I do not claim that the fact that a particular word has a certain meaning can be profitably construed as a function, inter alia, of the meanings of sentences in which it occurs. Nor am I claiming that the *concept* of sentence meaning is derivative from the *concept* of word meaning.[10]

It is common in many spheres of thought to find an opposition between the order of concepts and the order of facts or things, whether the latter be a causal, compositional, explanatory, or some other kind of order. For example, according to a popular position in the philosophy of science,

---

[10] Cf. Dummett 1973, 4–6.

microfacts and processes (atomic structure, electron movements) are responsible for observable macrophenomena like rusting and the movements of electric motors, and so are prior to the macrophenomena in the order of causality and causal explanation. Nevertheless, our concepts of the microphenomena are necessarily derived, at least in part, from the ways in which they enter into the explanation of the macrophenomena and so are posterior in the order of conceptual analysis to concepts of macrophenomena. This is an exact parallel to my position on the relation of sentence meaning and word meaning. On my view sentence meaning ("macro"-phenomenon) is explained by reference to its "micro"-structure—semantic and syntactic; but we cannot explicate our concepts of that microstructure except by reference to the ways in which aspects of the structure enter into the explanation of particular sentence meanings.

Here are some other examples of the same duality. According to Thomism, God is the cause of all other things, including human beings (God is prior in the order of causality), but our concept of God is derived from our concepts of human beings and other creatures (creatures are prior to God in the order of conceptual analysis). According to sense-datum theory, the concept of a physical object is derivative from concepts of sense-data, even though particular sense-data are caused by physical objects.

iv. Sentence Meaning as Illocutionary Act Potential

I now turn to identifying a category of *things done in communication*, such that a sentence's having a certain meaning can be identified with its being usable to do something of that sort. The view to be defended will be:

V. A sentence's having a certain meaning consists in its being usable to perform illocutionary acts of a certain type.

More concisely:

VI. Sentence meaning is illocutionary act potential.

If we look back at my preliminary way of identifying illocutionary acts, it will be clear that such acts are tailor-made for this semantic role. A specification of an illocutionary act embodies a specification of the *content* of an utterance. Our familiar *oratio obliqua* forms constitute the canonical way of reporting illocutionary acts; and such forms are precisely designed to report *what the speaker said*, inflating the ordinary use of 'say' a bit. Now there is an obvious and intimate connection between what the speaker said, and both speaker meaning (what the speaker meant by what he or she said) and linguistic meaning (in this case sentence meaning), what the sentence uttered by the speaker means. First of all, in one of the meanings of the protean expression 'what the speaker meant', the one under consideration here, it is just a formulation for what the speaker said. If you are told what he said, you have all you could ask for as an answer to "What did he mean?". Thus to specify the illocutionary act performed is to specify the *speaker meaning* of that utterance.

As for sentence meaning, the Use Principle (IV.) embodies the insight that a meaning of a sentence fits it to be used to say one sort of thing, carry one sort of content, rather than others. And if I am right in supposing that saying a certain sort of thing just *is* performing an illocutionary act of a certain type, then it follows right away that it is by virtue of having a certain meaning that a sentence is usable to perform illocutionary acts of a certain type. And that encourages us to take the further step of simply identifying having a certain meaning (on the part of a sentence) with having a certain illocutionary act potential. That is, to be sure, a *further* step. Sentence meaning could determine illocutionary act potential without being identical with it. But for the present I am concerned only to indicate the initial plausibility of this move. Its further virtues will be displayed in the detailed working out of the account, and in its confrontation with rival theories in the last chapter.

Indeed, the most obvious objection to VI. is that illocutionary acts are too tailor-made for the purpose. Illocutionary act potential is too close to sentence meaning to provide an illuminating account of it. To say that a sentence is usable to assert that grass is green is too close to saying that it means *grass is green* to throw any light on the nature of meaning. I feel the force of this objection. There is an obvious appeal to the project of explicating linguistic meaning in terms that are wholly nonintentional, not dealing with any sort of propositional content, and even wholly naturalistic (whatever that is supposed to mean). If we could do this, it would be a great achievement, it would make for greater ontological economy, and so on. But the question is as to whether it can be done. My judgment is that all such attempts to date, and there have been many, have failed badly.[11] In comparing the present theory with more reductive theories we have to consider what is feasible as well as what would be most attractive if we could have it.

That is one reason for resisting the seductive pull of reductionism and sticking with the present enterprise. But the virtues of the illocutionary act potential account of sentence meaning are not confined to "Well, it may not be much, but it's the best we can do". We must take care not to underestimate the much it is. Though it does not explicate semantic content in propositional-content-free terms, what it identifies sentence meaning

---

[11] Interestingly enough, Schiffer (1987) agrees that no attempt to explicate meaning, or any sort of propositional content, in physicalistic terms can succeed. He takes this as a reason to abandon the attempt to understand meaning. For my part, I prefer to keep meaning and reject physicalism.

with is conceptually different from sentence meaning in such a way as to throw real light on the matter. In a word what the theory does is to identify sentence meaning with usability to perform *acts* of a certain sort. Even though these are contentful acts rather than content-free acts, there is still a marked advance in understanding, and this for two reasons. (1) This is a way of cashing out the intuition (plausible supposition) that facts about language somehow supervene on, are derivative from, facts about what language users *do* in using the language, that is, facts about speech. And it does so, unlike perlocutionary act potential theories (as we shall see in the next section), in such a way that the act potentials really do match the sentence meanings with which they are identified. (2) Acts are not conceptually problematic or mysterious in the way linguistic meanings are. That is not to say that there are not deep problems about the nature, individuation, ontology, and so on, of acts that call for extended philosophical treatment. But at least we have in our ordinary modes of thinking a fairly secure grasp of what it is for an agent to perform an act, and more specifically what it is to say something. Overt actions are, to some extent, open to observation; we have fairly reliable ways of telling what action an agent is performing at a given moment; we have a pretty good idea of where to locate human actions on the ontological map. But linguistic meaning is mysterious and opaque in all these respects. What we can observe of a given meaningful unit (the way tokens sound or look) gives no clue as to what it is for that unit to mean so-and-so. It is by no means obvious how we tell what a word, phrase, or sentence means. (Don't say "Look in a dictionary". That just postpones the question. How does the dictionary maker tell?) And the ontology of meaning is not at all clear on the face of it. Are meanings abstract entities somehow related to their linguistic bearers? Are they ideas or other psychological units? Is it proper to take meanings to be entities of a certain sort at all?[12] And so on. By identifying sentence meaning with illocutionary act potential (and the meaning of subsentential units with the potential of making a certain contribution to sentence meaning), we will have taken a giant step in the direction of demystifying linguistic meaning and assigning it an intelligible place in the ontological economy.

v. Sentence Meaning and Perlocutionary Intentions

Even though the idea that sentence meaning amounts to the usability of the sentence to perform an utterance with a certain "content" can seem obviously true, it has been almost totally ignored by communication theorists prior to the last half of this century. Perhaps its neglect is due to the "too close to be illuminating" reaction I have just tried to defuse. In any event, it is striking that communication theorists have concentrated

[12] See Alston 1963b.

exclusively on the production of psychological effects on hearers (perlocutionary acts) as the semantically crucial category of communicative acts. For an expression to have a certain meaning is for it to be usable to affect a hearer psychologically in a certain way. Thus John Locke (1975, III, ii) took it that the "signification" of a word is to be found in the fact that it is regularly used as the sign of a certain idea in the mind of the speaker, that is, is presented to the hearer as a clue to the presence of that idea in the mind of the speaker, that is, is uttered in order to get the hearer to realize that an idea of that sort is in the mind of the speaker.[13] The most prominent current perlocutionary-based theory is the one initiated by H. P. Grice (1957, 1968, 1969) and further developed by Stephen Schiffer (1972) and Jonathan Bennett (1976).[14] It identifies a sentence's having a given meaning with there being a "practice" or "procedure" of uttering the sentence with a certain complicated sort of reflexive intention to produce certain kinds of psychological effects in hearers (Grice 1957, 1968), or, alternatively, with there being a certain "convention" or "conventional procedure" for using the sentence with such an intention (Schiffer 1972, Bennett 1976), or with there being a certain kind of regularity of using the sentence with such an intention (Bennett 1976). Since I presented the Griceian account of speaker meaning in Chapter 2, I will offer only a short recap here, as a basis for the account of sentence meaning. As pointed out in 2.2, though Grice, Schiffer, and Bennett all start with roughly the same account of speaker meaning, Grice and Bennett go directly from that to sentence meaning, while Schiffer makes a detour through an account of illocutionary acts. That detour was criticized at length in Chapter 2. Here I am concerned with the more direct route. Since my criticism of the perlocutionary potential account of meaning does not depend on the details of the view, I will slough over many interesting details.

Grice's account of speaker meaning (what a speaker means by uttering a certain sentence or other vehicle of meaning) is in terms of the speaker's intention to produce a certain effect in his audience by his utterance. Grice is clear that not any intention to produce an effect in the audience will do this trick. The kind of intention he arrives at is *an intention to produce an effect in a hearer (H) by means of the hearer's recognition of that intention.* (Call this an *M-intention.*) The suggestion then is that what the utterer (U) means by his utterance will be a function of what effect he M-intends to produce. Grice, followed in this by Schiffer and Bennett, concentrates on two kinds of effects, H's believing something and H's doing something. Grice would say, in his original 1957 version, that my meaning that the race will start in five minutes is a matter of my uttering a sentence with the

---

[13] For an updated and significantly revised version of Locke see Armstrong 1971.
[14] See also Loar 1981, chaps. 9 and 10, for an interesting discussion of this kind of theory.

M-intention of getting H to believe that the race will start in five minutes. (In a later version [1968] the intended effect has changed to H's believing that S believes that the race will start in five minutes.) And my meaning that H is to do action D is a matter of my uttering a sentence with the M-intention of getting H to do D (in a later version, H's believing that S intends (wants) H to do D).

As I pointed out in 2.2, this account of speaker meaning has been modified to an enormously complicated extent in Schiffer's hands, in order to take account of various counterexamples to its sufficiency. In Bennett 1976 we have a cutting of the Gordian knot that can be stated much more simply than Schiffer's constructions. It requires that there is nothing that U relies on to bring about the intended effect in A that U expects A to have a mistaken belief about (127). Let this be taken as done.

On this basis the meaning of a sentence can be construed, at a first approximation, as a matter of a regular "practice" or "policy" of using the sentence to mean so-and-so. In Grice 1968 he developed a refined version of this to take account of the facts that a sentence will often have more than one meaning and that there will often be more than one sentence that is regularly, or conventionally, used with a certain M-intention. Both these facts force us away from an account of sentence meaning in terms of a simple generalization of speaker meaning. The 1968 version handles this by replacing the idea of there being a practice of uttering sentence S with the M-intention of producing effect E, with the idea of members of the linguistic community *having in their repertoire the procedure* of uttering S with the M-intention of producing E. This leaves open both the possibilities just mentioned. For the fact that uttering S with that intention is one way of producing E is compatible with there being other ways involving other sentences, as well as with one's also having "in one's repertoire" the procedure of uttering S with some other M-intention to produce a different effect.

Bennett 1976, on the other hand, focuses on languages that do not involve synonymy or multivocality, and that do not involve figures of speech and other derivative uses of language (sec. 52). This permits him to revert to the simpler formulation for sentence meaning in terms of some sort of straight regularity connecting the utterance of a particular sentence and meaning so-and-so.[15] Moreover, Bennett avoids at least some of the counterexamples of the sort canvassed in 2.5 with respect to Schiffer's account of illocutionary acts by taking uttering S with a certain M-intention as only sufficient for meaning so-and-so, not also necessary (sec. 7). (More on this point below.)

---

[15] More precisely, this removes some of the need for such complications; as we have seen and will see in more detail in Chapter 7, in natural languages singular reference itself prevents a one-to-one lineup of sentence used and speaker meaning.

Since Bennett has given us the most sophisticated and impressive version of a Griceian approach to sentence meaning, I will concentrate on it for this critical comparison with the I-rule theory. It is a fearsomely complex and multifaceted account, and I will not be able to bring all that out here. Nevertheless, if I am to do it justice as a target of criticism, I must delineate its major lines. For one thing, Bennett argues that reliance on the "Griceian mechanism" to achieve communication is not necessary for meaning so-and-so in a community in which meaning regularities have been established. (The "Griceian mechanism" we may take to be H's realizing that U intended H to, e.g., believe that p on the basis of H's realization of this intention of U's.) He points out that a speaker, in attempting to communicate that p by uttering S, might instead rely on H's knowledge or belief that whenever S is uttered it is true that p. And he considers the possibility that this alternative explanation is preferable to the Griceian one, since it is more simple. He sketches out a "communication-system" he calls 'Plain Talk' in which though communication is often successful the speakers never rely on a Griceian mechanism but rely on something simpler like the regular connection of utterance of S and p.

He deals with this problem by formulating what he calls "sub-Griceian" conditions of meaning. He points out that Grice's original (1957) distinctions between natural and non-natural meaning can all be handled by a simpler condition for the non-natural side, namely, "*U intends to communicate P to A by offering intention-dependent evidence for P*". Or, more weakly, "*U thinks he is offering evidence and does not think that it is intention-free*". And if the utterance of S is evidence for p just because it (mostly) only occurs when p is the case, this makes it intention-dependent evidence, since there would be no such regularity if speakers did not generally have the intention to utter S only when it is true that p.[16]

Like Schiffer, Bennett weds this talk of regularities to a version of David Lewis's notion of a "convention". Roughly, on Lewis's view a convention is a behavioral regularity that a community maintains because the members mutually know that they have maintained it in the past and that it has solved a "coordination problem" for them. In order to adapt this to linguistic communication Bennett extends 'behavior' to encompass belief

---

[16] Strangely enough, at the outset of section 61, which is devoted to a summary evaluation of Griceian conditions for speaker meaning, Bennett writes: "That the intentions of human speakers are largely Griceian is beyond question" (200). At the same time, in attempting to go with the weakest possible conditions that are sufficient for speaker meaning, he emphasizes the sub-Griceian conditions. It is also worthy of note that the support adduced for the very strong claim just quoted is that "our linguistic resources let us directly express looped thoughts, and let us say that something is uttered in reliance upon others to have looped thoughts about it. Furthermore we have familiar kinds of communicative transaction—involving ambiguity, etc. . . . which cannot be understood except in Griceian terms." But these considerations support at most the claim that intentions of human speakers are sometimes Griceian.

acquisition. Thus the "coordination" involved is between S's intending to get A to believe that p on the basis of A's recognition of that intention, and A's coming to believe that p. This forms the basis of an account of sentence meaning, stated in a preliminary way at the outset of the book as: "'x means that P' is equated with 'There is a convention whereby the members of some community, when they utter or do x, mean by it that P'" (16).[17] But, surprisingly enough, in Chapter 7 Bennett argues at length that behavioral evidence that a certain behavioral regularity constitutes a convention is, at best, scanty, and insofar as there is any, it gives significant support to conventionality only in an attenuated sense. And although he is comfortable with the suggestion that a convention of using S to mean that p holding in a community would be sufficient to make S mean that p in that community, he is sufficiently committed to restricting himself to what can be validated by behavioral evidence that he shies away from couching his final formulation in terms of convention. Instead it runs like this. "I shall use the form 'S means P' as a shorthand for "There is a non-coincidental regularity such that whenever a tribesman utters a token of type S he means by it that P'", adding that "In practice these regularities would be imperfect . . ." (213). Though conventional regularities count as "non-coincidental", they by no means exhaust that category.

This Grice-Bennett position is not a reductive account of linguistic meaning to content-free notions any more than my account is. But it does aim to derive specifically *linguistic* semantic concepts from psychological notions like *intention*, notions that have a much wider application than the linguistic.

Now let's see how Bennett's perlocutionary intention (PI) account of sentence meaning stacks up against the IA potential account. First a concession. Bennett's gives an elaborate development of a way in which communication by means of the Griceian (or "sub-Griceian") mechanism *could* function in a society, and a way in which regularities in Griceian speaker meaning *could* endow communicative vehicles with meaning in the sense that they could be effectively usable for meaning that p or meaning that H is to do A, as that is Griceianly construed. To that extent such vehicles *could* play a perlocutionary role analogous to that often played by sentences in a language. Thus regularities in Griceian speaker meaning that p or that H is to do D are a sufficient condition for vehicles of complete thoughts having a perlocutionary equivalent of sentence meaning. But when we have a natural language of the sort we find in actual human societies, the situation is quite different. As an account of that the PI theory is markedly inferior to the IA potential account. There are two main reasons for this.

A. First, while the IA potential theory provides such a potential, and an

---

[17] In Chapter 8 I will say something about why I prefer my approach in terms of rules to this approach in terms of Lewisian conventions.

underlying I-rule, for every meaning of every sentence in a natural language, Bennett's PI theory falls far short of that. There are several respects in which it fails to do the whole job.

1. The first and most obvious is that it is severely limited in the range of meaningful sentences to which it applies. The theory is deliberately restricted to sentences that can be used to make assertions or issue "injunctions". And that leaves out a lot. Recurring to my classification of illocutionary forces, it fails to deal with sentences the standard use of which is to express attitudes—(a) 'That's lovely!', (b) 'How disgusting!'—make promises or other commitments—(c) 'I'll contribute $100'—or alter social status—(d) 'The meeting is hereby adjourned'. If these sentences were to be handled by Bennett's theory, they would have to be regularly used either to bring H to believe that p, for some p, or to get H to do D, for some D. But that is not the case. It would be a travesty to suppose that in a standard utterance of 'I pronounce you man and wife' U means that he pronounces the hearers man and wife, in that he has the central M-intention of bringing them to believe that they are pronounced man and wife or that U believes that he pronounces them man and wife. And correspondingly, the fact that the sentence means what it does could not be identified with there being a convention for using the sentence with such an M-intention. It would be equally absurd to suppose that (c) is standardly uttered to mean that U undertakes to pay A 5 percent interest per annum in the sense that U M-intends A to believe that U undertakes to pay A 5 percent interest per annum or . . . And again that implies that we cannot suppose that (c)'s meaning what it does can be a matter of there being a convention for using the sentence with such an M-intention. Bennett's theory as developed to date simply does not handle the distinctive meaning of such sentences. Nor can I see any way in which it could be beefed up to do that job.

Bennett, along with many others, seeks to make a virtue out of this weakness. Here is what he says, in a somewhat different connection, after announcing that he will seek merely sufficient conditions for meaning that are still "weak enough to be instructive" but will not "aim so high" as to go after necessary conditions.

I shall try to establish sufficient conditions which are weak enough to cover a large, central, basic class of instances of meaning. By 'central' I mean important in our everyday uses of language. By 'basic' I mean adequate as a basis for explaining all other kinds of meaning. . . . With a certain broadly Griceian [intending]—[meaning] conditional as my spearhead, I shall thrust through the centre of the conceptual area I want to occupy, there establishing a base from which one could easily range out and capture the rest of the territory. It would be more orthodox to advance on a broad front, invulnerable to flanking attacks and not committed to mopping-up operations after the main campaign is over; but the concept of meaning probably cannot be conquered in that way, within tolerable limits of complexity.

I shall omit the mopping up. It certainly could be done if my main conceptual thrust succeeds. This is a fairly small claim because that is a very large 'if'. (Bennett 1976, 23)

I find myself unimpressed by this apologia. First, because I have a theory that handles the whole territory in a unified manner "within tolerable limits of complexity". Bennett and other Griceians feel that such a theory does not provide the illumination that should be expected from an account of meaning. Earlier I made some response to the "too close to be illuminating" reaction. The second reason for not being impressed is that the extension to the rest of the territory is not so easy as Bennett supposes. I will document that in 9.10 and 9.11, where I look at some attempts to "capture the rest of the territory" from something like Bennett's "centre".

2. But the limitations of the PI approach are not restricted to what lies outside assertives and directives. Even within those categories it fails to distinguish between different species thereof. Within the assertive category there are differences between reporting that p, insisting that p, agreeing that p, conceding that p, announcing that p, and so on. Within the directive category there are differences between ordering H to do D, requesting H to do D, advising H to do D, suggesting that H do D, and so on. And there are corresponding differences in the (complete) meanings of sentences paradigmatically used for these purposes. This is most obvious with what Austin called "explicit performative" sentences that contain the illocutionary verb in the first-person simple present, like 'I advise you to do D' or 'I agree that p'. Chapters 4 and 5 indicated how such differences are handled in my account. That is, they indicated how the differences between the IA types are handled; and in the I-rule account of sentence meaning there is a straightforward transition from that to the account of the meaning of sentences standardly usable to perform IA's of those types. Bennett, on the other hand, does nothing to deal with these differences. All sentences with the potential of being used to assert that p are given the same account—as regularly used to mean that p, construed in a Griceian way. (Either that or the illocutionary force operator is put into the p, which implies that 'I agree that p' is regularly used to produce in H the activated belief that U agrees that p, rather than that p, contrary to Bennett's intentions, and contrary to the most plausible form of perlocutionary intention-based theory.) And all sentences with directive potential will receive the same treatment—as regularly used to mean that H is to do D. Thus the same account will be given of the meaning of 'I order you to do D', 'Would you please do D?', 'I advise you to do D', and 'I suggest that you do D', despite obvious differences in the meaning of these sentences. Surely an account of sentence meaning should do better than this. Here Bennett is

without recourse to the excuse that what is not being treated is of only marginal or derivative interest for communication. It is crucial for communication whether I am ordering, requesting, suggesting, or advising you to do D. And likewise for whether I am reporting, conceding, or announcing that p. Moreover, Bennett's aspiration for merely sufficient conditions will not help him here. Since these are cases in which we have the same Bennett-condition but different sentence meanings, the account does not provide even sufficient conditions.

There are other kinds of cases in which we get different meanings but the same central PI. Bennett, along with other Griceian theorists, seems to think that the only effective linguistic way of carrying out an M-intention to produce an activated belief that p in H is to utter a sentence that means that p. At least he takes a regularity of uttering a sentence to carry out such an intention as a sufficient condition for that sentence meaning that p. But consider the following sentences, any one of which might be used, with some regularity, to bring H to believe that p.

1. If you think about it, you will realize that p.
2. Isn't it obvious that p?
3. All the experts agree that p.
4. If you don't believe that p, you are just unacquainted with the relevant evidence.

But these sentences differ in meaning in important ways. Despite this, they all come out on Bennett's account as meaning that p. We must do better than that.

B. Second, these ways in which IA potential is more fully and closely connected with sentence meaning than PI reflect a deeper reason for the superiority of IA potential theory. I can introduce this by recognizing that typical human linguistic communication involves both illocutionary acts and perlocutionary intentions (with the latter often being realized). In a typical communicative situation U both, for example, asks for the butter and seeks to get someone to pass the butter to her. That being the case, let's ask which of the two aspects is the more fundamental. Here are two respects in which the illocutionary aspect gets the nod.

1. The speaker performs an IA in order to realize the PI, not vice versa. In the above example U asked H to pass the butter in order to get H to pass the butter, not vice versa. It would be absurd to suppose that U got H to pass the butter in order to ask H to pass the butter. By the time the butter gets passed, the point of asking H to pass it has been lost. And, in any event, there is no need to bring about the perlocutionary result in order to perform the IA. Mastery of the language and possession of one's faculties will suffice for that. Thus IA performance is more basic in the behavioral hierarchy.

Though this point can hardly be doubted, it is not sufficient to establish the point of most interest here—that linguistic meaning, assuming that it is supervenient on some aspects of what speakers do with the language, is supervenient on illocutionary activity rather than perlocutionary activity or intentions thereto. As far as anything said so far is concerned, it could be the case that the meaning of sentences becomes relevant only at a second stage of communication, the PI stage, rather than at the primary, IA stage. But we need not take that suggestion seriously. It is as obvious as anything can be that in choosing a sentence to use in performing an IA, one does so in the light of the meaning of that sentence. It would be futile to attempt an IA while ignoring the meaning of one's sentence. When one knows what one is about, one chooses a sentence with a meaning that fits it to perform an IA of the desired type, not one chosen at random. One asks for the butter, in English, by saying something like 'Please pass the butter', not any one of indefinitely many sentences with radically different meanings. Indeed, it was considerations like this that, in Chapter 6, were taken as providing the initial plausibility for the IA potential account of sentence meaning. Thus a consideration of how one is already entangled with meaning at the primary, IA stage of operation supports the idea that it is that stage to which we should look for a clue to the nature of sentence meaning.

While discussing relative priority, I should mention priority as to what is essential to communication. Here too IA's come off as more basic. Communication can take place even if the PI is not satisfied, while if no IA is performed, there is no (linguistic) communication, whatever effects one brings about on another person. Consider cases in which one fails to realize the sort of PI stressed by Griceans. U tells H that U has been home all that evening, but H does not believe him. Communication has still taken place, just by virtue of the fact that the claim has been made and understood by H. This suggests the further point that the most basic kind of PI in communication is what we might call an illocutionary one—to make clear to H what IA one is performing. So long as that goal is achieved, communication has been achieved, whatever further effects on H one might be aiming at. But this "illocutionary" perlocutionary act obviously presupposes the whole battery of IA concepts. Indeed, the aim at getting H to *realize* what IA one is performing presupposes that one has performed an IA of a certain type. And so this is another way in which the IA level is more basic than the PA level.

This basicality of the "illocutionary" PI ties in with the point that the suitability of using one sentence rather than another to achieve further effects on hearers is to be explained by the IA potential of those sentences. The Griceian attempt is to explain this by reference to a regularity of using a given sentence for that perlocutionary purpose, or by reference to a convention for doing so. But if that is the whole story, it leaves mysterious why such a regularity developed (where there is no "natural" connection between the intrinsic character of the sentence and the perlocutionary aim) or why there is any such convention. By inserting the IA stage into the picture (or rather by *recognizing* that it is there) we make this understandable. As soon as we realize that my uttering 'The meeting has been canceled' (often) leads H to come to believe this just because the linguistic system in the society is such that on hearing my utterance H realizes that I am *telling* her that the meeting has been canceled, then provided she is prepared to trust me on such matters, we see why and how the sentential vehicle is a suitable and often effective way of bringing about the aimed-lat result. Whereas when the IA stage is short-circuited and one attempts to connect the sentence directly with the PI, crucial questions are left dangling.

To be sure, the Griceian might point out that this leaves standing the thesis that some PI is essential to communication, even if its consummation is not. And I agree with this, at least so far as the "illocutionary" PI is concerned. There can be no interpersonal communication worthy of the name without U's both performing an IA and aiming at getting H to realize what that is. In Chapter 3 I built such an aim into the analysis of concepts of interpersonal IA's. But, of course, this is not the sort of PI stressed by Griceians, presumably just because it presupposes the basic role of IA's. And in Chapter 2 I pointed out various kinds of speech in which the kinds of PI's stressed in the Griceian account of speaker meaning are lacking. Remember the cases in which one makes an announcement because it is his job to do so but without caring whether anyone believes what he is saying or not.

In any event, I need not deny that PI's are essential to communication. My recommendation of IA potential theory over PI regularity theory of sentence meaning is sufficiently secured by the points that IA's serve as the means for securing perlocutionary effects, not vice versa, and that sentence meaning is crucial for the more basic, IA level of the proceedings. Indeed, there is another respect in which PI's are more basic for communication. It is just the respect in which the end is more fundamental than the means. Thus far I have stressed the converse fundamentality. The means are more basic in the structure of the means-end activity. It is at the base of the pyramid built up by relations of 'in order to'. But if IA's, at least in interpersonal communication, are, either always or usually, performed for the sake of achieving effects on hearers, then PI's constitute the rationale for the existence of the whole linguistic system that enables us to carry out those intentions by means of the IA performances the linguistic system makes possible. Putting this in terms of my theory, the I-rules in force in a society, and internalized by members thereof, would not enjoy that status were it not that they enable us to carry out PI's by means of the IA's they make possible. So PI's are prior in giving the whole system its point, even though IA's are prior in the utilization of the system. And even though it is at the IA stage of system utilization that we find the close connection with the meaning of sentences by virtue of which they can be used to perform one or another IA, and by means of that to achieve PI's.

To fully appreciate the case for the superiority of IA potential theory, we need to bring in both the main points I have been making. The first, "extensional" point makes clear that the IA potential theory does a much better job of "fitting" samenesses and differences in sentence meaning than the PI theory. But the second point, about relative priority, provides a deeper understanding of why this should be so. By "placing" both IA's and PI's in the total structure of communication, we can better see why it should be that sentence meaning and IA's are "made for each other", while PI's (of the "nonillocutionary" sort) only roughly model sentence meaning.

I need to add a few comments to round out this discussion.

A. I have given Bennett credit for showing, in an imaginative and ingenious way, that there could be communities in which speaker meaning can be constituted more or less as Grice supposes, by activity ("utterances" in a suitably broad sense) undertaken with M-intentions. But where we have a full-blown natural language, not only is it the case, as I have been arguing, that IA performance is more basic than PI's. We can also say that the PI's need not be Griceian. Where U can make use of a language, the sentences of which have established IA potentials by virtue of being governed by I-rules, U can perform an IA by choosing a sentence with the right IA potential, and seek to carry out a PI by means of that IA performance. There is no need for U to depend on H's realization of his intention to produce a certain effect in H by means of H's realization of that intention. He may have such a reflexive intention, but because of the semantic structure of the language, there is no need for him to do so. It would be an idle wheel. Bennett could acknowledge this without abandoning his theory.[18] After all, he recognizes "sub-Griceian" mechanisms, which require only a reliance on some way of producing the perlocutionary effect that is not independent of some intentions or other. His example of this concerns a regular correlation between an utterance type and the fact that p, rather than anything having to do with IA's. But the IA potentials of sentences are also not independent of speaker intentions in general, though they will be independent of the intentions of any given speaker. But if the Griceian account of speaker meaning is to be weakened to this extent, it lacks any distinctive thrust. Even relying on the IA potentials of sentences qualifies as using a "sub-Griceian" mechanism. If the Griceian program can be stretched so as to embrace my theory, I, obviously, have no objection to it.

---

[18] In conversation he has told me that he does, though I have not been able to find it in his book.

2. One thing that makes the Griceian program attractive to Bennett is that it is a source of suggestions as to how language originated. In Bennett 1976 he presents an intriguing account of how a full-blown language might develop, step by step, from a prelinguistic stage, an account that puts Griceian M-intentions at the origin of the process. I have already acknowledged that he has convincingly portrayed a real possibility there. IA potential theory makes no such pretensions. It plunges in medias res, examining a linguistic community as a going concern and seeking to understand what there is about the behavior of its members that underlies the semantic structure of its language. I don't suggest that it is an advantage of my theory that it has nothing to say about possibilities of language origins. Quite the contrary. It is clear that language must somehow have gotten started in human prehistory, and it would be a real achievement to throw light on how this happened, or even how it might have happened. Perhaps a Griceian approach is fruitful here. But the fact remains that once language becomes socially established and transmitted, Griceian M-intentions are not the place to look to find the behavioral substratum on which linguistic meaning supervenes. I have been spelling out the reasons for this judgment, and I will not rehash them.

Though IA potential theory does nothing, so far as I can see, to throw light on the origins of language, it does help us to understand the social transmission and internalization of linguistic competence. Since, on that view, it is I-rules that are most fundamental, first language learning can be thought of as initiated by the internalization of an initial body of such rules, each attached to a sentence (perhaps not as fully developed as a grammatically well formed sentence) as an unanalyzed unit. When that first set of I-rule sentence connections has been made, it provides a base from which sentence structure can be learned, after which the neophyte can attach I-rules to new sentences without being taught them individually. If the foundational stage of first language learning of semantics is a matter of internalizing I-rules, we can bring in what is known about the acquisition of other systems of regulative rules—from morality, etiquette, custom, ritual, and so on—in seeking an understanding of what goes on in the linguistic case.

vi. Two Difficulties in the Illocutionary Act Potential Theory

The decks are now cleared for the development of an IA potential theory of sentence meaning. Thus far I have presented only the sketchiest indication. There are many thorny problems to be solved before we have the theory in satisfactory shape. That task will mostly be deferred to the next two chapters. But before we embark on that I must address myself to a small and a large objection, either of which, if cogent, would spike the enterprise before it gets under way.

The small objection is this. Can't a given sentence be used to perform any illocutionary act whatever? I can always set up a special code in which I can use, for example, 'The sun is shining' to ask someone what time it is. Hence all sentences have the same (unlimited) illocutionary act potential, and differences in meanings of sentences cannot be traced to differences in illocutionary act potential.

The answer to this one is easy; that is what makes it a small objection. Sentence meaning is to be identified with *standard* illocutionary act potential, the potential a sentence possesses just by virtue of its linguistic characteristics, not any potential added to that endowment by ad hoc social arrangements. To be sure, the cogency of this answer depends on our ability to discriminate between what belongs to the language and what does not. But the whole enterprise of semantics (and, more generally, linguistics) depends on that, not just our theory. Note that this answer points forward to an account of what it is in the language that endows a sentence with one or more illocutionary act potentials, an account that will be provided in Chapter 7.

The large objection is this. Sentence meaning can be unqualifiedly identified with illocutionary act potential only if for each distinguishable sentence meaning there is exactly one illocutionary act type for the performance of tokens of which a sentence with that meaning is thereby fitted; and, vice versa, for each illocutionary act type there is exactly one sentence meaning that fits the sentence for being used to perform it. If this were true, then whenever I (correctly) use a sentence with a given meaning and thereby perform some illocutionary act it will always be the same act; and, vice versa, whenever I perform an illocutionary act of a particular type I will be using a sentence with the same meaning. But this is clearly not the case. Among the most obvious counterexamples are the cases with which Austin first introduced the term 'illocutionary act'. As we saw in Chapter 1, Austin pointed out that one could know just what I meant by 'It's going to charge', and still not know whether in uttering the sentence I was warning someone or just stating a fact (1962, 98). Again, the sense and reference with which I uttered 'Shoot her' may be clear and still it may not be clear whether I was ordering, imploring, urging, or advising the auditor to do so (1962, 101). In fact, Austin seems to make it part of his concept of an illocutionary act that it is a sort of speech act the exact character of which is *not* determined by the meaning (sense and reference) of the utterance, and which therefore is such that many different acts of this type can be performed by the utterance of a given sentence with one and the same meaning.

The phenomenon to which Austin drew attention in these passages is certainly a common one. For another example, when using 'The gate is open' in its most common meaning I might be warning, reminding, conceding, agreeing, remarking, or concluding that the gate is open, as well as just asserting this. We can see a failure of match in the opposite direction as well. We can have sentences with different meanings used to perform the same illocutionary act. If I can concede that the gate is open by saying 'The gate is open' (S₁), I can also concede that the gate is open by saying 'I concede that the gate is open'. The latter sentence clearly does not have exactly the same meaning as S₁. The presence of the additional term 'concede' ensures that.

vii. Intensifying the Difficulty

One may try to save the illocutionary-act-potential thesis in the face of these facts by stoutly maintaining that, contrary to our normal intuitions, a sentence has as many different meanings as there are distinguishable illocutionary acts it can be used to perform. According to this position we would be using S₁ in different senses, depending on whether it is being used to report, to conclude, to agree, or to admit that the gate is open. It could then be claimed that, like many other subtle differences in meaning, these differences are not commonly noted. I shouldn't wish to maintain that this move is obviously mistaken. I don't take ordinary "intuitions" as a completely adequate guide to the way in which meanings should be assigned to an expression; and I wouldn't do so even if these intuitions were considerably more definite and more consistent than is in fact the case. What is crucial for deciding this kind of question is what total semantic description of the language would best do the job, and that determination is a long way off. However, in the present case ordinary intuition speaks loudly and with considerable unanimity, and I am loath to contravene it just to save a theory. So I will not take this way out.

Nor will I adopt the most obvious way of fitting the theory to the facts, namely, by supposing each sentence meaning to be identical with a range of illocutionary act potentials, rather than with a single potential. Such a modification would not rob the IA potential theory of its distinctive force. Nevertheless, I do not believe that all the potentials associated with a given sentence are associated with it in the same way. And by bringing out the differences we will show how to single out that unique IA potential with which the meaning of a given sentence may be identified.

I can best approach this point by further intensifying the difficulty. Those who stress the fact that IA potential goes beyond meaning always focus on the illocutionary force aspect and fail to note that the same point holds of the propositional content. But the phenomenon is just as common there. Given appropriate contextual support I can express any of innumerably many propositional contents by the sentence 'It will', for example, that a certain bull is going to charge, that the interest rate will go down, that a certain ladder will hold steady, and so on. We get an even wider range of propositional content potentials with sentences the meanings of which specifically fit them for giving answers to yes-no questions, for example, 'Yes'. The propositional content expressed by 'Yes' will be whatever propositional content was expressed in the question to which it is a response. And since no limit can be put on that, 'Yes' can be used to express *any propositional content whatever*—surely a limiting case of the underdetermination of IA potential by meaning. Here, even more obviously, it would be inadmissible to respond to the difficulty by distinguishing different senses for each propositional content the sentence can be used to express. It would be an insane semantics that would assign a different meaning to 'Yes' for each proposition assertable in English.

The underdetermination of propositional content by sentence meaning is equally striking in the referential component. Let me digress from the main line of argument long enough to explain how I am thinking of a total propositional content as consisting of different "aspects". When one expresses a proposition that is "about" one or more entities, he will be *referring* to those entities. If the proposition is *his garden gate's being unlocked*, he is referring to his garden gate; if the proposition is *Jim's being married to Sally or Sam's being married to Jane*, he is referring to Jim, Sally, Sam, and Jane. We will say that the proposition involves a *reference* to those entities; this aspect of the proposition will be termed its "referential aspect". All the other contributions to the content of a proposition I lump together under the heading of "conceptual content". This includes both the predications involved (the gate's being *open* rather than *closed*) and the conceptual content of the referring devices used to pick out the referents. Consider utterances of the sentences (a) 'My garden gate is open', (b) 'My garden gate is closed', and (c) 'That gate is open'. (a) and (b) will differ in conceptual content by virtue of the different predicates involved. They may or may not differ in reference, depending on whether the same gate is referred to. (a) and (c) may or may not differ in reference, but even if they do not, they differ in conceptual content by virtue of the difference in the concepts expressed by the referring expressions used. To sum up, the referential aspect of a proposition is given solely by the *identity* of the referents. Everything else is assigned to conceptual content.

The above examples of multiple propositional contents for a given meaning had to do with conceptual content. The most obvious cases of underdetermination of predicative content by meaning involve sentences that have the special role of responding to prior utterances that make explicit that content. But underdetermination of *reference* by meaning is a much more pervasive phenomenon. It is generally the case that the meaning of one's referring expression does not determine a particular referent. The expressions we most commonly use to refer to particular objects can, each of them, be used without change of meaning to refer to any one of an indefinite plurality of objects. "Definite descriptions" like 'the gate' can be used to refer to any particular gate; 'he' can be used to refer to any male human being, as well as to male animals of other species and to other things as well. 'I' can be used by any speaker to refer to himself or herself; a proper name like 'Sam' can be used to refer to anything to which the name has been attached.[19] Thus a sentence containing a referring expression like these is usable to perform any one of an indefinitely large plurality of illocutionary acts differing in the precise identity of the referents. I can use 'The gate is open' to assert that my garden gate is open, that Sam's front gate is open, that the gate we are now looking at is open, and so on. And where the referring expression is of more general application, the variety of possible illocutionary acts is even greater. 'It's very large' can be used to assert largeness of anything of which largeness can be intelligibly predicated.

Here again we cannot evade the problem by distinguishing senses. Clearly 'he' does not have as many different senses as there are entities to which it can be used to refer. If it did, its meaning would constantly be augmented as new referents come into existence; and speakers would constantly be learning new meanings of the word as they use it to refer to further individuals. But in fact there is a constant meaning of the pronoun; once speakers have mastered that, they are in a position to use the word to refer to any of an indefinitely large plurality of objects.

While we are intensifying the difficulty, we may as well point out that a sentence may be too "rich" as well as too "poor" for an illocutionary act type a token of which it has been used to perform. Or, coming at the point from the other end, an illocutionary act the sentence has been used to perform may be "overspecified" by the sentence, as well as "underspecified". The phenomena cited thus far all exhibit the second term of each contrast. 'The gate is open' is too poor for *admitting* that *my garden* gate is open and too poor on three counts. The meaning of the sentence does not tie us down to the illocutionary force, the particular referent, or the full conceptual content of that illocutionary act type. The illocutionary act is "underspecified" by the meaning of the sentence employed. But we may also truly apply an illocutionary act concept to a speaker without embodying in that concept the full richness of the meaning of the sentence employed. Thus when my sentence was 'I admit that my garden gate was unlocked', I may be correctly said to have asserted of a certain gate that it was unlocked. That illocutionary act description leaves out the precise illocutionary force that was carried by the sentence and identifies the referent in even less specific terms than the expression referring to it. Clearly the illocutionary act performed on a given occasion can be underspecified in

---

[19] It is a matter of controversy whether there are any referring expressions the meaning of which uniquely determines a referent. Popular candidates are Russell's "logically proper names", definite descriptions like 'the inventor of the wheel', and terms for points in a coordinate system, like '1960 A.D.'. My point here is that for most of the referring expressions in common use meaning does not determine reference.

various ways and to various different extents. In this last case I might also be said to have admitted that something is unlocked, to have asserted something about a gate, and so on. Thus a given sentence, by virtue of having a certain meaning, may be used to perform tokens of various too poor illocutionary act types, as well as tokens of various too rich illocutionary act types. This further increases the misfit between sentence meaning and illocutionary act potential.

viii. Matching Illocutionary Act Types

I have been deliberately intensifying the problem, partly to set it in the truest light possible, but also partly because I think that by seeing the full extent of the difficulty we will be in a better position to find a solution. For one thing, once we realize how pervasively the misfit affects propositional content as well as illocutionary force, we will be encouraged to think that there must be some solution. Presumably no one doubts that there is some intimate connection between the meaning of a sentence and its capacity to express a certain proposition.[20] Those who are anxious to separate illocutionary force from meaning display no such tendency with respect to the relation of propositional content and meaning. If Austin had used the "propositional content" terminology, he would undoubtedly have taken the "carrying" of such content to be an aspect of the "locutionary act" (uttering a sentence with a certain "sense and reference"). Therefore, if the fact that propositional content can vary while meaning remains fixed does not prevent sentence meaning from being intimately related to proposition expression capacities, a like variability in illocutionary force should not prevent sentence meaning from being intimately related to it also.

Furthermore, in extending the difficulty we have pointed the way to a solution. Think back to the case in which the propositional content of an utterance goes beyond what is embodied in the sentence meaning. What enables us to say more than is contained in the sentence meaning is that we get support from the context. In the cases of additional conceptual content cited above, that content had already been carried by sentences uttered earlier in the conversation—the question being answered or the statement being agreed with. That leaves a speaker free to simply use some device for hooking onto that previous utterance: 'Yes' or 'That's right'. The general point is that where appropriate contextual support is available one need not use a sentence with a meaning rich enough to determine all the content of what one is saying. This point is also exemplified by the other cases in which the sentence is too poor. We are able to carry out successful references with expressions whose meanings do not uniquely identify the referent because we can depend on contextual cues to fill the

---

[20] At least no one who makes use of all these concepts.

gap. Why should we not treat variability of illocutionary force in the same way? Here too we are able say something with a given illocutionary force without using a sentence whose meaning confines us to that, where the context of utterance in some way makes sufficiently clear with what force our utterance is to be taken.

Thus we see that the underdetermination of illocutionary act by sentence meaning is not in any way an exceptional or mysterious phenomenon. On the contrary, it is a well-understood general feature of speech, an exemplification of the principle of least effort. Where sufficient contextual indications are available, there is no need to use a sentence rich enough to determine the full content of what we say.

But how do these considerations show us how to modify the IA potential theory of sentence meaning in such a way as to take account of this variability? Here our discussion of overspecification and underspecification is helpful. Underlying that discussion is the general point that an illocutionary act, like anything else, can be conceptualized in many different ways; a particular illocutionary act is a token of many illocutionary act types. One and the same illocutionary performance may be correctly described as asserting that a certain gate is unlocked, admitting that a certain gate is unlocked, admitting that my garden gate is unlocked, admitting that something is unlocked, and so on. Thus an illocutionary act may be specified in terms that bring in exactly as much content as is contained in the meaning of the sentence employed, in terms of more content or in terms of less content. The act may be exactly described, as well as underdescribed or overdescribed, for the meaning of its sentential vehicle. If the sentence 'The gate is open' is used in a particular instance to admit that my garden gate is open, that illocutionary act will be "exactly described" as *asserting that a certain gate is open*; it will be overdescribed (in its illocutionary force) as *admitting that a certain gate is open*. And it may be underdescribed (in its propositional content) as *asserting that something is open* or as *asserting something of a certain gate*; while it may be overdescribed in its propositional content as *asserting that my garden gate is open*.[21] A description may be too rich, or too poor, in more than one respect simultaneously, as *admitting that my garden gate is open* (too rich in illocutionary force and propositional content). Indeed, a description may be too rich in one respect and too poor in another, as in *admitting that something is open*.

What I have just been calling a "description" or a "specification" de-

[21] Some of these phrases, particularly "asserting that something is . . ." and "asserting that a certain F is . . .", are subject to more than one interpretation. The first one, for example, could be used to mean "asserting that there is something that is . . ." as well as used to mean "asserting with respect to something in particular that it is . . .". I will always be using such phrases in the second way, using them to report in quite unspecific terms a singular utterance that is about some particular, not to report an existentially quantified utterance. Sometimes I will convey my intentions less ambiguously by using the *de re* form, for example, "asserting of a certain gate that it is open".

termines a certain illocutionary act *type*. An illocutionary act type that contains exactly as much content as a certain sentence meaning may be termed the "matching illocutionary act type" for that sentence meaning. Thus, if we restrict ourselves to the most basic meaning for each of the following sentences, the matching illocutionary act type in each case can be specified as follows:

'The gate is unlocked'—asserting that a certain gate is unlocked.
'It's unlocked'—asserting that something is unlocked.
'My garden gate is unlocked'—asserting that a certain gate leading into a certain garden belonging to the speaker is unlocked.
'Start it now'—telling someone to initiate something just after the utterance.
'I order you to start it now'—ordering someone to initiate something just after the utterance.
'Start the engine now'—telling someone to put a certain engine into operation just after the utterance.

We can now see how to modify VI. (the IA potential principle) so as to escape the difficulty of multiple IA potentials. We identify a sentence meaning with its *matching illocutionary act potential,* that is, with the potential to perform illocutionary acts of the type that exactly matches that meaning. That potential exactly mirrors the meaning; it must, for it was specifically selected to do so. Nor can there be any danger that there is more than one illocutionary act type (potential) that embodies just the same content as that meaning. Hence we may replace VI. with:

VII. *What it is for a sentence to have a certain meaning is for it to be usable to perform illocutionary acts of the matching type (that is, to have the matching illocutionary act potential).*

Now let's see if we can be more explicit as to what it takes for a given illocutionary act type to match a given sentence meaning. So far the account has been in terms of including the same "content", and it would be desirable to go beyond that metaphor. We have been identifying some respects in which the "contents" might differ, and we can build on that to construct a more analytical account. To wit, we have considered three ways in which an illocutionary act type may or may not match a sentence meaning in specificity: illocutionary force, identification of referents, and conceptual content. The above list of matching illocutionary act types was presented as intuitively matching the respective sentence meanings in these respects. I will now develop a principle of identification that yields such matching.

In seeking a matching illocutionary act type for a given sentence meaning we are looking for a type such that a sentence is fitted to perform a token of that type, just by virtue of its having that meaning. Or rather, since this formula would include types that are poorer than the meaning, we are looking for the richest type that satisfies this condition. It is just by virtue of meaning what it does that 'The gate is open' is usable to assert that a certain gate is open. To render it usable to *admit* that a certain gate is open, or to assert that *my garden gate* is open, special contextual support is needed. These considerations encourage us to adopt the following definition.

D11. *I is the matching illocutionary act type for sentence meaning M iff I is the most inclusive type such that a sentence with meaning M can be used to perform tokens of I just by virtue of having that meaning.*

Unfortunately this simple formula doesn't work. It founders, as will so many other simple formulations, on the complexities of reference. If references were invariably effected by expressions each of which is tied by its meaning to one unique referent (what Russell called *logically proper names*), the formula would work. We could then specify the referential, as well as the other, aspects of a matching illocutionary act type so that, given the meaning of the sentence (including the meanings of the names involved), illocutionary acts of that type can be carried off whatever the context. But, as we have noted, that is not the way singular reference is normally effected in natural languages. The standard procedure is to use some expression that is fitted by its meaning to refer to any of an indefinitely large plurality of items, the particular referent on a given occasion of use being determined, if at all, by contextual features. That is why in all the above examples the matching illocutionary act description involves an indefinite specification of referents—'a certain gate', 'something', 'a certain garden gate belonging to the speaker', 'someone named Sam', and so on. For if the sentence contains referring expressions of the usual sort, like 'the gate', then if the putatively matching illocutionary act description specified some particular gate, person, or whatever, the illocutionary act type thus specified would be too specific. The meaning of, for example, 'The gate is open' does not suffice to pick out any particular gate as referent, and hence the sentence is not fitted just by its meaning to perform illocutionary acts of that maximally specific type.

Now for why this torpedoes D11. Even when we present the referent in unspecific terms ('a certain gate') and thus do as much as we can to match the referential unspecificity of the meaning of the referring expression ('the gate'), we have still failed to specify an illocutionary act that the sentence can be used to perform without any contextual support. For a referring expression of the standard type cannot perform its referential function *at all* without contextual indication of the particular item that is referred to on that occasion.

For such referring expressions there is no such thing as a context-independent reference. The meaning of a typical referring expression fits it to be used for a certain kind of job, where further conditions are required in each case to enable it to carry through the job. The meaning of the expression makes provision, so to say, for its own transcendence. Hence the meaning of 'The gate is open' does not, *by itself*, make it possible to use that sentence to *assert of a certain gate* that it is open. For unless the context of utterance suffices to pick out some particular gate as the one that is being said to be open, no illocutionary act of that (not fully specific) type will have been performed.

Another way of making the point is this. Where singular reference is not involved, the matching illocutionary act description determined by D11. can be the fullest description of an illocutionary act actually performed by uttering the sentence. In uttering 'All crows are black' (and assuming, contrary to Putnam, that nothing similar to singular reference is involved in this assertion), I may just be performing an illocutionary act of the matching type—asserting that all crows are black—and that's all. I may be doing nothing illocutionarily that falls under a more specific description, like *agreeing* that all crows are black. But with sentences containing typical singular referring expressions this is not possible. I cannot just perform the matching illocutionary act yielded by D11. The predicate 'asserted of a certain gate that it is open' cannot be true of me unless some more specific predicate of the form 'asserted of gate G that it is open' is true of me, where 'G' picks out some particular gate. Hence even the referentially unspecific illocutionary act type does not match the sentence meaning in the way specified by D11.

Nevertheless it is clear that this type comes as close to a match as possible. And so if we are to have matching types for sentence meanings that are built up, in part, out of the meanings of referring expressions, we will have to rethink what it takes to have a matching illocutionary act type. Let's see if we can find some way in which the usability of 'The gate is open' (G) to assert that a certain gate is open is fully determined by its meaning, a way in which its usability to, for example, admit that my garden gate is open is not fully determined by its meaning. We can accomplish this by taking the standpoint of the hearer. If I know the meaning with which U is uttering G and know that U intends to engage in communication, what does that tell me about the illocutionary act he is performing? So long as we put the question in that way we will not get beyond the above result. In standard referential cases this will not, for reasons just given, be enough to tell me that U has *succeeded* in performing a token of what we have been calling the matching illocutionary act type, for that itself will not tell me that the speaker has succeeded in picking out a particular gate. However, even here knowledge of the sentence meaning is sufficient to enable the addressee to know that U *intends* to perform an illocutionary act of that matching type.[22] And in this respect the matching type is distinguished from those that are too rich. Just by knowing that U is using S with its normal meaning, and intends to be communicating, I can know he *intends* to be saying of some particular gate that it is open. But just by knowing that, I cannot know that he intends to be saying of my garden gate that it is open or that he intends to be admitting that a certain gate is open.

So let's modify D11. to read:

D12. I is the matching illocutionary act type for sentence meaning M iff I is the most inclusive type such that an addressee, just by knowing that U is uttering a sentence with meaning M and intends to be communicating, can thereby know that U intends to be performing a token of I.

Having developed a criterion that handles the points brought out thus far, we must next consider some other respects in which illocutionary acts that a sentence can be used to perform when uttered with a certain meaning may fail to match that meaning; and then we can consider whether our formula has to be modified to accommodate those dimensions of mismatch.

1. *Figurative speech.* Here a sentence meaning is exploited not to produce a token of what we would call the matching illocutionary act, but rather to say something derived from that via a figure of speech. When Ross, in Act I, scene ii of *Macbeth*, says ". . . the Norweyan banners . . . fan our people cold", he is not saying, as he would be if speaking literally, that some Norwegians are flapping their banners near some Scotch so as to reduce their temperature, but rather that the Norwegian army is striking dread in the inhabitants of Scotland. Again, when Hamlet, in Act II, scene iv, speaks of his mother and uncle "honeying and making love over the nasty sty", he is not saying that they have set up a bed over a pigsty. He is rather negatively evaluating their activity by metaphorically speaking of their bed as a pigsty.

2. *Parasitic uses of sentences.* These include such things as making requests in dramatic productions and speaking ironically. If I say in the course of a play, "Would you please look up Susie's telephone number?", I am not seriously requesting anyone to look up anyone's telephone number. I am only doing this "in the play". But again I exploit the ordinary meaning of the sentence in doing so. Again, if I say, ironically, "What a beautiful day!", meaning thereby to remark on the foul weather, I have exploited

---

[22] This claim is subject to certain qualifications that will be brought out shortly and embodied in a revised formulation.

the ordinary meaning of the sentence to perform an illocutionary act with a propositional content that is contrary to that of the matching illocutionary act type.

In taking these to be mismatches, I assume that the sentence in each case is used with its normal meaning, a meaning that is associated with a matching illocutionary act type different from the one being performed figuratively or parasitically. This assumption may be challenged, particularly for the figurative cases. If I am not saying that those banners (literally) reduced the temperature of some Scotchmen, then I don't utter the sentence with its normal meaning. My answer to that is that unless I were using the sentence in that sense I would have no basis for my figurative extension.[23] I do not, however, wish to argue that question here. If any of my cases do not involve using one's sentence with its normal literal meaning, they pose no problem for V. So let's proceed to consider such cases on the assumption that they do involve a mismatch.

As such they pose two problems for my account. (1) Are nonmatching illocutionary acts of the sorts just discussed excluded by principle VI.? (2) Do cases like these raise any difficulties for the use of VI. to identify a unique matching illocutionary act type for a particular sentence meaning? Problem (1) can be quickly dispatched. Clearly, just knowing that U is uttering S with some standard meaning does not suffice to assure me that U intends to be making some figurative extension or to be speaking ironically. Additional information is needed for these determinations. So there is no danger of VI. implying that the illocutionary act performed in one of these cases is of the matching type for the sentence meaning in question. But (2) is a bit stickier. If when U makes a figurative use of "the Norweyan banners . . . fan our people cold", U is using the sentence in its most basic meaning, then clearly an addressee cannot, just by knowing that, know that U intends to be performing the matching illocutionary act. For in this case U has no such intention. Nor just by knowing that U is using "What a beautiful day!" in its most basic meaning can one tell that U intends to be performing the matching illocutionary act rather than speaking ironically.

This indicates that we must add to the information that the addressee, H, needs in order to determine that U intends to be performing the matching illocutionary act. This further information must rule out the possibility that U intends to be performing some figurative or parasitic illocutionary act instead. Let's consider how best to specify that. Reflecting on figurative uses and (what I have been calling) parasitic uses, we can dis-

---

[23] For reasons to suppose that figurative speech involves using words and sentences in some established sense, and hence that the figurative-literal difference is a difference in what use one makes of certain semantic resources, not a difference in those resources themselves, see Searle 1979 and Alston 1980c.

cern an important common feature. In both sorts of cases the content of the illocutionary act performed is derivative from the content of another illocutionary act performable by uttering the sentence in question. In metaphorical utterances like those cited above what one is saying is derivative from the content of what one would be saying in a literal use of the sentence, in which one is performing the matching illocutionary act. Thus in saying 'Harry is a tower of strength', where Harry is a human being, what one asserts is derivative from what one would assert if one said of a tower named Harry that it is a tower of strength. One couldn't understand the metaphorical use unless one understands and "makes use of " the literal use. Often the derivation is best understood as involving only part of the content of the illocutionary act performed figuratively. Consider Macbeth's saying "Sleep knits up the ravell'd sleave of care". That complete sentence makes no sense if all its terms are used literally. Here what the understanding derives from is what one would be saying if the predicate 'knits up a ravell'd sleave' were predicated of a human being. But in either sort of case it is clear that figurative uses contrast with literal uses in that the understanding of the former goes through the understanding of some other use of the sentence, or part thereof, whereas the understanding of literal uses does not.

And parasitic uses exhibit a parallel derivativeness. If I say 'Has my wife gotten back home?' in a play, the audience could not understand that utterance except by using its understanding of what would be said by someone who literally and seriously asked whether his wife had returned home. In the play one is *imitating* that more basic use of the sentence or, as one might say, *pretending* to be making that use but not really doing so. The function of 'Has my wife returned home?' in the play depends on the audience's being prepared, by a "willing suspension of disbelief ", to take me as asking my addressee whether my wife has returned home, while realizing that I, the actor, am not *really* doing that. And the ironical 'What a beautiful day!' is understood as a certain kind of transformation of what one would be saying if one seriously opined that the day is beautiful.

Let's use the term *straightforward* use of a sentence for one that does *not* exhibit the kind of derivativeness I have been illustrating. We can then exclude figurative and parasitic illocutionary acts as candidates for matching illocutionary acts by beefing up VI. to require the addressee to know that the speaker is making a straightforward use of the sentence in question.[24]

But this is not the end of the modifications required. Another complication is provided by what has come to be called *indirect speech acts*. I ask you

[24] For an excellent treatment of ways in which an illocutionary act goes beyond what is embodied in the meaning of the sentence uttered, a treatment that makes many more distinctions than the above, see Kent Bach's "Semantic Slack: What Is Said and More", in Tsohatzidis 1994. This note is also relevant to the discussion of illocutionary rules in 7.4 and 7.6.

whether you can reach the salt, thereby (indirectly) requesting you to pass the salt. Or I tell you that you are standing on my foot, thereby (indirectly) requesting you to get off my foot. In these cases the sentence is used to perform some illocutionary act of a type quite different from its matching illocutionary act type. Just how this phenomenon is related to the present problem depends on just how it is to be construed, and that is currently a matter of controversy. Our main concern here is whether we should say, in the first case for example, that U is both asking a question and making a request. If so, since the matching illocutionary act for the sentence 'Can you reach the salt?' would be *asking one's addressee whether she or he can reach the salt*, U would be intending to perform that matching act, and the original formulation would apply correctly to the case. The addressee, by knowing the meaning with which the sentence is uttered, would know that the speaker intended to be performing the act we would want to count as the matching illocutionary act. But suppose the right diagnosis is that the speaker is only requesting the addressee to pass the salt and not asking the above question at all. If so, the knowledge of the sentence meaning would not enable H to know that U intended to perform what we want to consider the matching interrogative act. H would also have to know that U was not (merely) performing some other illocutionary act "indirectly" related to that interrogative act. To be on the safe side, let's assume this second construal. That will require us to add to the list of what H must know in order to know that U intends to perform the matching illocutionary act, that U *not be performing an indirect illocutionary act*. To put it positively and more concisely, that U is making a *direct use* of the sentence.

In the light of all this we can reformulate D12. as follows.

D13. *I is the matching illocutionary act type for sentence meaning M iff I is the most inclusive type such that an addressee, just by knowing that U is uttering a sentence with meaning M and intends to be making a straightforward, direct use of that sentence, can thereby know that U intends to be performing a token of I.*

There are also noncommunicative uses of sentences to do such things as practice pronunciation, vocalize for the sheer joy of doing so, and test microphones. But we need not take any account of this in our formula for picking out the matching illocutionary act. These uses fall completely outside the territory by reason of the fact that they do not involve using a sentence, word, or phrase with one meaning rather than another. Whereas what a matching illocutionary act *matches* is a *sentence meaning*. I will have to bring noncommunicative uses of language into the picture when I discuss how to formulate illocutionary rules, rules being governed by which give a sentence its IA potential.

In the light of the points brought out in this section, let us examine the prospects of asserting the converse of our matching IA potential principle, VII., namely,

VIII. For any illocutionary act type there is a certain sentence meaning (the matching sentence meaning for that illocutionary act type) such that a sentence's being usable to perform an illocutionary act of that type is its having that meaning.

In other words, can we find for each illocutionary act type a sentence meaning that it matches?

First, I want to restrict this question somewhat. Clearly, if there are illocutionary act types we do not at present have the resources to specify, there will be no matching sentence meaning possessed by any sentences in any existing human languages. The only question that would remain would be as to whether for any illocutionary act type it is possible that there should be a sentence meaning that it matches. But for present purposes the question will be restricted to illocutionary act types we are capable of specifying.

What is suggested by the preceding discussion is that there will be a matching sentence meaning for any illocutionary act type so far as its illocutionary force and conceptual content is concerned, but not for the referential aspect, so long as we are restricted to the most common sorts of referring expressions. Let me elaborate.

It would seem that for any illocutionary force and conceptual content we can specify, there is some way of constructing a sentence so that its meaning will determine that content. As for the conceptual content, we can simply take the terms we used to specify that content in our illocutionary act description and put them (perhaps with suitable grammatical transformations) into the sentence in question. As for illocutionary force, if all else fails we can attach the I-verb in question to a sentence so as to construct a performative formula.[25] The reader is invited to take our previous examples of illocutionary acts performed with sentences that did not embody all the illocutionary force or conceptual content and try in each case to construct a sentence with a meaning that matches the illocutionary act in these respects. If she found this impossible at any point I should be surprised. But on the referential side this will not be possible with ordinary referring expressions. For, as we have seen, the meanings of such expressions underdetermine particular references, the rest of the determination being carried by contextual features. Hence if the illocutionary act type carries a specification of a particular referent—*asserting that Alston's garden gate is open* (where 'Alston' picks out exactly one person on that oc-

---

[25] The exceptions to this will not hamper us in practice. See the discussion of expressing in 4.6.

casion of use)—we shall not find any ordinary natural language sentence the meaning of which exactly matches that illocutionary act type. For there is no expression the meaning of which ties it to referring to that person and only to that person. That is not the way typical referring expressions work in natural languages. Certainly 'Alston' and 'Alston's garden gate' are not expressions that work this way. Each is fitted by its meaning to be used to refer to any one of innumerable persons or gates. We will be able to construct a sentence the meaning of which matches a given illocutionary act in its referential aspect only if, for each possible referent, we can find an expression the meaning of which ties it to that referent alone. I shall not try to decide whether this is possible, but I very much doubt that it is feasible for natural languages.

To sum all this up, a given sentence can be used with one and the same meaning to perform illocutionary acts of indefinitely many types. Furthermore, it can be standardly or normally used to do so, apart from any special ad hoc arrangements. This is because the sentence meaning by itself does not suffice to determine all the features of the illocutionary acts the sentence can be used to perform. The meaning makes an essential contribution to that determination, but the conventions and practices of speech are such as to make provision for sentence meaning to interact with contextual indications to produce illocutionary acts the content of which go beyond that meaning. That makes it possible for one's utterance to carry illocutionary force or conceptual content or references to particular individuals that are not contained as such in the meaning of the sentence. It also makes possible figurative uses in which one plays variations on the sentence meaning to produce new propositional contents. And it makes possible the lifting of the whole system of illocutionary act types into a new dimension, like drama, in which they have, as a whole, a new sort of force that is systematically related to the original one. But recognizing this diversity, we can still hold on to the crucial identification of sentence meaning with illocutionary act potential by singling out for each sentence meaning a *matching illocutionary act type*, because that illocutionary act type has a content that precisely matches the content of that sentence meaning. In this way the illocutionary act potential theory of sentence meaning can be rescued from the difficulties posed by multiple illocutionary act potentials.

I have been concentrating on ways to accommodate multiple IA potential without distinguishing different sentence meanings. But I do not want to handle every case of multiple IA potential in these ways. Many sentences do have more than one meaning, and sometimes the fact that a sentence can be used to perform illocutionary acts of more than one type reflects that. 'He got a good hand' can be used (1) to assert of a certain male human being that he received a lot of applause, (2) to assert of a certain male human being that he received a favorable collocation of cards in a deal, and (3) to assert of a certain male human being that he engaged a desirable worker. Surely three different meanings of the sentence correspond to these differences.

If I intended the IA potential thesis to be a reductive definition of sentence meaning, it would be viciously circular. For the explanation of 'matching illocutionary act type' is itself in terms of sentence meaning; the illocutionary act type that matches a given sentence meaning is one such that just by knowing that P uttered a sentence with that meaning . . . And the supplementary directions we have given as to what is to be excluded from the matching illocutionary act type themselves employ the concept of sentence meaning. Thus we have said that we must exclude from the matching illocutionary act type any content that is not explicitly carried by the *semantic structure* of the sentence; we have said that we must restrict ourselves to illocutionary act types performable just by exploiting the *literal meaning* of the sentence; and so on.

I might reply to this difficulty by pointing out that my final account of the nature of sentence meaning will not be in terms of IA potential but rather in terms of the sentence's being governed by certain kinds of rules. But though this is correct, it will, at best, postpone the difficulty; for the account in terms of rules itself employs the concept of sentence meaning. The crucial point to make is that my thesis is not intended to be a conceptual analysis of the classical type, or a reductive definition. It is a hypothesis as to the *nature* of sentential meaning, as to the psychosocial substance of the fact that a sentence has one or more meanings. I initially identified sentence meaning in 6.1 by the axioms of meaning that are in "functional" terms. The meaning of a given sentence is that which one will know (in a practical, know-how way) just by virtue of being fluent in the language; it is that which one must know (again in a practical sense) in order to know what is being said by an utterance of the sentence; it is that which is determined by the meaningful components of the sentence plus its structure; and so on. This preliminary, pretheoretical identification is in terms of the place sentence meaning occupies in one or another system—the structure of the language, the knowledge of the fluent speaker, the way that knowledge guides speech and understanding of speech, and so on. The IA potential thesis is a claim about the intrinsic nature of that which stands in these functional relations. As such it is analogous to theoretical hypotheses in science concerning the underlying nature of some functionally identified property, process, or substance, rather than to philosophical attempts to lay bare our concept of T or to bring out the meaning of the term 'T'. It is more like a hypothesis as to the real nature of what is functionally identified as valence, heat, magnetism, or fragility. And it should be evaluated in basically the same way. The identification of heat with the kinetic energy of molecules is not invalidated if, at a given stage of the game, we have to make use of the concept of heat to determine just what average kinetic energy to identify with a given intensity of heat. In the same way the IA potential theory of meaning is not invalidated by the necessity to use our pretheoretical concept of sentence meaning in determining just what IA potential constitutes a given sentence meaning.

ix. Illocutionary Rules

The next step in the development of the theory of sentence meaning is to determine what constitutes an IA potential of a sentence. By virtue of what is a given sentence standardly usable to perform one kind of illocutionary act rather than another? It is clearly not the phonetic, phonemic, or syntactic constitution of the sentence. We could be clear about all that and still be blankly ignorant of the IA potential. We could truly say that it is the (a) *meaning* of the sentence that gives it a certain IA potential. Since I am identifying the meaning with an IA potential, I could hardly deny that the former is sufficient for the latter. A fact is a sufficient condition for any fact with which it is identical. But this would reverse the order of explanation I am interested in. As I made explicit earlier, I take linguistic meaning to be something that is not at all transparent on the surface and that needs explication in more pellucid terms. I seek to use the notion of IA potential to throw light on sentence meaning, not vice versa. Hence I must look elsewhere for an account of what endows a sentence with a certain IA potential.

Fortunately, the material for this is ready to hand in the account of illocutionary acts developed in Part I. Several ways of bringing out the nature of illocutionary acts were suggested, but the favored account was in terms of uttering a sentence *as subject to a certain rule*. This suggests an answer to the present question. For a sentence to have a certain IA potential is for that sentence to be governed by, subject to, a certain rule. Such rules I will call *illocutionary rules*. The next two chapters will take up this suggestion and develop an account of sentence meaning as illocutionary rule governance.

CHAPTER SEVEN

Illocutionary Act Potential
and Illocutionary Rules

i. IA Potential as Subjection to Illocutionary Rules

As briefly indicated at the end of the last chapter, the account of the nature of illocutionary acts in Part I provides an obvious answer to the question of what it is by virtue of which a sentence has a certain illocutionary act potential. For the account of illocutionary acts developed there was largely in terms of S's R'ing certain conditions in uttering a sentence. And our favored account of R'ing conditions was in terms of S's placing his utterance under a certain rule. The explicit formulation was this.

> **D8. In uttering S, U R's that *p*—In uttering S, U subjects his utterance to a rule that, in application to this case, implies that it is permissible for U to utter S only if *p*.**

This naturally suggests that what renders a sentence standardly usable to perform an illocutionary act of a certain type is that the sentence is governed by a certain rule—the one subjection of an utterance to which renders that utterance an illocutionary act of that type. If to ask someone for a glass of water is to utter a sentence and, in doing so, to subject one's utterance to a rule that lays down certain requirements for correct or permissible utterance, then what it takes for a sentence to be standardly usable to make that request is for it to be governed by such a rule, one that imposes those requirements as necessary conditions for the permissible utterance of that sentence. Calling such rules *illocutionary rules*, we get the simple formula:

IX. A sentence's having a certain illocutionary act potential consists in its being subject to a certain illocutionary rule.

Combining that with VI. we get:

X. A sentence's having a certain meaning consists in its being subject to a certain illocutionary rule.

In the course of this chapter we will see that things are considerably more complicated than this simple picture will suggest. In particular, we will be forced to qualify the principle that to perform an IA that matches a certain sentence meaning is simply to R those conditions that are required by the I-rule governance by which gives the sentence that meaning. In Chapter 3 I pointed out that when U says that a certain garden gate is open, U is R'ing, with respect to a particular garden gate, G, that it is open. But it is absurd to suppose that the sentence 'The garden gate is open' is correctly uttered only when G is open. That sentence is legitimately used to assert that any one of indefinitely many garden gates is open. And in this chapter we will see the need for complications to deal with other discrepancies as well. But, surprisingly enough, this does not enforce any modification of IX. and X. The identification of sentence meaning, matching IA potential, and I-rule governance will stand fast.

ii. Linguistic Meaning as Rule Governance

Before embarking on the quest for a satisfactory conception of illocutionary rules, let's pause to consider the general idea that linguistic meaning is a matter of rule governance.[1] The following passages exemplify the support for this idea.

> The meaning of a word or a combination of words is, in this way, determined by a set of rules which regulate their use. . . . Stating the meaning of a sentence amounts to stating the rules according to which the sentence is to be used. (Schlick 1936, 341)

> . . . to talk about the meaning of an expression or sentence is not to talk about its use on a particular occasion, but about the rules, habits, conven-

---

[1] Much of this section is taken from Alston 1974.

tions governing its correct use, on all occasions, to refer or to assert. . . .
(Strawson 1971, 9)

It is quite clear that, in some sense, one who knows a natural language tacitly knows a system of rules . . . the semantic component [of a description of a language] is a statement of the rules by which he [the user of a language] interprets sentences as meaningful messages. (Katz 1966, 100, 111)

I have said that the hypothesis of this book is that speaking a language is performing acts according to rules. The form this hypothesis will take is that the semantic structure of a language may be regarded as a conventional realization of a series of sets of underlying constitutive rules, and that speech acts are acts characteristically performed by uttering expressions in accordance with these sets of constitutive rules. (Searle 1969, 36–37)

Indeed, I might well have included this conviction among my axioms of meaning in 6.1. Better late than never.

A7. A linguistic expression means what it does by virtue of being governed by a rule or convention.

Here are some remarks that are designed to exhibit the initial plausibility of A7.

Whatever else may be true of linguistic meaning, it is clear that the fact that a given word, phrase, or sentence in a language has a certain meaning is in some way dependent on facts about the society in which that language is spoken, rather than on any intrinsic features of the expression (as an acoustic or orthographical type), and rather than on any nomological connections in which such physical types stand. This is shown by the mere fact that the same acoustic type, for example, 'low', can have very different meanings in different languages, for example, French ('l'eau') and English ('low'). Consider further the fact that it is possible to change the meaning of a word in a language by an explicit agreement or by (a successfully enforced) fiat. Thus we could, if enough of us so chose, change the meaning of 'snow' from what it is now to the meaning currently possessed by 'fire'. It seems that any fact that is dependent on the constitution of a society, and moreover dependent in such a way that it could be changed by agreement, convention, or decree, must be a fact about what rules (conventions, norms) are in force in the society; for this is the kind of fact that behaves in just this way. Both the above points hold for the fact that in the United States the right side of the road is the one on which to drive.

More direct indications of the "rulish" character of semantic facts come from the pervasive application of rule-derived distinctions to the semantic side of the use of language.[2] One may use the *right* or the *wrong* word, the *correct* or *incorrect* phrase, to say what one set out to say. If one is learning a language one is often corrected by one's tutors, told that one is not to say _____ in those circumstances, or that what one *can* say is _____. One may *misuse* expressions to the point at which what one says does not make sense. Such metatalk reflects the presence of rules governing speech. It is where rules are in force—permitting some moves, forbidding others, requiring others—that one can speak of a certain action in a certain context as being right or wrong, correct or incorrect, that one can speak of what a person can, must, or must not do, that one can be said to *misuse* something. These considerations lend powerful credence to the ideas that when a person learns a language what he learns is a system of rules, that what makes someone a fluent speaker of a language is the practical mastery of a set of rules, and that what a linguist is trying to uncover when she sets out to describe the language is just that system of rules.

Remember axiom A2.

A2. *The fact that an expression has a certain meaning is what enables it to play a distinctive role (enables it to be used in a certain way) in communication.*

In the last chapter I succumbed to the temptation to inflate A2. into a statement of what linguistic meaning consists in. This is what I called the "Use Principle".

IV. An expression's having a certain meaning consists in its being usable to play a certain role (to do certain things) in communication.

I will yield to a similar temptation here, propounding a Rule Principle concerning the nature of linguistic meaning, confining myself here to sentences.[3]

XI. A sentence's having a certain meaning consists in its being subject to a certain rule or convention.

This is obviously just a generalization of X., the Illocutionary Rule Principle.

---

[2] A proper defense of the rule theory of linguistic meaning would appear as just one facet of a defense of the more general contention that a language is best conceived as being a system of rules—syntactical and phonological as well as semantic. All the points in this section apply equally to the phonological and syntactic aspects of language.

[3] I will do something to justify this transition in 9.2.

It may strike one as implausible to suppose that a sentence's having a certain meaning can consist both in what it is usable to do in communication and in what rule(s) it is subject to. Aren't these quite different matters? To specify what a gun is standardly usable to do is one thing; to specify the rules governing its use is another. But that is because what a gun is standardly used to do is not itself rule-constituted. There is no rule, or system of rules, that must hold in order for it to be possible that there is such an activity as shooting guns. In this it differs from a rule-constituted activity like trumping a trick in bridge. If it were not for the rules of bridge there could be no such activity as trumping a trick. The upshot of our discussion of illocutionary acts is that they are like trumping a trick, and unlike shooting a gun, in this respect. To perform an illocutionary act is to utter a sentence, subjecting one's utterance to a rule that implies certain conditions of correctness for this utterance. Apart from such rules there could be no such activity. Hence if sentence meaning consists in being usable to do things of that sort, it is by no means surprising that it should also consist in being subject to a certain kind of rule. Once we spell out what it takes for a sentence to be usable to perform illocutionary acts of a certain type, a spelling out encapsulated in IX., it becomes clear that III. and X. are different ways of saying the same thing.

iii. Some Versions of Semantic Rules

I can provide a useful contrastive background for our illocutionary rule theory of sentence meaning by critically examining some attempts to indicate the sorts of rules that give linguistic expressions their meanings. These are chosen to illustrate defects I am concerned to avoid.

I. Rudolf Carnap (1942, 246)[4]
    A. Rules of truth:
        1. pr_1 (in_1) is true if and only if Chicago is large.
        2. pr_2 (in_1) is true if and only if Chicago has a harbor.
    B. Rules of designation:
        1. in_1 designates Chicago.
        2. pr_1 designates the property of being large.
        3. pr_2 designates the property of having a harbor.

---

[4] Unlike the other authors quoted in this section, Carnap does not proffer his rules as exemplifications of the rule theory as I have construed it. Or at least it is not clear that he is doing so. However, I wanted to include Carnapian rules as representative of the "formal semantic" tradition in which there is much talk of linguistic rules, semantic and otherwise. For whatever the intentions of formal semanticists, it is of interest to determine whether the sorts of rules they envisage *can* illustrate the way in which having a meaning consists in being governed by rules. Much of what I have to say about Carnap's rules also applies to later developments in formal semantics. See David Lewis 1972 and the literature referred to there.

II. Rudolf Carnap (1947, 4–56)
  A. Rules of designation for individual constants:
    1. 's' is a symbolic translation of 'Walter Scott'.
    2. 'w'—(the book) Waverley.
  B. Rules of designation for predicates:
    'Hx'—'x is human (a human being)'
    'RAx'—'x is a rational animal'
    'Fx'—'x is (naturally) featherless'
    'Bx'—'x is a biped'
    'Axy'—'x is an author of y'
  C. Rule of truth for the simplest atomic sentence:
    An atomic sentence in S_1 consisting of a predicate followed by an individual constant is true if and only if the individual to which the individual constant refers possesses the property to which the predicate refers.
  D. Rule of truth for 'v':
    A sentence 'pvq' is true in S_1 if and only if at least one of the two components is true.
III. Max Black (1962, 66)
  "Monday" may be replaced by "the day before Tuesday" and vice versa.
IV. J. J. Katz (1966)
  A. Dictionary entries (p. 155)
    bachelor—N, $N_1 \ldots, N_k$
    (1) (Physical object), (Living), (Human), (Male), (Adult), (Never married): SR
    (2) (Physical object), (Living), (Human) (Young), (Knight), (Serving under the standard of another): SR
  B. Projection rules (p. 166):
    Given two readings,
    R_1: (a_1), (a_2): $\ldots$, (a_n) : SR_1
    R_2: (b_1), (b_2): $\ldots$, (b_m) : SR_2
    such that R_1 is assigned to a node X_1 and R_2 is assigned to a node X_2. X_1 dominates a string of words that is a head and X_2 dominates a string that is a modifier, and X_1 and X_2 branch from the same immediately dominating node X, *then* the derived reading R_3: (a_1), (a_2) : $\ldots$, (a_n), (b_1), (b_2), $\ldots$, (b_m); SR_1 is assigned to the node X just in case the selection restriction SR_2 is satisfied by R_1.

It is my contention that none of these formulations is wholly satisfactory as an illustration of the way in which having a certain meaning *is* being governed by a certain rule. To substantiate this charge, and to provide some guidance for my own efforts, I will lay down three requirements that a rule must satisfy in order to be suitable for the task at hand.

(1) *Distinctiveness*. It must be a rule in some distinctive sense, as contrasted, for example, with definitions, empirical generalizations, and nomological principles. The word 'rule' is used rather freely, especially in learned and quasi-learned discourse; and many items so called do not count as belonging to the category of rules, rather than to some of the others just mentioned.[5] If the rule theory is to be supported by the rationale sketched above, the rules involved will have to be such that, unlike empirical generalizations and natural laws, they have implications as to the conditions under which a certain kind of behavior is right or wrong, correct or incorrect;[6] and they will have to be such that they are modifiable at will. An adequate formulation of a rule will represent it in such a way that these implications are made clear.

The examples from Carnap do not satisfy this requirement. His formulations do present facts about a language (assuming we know how to interpret the connectives 'designates' and '—', the author not being very forthcoming on this), but as they stand they do not formulate *rules* in any distinctive sense of the term. If it is a fact that in a certain language pr_1 designates the property of being large, then it follows from the rule theory that this is the case because there is some rule governing the employment of pr_1 in that language. But Carnap does not tell us what that rule is. He does not specify what may, must, or must not be done with pr, or the conditions under which it may, must, or must not be uttered. His formulation does nothing to make explicit the conditions under which behavior involving the expression is correct or incorrect, right or wrong. The same comment is to be made for his "rules of truth". They make explicit the necessary and sufficient conditions of a sentence's having the property of being true, but they do not make explicit what moves with the sentence are permitted, required, or forbidden. Thus they are not formulations of *rules* in any distinctive sense, any more than any other statements of necessary and sufficient conditions like "Lead melts if and only if it is heated to 327 degrees F".[7] The same comments apply to the dictionary entry in the quotation from Katz.[8] In all these cases we are presented with se-

---

[5] To illustrate this with something outside semantics, Arthur Koestler 1968 develops an extremely general notion of the "holon". One of his general principles is: "Functional holons are governed by fixed sets of rules and display more or less flexible strategies" (342). In applying this to atoms conceived as holons he speaks of "the rule-governed interactions between nucleus and outer electron shells" (62). However, it is clear that these "rules" are more felicitously called "natural laws". They are not rules in a distinctive sense in which the fact that a rule holds sets up implications as to what behavior is right or wrong, correct or incorrect.
[6] This requirement would seem to prevent Searle from counting his "constitutive" rules as rules (1969, 2.5). See the discussion of this in 8.2.
[7] The same stricture applies to the popular view that the meaning of a predicate is a "function" from possible worlds (perhaps together with other items) to extensions (see Lewis 1972). Such formulations do not make explicit what may or may not be done with any expression.
[8] Katz says, "Accordingly we may regard the dictionary as a finite list of rules, called 'dictionary entries', each of which pairs a word with a representation of its meaning in some normal form" (1966, 154).

mantic statements that the rule theory aims to explicate in terms of rules, rather than the rules themselves; we are given the explicandum, not the explicans.

(2) *Translinguistic connection.* It must effect a connection between a linguistic expression and what, in these matters, is quaintly called "the world", that is, between the expression and those states of affairs, largely though not exclusively nonlinguistic, which the expression is used to talk about. For the meaning of an expression is what enables it to be used in talking about one thing rather than another. This is the point that lies behind the Carnap-Morris view that semantics, as contrasted with syntactics on the one side and pragmatics on the other, is concerned with the relation between symbols and their "designata"; it also lies behind the popular view that for a bit of language to have a meaning is for it to "refer" to something. These latter formulations reflect the point in much too restrictive a way, for it is not the case that all meaningful linguistic expressions designate or refer to something, in any distinctive senses of the terms 'designate' and 'refer'.[9] Any formulation that, like those just mentioned, views all meaningful linguistic expressions as performing the same semantic function is bound to fail. Members of structurally different linguistic categories perform different semantic functions; that is what linguistic structure is all about. My own formulation in terms of "what an expression is used to talk about" is overgeneralized in a different way. It characterizes all meaningful linguistic expressions in terms that are distinctively appropriate to sentences. It is a sentence that is usable to say something, to "talk about something". A subsentential unit like a word cannot be the vehicle of a complete message, except where used elliptically for a sentence. The least complicated unconfused way of formulating the present requirement is one based on a distinction between sentences and their meaningful components. Using that distinction we can say that (a) it is by virtue of having a certain meaning that a *sentence* is rendered usable for saying one thing rather than another, and (b) it is by virtue of having a certain meaning that a *word* is rendered usable to make a certain distinctive contribution to what is sayable by various sentences in which it occurs. Sentence meaning ties a sentence to a complete communicable content, while word meaning ties a word to something that is potentially a part of many complete communicable contents. And since these "contents" generally have to do with extralinguistic matters, semantic rules will, in general, have to relate the expression to the extralinguistic world.[10]

---

[9] So far as 'refer' is concerned, I agree with Strawson that no linguistic expression refers to anything. It is rather that some expressions are such that one can use a given expression of that type to refer to various things on various occasions. But that is another story.

[10] The necessity for this requirement is also indicated by the oft-noted point that one could have practical mastery of an indefinite number of purely intralinguistic rules that govern a particular language, e.g., Japanese, and still not know the meanings of any Japanese words or

Not all semantic rules have to be of this form. Once some expressions have been given meaning by translinguistic rules, the meanings of other expressions can be specified by rules of intersubstitutability, as in the classic form of definitions. If we have already specified the meanings of 'female' and 'fox', then the meaning of 'vixen' can be given by formulating a rule that permits the substitution of 'vixen' for 'female fox'. This is unproblematic. The real difficulty comes in giving appropriate formulations of the basic semantical rules, those that do not presuppose other semantic rules. And for those the present requirement holds.

Among our examples II. (A1. and B.), and III. run afoul of this requirement. What they present as semantic rules are simply definitions of the standard replacement type. Whether it is explicitly formulated as a rule, as in the Black example, or not, as in the Carnap examples, it equally fails to satisfy the present requirement.

(3) *Scope.* The rules must govern first-level speech behavior, rather than (just) secondary metalinguistic activity on the part of grammarians, lexicographers, and other persons involved in describing and theorizing about language.

This requirement, like (1), stems from the basic rationale for the rule theory. What emerged from those considerations was the thesis that a language consists of a system of rules, and that what one learns when one learns a language is the practical mastery of that set of rules. More specifically, with respect to the semantic side of language the upshot was that in learning the meanings of words and in learning how to interpret sentences in a language, one acquires practical mastery of rules and comes to act in the light of them. Rules such that learning a language consists in acquiring a practical mastery of them must govern activities engaged in by any fluent speaker of the language, such as making assertions, requests, and promises, asking questions, and expressing feelings and attitudes.

With the possible exception of IV. all our examples that are rules in a distinctive sense govern first-level speech.[11] The status of the Katz rules is not so clear. In Katz and Fodor 1963 the authors maintain that the use of

---

be able to understand Japanese sentences and use them properly in communication. By virtue of knowing such rules one could know how to construct grammatical phrases and sentences and how to avoid constructing ungrammatical ones; one could know which substitutions could be made without changing meaning, and what sentences are paraphrases of a given sentence. One could know all this on the basis of intralinguistic rules, but if such rules were all that one had mastered, one would not know the meanings of any Japanese words or sentences. But this familiar line of argument, unlike the one presented above, does not proceed on the basis of any positive notion of the nature and function of linguistic meaning.

[11] Turning again to the popular idea that a meaning is a function from possible worlds to extensions, it would seem that insofar as the statement of such a function can be construed as a rule in a distinctive sense of the term, it will govern only very sophisticated higher-level behavior, namely, assigning extensions to expressions in various possible worlds.

a projection rule like IVB. is an essential part of the fluent speaker's exercise of his fluency.

> What the fluent speaker has at his disposal . . . are rules for applying the information in the dictionary which take account of semantic relations between morphemes and the interaction between meaning and syntactic structure in determining the correct semantic interpretation for any of the infinitely many sentences the grammar generates. (493)

Again, Katz in 1966 speaks of the "semantic component" as "a statement of the rules by which he (a speaker of the language) interprets sentences as meaningful messages" (111). But sometimes the relation between the rules formulated by the linguist in describing the language and the rules utilized by the native speaker of the language is specified as something short of identity.

> Hence, for the semantic component to reconstruct the principles underlying the speaker's semantic competence, the rules of the semantic component must *simulate* the operation of these principles by projecting representations of the meaning of higher level constituents from representations of the meaning of the lower level constituents that comprise them. (Katz 1966, 152, my emphasis)

> Thus, these rules (projection rules) provide a *reconstruction* of the process by which a speaker utilizes his knowledge of the dictionary to obtain the meanings of any syntactically compound constituent, including sentences. (161–162, my emphasis)

Whatever the exact intent of these authors, there are some problems here. First, although we can well imagine a *hearer* interpreting sentences by constructing readings for those sentences in the manner indicated by the projection rules, it is not clear how such rules would be used by the *speaker*. She is going in the opposite direction; she doesn't assign a "reading" to a given sentence, but (if she does anything at all of this general character) she finds a sentence to match a given "reading". Thus if she uses any rules of this ilk, they will have to be differently constituted. Second, even if a hearer does, in some sense, make use of the projection rules, it is not clear that they function as rules in the distinctive sense explained above. If hearers derive readings for sentences in anything like the way described by Fodor and Katz, they don't do so consciously. And it is not clear that "rules" governing unconscious cognitive operations are rules in our distinctive sense, in which they determine certain moves as right or wrong, correct or incorrect. Perhaps they are better understood as describing the normal operation of a *mechanism*, in which case they would no more furnish a basis for accusing someone of a rule violation than would an account of the normal operations of a gasoline engine. A linguist might consciously construct a reading for a sentence by using projection rules, but then the rule would not be governing first-level speech.

After elaborating my account of sentence meaning in terms of illocutionary rules I will return to these requirements and point out that illocutionary rules satisfy all of them.

iv. Progressive Complication of Illocutionary Rules

I now return to the task of developing a way of formulating I-rules that will enable them to do the jobs I have assigned to them. To guide this investigation I will make explicit the constraints these formulations must satisfy.

1. An I-rule lays down necessary and sufficient conditions for the utterance of the sentence it governs. This is required because of the basic rationale for such rules—that they specify conditions under which utterances are correct or incorrect, right or wrong, permissible or impermissible. They must specify sufficient conditions if they are to determine that a given utterance is correct, and they must specify necessary conditions if they are to determine that a given utterance is incorrect.

2. Being governed by a certain I-rule endows a sentence with a certain meaning.

3. And since I am assuming an IA potential account of sentence meaning, it follows from that and 2. that being governed by a certain I-rule endows a sentence with a certain IA potential, the potential for being used to perform IA's of the *matching* type, as we saw in Chapter 6.

4. And, following the D8. definition of R'ing, what it is for U to R that p in uttering sentence S, is for U to utter S as subject to an I-rule that requires that p as a condition of correct utterance. In the course of this chapter we will see that in order to maintain 1., 2., and 3., we will have to move beyond the simplest understanding of 4., in which there is an identity between what is required by the I-rule governing S and what is R'd by U in performing an IA of the matching type. But we won't get into that until Section v, where we treat reference and ellipticity.

In this section I will deal with certain difficulties for construing I-rules as satisfying constraint 1., none of which needs such radical surgery. To lay these out consider the following features of speech that seem to imply that one can be completely in order in uttering a sentence, S, while not conforming to what is required for permissible utterance by an I-rule that governs that sentence.

A. As I have noted earlier, it is always possible to make a nonillocutionary use of a sentence, as when one is testing a microphone, provided the speaker does so in a situation where it would not be taken as obvious that she was making some illocutionary use instead. In such a situation one can legitimately say 'Grass is purple' even though grass is not purple. Hence, how can it be required for permissible utterance of 'Grass is purple' that grass be purple?

B. There are figurative uses of a sentence, in which the speaker is doing something that is derived in some systematic fashion from the matching illocutionary act potential. I may be speaking metaphorically when I say 'The door is open', meaning thereby that the time is propitious for suggesting a resolution of a conflict. In that case my utterance could be perfectly in order even if no door at all is open.

C. There are also what we might call "parasitic" uses. If I am speaking a line in a play in saying 'My wife is angry', my utterance may be perfectly in order even though my wife is not angry. Again, I may be speaking ironically when I say 'What a nice day!', meaning that the weather is terrible. Both these cases are parasitic on more straightforward uses of sentences to assert seriously that one's wife is angry or to remark sincerely that it is a nice day.

D. Many sentences in natural languages have more than one meaning ("multivocality") and, correspondingly, more than one illocutionary act potential. Consider 'A good hand is much appreciated'. This sentence has the following meanings. *A round of applause is much appreciated. A favorable collocation of cards in a card game is much appreciated.*[12] But obviously neither of these underlined conditions can be required for correct utterance. For if U is employing the sentence in the first sense, the second condition is not required, and vice versa for the other.

D., multivocality, poses somewhat different and more complex problems than the other three. We can handle A.–C. in a simple way by a restriction on the sphere in which the I-rule applies. They all have to do with the possibility of using even a univocal (only one meaning) sentence to do something other than what its meaning in the language most directly fits it to do. The meaning of 'The door is open' (S) consists in what we can call a "basic" or "literal" illocutionary act potential—usability to *assert of a certain door that it is open*. This is its matching IA potential. But since S can, with suitable arrangements, legitimately be used to do various other things, the necessity and sufficiency of the condition that *the door in question is open* holds only within a certain sphere of activity. It holds only when the speaker directly exploits the literal meaning of the sentence, only when that game is being played. When something else is afoot, this requirement does not apply. The game analogy was deliberate. As intimated at the end of Chapter 3, it is typical of rules of games to be applicable only when the game is being played. When we are playing bridge, I

---

[12] There are more meanings than this, but these two will serve for purposes of illustration.

am required to follow suit if possible. But if we are just successively throwing cards on the table to see what patterns they will make, I am subject to no such requirement.[13] Analogously, an I-rule applies only when the game of *directly exploiting the meaning of the sentence for communicative purposes* is being played. One isn't playing that game when testing a microphone or when speaking figuratively or in a play.

This ties in with the point that the speaker has some say as to whether the relevant I-rule applies to a particular utterance of the sentence. I-rules do not apply willy-nilly to actions of a certain sort, the way moral rules or traffic regulations do. This is because, within limits, I can choose whether I am engaging in the relevant activity at the moment at which I utter the sentence. This is only within limits, because unless I give or exploit some indication that I am not playing *the direct exploitation of meaning* game, I may rightfully be taken to do so.[14] In the same way a batter who, without having previously called time out, takes a healthy swing at a pitch and then claims he was merely loosening up will not be allowed to get away with it. He was playing baseball at that moment, whatever his protestations.

How are we to build this point into our formulations of I-rules? By incorporating into each formulation a specification of the sphere of activity within which the rule applies. Thus an I-rule for 'The door is open' could be reformulated as:

R2: SI may be uttered in the *literal, first-order, communicative* use of language *iff* the door in question is open.

Here "literal" rules out figurative uses; "first-order" rules out parasitic uses; and "communicative" rules out nonillocutionary uses.

Rather than putting all this into each rule, I will formulate the rules subject to the tacit assumption that they will apply only to the kind of speech activity in question. This is what we do in giving rules of games. The whole set of rules is thought of as rules for playing tennis, rules to which one is subject only when playing tennis. But we don't bother to preface each rule with "When playing tennis . . .". The choice between these alternatives is a matter of bookkeeping, rather than anything more substantive.

This way of formulating I-rules may give rise to worries about circularity, similar to those we encountered in Chapter 6 in connection with the notion of a matching illocutionary act. We have been using semantic terms like 'literal' and 'exploiting the meaning of' in demarcating the sphere within which the rule applies. But doesn't that mean that an account of

---

[13] There are also analogues outside games strictly so called. The requirement of asking for permission to speak applies when one is participating in a certain kind of deliberative assembly, but not at a dinner party.

[14] See 5.9 for more on this.

sentence meaning in terms of subjection to I-rules is infected with vicious circularity? No, it does not.

1. First and most important, there is the point that we do not seek to give a classical *definition* or reductive analysis of the concept of sentence meaning. For more on this see the last paragraph of 6.8.

2. But even if we did, there would be no circularity. In this respect the present problem is unlike that raised by the fact that the notion of a matching illocutionary act appears in the account of sentence meaning. That would introduce circularity if a classical, reductive definition of sentence meaning were aimed at, as I pointed out in 6.7. But the restrictions on the sphere of activity in which the rule applies pose no such threat. For what appears in the analysis of sentence meaning is not any particular illocutionary rules, but rather the general concept of an illocutionary rule. *What it is for a sentence to have a certain meaning is for it to be subject to a certain illocutionary rule.* The general concept of an illocutionary rule does not contain any of the semantic concepts in question. It is simply the concept of a rule that is such that by being subject to the rule a sentence possesses a certain illocutionary act potential. We can grasp that general concept without getting into the question of how to formulate such rules or how to specify the activities to which they apply.

Note that although this restriction on I-rules enables us to formulate a rule such that subjection to the rule renders a sentence usable to perform the matching IA, it does not help us to understand how the R'ing involved in a figurative or parasitic IA is related to I-rule subjection. We will tackle that problem in Section viii.

Next, let's consider how to deal with difficulty D.— *multivocality*. When one is using the sentence to perform one of the illocutionary acts in its potential, one is not R'ing the conditions that pertain to the other acts, except insofar as there is overlap. Hence there is not a rule in force that requires the conditions associated with any one of the acts as necessary for permissible utterance.

In thinking about this we may be struck by the fact that even though 'A good hand is much appreciated' can be used to make either of the two assertions mentioned, it cannot be used in any old context to make each of them. If the immediately preceding conversation concerned Strasnick's recent piano recital, and nothing has been said about Strasnick's involvement in card games, then it would be out of order to use that sentence, without special notice, to assert that a favorable collocation of cards is much appreciated. This may encourage us to think that wherever we have a sentence with multiple IA potentials, those potentials are distributed among types of contexts in such a way that the sentence will be correctly used to perform illocutionary act I_1 only if the context of utterance is of type C_1. If that were the case, the illocutionary rule for 'A good hand is much appreciated' (S2) could be of this form.

R3: S2 may be uttered in contexts of type C_1 *only if*:
   A. A lot of applause is much appreciated.
R4: S2 may be uttered in contexts of type C_2 *only if*:
   A. A favorable collocation of cards is much appreciated.
. . . .

But this move will not work for the following reasons. First, it is dubious that illocutionary act potentials are correlated with types of context in the way required. The method will not work if there are contexts in which a sentence could properly be used to perform more than one illocutionary act in its potential. In that case a condition that is associated with one of these acts and not the other is not required for permissible utterance of the sentence in that context. Hence no rule of the form just exemplified will be applicable. And it seems that there are such contexts. In the course of discussing someone's recent behavior I say "A normal person wouldn't have done that", where nothing in the context indicates either that I am asserting that the *average* person wouldn't have done that or that I am asserting that a *well-adjusted* person wouldn't have done that. Is it not still legitimate for me to be making either of those assertions? No doubt, it would have been better for me to give some clue to my audience as to how I am using the word 'normal'. But we do allow this sort of thing, perhaps because it is always possible for the speaker to subsequently use a less ambiguous sentence to explain her intent if it appears that she was misunderstood.

But suppose there is no context in which more than one illocutionary act can be correctly performed by a given sentence. There is another reason for avoiding building contextual restrictions into illocutionary rules. There is not, in general, any way of specifying the type of context appropriate for a given illocutionary act type, except by utilizing the concept of that type, or something uncomfortably close to it. In what sort of context is it permissible to use 'A good hand is much appreciated' to assert that a lot of applause is much appreciated? I don't know of any general specification that will work except "contexts in which it is appropriate to use the sentence to assert that a lot of applause is much appreciated". And if so, this style of formulation winds up saying, trivially, that in a context in which condition A is required for correct utterance, condition A is required for correct utterance.

Note that the difficulty could be easily resolved if each I-rule simply states a sufficient condition of permissible utterance. Then we would have a separate rule for each distinct meaning of the sentence. But since this would violate the first constraint on I-rules, I will not pursue it.

We have been running into dead ends. But there is an effective solution to our dilemma. I have been neglecting the point that on my theory of sentence meaning subjection to an I-rule endows a sentence *with a certain meaning*. The application of this principle to a multivocal sentence would not be a single I-rule that covers all the sentence's meaning, but a different I-rule for each sentence meaning.[15] Each I-rule would specify sufficient and necessary conditions for correct utterance, not for the sentence *überhaupt* (with the restrictions of sphere of application already specified in this section) but for the sentence when used with a particular one of its meanings. Thus one of these rules for S2 would read:

R5: S2, when used to mean that a lot of applause is much appreciated, may be uttered iff a lot of applause is much appreciated.

This might seem to give rise to circularity, analogous to that which seemed to arise from the restriction of the sphere of application of I-rules to the "literal, first-order, communicative use of language". For R5 requires us to specify the relevant meaning of the sentence within the I-rule subjection to which is supposed to endow the sentence with that meaning. But the threat is toothless for the reasons given in connection with that restriction. First, there can be no circularity because no definition or reductive analysis of sentence meaning is intended. Second, even if this were intended, there would be no circularity because the analysis of sentence meaning would make no reference to the content of any particular rule but only to the concept of *being subject to (some) I-rule*.

Since the theory is designed specifically for intentional IA's (even if there can be unintentional specimens), the restriction of each rule to the sentence used with meaning M1 is, in effect, a restriction to utterances of the sentence with a certain speaker intention. Indeed, in 3.6 we already laid it down that interpersonal IA's require a certain intention of the speaker, an intention that the audience, H, should realize what IA he is performing, which amounts in practice to intending that H realize what conditions he is satisfying. It was tacitly assumed there that the successful carrying out of this intention would be effected, when it is, by H's knowledge of the language, more specifically by H's knowledge of the meaning of the sentence uttered. But now that we have taken multivocality seriously, we see that in those cases (which are very common in natural languages) a general knowledge of the semantic status of the sentence in the language will not suffice. H must also know which of the meanings of the sentence U means to be exploiting. And this means that there is a further requirement on U here, to see to it that H is given sufficient clues as to which of the meanings it is with which U is using the sentence on that occasion. Adding this to R5 we get:

[15] In 7.5 I will discuss a way of formulating a single I-rule for a multivocal sentence, a way that runs into a fatal difficulty that will be first explained in connection with problems of reference.

R6: S₂, when used by U to mean that a lot of applause is much appreciated, may be uttered iff:
1. A lot of applause is much appreciated.
2. U takes reasonable precautions to see to it that H is given an indication of which meaning it is with which U employs the sentence on this occasion.

v. How to Handle Ellipticity and Singular Reference

There are two additional complications—E. ellipticity and F. reference—that pose more serious and far-reaching problems, especially the latter.

E. Ellipticity. I may be speaking elliptically, as when I say 'She's coming' in answer to the question 'Is she coming to the party?'. In saying what I did in that context I R'd that she is coming to the party, but it would be a mistake to make it a requirement for permissible utterance of 'She's coming' that the person referred to by 'she' is coming to the party referred to in the above context. 'She's coming' can be used elliptically to assert of any female person (or object treated as such, like a ship) that she is coming to any one of a variety of destinations.

F. Singular reference. Since, as I have repeatedly noted, reference is underdetermined by meaning, I can quite properly use 'The door is open', in its standard meaning, to say of any one of indefinitely many doors that it is open. But when I do so in a particular case, I say of a specific door, D, that it is open and hence R that D is open. But obviously the I-rule governing the sentence doesn't require as a condition of permissible utterance that D be open. If it did, the sentence would not be usable to assert this of each of indefinitely many other doors.

I treat E. and F. in the same section because of the following similarity. The matching IA type for a sentence that involves singular reference by a typical referring expression, or that is typically used elliptically, is a *determinable*. For 'The door is open', it is *asserting that a certain particular door is open*. That type is restricted to no one particular door. The same point can be made of sentences containing pronouns like 'I', 'she', 'this', 'you', other "incomplete" definite descriptions like 'the door', proper names each of which can be used as the name of indefinitely many items, and definite descriptions containing referring expressions of the above types, for example, 'the cabinet John gave me'. Turning to sentences apt for ellipsis, for 'Yes' the matching IA type is *giving an affirmative answer to a yes-no question*. Doing that is obviously not restricted to a particular propositional content. It can involve any proposition that can be the content of a yes-no question, that is, any proposition whatever. But, as pointed out in 6.8, one cannot perform a determinable IA type without performing some determinate thereof. I can't "assert that a certain particular door is open" without asserting that of one unique door.[16] Nor can I give an affirmative answer to a question without asserting some particular proposition in doing so. This means that both E. and F. are such that one cannot perform a token of the matching (determinable) IA type without performing a token of a determinate IA type that involves R'ing something more specific than what is required by the I-rule governing the sentence. And that is why they pose problems for our account. This problem is not, as with A.–D., that the obvious I-rule in each case requires something without which the sentence can be permissibly uttered. It is rather that the obvious I-rule requires something less than is R'd in a standard use of the sentence with the meaning in question.

Thus the problem with E. and F. is, in a way, the opposite of that with A.–D. With the latter the problem is that there are correct employments of the sentence in question in which what is R'd is either nothing (A.), or something quite different from what is required by an I-rule constructed on the basis of the (or a) matching IA type (B.–C.), or less than the obvious I-rule would require (D.) So to handle A.–D. we had to qualify or reconstrue I-rules in such a way that they do not unqualifiedly require what is R'd when one performs the (or a) matching IA type. What these cases show is that building the I-rule by unqualifiedly requiring what is R'd in performing the (or a) matching IA type results in requiring "too much", or the wrong sort of thing. Hence the solution is to put restrictions on the contexts in which that is required. But E. and F. pose quite different problems. Here what is required by the I-rule is rather "too little". It is too unspecific to give us all that is required for a determinate of that determinable type.

Hence we are faced with the problem of how to formulate an I-rule that will give the sentence the potential to be used to perform any one of indefinitely many determinates that fall under the determinable matching IA type. The general line of the solution is clear. Since the meaning of the sentence determines only an unspecific type, a contribution from the context is needed to convert this into a specific determinate form thereof. And the I-rule will have to make provision for this without requiring any particular exploitation of that provision. For it has to render the sentence usable for performing *any* of the determinates that fall under the determinable matching IA type. Let's see how this works out for our two types of cases, beginning with ellipticity.

Since the present problem concerns how to formulate rules governing

---

[16] There is an obvious construal of the phrase "assert that a certain particular door is open" in which I can do this by a standard employment of 'There is a certain particular door that is open'. Here I perform the IA in question without making any assertion about any particular door. But in using 'assert that a certain particular door is open' to give the matching IA type for 'The door is open', I understand that phrase in such a way that one can't be asserting that some particular door is open without asserting *of* some particular door that it is open.

sentences, we are not concerned with cases of ellipticity that do not involve sentence utterance. But to apply this point some tough calls are required as to what counts as a sentence. In answer to "Would you like tea or coffee?" I reply "Tea". My utterance was elliptical for "I would like tea", but is what I uttered a sentence? Rather than clutter this presentation with a critical discussion of sententiality, I will rule for present purposes that anything used elliptically for a sentence will thereby count enough as a sentence (or sentence surrogate) to have a meaning dependent on an I-rule. So when 'tea' is used as in the above, rather than as a constituent of a sentence, we will think of it as functioning as a sentence surrogate and as such governed by an I-rule, as much as a stronger candidate for sentencehood like 'Yes". Consider "Yes" in answer to "Is lye an alkali?". We may say that the matching IA type for 'Yes' in its standard meaning is *giving an affirmative answer to a yes-no question*. This is a determinable IA type, each determinate falling under which would be an assertion of an answer to a particular question. And the I-rule governing the use of 'Yes' with that meaning is:

R7: "Yes" may be uttered in the literal, first-order, communicative use of language *iff*
A. There are contextual indications of a particular yes-no question to which 'Yes' is offered as an answer.
B. The correct answer to this question is affirmative.

Here A. requires that the context indicate a particular yes-no question as the one to which this utterance of "Yes" is an answer. If that condition is satisfied, the question so indicated provides the propositional content of the assertion made by "Yes". That is, it provides the propositional content of the declarative sentence for which 'Yes' is elliptical. And B. requires the truth of that proposition. 'Yes' carries more definite indications of what sort of thing to look for to discover the determinate IA type in a particular case than other elliptical expressions like 'Tea'. There the sentence for which it is elliptical could be anything into which 'tea' fits grammatically—'That's tea', 'A major agricultural product of India is tea', 'I am drinking tea'. . . . .

Now for the reference problem, F. It would greatly simplify matters if we could handle this in the same way as E. This would involve treating a particular utterance of 'The door is open' as elliptical for a sentence that picks out a particular door by a "logically proper name" of that door, an expression that is restricted by its meaning to referring to that door and only that door. But we can't, because in general we cannot find any such expression in a natural language. We can, occasionally, pick out a particular individual by a purely qualitative definite description ('the first human being to make fire'). But that is the exception rather than the rule. Most singular referring expressions in natural languages are suited by their meaning to be used to refer to each of many particular individuals.

How, then, are we to formulate a rule that will render 'The door is open' (S_1) usable to assert of any particular door, D, that it is open? Since we can't require any particular door to be open, we must find some appropriate generalization of that requirement, a generalization that can be conformed to in a particular case only if some particular door is open. The simplest move would be to existentially generalize the condition associated with a particular singular assertion of this class, such as the assertion that D is open. This would give us:

R8: S_1 may be uttered *iff* there is an x such that:
    A. x is a door.
    B. x is open.

But this is grotesquely unsuitable for the purpose. If I were to utter a sentence R'ing those and just those conditions, I would not be making an assertion about a particular door or about any other individual thing. I would be asserting that there is at least one open door in the world. R8 is a suitable rule for a sentence like 'There are open doors' or 'Some doors are open'.

Clearly, R8 gets too far away from requiring of some particular door that it be open; it misses singular reference altogether. We need to find a generalized requirement such that when someone subjects his utterance to this requirement in a particular case, he will thereby be R'ing that some particular door is open, that is, a rule that, as I put it first in 3.5, requires, *in application to this case*, that D is open. The I-rule must require something of the speaker that will ensure that his assertion is about (or at least is intended to be about) some particular door. And this requirement must be such that the unique door picked out in any particular application of the rule must be the one referred to by the speaker. But what uniqueness requirement will do this trick?

The simplest suggestion is that the x in question be the one referred to by the speaker.

R9: S_1 may be uttered by U at time t *iff* there is exactly one x such that:
    A. x is a door.
    B. U refers to x at t in uttering S1.
    C. x is open.

As presently formulated this rule seems to give the speaker unrestricted license to refer to any door he pleases when uttering S_1, whatever the circumstances. But, just as in the multivocality case, we can't suppose the linguistic community to be that permissive. One is out of order if he uses, or tries to use, 'the door' to refer to door d_1 when the context plainly points to d_2 as the door under discussion, or even when nothing in the context gives any clue as to what door U is talking about. Therefore let's enrich condition B. as follows.

R10: S_1 may be uttered *iff* there is exactly one x such that:
   A. x is a door.
   B. In uttering S1, U refers to x.
   C. U takes reasonable precautions to see to it that the audience is in a position to determine which x it is to which he is referring.
   D. x is open.

It is clear that when one utters S_1 as subject to this rule *and conforms to at least A. and B.*,[17] one will thereby be asserting that some particular door is open. For by virtue of conforming to A. and B., there is some particular x to which one is referring and which is a door, and by virtue of uttering S_1 as subject to the rule, one is R'ing that this door is open, as well as R'ing that it is a door and that one is referring to it. Hence, since S_1 is the right sort of sentence for the purpose, one is asserting that that door is open.

It is natural to feel that this is too easy a way out. Reference is itself a major problem in philosophy of language, and it would add to the significance of this book if it presented an adequate account of reference as a spin-off from the IA potential theory of meaning. And at an earlier stage of this enterprise I thought, mistakenly I now see, that I had a way of doing that. Since the reason this doesn't work turns out to be instructive, I will briefly indicate how that goes.

First, the attempt. Referring is, by almost common consent, not an autonomous speech act. I can't just refer to Susie and let it go at that. When I refer to something I do so in the course of performing some illocutionary act that has to do with that something. I refer to a certain paper you are working on in promising to read it, or in commending you for having finished it, or in exhorting you to finish it, or in remarking that it is longer than necessary. But since, on my theory, an illocutionary act gets its content from what the speaker R's, the act will have to do with a certain individual just in case the speaker is R'ing various conditions concerned with that individual. I refer to my wife in saying 'She's my chief support' *iff* my wife is the one I R to be my chief support. A particular pile of papers is

---

[17] After we get this rule into more satisfactory shape, we shall have more to say about the roles of rule subjection and rule conformity in performing singular illocutionary acts. One objection to this formulation is that it fails to conform to my general model that it is rule subjection rather than rule conformity that is required for performing the matching illocutionary act.

what I refer to when I say 'Take it away' *iff* that pile of papers is what I R that I want taken away and what I R that it is possible for the addressee to take away. This suggests that we can explain what it is to refer to x in a speech act by saying that it is to R that ... x ... in performing that speech act. Let's apply this idea to the task of formulating an I-rule for S₁ that will both fit it for saying of any door that it is open, and be such that it can be conformed to in a particular case only by saying of a particular door that it is open.

R11: S_1 may be uttered *iff* there is exactly one x such that:
A. x is a door.
B. In uttering S₁ U R's that x is open, taking reasonable precautions to see to it that the audience is in a position to determine which x it is which U is R'ing to be open.
C. x is open.

Now for why this doesn't work. It runs into conflict with my favored way of explaining R'ing, in terms of subjecting one's utterance to a certain I-rule. To see this, ask whether that explanation can be used to specify what it is for U to R that the unique x in question is open. If it can, what I-rule is such that by virtue of subjecting the utterance to it U R's that that x is open? Remember that R11 does not require U to R, with respect to any particular x, that it is open; it requires only that there be some particular x or other of which U R's this. That is why D8, the explanation of R'ing in terms of rule subjection, included the saving phrase "in application to this case". This suggests that when U does R that x is open, for some particular x, the rule requires, *in application to that case*, that U does so R. But by virtue of what does R11 require that in application to that case? Not, as we have seen, by its explicit content. Clearly, there is this further requirement here only because this x is the one U R's to be open. And see where this has brought us. The rule, in application to this case, requires that U R's *that* x to be open, because and only because that is the one that U does R to be open! So far from the R'ing being explained or constituted by subjection to that rule, the requirement in question is laid on U by the fact that U R's that the x in question is open. So the R'ing is what lays this requirement on U to R that x is open, rather than the subjection to this rule being what engenders the R'ing. The explanation is going in the opposite direction. Hence we cannot both recognize that in uttering S₁ U R's that this particular x is open *and* hold that R'ing is (always) a matter of subjecting one's utterance to an I-rule.

Hence this way of dealing with the problem of singular sentences does not work so long as D8 is accepted as an explanation of what it is to R. We could, of course, keep this way of formulating I-rules for singular sentences by abandoning D8 and going back to the earlier account of R'ing that p, the one in terms of laying oneself open to blame or other negative sanction in case of not-p. But I am too convinced of the conceptual necessity of rule governance for being rightly liable to blame for that tactic to appeal to me. I could not in good conscience turn my back on the dependence of such normative statuses on rules. That is why I included my fourth constraint on I-rules at the beginning of iv. Hence I will forego any benefits to be gained by the approach to reference I have just been discussing.

I can now make good on my promise in Section iv to explain why my earlier attempt to construe a multivocal sentence as governed by a single I-rule doesn't work. The suggested rule was as follows (assuming that 'A good hand is much appreciated' has only two meanings):

R12: 'A good hand is much appreciated' may be uttered *iff* at least one of the following sets of conditions holds.

A.

1. A lot of applause is much appreciated.
2. U R's 1., taking reasonable precautions to see to it that his audience is in a position to ascertain this.

B.

1. A favorable collocation of cards is much appreciated.
2. U R's 1., taking reasonable precautions to see to it that his audience is in a position to ascertain this.

The attempt here was to use the requirement of R'ing in each case to specify a condition such that if it is satisfied U is making use of one of the meanings of the sentence rather than another. And so, depending on which initial condition is R'd, U will be subject to the right set of conditions for his communicative intent. And since this maneuver depends on putting R'ing in the I-rule it falls victim to the difficulty we have seen to afflict its kin in the referential case. In both cases, we cannot construe the R'ing required by the rule in a particular case in terms of rule subjection, for it is only by R'ing that p that the requirement that U R's that p is imposed on him. Again, the R'ing explains (that piece of) the rule subjection rather than vice versa.

To return to reference, these considerations force us back to using an unexplicated concept of reference in the I-rule formulations. Now that we have grasped that nettle, there are some further points that need to be made.

(1) I must return to the distinction between *de dicto* and *de re* illocutionary acts. To assert that a certain door is open in the *de dicto* sense it is sufficient to subject one's utterance to R10, to take the conditions required by R10 as necessary for correctness. It is not necessary to satisfy any of those conditions. R'ing those conditions is sufficient for *purporting* to refer to a certain door and asserting of *it* that it is open. But to assert that a certain door is open in the *de re* sense (less ambiguously put as 'S asserted *of a certain door* that it is open') is to *succeed* in referring to a certain door and to assert of that door that it is open. This requires not only subjecting one's utterance to R10 but also satisfying at least requirements A. and B. For one has succeeded in referring to a particular door (in the context of this illocutionary act) only if there *is* exactly one door such that one R's it to be open, taking reasonable precautions.... Merely subjecting one's utterance to the rule takes one only as far as intending or purporting to refer to a particular door.

(2) The same utterance can, of course, involve both ellipticity and reference. Consider an elliptical sentence like "She's coming". In addition to being elliptical for a sentence that makes explicit to what she is coming, this sentence and the one for which it is elliptical contain two references underdetermined by meaning. The first is the reference of 'She'. The second will be more explicit in the sentence for which this one is elliptical, for example, 'She's coming to the party'. Which party is being referred to is not determined by the meaning of 'the party'. This means that the I-rule governing 'She's coming' will have to make requirements on the speaker to see to it that both these modes of indeterminacy (elliptical and referential) are resolved. That will give us a rule like this.

> R13: 'She's coming' may be uttered by U in a literal, direct, first-order communicative use of language *iff*:
>
> A. Something in the context indicates what the sentence 'She's coming' is used as elliptical for, where that sentence makes explicit what destination the referent of 'she' is being said to come to.
>
> B. There is exactly one x and exactly one y such that:
>
> 1. x is a female or something (like a ship) treated as a female person.
> 2. y is a destination.
> 3. U refers to x and to y in uttering 'She's coming', taking reasonable precaution to see to it that the audience is in a position to determine which x and which y is being referred to.
> 4. x is coming to y.

These requirements render the sentence usable to make a determinate assertion that falls under both the ellipticity and referential determinables.

(3) To return once more to reference, since I have adjured any attempt to tie this treatment to a theory of reference, I leave open the many questions that come up in the attempt to develop such a theory. I have views on the subject, but this is not the place to present them. Nevertheless, since I-rules are rules subjection to which constitutes a sentence's meaning so-and-so, their content has to reflect the semantics of different kinds of referring expressions. 'The door is open' involves what may be called an "incomplete definite description", one that needs contextual support to achieve unique reference. As such it is typical of ordinary referring devices in that meaning underdetermines reference. But although this feature is common to practically all such devices, the details of the I-rules associated with them will differ. Where a proper name is involved, as in 'John has left the country', we find among the rules a requirement that the unique x be named 'John', rather than that it have a certain property or be of a certain kind. This requirement is flexible enough to allow, in certain cases, for ad hoc naming by the speaker, though not so flexible as to allow that anything goes.[18] Then there are pronouns, where the descriptive content is minimal, or has even evaporated altogether. In 'She's coming', the relevant requirement is that the x in question be female or something treated as female. While with 'It's open', the referring device leaves the field wide open for the identity of the referent, though the predicate confines it to something that can be intelligibly spoken of as "open".

I am not able to give here a complete systematic treatment of the ways the differences in referring expressions affect the content of I-rules. That would involve going into grammar much more than I am prepared to do in this book. I aspire only to give a few illustrations of such differences. But there is one unusual case that I should comment on, especially since it has shaped philosophical treatments of definite descriptions out of all proportion to its incidence in natural languages. This is the case of definite descriptions whose meaning does, or might, uniquely determine a referent, as 'the inventor of the wheel', or 'the tallest man in the history of the species'. It is not guaranteed that such expressions uniquely refer. There may have been no single person who did what is properly called 'inventing the wheel', or it might have been invented simultaneously in widely

---

[18] One may think that this requirement conflicts with a Kripke-Donnellan sort of view of proper names, according to which the use of a proper name is perfectly all right, so long as it is causally connected in a certain way with certain kinds of previous uses of the name. No particular mental attitude on the part of the speaker is required. But remember that R'ing that p need not involve any conscious mental act. It is enough if the speaker take on a disposition to recognize something wrong with the utterance if the x in question is not named 'John'. Moreover, if the view in question really does make no demands on the mental attitudes of the speaker, I hold that it goes too far. At least U would have to intend to be hooking onto certain (which?) previous uses of the name.

separated places. And there may be an n-way tie for tallest man. But still, it seems that if such an expression does uniquely pick out someone, it needs no contextual support to do so. The meaning plus the relevant facts of application are sufficient. Note that these cases must be sharply distinguished from those very numerous cases, sloppily assimilated to the above by many philosophers, in which the reference essentially depends on more typical referring expressions within the definite description—such as 'my computer', 'the tallest man on the team', 'Aristotle's first philosophical writing', or 'the desk in the next room'. In these cases meaning does not uniquely determine reference just because the identity of me (the owner of the computer), the team in question, the particular person named Aristotle being referred to, or the location of the "next room" is not determined by meaning alone. Neglecting this fact, ever so many philosophers have been led into supposing that it is very common for definite descriptions to have a unique reference just by virtue of their meaning, whereas that is a very unusual phenomenon.

However, where we do have such a case, it looks as if the I-rule governing a sentence containing it, such as 'The inventor of the wheel was a genius', will be atypical of the I-rules I have been laying out for singular sentences. For it will not have to deal with problems that stem from the fact that the sentence is usable to say of any one of many different people that they are genuises. But still it will have to allow for the absence of unique reference. And so the I-rule would read:

R14: 'The inventor of the wheel was a genius' may be uttered *iff* there
is exactly one x such that:
1. x invented the wheel.
2. x is a genius.

This is much simpler than the I-rule for 'The door is open'. But at a cost. For it turns out that the meaning thus engendered for 'The inventor of the wheel was a genius' makes it not a singular statement (a statement about some particular object), but an existentially quantified statement. With 'The door is open', even though what the I-rule requires is in the uniquely existentially quantified form, the singular character of any assertion the sentence is standardly usable to make is preserved by the requirement that U refers to some particular door. But we have no such saving clause in the rule for 'The inventor of the wheel was a genius'.

Interestingly enough, this result dovetails nicely with the implausibility of supposing that when someone who has no connection with whoever invented the wheel and indeed knows nothing of such a person, if any, except that he invented the wheel, assertively utters this sentence, understanding what he is saying, this shows that he has a certain person "in mind". Hence we are loath to suppose that such an assertion could be a *de re* assertion, *de* the inventor of the wheel. If the assertion is really a disguised existentially quantified one, that would explain this intuition.

vi. Reference, Ellipticity, and R'ing as Rule Subjection

I rejected the above attempt to formulate I-rules without using 're-fer' (exemplified by R11) because it failed constraint 4., which requires compatibility with the account of R'ing in terms of rule subjection. But doesn't the above account of reference run afoul of the same constraint? Isn't it just as true here that when one issues a determinate form of asserting that a certain door is open, one R's something, namely, that the particular door being referred to is open, that is not required by the I-rule governing one's sentence (e.g., 'The door is open')?

No, the cases are fundamentally different. With reference and ellipticity,the formula "R'ing that *p* is subjecting oneself to a rule that, *in application to this case*, requires that *p*" holds, though it doesn't for the rejected I-rules for reference and multivocality. But I need to explain how this is.

First, let's recall the point that a determinable IA type can be exemplified only by performing an act that exemplifies one of the determinate forms of that determinable. For I-rules governing both elliptical and (the usual kind of) singular sentences, the matching IA type is a determinable—giving an affirmative answer to a yes-no question marked out by the context or saying of some particular door that it is open. In each case the I-rule requires that some determinate form of the determinable IA type be performed by each utterance of the sentence, but, obviously, it doesn't require any particular determinate. And so when U says 'The door is open', thereby asserting openness of some particular door, U R's that that particular door is open, but this R'ing is not a matter of just subjecting the utterance to that I-rule. For one could be placing the utterance under R10 and R'ing that some other particular door instead is open. So how are we to construe that R'ing in terms of rule subjection?

What we need to do is to understand how the "in application to this case" clause of D8. works. The key is that the requirement that a particular door, D, be open is engendered by the *satisfaction* of the B. portion of the existential requirement laid down by R10. Since U satisfies the requirement that there be exactly one *x* to which U refers by referring to D, U thereby subjects himself, in this instance, to the requirement that D be open. To spell this out more fully, let's restate what R10 requires for permissible utterance in the appropriate sphere of activity.

There is exactly one *x* such that:

A. *x* is a door.
B. In uttering S1, U refers to *x*.

C. U takes reasonable precautions to see to it that the audience is in a position to determine which x it is to which he is referring.

D. x is open.

If U satisfies this requirement by, inter alia, referring to door O, he thereby subjects his utterance to the requirement that O is open as well as being a door. A complete conformity to R10 is not necessary for this. Satisfaction of condition D. is not required. If it were, then U could not assert of O that it is open unless U were speaking truly. And we don't want to deny that U can falsely assert that O is open. Satisfaction of C. is not necessary either. Suppose that one *has a particular door in mind* (whatever it takes for that) and asserts it to be open, but neglects to do anything to make sure that the audience can tell which door one is talking about. In that case there is certainly something wrong with one's performance, but has the speaker failed to assert of a certain door (the one she has in mind) that it is open? I cannot see that she has failed.[19] She has failed to communicate the intended message to her audience, but I have been arguing all along that such success is not necessary for illocutionary act performance. Thus, when H expresses puzzlement as to what he was saying, U might say "Didn't you hear me? I said that that door over there [pointing] is open." This implies that U was asserting that, even though he culpably failed to make this clear to H.

This verdict might seem to be in conflict with the dictum in 3.6 and elsewhere, that a necessary condition of an interpersonally directed IA is that the speaker utter a sentence with the intention of getting the hearer to realize that the other conditions of the IA are satisfied. But there is no conflict. What I have just rejected is the requirement that one of the conditions U is R'ing be satisfied. But it still remains that U will, if the IA is directed to a hearer, *intend* that the hearer realize that all the conditions that are necessary for the IA have been satisfied. It is just that the "taking reasonable precautions" condition is not one of those; only the *R'ing that one is taking reasonable precautions . . .* has that status.

What about condition A.? Must that be satisfied in order that one makes a singular assertion in uttering 'The door is open'? Certainly one has not made a standard use of 'The door is open' unless one R's of some particular *door* that it is open. We shall see in 7.8 that there are cases in which A. is not satisfied and yet U says of *something* that it is open. But for now let's take it that the satisfaction of A. is part of what engenders a requirement about O in particular.

There are several things to note about this situation. First, since U's

---

[19] By looking back at 3.8 and 3.9 you will see that the accounts of *de re* IA's given there included no analogue of this "taking reasonable precautions . . ." requirement.

R'ing that O is open depends on a partial satisfaction of what is required by the relevant I-rule, we can no longer hold that R'ing is solely a matter of I-rule subjection. Some rule satisfaction comes into the picture as well.

Second, the requirements to which U subjects himself in asserting that O is open are stratified. By virtue of uttering 'The door is open' in its standard meaning (in the literal, first-order, communicative use of language) he subjects himself to what is required by the rule governing 'The door is open' in that meaning, R10. But then by virtue of satisfying part of those requirements, the further requirements are engendered that O is a door, is referred to by U, and is open.

Third, thus far we have considered the case in which U not only R's what is required by R10 but also satisfies part of that requirement. But what about the case in which U subjects his utterance to R10 but fails to satisfy A. and B.? What do we say about that? Here the distinction between *de re* and *de dicto* becomes relevant. U's R'ing what is required by R10 is sufficient for a *de dicto* assertion that a certain door is open. But for a *de re* assertion U must succeed in referring to a particular door and R it to be a door and to be open. Thus our stratification of requirements gives us a neat way of making the *de re*–*de dicto* distinction.

Note the relationship between the *de dicto*–*de re* distinction and the determinable-determinate distinction, as applied to IA's involving singular reference. The distinctions are not coextensive. A determinable referential IA can be *de dicto* or *de re*, or both. I have just brought out the *de dicto* version—to subject one's utterance to R10 (if the sentence is 'The door is open') and to R what that rule requires. To perform a *de re* version of that determinable IA is to do that *and* satisfy at least the first half of that requirement. But, and here is the connection between the two distinctions, to exemplify the *de re* version one must also perform a token of a determinate IA type that falls under that determinate. That involves asserting *of some particular door, O,* that it is open. Thus although a determinable referential IA can be *de dicto* or *de re*, or both, a determinate form there is necessarily *de re*. Another respect in which the distinctions are not coextensive is this. One cannot exemplify the determinate IA type without thereby exemplifying the corresponding determinable one. I cannot assert that O (a particular door) is open without asserting that some particular door is open. But as I distinguished *de dicto* and *de re* in 3.9 in terms of whether U says something of a proposition or of an object, we cannot say that one cannot perform a *de re* assertion without thereby performing the corresponding *de dicto* assertion. Nevertheless the connection remains. The partial satisfaction of the I-rule that is required for a successful performance of the determinate IA is also just what is required for a *de re* assertion.

The above account of singular IA's has an exact parallel with elliptical sentences. The matching IA for 'Yes' is a determinable IA, *giving an affir-*

mative answer to some yes-no question marked out by the context, and the I-rule for "Yes" requires U to perform some determinate under this determinable (give an affirmative answer to some particular question), but does not require an answer to any one question rather than another. Again, if U satisfies the requirements of that I-rule, again except for the provision of sufficient clues for the audience and the truth of the answer, U thereby subjects himself to the requirement of the correctness of an affirmative answer to the particular question selected. Again, we have the same stratification of requirements, the latter dependent on a satisfaction of the former that are laid down by the relevant I-rule. The only lack of parallel is the absence of any analogue for a *de dicto* singular IA. Whereas with a failed attempt at reference there is still an IA, though only *de dicto,* we do not credit someone who says "Yes" to no particular question with having asserted anything at all. No doubt, we could, in which case there would be a "de dicto" elliptical statement. This does not seem to be a deep difference.

So far so good. But I have still not answered the question of how to reconcile this analysis of determinate IA's with the D8. account of R'ing. The above account makes it clear not all the R'ings consist in a mere subjection to the I-rule governing the sentence. D8. does include the qualification, "in application to this case". Taken strictly, this implies that R10, in application to the above case where the assertion was that O is open, requires "in application to that case" that O be open. But is that tenable? How can R10, in application to that case or otherwise, require that D be open, when nothing at all is said about D or any other particular door in the formulation of R10? Moreover, can one and the same rule require something different for different cases while remaining the same rule?

A better construal of the situation would be that when U satisfies the relevant requirements made on him by R10, another rule comes into play, one tailored to the situation engendered by those satisfactions. We might think of this as a rule governing a restricted subset of utterances of the sentence, rather than governing utterances of the sentence in general. Let's use a lowercase 'r' for such rules. We can say that by virtue of U's satisfying the A. and B. portions of R10 with respect to O, U thereby becomes subject to an 'r' rule that reads as follows:

> r10A. 'The door is open' may be uttered by U in the situation in which U satisfies A. and B. of R9 with respect to O only if:
> A. O is a door.
> B. U refers to O.
> C. U gives the audience, H, sufficient indications of what it is to which U is referring.
> D. O is open.

This enables us to construe everything that U R's in asserting that a certain door is open as a matter of U's subjecting his utterance to a certain rule. The only modification is that the rules mentioned by this formulation range over not only I-rules but also the derivative r-rules. r-rules, unlike I-rules, do not endow sentences with meanings. Instead, subjection to them is engendered by something a speaker does on the basis of I-rules. They are creatures of speech, not language. The meaning of 'The door is open' remains the same, whether or not U satisfies A. and B. of R10, and thereby engenders r10A.

The introduction of r-rules adds to the role of the speaker in determining the requirements to which she is subject. All along we have been balancing the demands of society and the free choices of individuals. Both come into the requirements imposed by I-rules. By virtue of the constitution of the language, a social institution, a given sentence is governed by one or more I-rules. You and I have no say in that, except to the very limited extent that we make additions to or modifications in the language. But even with I-rules the speaker has some autonomy. It is up to the speaker whether she is making a communicative, first-order, literal use of the sentence, or some use that contrasts with that in one or another way. But with r-rules we take a further step toward individual autonomy. r-rules are not socially established in the way I-rules are. If no one ever satisfied the relevant requirements of, for example, R10, no rule like r10A would ever come into play. The constitution of the language makes provision for its possibility, but whether that possibility is realized depends on what happens in speech. Here the social side of the contrast is reduced to a minimum. It merely sets up provisions for the possible sway of r-rules, whenever some speaker satisfies the condition for realizing such a possibility.

I hope it will introduce more light than darkness into the situation if I briefly relate this treatment of sentences containing singular referring expressions of the ordinary sort to David Kaplan's (1989) well-known distinction between *character* and *content* for sentences containing indexicals. What I call the meaning (IA potential) of a sentence containing singular referring expressions corresponds to Kaplan's character. It is constant across contexts of utterance and can be represented by a function from contexts to content (roughly what is said). Kaplan's content for such a sentence is closely related to what I have referred to as the content (in my sense) of the referentially determinate *de re* IA performed by uttering the sentence. The main differences from Kaplan's treatment are these. (1) Kaplan does, and I do not, allow for "content" that is less determinate than a fully determinate proposition (e.g., *It is raining* with location and time unspecified.) (2) Whereas my account is designed to cover sentences generally with all kinds of IA potential, Kaplan's is restricted to sentences with the potential to be used in making true or false statements. Hence his treatment is within the Fregean tradition of taking truth values as "extensions" of sentences and has nothing to say about sentences with quite different IA potentials. (3) Connected with this, Kaplan's conception of content is restricted to what I call "propositional content" and ignores illocutionary force. But within the assertive segment of the territory, and allowing for difference (1), his "character" and "content" correlates with my meaning and (determinate) IA potential.

vii. IA Analysis in Terms of Rule Subjection and in Terms of R'ing

The next item on the agenda is to explore some complications in the ways we can, and cannot, use subjection to I-rules and r-rules to provide analyses of IA concepts in addition to analyses of those concepts in terms of R'ing.

This discussion will be limited to the R'ing portion of what I will call an R'ing analysis of a given IA concept. As a prelude to that I remind the reader of those features of R'ing analyses other than specification of what U R's. (Some of these also apply to analyses in terms of rule subjection, as noted.)

1. For assertives there is the requirement on the sentential vehicle that it explicitly and exactly express the proposition being asserted. This requirement bears on the character of the underlying sentential act, not on the content that makes the IA what it is. When a rule subjection analysis is not in terms of a specified sentence, this requirement also applies. Where a particular sentence is specified, the I-rule for an assertive will not hold of the sentence unless it is of the right character for the job.

2. There is the blanket requirement for interpersonal IA's that U intend H to realize that the other conditions for the IA performance have been satisfied. Again, this has no bearing on the content of the IA, what distinguishes one IA type from another. I have already ruled that this will not be made explicit in any analyses I give but will be tacitly understood as applicable to any IA's directed to other persons. This tacit requirement will hold for both kinds of analysis of IA concepts.

Despite these tangential accretions the substance of an R'ing analysis of IA's is wholly contained in the specification of what U is R'ing, and, in the rule analysis, in a specification of what the rule requires.

In Chapters 3–5 I provided analyses of IA concepts in terms of R'ing. Now that I have developed models for formulating I-rules, I am in a position to provide alternative analyses of IA types in terms of subjection to I-rules. And there is another way in which the developments in this chapter and in Chapter 6 give rise to additional tasks. We have seen that many, indeed most, matching IA types are less than fully determinate, and such that they can be instantiated only if some determinate form thereof is instantiated. We need to look into how these determinable IA types, as well as the determinates that fall under them, are to be analyzed, in both styles. And third, the *de re–de dicto* distinction needs to be applied to these variations.

I will begin by tackling all these problems more or less simultaneously, by considering how to give a rule subjection analysis of the unspecific IA type *asserting that a certain door is open*, considering how this can be given *de re* and *de dicto* versions. We can then move on to further problems. I begin with an analysis that does not specify a particular sentential vehicle.

I₁₇. U asserted that a certain door is open in uttering S *iff* U subjected his utterance of S to the following rule:

R₁₅: S may be uttered by U *iff* there is exactly one *x* such that:
    A. *x* is a door.
    B. U refers to *x*.
    C. U takes reasonable precautions to see to it that the audience is in a position to determine which door it is to which U is referring.
    D. *x* is open.

R₁₅ has the same content as the rule formulated in Section v as the I-rule governing 'The door is open', I₁₀. The switch to the sentential variable 'S' is necessary for a fully general analysis of the IA type. For one can perform that IA as subject to such a rule by uttering many other sentences, for example, 'La porte est ouverte'. But this move is not entirely satisfactory. It is always possible to make this assertion elliptically, without uttering any sentence subject to a rule that lays down such requirements. If I am asked 'Is the door open?', I can assert that it is just by saying 'Yes'. Likewise, one can be speaking metaphorically or ironically in making the assertion, and here too no sentence subject to such a rule would be involved. But this can be handled by putting the restriction to a certain use of language in the analysandum.

In the literal, first-order, use of language, U asserted that a particular door is open.

This implies that the IA type being analyzed does not include any assertions performed by the use of figurative devices, ellipsis, or derivative means.

But still more problems loom. One can satisfy the enriched analysandum of I₁₅ by uttering a sentence considerably more specific than 'The door is open', such as 'Our kitchen door is open' or 'The door to the bank is open', or . . . We cannot solve this difficulty by further amending the analysandum to read 'U asserted that a certain door is open and performed no IA of a more specific type that involves asserting openness of one particular door'. For that would restrict the analysandum to *de dicto* assertions that are not also *de re*.[20] Hence, for generalized rule subjection analyses of referentially determinable types, there seems to be no alternative to adding a particular sentential vehicle to the analysandum. This has the disadvantage of requiring a different analysis of the IA type for each matching sentence type, but there would seem to be no way around this.

The same restriction applies to determinable IA types that match elliptical sentences. *Giving an affirmative answer to a certain contextually determined yes-no question* can obviously be performed by any one of indefinitely many sentences, each of which spells out an affirmative answer to the question picked out by some context or other. And so although that IA type matches the standard meaning of 'Yes', we cannot say that it is performed if *and only if* U subjects his utterance to the I-rule that governs 'Yes'. Here too an I-rule subjection analysis is available only for the IA type as performed by a particular (elliptical or nonelliptical) sentence.

We got into the above difficulties because the IA type was determinable. For any such type there are many determinate nonsynonymous sentences that can be used to perform tokens of that type. Hence the IA type in question, in abstraction from some particular sentential way of performing it, is not paired with any unique I-rule. But what about fully determinate IA types, whether they involve singular reference or not?

In Chapters 3–5 we were working with IA types that were fully determinate referentially because we were presupposing unique reference in specifying the type. In dealing with *adjourning the fall meeting of the University Senate* we assumed a normal situation in which contextual features made it possible to use 'the University Senate' to pick out a particular University Senate and 'the fall meeting' to pick out a particular autumnal meeting thereof. And we made the same assumption for the expressions when they occur in the conditions R'd in performing the IA. The specific account in terms of R'ing was (reformulated to take account of later developments):

I16. U declared the fall meeting of the University Senate adjourned in uttering S iff U R'd that:
    A. The fall meeting of the University Senate is currently in session.
    B. U has the authority to terminate that meeting.
    C. Conditions are appropriate for the exercise of that authority.
    D. By uttering S, U brings it about that that meeting is terminated.

By assuming a context in which the referring expressions secure unique reference, we can give a straightforward analysis of the IA type in terms of

---

[20] We could, of course, maintain the analysis by switching to an analysandum so restricted, but I will not explore that possibility.

R'ing. But an I-rule subjection analysis is another matter. Look what happens when we try.

I₁8. U declared the fall meeting of the University Senate adjourned in uttering S *iff* in uttering S, U subjected the utterance of S to a rule that requires:
   A. The fall meeting of the University Senate is currently in session.
   B. U has the authority to terminate that meeting.
   C. Conditions are appropriate for the exercise of that authority.
   D. By uttering S, U brings it about that that meeting is terminated.

Remember that (a) the referring expressions in the conditions are presupposed to be so used to achieve unique reference, and (b) there are (virtually) no referring expressions in ordinary language that are restricted by their meaning to exactly one referent. But, assuming that the rule in question is an I-rule that specifies a meaning of a sentence, this implies that (in most cases) we would search in vain for a substitution for the variable 'S'. Such a substitutend would have to be such that its literal use is forbidden, incorrect, provided it is not used with respect to the particular meeting of the particular University Senate mentioned in those rules. But there is no such sentence available in English or other natural languages. Certainly 'I declare this meeting adjourned', or 'I declare the fall meeting of the University Senate adjourned' will not qualify. For each of them can be used with complete propriety to declare any of innumerable different fall meetings of University Senates adjourned. And so for any other ordinary sentence used for that purpose. In other words, there is no way to use the I-rule subjection account to specify what it is to adjourn that meeting of that University Senate. One might claim that we could assign a proper name, namely, 'S' to that particular meeting of that particular University Senate, and that the sentence 'I declare S adjourned' would then by its meaning have the sole potential of being used to declare that particular meeting adjourned. But that would be the case only if 'S' just by virtue of its meaning is usable only for an IA of that type. And that depends on how we are to specify the meaning of a proper name. Without going properly into that thorny question, I will just say that it is very dubious that there could be anything in the semantics of a language that would restrict this name to one application. Certainly the usual proper names in natural languages do not work that way. And for good reason. If the language contained a different proper name for each individual item we have occasion to refer to, the language would become so unwieldy as to be useless. There are good reasons why referring expressions in natural languages have the chameleon-like semantic character they do, needing contextual support to achieve each unique reference. Hence, as far as workable languages are concerned, the above verdict stands. The rule subjection analysis just formulated would make the IA impossible.

This puts a crimp in the project of giving both R'ing and rule subjection analyses of all IA types. But the limitations thus revealed are based on fundamental features of natural language and are hence something any theory must accommodate. And note that no limitations are entailed for the assignment of I-rules to sentences, or sentence meanings. If we had sentences that are semantically fully referentiallly determinate, we could construct I-rules for them. But since we lack such sentences, there is no call for such I-rules.

How about analyses in terms of R'ing? Are they always available for any IA type, regardless of the sentential act underlying it? In Chapters 3–5 we saw how to do this for determinate IA types, both referential and nonreferential. But we didn't encounter determinable types until they were forced on our attention by the need to identify types that match sentence meanings. And how about them? Here there is a straightforward derivation of the IA analysis from the I-rule governing a matching sentence meaning. The details of this will vary depending on whether the type is *de re* or *de dicto*, a topic that is next on the agenda. As a simple illustration, consider *asserting that something is malleable*. The matching sentence is 'It's malleable'. The specific content of the I-rule governing that sentence is:

R16 'It's malleable' may be uttered *iff* there is exactly one x such that:
    A. U refers to x.
    B. U takes precautions to see to it that the audience is in a position to determine what x it is to which U is referring.
    C. x is malleable.

On the general principle that performing IA (I) involves R'ing what is required by the I-rule governing the sentence uttered in doing (I), we can say that *asserting of something that it is malleable* is a matter of there being exactly one x such that U R's that (a) U refers to x, (b) U takes reasonable precautions to see to it that the audience is in a position to determine what x it is to which U is referring, and (c) x is malleable. This will constitute making that assertion, regardless of what particular sentence is used to do so. At least that account is sufficient for a *de dicto* assertion.

Now I bring the *de re–de dicto* distinction more fully into the discussion. In 3.9 I explained how to do IA analyses in terms of R'ing for both *de re* and *de dicto* determinate IA's. Let's recall this, using *asserting that John is tall* as our example. The difference came in whether the crucial R'ing is (a) R'ing with respect to John that he is tall (*de re*) or (b) R'ing with respect to the proposition that [John is tall] that it is true (*de dicto*). Thus determinate IA types are *de dicto* or *de re*, depending on whether the R'ing involved is *de dicto* or *de re*. As we will see now, R'ing analyses for determinable IA's pose additional problems. Remember that we are making the *de re–de dicto* distinction only for IA's that involve singular reference.

Continuing with the procedure of deriving the R'ing analyses from rule subjection analyses, let's go back to R10, the rule governing 'The door is open'. That read as follows:

> R10: 'The door is open' may be uttered *iff* there is exactly one *x* such that:
> A. *x* is a door.
> B. U refers to *x*.
> C. U takes reasonable precautions to see to it that the audience is in a position to determine which door it is to which he is referring.
> D. *x* is open.

The simplest way of giving a rule subjection account of the matching IA would be:

> I19. U asserted that a certain door is open in uttering 'The door is open' *iff* U subjected his utterance to R10.

The extrapolation to the R'ing form would have it that U performs an IA of that type iff U R's that there is exactly one *x* such that A.–D. above are true of it. That will suffice for exemplifying the determinable IA type. To perform a determinate form thereof, as I said in Section vi, one must also satisfy the condition that there is exactly one *x* of which A. and B. are true. That will give us a *de re* assertion of a particular door that it is open.

Note that the above account of a *de re* IA involving partial satisfaction of, as well as subjection to, a relevant I-rule enables us to answer another question—"Are there different I-rules for *de re* and *de dicto* IA's?". I am unable to find any such difference, and the above account relieves us of the necessity of doing so. The difference comes not from different I-rules, but from differences in how they bear on the IA performance. Whereas a *de dicto* IA requires only subjection to the rule, the *de re* version also requires partial satisfaction of the rule, along with further R'ing to which that gives rise. This provides a neat way of distinguishing *de dicto* and *de re* IA's in terms of I-rules.

In the light of the above, here are both R'ing and rule subjection analyses of *asserting of some particular door that it is open*, of both *de dicto* and *de re* forms.

I20. U asserted of some particular door that it is open in uttering S iff in uttering S:
   A. U R'd that there is exactly one x such that:
      1. x is a door.
      2. U refers to x.
      3. U takes reasonable precautions to see to it that the audience is in a position to determine which door it is that U is referring to.
      4. x is open.
   B. There is exactly one x such that:
      1. x is a door.
      2. U refers to x.

This analysis is of the *de re* type since it requires that U succeeds in referring to a particular door and hence that A.1. and 2. are satisfied as well as R'd. For the *de dicto* version we omit condition B.

Now for a rule subjection analysis. Remember that this requires that a particular sentential vehicle is specified. The *de dicto* version is quite simple. It is I19 above.

I19. U asserted that a certain particular door is open by uttering 'The door is open' *iff* U subjected his utterance to R10.

For the *de re* version there are two alternatives. The first is wholly in terms of an R-rule, at the cost of requiring partial satisfaction of the rule, as well as subjection thereto. This involves only an addition to the *de dicto* version.

I21. U asserted that a certain particular door is open by uttering 'The door is open' *iff* U subjected his utterance to R 10, satisfying A.1. and 2.

Alternatively, we can do it purely in terms of rule subjection, at the cost of introducing r-rules as well as I-rules.

I22. U asserted that a certain particular door is open by uttering 'The door is open' *iff* U subjected his utterance to R10, and by virtue of satisfying A.1. and 2. of R13, U subjects his utterance to an r-rule that requires of some particular door, O, that (a) O is a door and (b) U refers to O.

The analysis of IA's in elliptical speech can be modeled on the above treatment of reference. Here too we can think of the R'ing being determined both by subjection to an I-rule and by subjection to an r-rule that is engendered by partial satisfaction of the I-rule governing the elliptically used expression.

Robinson asks me, "Are you going to the next session?". I reply "Yes". By doing so I assert that I am going to the next session, as well as give an affirmative answer to the question. In performing the former IA, I R that I am going to the next session.[21] The present question is one of understanding how to construe the fact that I R'd that I was going to the next session by saying "Yes". It is clear that subjecting my utterance to the I-rule governing 'Yes' (R7) doesn't do that. Again, just as with referential problems, by satisfying part of what the I-rule governing 'Yes' requires, the requirement that something in the context picks out a yes-no question to which this utterance of 'Yes' is an answer, I have thereby subjected myself to a rule that requires that I am going to the next session. This r-rule is, of course, identical to the I-rule governing 'I am going to the next session'. So all the R'ing here can be construed as a matter of subjecting my utterance to rules, both to an I-rule governing the sentence uttered and, by satisfying part of that, to an r-rule thus engendered. An alternative to bringing in r-rules would be to take the R'ing involved to be purely determined by subjection to I-rules, but where this involves an I-rule governing the sentence for which the expression uttered is elliptical, as well as the I-rule governing what is uttered.

viii. Some Additional Problems for IA Analysis

There is one problem about the above account of I-rules for singular IA's, at least for those using definite descriptions, and perhaps for all others as well. It has to do mostly though not entirely with *de re* versions thereof. As I have been laying things out, the rule for 'The piano needs dusting' would require that there be exactly one x such that it is a piano and U refers to it. Correspondingly, U performs the *de re* IA of telling someone that a certain piano needs dusting only if U R's *that there is exactly one x that is a piano and that U refers to* and only if the italicized condition holds. In other words the relevant I-rule requires that U commit himself to referring to an entity that "falls under" whatever referential device he is using, and the *de re* IA requires that he actually refers to an entity that satisfies that condition. The problem comes from some interesting phenomena pointed out in Donnellan 1966. There he maintains that one can succeed in referring to x by a definite description even if x fails to satisfy that description. His initial example involved the sentence 'Smith's murderer is

---

[21] Of course, we have questions here as to how 'the next session' refers to a particular session (of something or other) rather than to one of innumerable other sessions of something or other. But ignore those referential problems for the purpose of this example, and assume a unique reference of this phrase throughout.

insane'. If this sentence were uttered by Brown, a spectator at the trial of Jones, who has been charged with Smith's murder, and it is clear that Brown means to be referring to Jones, who is testifying at the moment, and does not mean this reference to hang on whether Jones actually committed the murder (though Brown believes that he did), then Brown succeeded in referring to Jones and saying of him that he is insane, even if in fact Jones is innocent, and the definite description Brown used does not apply to Jones. Hence on my account, *Brown asserted that Smith's murderer is insane* is true only in the *de dicto* version and false in the *de re* version. Donnellan presents another example in which on my account U didn't even make the *de dicto* assertion. There U, and everyone else in the relevant community, knows that Bertrand is not the real king but a pretender, yet it is customary at the time to refer to him as "the king". U tells someone "The king is in his counting house". Here U isn't even R'ing that there is a unique *x* that is the king and that U is referring to; much less is that the case. On my account he is asserting that the king is in his counting house neither in the *de dicto* nor in the *de re* version.

I hinted above that although in Donnellan 1966 he confines himself to definite descriptions, the phenomenon extends more widely. It is found with proper names too. On my analysis an assertion of the form 'N is P' (where 'N' is a proper name) involves R'ing that there is exactly one *x* such that *x* is named 'N' and U refers to it. Nevertheless one can succeed in referring to something by a name where this is not true, and even where U and the audience realize that it is not true. The analogue to the first D-case above would be one in which, mistakenly believing that the man talking to Susan is named 'Joe', I say (where it is clear that I am speaking of the man talking to Susan) "Joe looks excited". Here I succeeded in saying of that man that he looks excited, even though he is not named 'Joe'. This would be a *de dicto*, but not a *de re*, case of asserting that Joe looks excited. For an analogue to the second case, just change it to an alias ('Smithers') gone awry, so that everyone in the relevant community has discovered it but people are still referring to the person by that name. Here when I say "Smithers just drove off ", I did succeed in saying that of this person, even though, on my account, I performed neither a *de dicto* nor a *de re* assertion that Smithers drove off.

Let's be straight as to just how this poses a problem for my theory. It is not that these are straightforward counterexamples. Where my theory implies that a certain IA type is not exemplified, that is likewise the natural intuitive judgment. It is clear that Brown did not assert, of Smith's murderer, that he is insane. It also clear in the second case that U did not assert that the king is in his counting house (in any sense of that more robust than 'U asserted of someone that he is in his counting house by uttering the sentence 'The king is in his counting house''. So what is the problem? It is that Donnellan's cases (hereafter D-cases) are not handled by anything

I have yet developed. These are cases of someone's making a genuine singular assertion by a sentence using a definite description to pick out the entity the assertion is about. But my only patterns of analysis for IA's that involve definite descriptions are typified by I19 and I20. And neither of those fit the D-cases.

Does this mean that we must devise different I-rules for sentences used in D-cases? I think not. In the first case Brown subjects his utterance to the standard rule for the sentence used but, on a *de re* construal, violates it. Whereas in the second case U violates the rule on either construal. But that is the right verdict. These speakers have done something other than conform to the rule for a literal, first-order, communicative use of these sentences. But then how is it that they succeeded in making a singular assertion? We may look to figurative speech for a useful analogue. When Ross says in Act I, scene ii of *Macbeth* ". . . the Norweyan banners flout the sky and fan our people cold", he is violating an appropriate I-rule for the literal assertive use of that sentence. He is not asserting that some Norwegians, by waving their banners, are reducing the temperature of some Scotchmen. He is, rather, asserting that the Norwegian army is striking fear in the Scotch. As in other figurative speech, he is using the literal meaning of the sentence as a base from which to make an ad hoc, creative departure, in this case by means of an analogy between reduction in physical temperature and fear. That is the way I suggest that we view D-cases. I don't suggest that they constitute figurative speech but that they are like figurative speech in using language in a way that is based on its literal employment but involving an intelligible departure therefrom. This can be either intentional, as in the second D-case, or unintentional, as in the first D-case. In both cases the literal meaning of the sentence is a point of departure for doing something else with it, referentially. In both cases the content of the definite description fits into the context well enough to permit identification of the intended referent. Since Jones is on trial for Smith's murder, and the interlocutors have been observing his testimony, it is clear to whom Brown is referring, whether Jones is guilty or innocent. In the second case, because of the unspoken convention to keep referring to the pretender as 'the king', it is clear to all concerned to whom U is referring, though he is not, in fact, the king. Contextual support makes the reference clear, even in the absence of conformity to the relevant I-rule. To accommodate D-cases in my standard I-rules for sentences containing definite descriptions, I will think of D-cases as being "derivative" uses of speech, thereby excluding them from the scope of I-rules, which is restricted to "literal, *first-order*, communicative uses of language".

Next we have the question of whether the matching IA type for a typical singular sentence meaning should be construed as *de re* or as *de dicto*. Both have their claims. First, it is clear that the matching illocutionary act type for a singular sentence like S$_1$ ('The piano needs dusting') is not *saying of a certain piano that it needs dusting* on a fully *de re* construal. On that reading the IA report asserts a relation between U and a certain object (which is a piano); and U can be related to that object by saying of it that it needs dusting however U refers to it. But we have not made full use of the semantic potential of the sentence unless we refer to something *as a piano* and then say that it needs dusting. On the other hand, the matching IA cannot be purely *de dicto*. For that would leave open the possibility that U fails in his attempt to refer to a certain piano. And remember that in 6.7 we selected the matching type for a given sentence meaning by determining what is the *richest* type that is such that just by knowing that U uttered S with that meaning, and was intending to be making a literal, first-order, communicative use of S, a hearer could tell that U *intended* to be performing an illocutionary act of that type. That criterion requires an IA type that involves successful reference. Just by knowing that U is making a literal, first-order communicative use of 'The piano needs dusting', in its basic meaning, one can know that U *intends* to successfully pick out a certain piano and say of it that it needs dusting. As far as referential success is concerned, the *de re* type is the richer one. Hence in this respect it is the *de re* type that qualifies as matching.

The conclusion is clear. The matching IA type for singular sentences takes something from both sides of the distinction—referential success from the *de re* and character of mode of reference from the *de dicto*. We can best think of it as a *de re* type with an additional stipulation of the mode of reference. I won't bother to illustrate such a mixed type in the examples of IA analysis that are coming up in Section x. It will be clear how to modify those examples of singular IA types to get what is needed.

The other loose end still dangling is this. In Section iv I indicated how to avoid counterexamples to I-rules from figurative and other forms of speech that are derivative in one way or another from a straightforward literal use of the semantics of the language. The device was to restrict the scope of I-rules to what I called "first-order, literal use of language". That enabled us to formulate I-rules that endow sentences with their meaning(s) in the language. But it did not touch the question of how to analyze IA's that are performed figuratively, ironically, or in some other semantically derivative way. When, speaking ironically, I remark that the current impeachment proceedings are stupid by saying 'That's a brilliant thing to do', I perform an IA with a particular propositional content, as I do if I say, figuratively, that Jones is in big trouble by saying 'Jones fell into a swamp'. There is no difficulty in providing R'ing analyses of such IA's, so long as the act involves a definite propositional content. But how about rule subjection analyses? In neither of these cases does someone do what she is doing by subjecting her utterance to any R-rule governing the sentence uttered. And, that being the case, how is the R'ing involved related to rule subjection?

To be more explicit about the boundaries of the present territory, it comprises IA's made with sentential devices the standard meaning (I-rules) of which does not lay down what is R'd in this illocutionary use of them, not even indeterminately, as we saw to be the case with reference and ellipticity. This is not a sharp distinction, because with metaphor and irony and other derivative uses the standard meaning of the sentence used does play a role. But with reference and ellipticity the deviations from I-rules are "provided for" by those rules to a much greater extent than with the cases we are now considering. These cases involve much freer play by the speaker in moving from the standard meaning of the sentence to the propositional content of the IA. I will now consider how this works in various regions of the territory.

(1) I begin with figurative speech. I won't attempt a comprehensive treatment of figures of speech, something that would require another book. Instead I will concentrate on two types that present different profiles— *metaphor* and *irony*.

With respect to metaphor, I first need to distinguish those cases in which the speaker does and those in which she does not purport to be performing a fairly definite illocutionary act. I don't suppose there is a sharp dividing line between these. The clearest cases of the former are those in which there is an obvious literal paraphrase. Take Churchill's famous utterance in his Westminster College 1946 address: "An iron curtain has descended across the continent". Here there is no question as to what Churchill meant to be asserting, and it is clear how to specify that literally, at least roughly. "The Soviet Union has put strong obstacles in the way of the free exchange of people, goods, information, and ideas between eastern and western Europe." At the other extreme we have figurative utterances the producer of which has no one definite message in mind. The sentence is, so to say, tossed at the hearer to make of what he will. 'We are all in the arms of Mother Nature' might be so intended. And there are many intermediate cases. Since our present topic concerns what is involved in performing IA's in figurative speech, the discussion will be confined to cases near the more definite end, where a particular propositional content can be identified.

To return to Churchill, he obviously was not subjecting his utterance to the requirements of the I-rule governing the literal use of "An iron curtain has descended across the continent". Nevertheless he was making an assertion, the content of which is given by what he was R'ing. And how is that determined in terms of rule subjection? By the I-rule governing a sentence that could be used to give a (more or less exact) literal paraphrase, like the one above, that makes explicit what was asserted. Churchill performed the IA the R'ing content of which is determined by what is required by the I-rule governing this literal paraphrase.

Metaphorical speech is like ellipticity, in that we move from what was uttered to some sentence not uttered and take the I-rule governing the latter as supplying conditions R'd in the IA performed. But it is unlike yes-no questions in that we are left without very definite guidance from what is uttered in finding the sentence governed by the appropriate I-rule. True enough, the sentence uttered is the basis for that search. We take it as a "model" or "analogue" of what the speaker is saying. But there are no cut and dried directions for finding what is being modeled. There are, in principle, many ways of taking 'iron curtain' or 'walking shadow' (in "Life's a walking shadow") as a model of what is being said, just because any item is similar in different ways to many other things. The interpretation of metaphorical utterances places more of a burden on the imaginative powers of the hearer.

(2) Irony involves more definite guidance in finding the relevant I-rule. In contrast to the "free floating" character of metaphor, there is a rough algorithm for computing the propositional content of an assertion: *find the opposite of what would be asserted by a literal use of the sentence uttered*. This is rough because there is often more than one opposite, but in such cases one candidate is often rendered most salient by something in the context. If one says, ironically, 'What a beautiful day!', this principle leads us to construe the utterance as subject to a rule that requires that the day of utterance be rainy or gloomy or terribly cold, depending on contextual indications, or disagreeable in some other way.

(3) Next are parasitic uses, the paradigm of which is speeches in dramatic performances. These can be treated very simply. Unlike (1) and (2), we are not required to move to other sentences governed by other I-rules. Instead we stick with the sentence uttered ("Thank you for your help") and with the matching IA, the one performed by a literal, first-order, communicative use of that sentence. Although the actor is not seriously performing an IA act of that type (seriously thanking someone for having helped him), he is doing something maximally close to that in content, namely, *pretending to perform an IA of that type*. All the details are the same. The array of conditions R'd doesn't have to be changed at all. We take the whole package from the first-order employment of the sentence and transform it from serious involvement to a pretense of just the same involvement. In terms of R'ing there is a transformation of seriously R'ing that p, for relevant p's, to pretending to R them.

ix. IA's, I-rules, IA Potential, and Sentence Meaning

In the last few sections I have uncovered a number of complications in my earlier identification of R'ing and I-rule subjection, as well as variations in what is possible by way of IA analysis. The time has come to review these in a summary fashion, and reconsider their bearing on the fundamental theses of this book: (1) The rule subjection account of R'ing (R4); (2) sentence meaning = IA potential = I-rule governance.

First a review of when R'ing, and hence IA performance so far as it is constituted by R'ing, is and is not wholly constituted by the subjection of the sentence uttered to an I-rule. What we have seen is that I-rule subjection is not the whole story in the following cases.

A. The use of sentences that contain singular referring devices of the usual sort in which meaning does not determine reference.
B. The use of elliptical devices.
C. Figurative speech.

In such cases although the I-rule governing the sentence uttered is the basis of whatever IA is performed, it does not suffice to fully determine it. In A. and B. we found two ways of marking this partial determination and what is needed to complete it. First, if U not only subjects his utterance to an I-rule but also satisfies part of it, that satisfaction will complete the determination of the IA by engendering certain further requirements on the speaker and correlated R'ings. Alternatively, we could preserve the thesis that R'ing is always a matter of rule subjection by thinking of the satisfaction of the I-rule just mentioned as engendering a much more specific "r-rule" for the utterance, a rule that makes specific requirements for the specific features of that utterance. An r-rule, unlike an I-rule, does not endow the sentence (type) with a meaning, but rather, in the referential cases, endows the utterances with a particular reference and, in the elliptical case, fills out the propositional content of the utterance.

Figurative speech is a different ball game. Here there is a move to a more or less different propositional content from that determined by the I-rule governing the sentence uttered. When I say 'Religion has been corroded by the acids of modernity' and mean what is typically meant by saying that, the content of my IA is not concerned with acids and corrosion in the literal sense of those terms, though it does have to do with religion and modernity. What is going on here is that what is literally meant by a sentence of the form 'x is corroded by the acids of y' is used as a "model" or "analogue" for what is being said here of religion and modernity. To get an I-rule into the picture we have to take the speaker to be subjecting his utterance to an I-rule that would govern a literal paraphrase of the utterance, something like 'Developments in modern society (culture) have weakened the hold of religion on the populace'. The IA performed, and the R'ings involved, have a content determined by the I-rule governing a sentence like that. We have an I-rule substitution rather than the filling out of the content of an I-rule. Irony, as we have seen, presents a similar picture of moving to a different I-rule, though there we have a more definite way of determining what that alternative I-rule is.

Derivative cases like lines spoken in a play are still different. Here there is no alteration or enrichments of content. 'The guests have arrived' is used to express the same propositional content in a play and in real life. It is rather that whereas the speaker is seriously R'ing the relevant conditions in the former, she is only pretending to in the play.[22]

Thus the above cases involve importantly different mechanisms. But there are common elements. Most basically, the IA performed (at least the most specific IA performed) is not the one that is constituted by R'ing exactly what is required by the I-rule governing the sentence uttered. Put otherwise, the most specific IA performed is not the matching IA for the meaning with which the sentence is uttered. The way we arrive at the specific IA performed from the meaning (I-rule) of the sentence uttered is different for the different cases. But a common aspect is that what is rule-required, and hence R'd, in each case is a joint function of the I-rule governing the sentence uttered and features of the context and speaker intention that indicate, in one way or another, some addition to or departure from what is required in general by that I-rule. If there were no indications that someone is speaking ironically or metaphorically (and in metaphor which analogies are being exploited) or that a dramatic production is going on, one would be hard pressed to communicate effectively in these modes of speech. As for reference, the I-rules contain a requirement that the audience is given sufficient indication of which particular so-and-so the utterance is about. And in other cases it is usually obvious from the context how to fill out the content. The general principle throughout is that where what one is saying cannot be wholly gleaned from knowing the meaning of the linguistic devices employed, there must be a sufficient basis elsewhere to fill that out or communication will not be secured.

Thus there are numerous cases in which the simple equation of R'ing with subjection of utterance to I-rule must be qualified. And given the prevalence of singular reference in speech, these cases would take up a large proportion of speech, even without the other types enumerated above. It is only where none of these is exemplified that the I-rule subjection account of R'ing can remain unmodified. This is largely confined to assertives without singular reference, like asserting that lemons are yellow.

But now what about the thesis that sentence meaning = IA potential = governance by an I-rule? Here the original thesis can be retained, so long as we remember that a potential for a use does not necessarily fully determine a use. Even if, in referential and elliptical cases, *performing* the matching IA requires something beyond subjecting one's utterance to the ap-

---

[22] Needless to say, a given utterance can display more than one of these phenomena. When speaking a line in a play I can be making a reference to another character and speaking elliptically or metaphorically.

propriate I-rule, it does not follow that I-rule governance is insufficient for giving the sentence a *potential* for that. After all, the rule lays down the appropriate recipe for such a performance. The I-rule, by virtue of laying down those requirements, is all it takes to make the sentence an appropriate one for doing this. Whether I actually conform to what the rule requires is not a matter of *what* rules apply. Even if we added more rules there would still be the further issue of whether they are conformed to. Thus in laying down requirements, the I-rule does as much as a rule could do to render the sentence *usable* for an act of conforming to *those requirements*. The rule governance is all one could ask from the *language* in the way of a potential. It is up to the speaker whether this potential is fully actualized. We can't expect a *potential* to determine its own realization.

What about the other cases, particularly figurative speech? There it is not true that even complete conformity to the I-rule that gives the sentence a meaning is sufficient for performing an IA of the type performed. On the contrary, in these cases the IA performed is often not of the matching type, even partially, but of one related to that type in a certain way. Nevertheless the point remains that the established meaning of the sentence that flows from the I-rule governance provides the basis from which these figurative extensions are made, whether by analogy (metaphor) or contrariety (irony), or otherwise. The final IA product less closely follows the I-rule governing the sentence than in the referential and elliptical cases, but still the I-rule (standard meaning) provides an appropriate launching for those figurative flights of fancy. And so we can say even in these cases that sentence meaning = IA potential = I-rule governance.

It may be helpful to give a brief summary of the restrictions we discovered in vii on the analyses that are possible for one or another IA type. The first point is that an R'ing analysis is possible for any IA type without restriction, even those performed figuratively. It is with rule subjection analyses that things are more spotty. First, there is the distinction between determinable and determinate IA types. With respect to determinables there are two points. First, such IA types cannot receive a rule subjection analysis without specifying the sentence performed. And where the indeterminacy is due to reference, the *de re* version does, while the *de dicto* version does not, require the analysis either to specify that the relevant I-rule is at least partially conformed to as well as the utterance's being subject to it, or to specify an r-rule to which the utterance is subject. Where the indeterminacy is due to ellipticity, there is no *de dicto–de re* distinction applicable, unless reference is also involved, and the above requirements for a *de re* referential case apply. With a referentially determinate IA type, natural languages lack in most cases any sentence with a meaning such that the governing I-rule restricts the sentence to a unique referent for the referring expressions(s) involved. Hence an I-rule subjection analysis is not available here. When an IA of a determinate IA type is performed elliptically, no issue arises from the ellipticity for its analysis. For here, unlike the referential case, the ellipticity does not enter into the constitution (content) of the IA type, only its means of performance. This last point can also be made for IA's performed figuratively. But in both the elliptical and the figurative case, if the (complete) IA is to be analyzed in terms of rule subjection (and possibly partial conformity if singular reference is involved), it would have to be in terms of the I-rule governing the sentence for which the elliptical expression is elliptical, or in terms of the literal paraphrase of the metaphor.

Finally, note that I-rules satisfy the constraints on rules I enumerated in Section iii.

(1) Distinctiveness. Since I-rules lay down necessary and sufficient conditions for correctness of sentence utterance, in a certain sphere of activity, they embody the distinctive character of which I was speaking. They have implications for the conditions under which a certain kind of behavior is right or wrong, correct or incorrect; and they are such that they are modifiable at will.

(2) Translinguistic connection. The conditions I-rules lay down have to do with extralinguistic states of affairs, except in those special cases in which the matching IA has to do solely with language. Thus by virtue of subjecting one's utterance to such a rule one is enabled to make one's speech deal with the world beyond language.

(3) Scope. The rules govern first-level speech behavior and not just higher-level speech about language and speech.

x. Sample I-Rules and IA Analyses

We have now forged the tools we need to construct I-rules and analyses of IA concepts from all the major IA categories. In order to prevent the list from becoming intolerably prolix, I will observe certain restrictions. First, the analyses will be tailored to the literal, first-order use of language. There will be no attempt to explore figurative or other derivative ways of performing IA's. Second, I will ignore any multivocality that may attach to the sentences cited. Since on my treatment a multivocal sentence is subject to a different I-rule for each distinguishable meaning, the account of its I-rule governance for a particular meaning will be indistinguishable from the treatment of a univocal sentence. Third, except for one example, I., without singular reference or ellipticity, the sentences will all have determinable meanings. For each sentence I will give an analysis of the (determinable) matching IA type. For II.–V. I will follow that with an analysis of a determinate type that falls under that determinable; that should be sufficient to give the idea of how to move from the determinable to a corresponding determinate. The analysis of a determinable type (as well as the analysis of an IA type matching a nonreferential sentence) can take both I-rule subjection and R'ing forms, the former requiring the mention of a particular sentential vehicle. But a referentially determinate type is susceptible only of an R'ing analysis. The rule subjection analyses of *de re* determinable IA types will be in terms of subjection to an I-rule and partial satisfaction of its requirements. It should be clear from the above discussion how to convert the partial satisfaction of an I-rule to an r-rule subjection form. Fourth, the main addition this section makes to the scattered examples of I-rules and IA analyses in iv–ix is the application of the analytical tools I have developed to the analysis of IA types from all major categories. Fifth, with all determinable IA types that involve singular reference, I will give the analysis of the *de re* version. The *de dicto* version is easily derived from the rule subjection version by omitting the requirement of partial satisfaction, and from the R'ing version by omitting the B. condition. Sixth, I restrict myself to intentional IA's, if, indeed, that is a restriction. Seventh, in the interest of concision, for the analysis of assertive types that do not specify a sentence I will tacitly assume the requirement that the sentence explicitly present the proposition asserted, and for IA's generally I will tacitly assume the requirement for interpersonally directed tokens that U intend that H realize that the other conditions are satisfied. I-rules are indicated by 'R' followed by a number, IA's to be analyzed by 'I' followed by a number. A rule subjection analysis is prefaced by 'RS', an R'ing analysis by 'R'. An R'ing analysis of a referentially determinate IA type will be prefaced by (RD). In order to keep a uniformity of number for each correlated I-rule and IA, I will skip over some R numbers, beginning both R's and I's with 23, thus maintaining at least for the I's a continuity with the successive numbers in the book up to this point.

Assertives

I.

R23. 'All lemons are yellow' may be uttered *iff* all lemons are yellow.
I23. *Asserting that all lemons are yellow.*
    (RS). U asserted that all lemons are yellow, in uttering S *iff* U subjected her utterance to R23.
    (R). U asserted that all lemons are yellow in uttering S *iff*:
        A. In uttering S, U R'd that all lemons are yellow.

II.

R24. 'The stove is on' may be uttered at *t iff* there is exactly one *x* such that:
    A. *x* is a stove.

B. U refers to *x* in uttering 'The stove is on' at *t*.

C. U takes reasonable precautions to see to it that the audience is in a position to determine which stove it is to which he is referring.

D. *x* is on at *t*.

I24. *Asserting that a certain particular stove is on.*

(RS) U asserted that a certain particular stove is on, in uttering 'The stove is on' at *t iff* U subjected his utterance to R24, satisfying at least requirements A. and B.

(R) U asserted that a certain particular stove is on, in uttering S at *t iff*:

A. U R'd that there is exactly one *x* such that:
1. *x* is a stove.
2. U refers to *x* in uttering S at *t*.
3. U takes reasonable precautions to see to it that the audience is in a position to determine which stove it is that U is referring to.
4. *x* is on at *t*.

B. There is exactly one *x* such that:
1. *x* is a stove.
2. U refers to *x* in uttering S at *t*.

(RD) U asserted that his kitchen stove is on in uttering S at *t iff* in uttering S at *t* U R'd that:

A. His kitchen stove is on.

B. U took reasonable precautions to see to it that the audience is in a position to determine that it is his kitchen stove that U is R'ing to be on.

(Remember that in these analyses of referentially determinate IA types, we assume that all referring expressions in both the analysandum and the analysans are so used as to have unique reference.)

III.

R25. 'The key is on the table' may be uttered at *t iff* there is exactly one *x* and exactly one *y* such that:

A. *x* is a key.

B. *y* is a table.

C. U refers to *x* and *y* in uttering 'The key is on the table' at *t*.

D. U takes reasonable precautions to see to it that the audience is in a position to determine which key and which table it is to which he is referring.

D. *x* is on *y* at *t*.

I25. *Asserting that a certain particular key is on a certain particular table.*
(RS) U asserted that a certain particular key is on a certain particular table, in uttering 'The key is on the table' at *t iff* U subjects
his utterance to R 25, satisfying at least requirements A. and B.
(R) U asserted that a certain particular key is on a certain table
in uttering S at *t iff*:

    A. U R's that there is exactly one *x* and exactly one *y* such
       that:
       1. *x* is a key.
       2. *y* is a table.
       3. U refers to *x* and *y* in uttering S at *t*.
       4. U takes reasonable precautions to see to it that the
          audience is in a position to determine which key it is
          that he is R'ing to be on which table.
       5. *x* is on *y* at *t*.
    B. There is exactly one *x* and exactly one *y* such that:
       1. *x* is a key.
       2. *y* is a table.
       3. U refers to *x* and *y* in uttering S at *t*.
(RD) U asserted that Joan's key is on her kitchen table in uttering
S at *t iff* U R'd that:

    A. Joan's key is on her kitchen table at *t*.
    B. U takes reasonable precautions to see to it that the au-
       dience is in a position to determine that it is Joan's key
       that U is R'ing to be on her kitchen table at *t*.

IV.

R26. 'I concede that the door is open' may be uttered at *t iff* there is
exactly one *x* such that:
A. *x* is a door.
B. U refers to *x* in uttering 'I concede that the door is open' at *t*.
C. U takes reasonable precautions to see to it that the audience
   is in a position to determine which door it is to which U is
   referring.
D. *x* is open at *t*.
E. *x*'s being open at *t* is a fact that is, or might be thought to be,
   unfavorable to U in some way.
I26. *Purporting to concede that a certain particular door is open.*
(RS) U purported to concede that a certain particular door is
open, in uttering 'I concede that the door is open' at *t iff* U subjected his utterance to R26, satisfying at least requirements A.
and B.

(R) U purported to concede that a certain particular door is open, in uttering S at *t iff*:

    A. In uttering S at *t*, U R'd that there is exactly one *x* such that:

        1. *x* is a door.

        2. U refers to *x* in uttering S at *t*.

        3. U takes reasonable precautions to see to it that the audience is in a position to know which door it is to which U is referring.

        4. *x* is open at *t*.

        5. The fact that *x* is open at *t* is, or might be thought to be, unfavorable to U in some way.

    B. There is exactly one *x* such that:

        1. *x* is a door.

        2. U refers to *x* in uttering S at *t*.[23]

(RD) U purported to concede that his front door is open, in uttering S at *t iff* U R'd that:

    A. His front door is open at *t*.

    B. U takes reasonable precautions to see to it that the audience can tell that it is his front door that U is R'ing to be open at *t*.

    C. The fact that his front door is open at *t* is, or might be thought to be, unfavorable to U in some way.

Directives

V.

R27. 'Clean up the room' may be uttered by U at time *t iff* there is exactly one *x* and exactly one *y* such that:

    A. *x* is addressed by U at *t*.

    B. *y* is a room.

    C. U refers to *x* and to *y* in uttering S at *t*.[24]

    D. U has authority over *x* with respect to activities like cleaning *y*.

    E. It is possible for *x* to clean *y*.

    F. By uttering 'Clean up the room' at *t*, U lays on *x* an obligation to clean *y*.

    G. U uttered 'Clean up the room' at *t* in order to get *x* to clean *y*.

---

[23] The fact that A.1. and 2. are also required as such and not just as R'd by U, whereas 3., 4., and 5. are not, reflects the difference between referential and predicative conditions. The former, but not the latter, are required for the singular IA.

[24] From now on any condition that U refers to something or other, as well as any condition (in the analysis of referentially determinate IA's) that presupposes unique reference, will be tacitly thought of as followed by a condition to the effect that U takes reasonable precautions to see to it that the audience is in a position to determine what it is to which U refers.

I27. *Ordering someone to clean up a certain room.*

(RS) U ordered someone to clean up a certain particular room, in uttering 'Clean up the room' at *t iff* U subjected her utterance to R27, satisfying at least requirements A., B., and C.

(R) U ordered someone to clean up a certain particular room, in uttering S at *t iff*:

    A. In uttering S, U R'd that there is exactly one *x* and exactly one *y* such that:

        1. *x* is addressed by U at *t*.

        2. *y* is a room.

        3. U referred to *x* and *y* in uttering S at *t*.

        4. U has authority over *x* with respect to activities like cleaning *y*.

        5. It is possible for *x* to clean *y*.

        6. By uttering S at *t*, U lays on *x* an obligation to clean *y*.

        7. U uttered S at *t* in order to get *x* to clean *y*.[25]

    B. There is exactly one *x* and exactly one *y* such that:

        1. *x* is addressed by U at *t*.

        2. *y* is a room.

        3. U refers to *x* and to *y* in uttering S at *t*.

(RD) U ordered her maid to clean the dining room in uttering S *iff* in uttering S U R'd that:

    1. It is possible for her maid to clean the dining room.

    2. U has authority over her maid with respect to activities like cleaning.

    3. By uttering S at *t*, U laid on her maid an obligation to clean the dining room.

    4. U uttered S at *t* in order to get her maid to clean the dining room.

VI.

R28. 'Please hand me the newspaper' may be uttered by U at *t iff* there is exactly one *x* and exactly one *y* such that:

    A. *x* is addressed by U at *t*.

    B. *y* is a newspaper.

---

[25] So long as we were dealing with assertives, we had a requirement that S be appropriate for the purpose. We required that S either explicitly present the proposition being asserted or be used as a substitute for a sentence that does so. Because of considerations brought out in the discussion of unintentional illocutionary acts in 5.9, there is a general need for some kind of restriction on S for all illocutionary acts, viz., that it be "suitable for the purpose", either by virtue of its meaning or by virtue of its being used as a substitute for a sentence that is suitable by virtue of its meaning, where in the latter case some indication is given of that. Rather than further loading down these rather complicated formulations, I shall tacitly assume a restriction like this throughout.

C. U refers to x and to y in uttering 'Please hand me the newspaper' at t.
D. U has some interest in x's handing y to U.
E. It is possible for x to hand y to U.
F. By uttering 'Please hand me the newspaper' at t, U lays on x a weak obligation to hand y to U.
G. U utters 'Please hand me the newspaper' at t in order to get x to hand y to U.

I28. *Asking someone to hand one a certain particular newspaper.*
(RS) U asked someone to hand her a certain particular newspaper, in uttering 'Please hand me the newspaper' at t, *iff* U subjected her utterance to R 28, satisfying at least requirements A., B., and C.
(R) U asked someone to hand her a certain particular newspaper, in uttering S at t, *iff*:
A. In uttering S at t, U R'd that there is exactly one x and exactly one y such that:
1. x is addressed by U at t.
2. y is a newspaper.
3. U referred to x and y in uttering S at t.
4. U has some interest in x's handing y to U.
5. It is possible for x to hand y to U.
6. By uttering S at t, U lays on x a weak obligation to hand y to U.
7. U utters S at t in order to get x to hand y to U.
B. There is exactly one x and exactly one y such that:
1. x is addressed by U at t.
2. y is a newspaper.
3. U referred to x and to y in uttering S at t.

Expressives

VII.

R29. 'Thanks for recommending me for that job' may be uttered by U at t *iff* there is exactly one x and exactly one y such that:
A. x is addressed by U at t.
B. y is a job.
C. U referred to x and to y in uttering 'Thanks for recommending me for that job' at t.
D. x recommended U for y prior to t.
E. U is grateful to x for recommending U for y.

I29. *Thanking someone for recommending one for a certain job.*
(RS) U thanked someone for recommending him for a certain job, in uttering 'Thanks for recommending me for that job' at t,

iff U subjected his utterance to R29, satisfying at least requirements A., B., and C.

(R) U thanked someone for recommending him for a certain job, in uttering S at *t*, *iff*:

    A. In uttering S at *t*, U R'd that there is exactly one *x* and exactly one *y* such that:

        1. *x* is addressed by U at *t*.

        2. *y* is a job.

        3. U referred to *x* and *y* in uttering S at *t*.

        4. *x* recommended U for *y* prior to *t*.

        5. U is grateful to *x* for recommending U for *y*.

    B. There is exactly one *x* and exactly one *y* such that:

        1. *x* is addressed by U at *t*.

        2. *y* is a job.

        3. U referred to *x* and *y* in uttering S at *t*.

VIII.

R30. 'I don't approve of that' may be uttered *iff* there is exactly one *x* such that:

    A. *x* is a possible object of approval or disapproval.

    B. U refers to *x* in uttering 'I don't approve of that'.

    C. U disapproves of *x*.

I30. *Expressing disapproval of something.*

(RS) U expressed disapproval of something in uttering 'I don't approve of that' *iff* U subjected his utterance to R30, satisfying at least requirements A. and B.

(R) U expressed disapproval of something, in uttering S, *iff*:

    A. In uttering S, U R'd that there is exactly one *x* such that:

        1. *x* is a possible object of approval or disapproval.

        2. U referred to *x* in uttering S.

        3. U disapproves of *x*.

    B. There is exactly one *x* such that:

        1. *x* is a possible object of approval or disapproval.

        2. U referred to *x* in uttering S.

Commissives

IX.

R31. 'I promise to drive you to the meeting' may be uttered by U at *t* *iff* there is exactly one *x* and exactly one *y* such that:

    A. *x* is addressed by U at *t*.

    B. *y* is a meeting.

C. U refers to x and y in uttering 'I promise to drive you to the meeting' at t.

D. It is possible for U to drive x to y.

E. x would prefer U's doing so to U's not doing so.

F. At t U intends to drive x to y.

G. By uttering 'I promise to drive you to the meeting' at t, U lays on U an obligation to drive x to y.

I31. *Purporting to promise someone to drive him to a certain meeting.*[26]

(RS) U purported to promise someone to drive him to a certain meeting in uttering 'I promise to drive you to the meeting' at t *iff* U subjected his utterance to R31, satisfying at least requirements A., B., and C.

(R) U purported at t to promise someone to drive him to a certain meeting in uttering S *iff*:

A. In uttering S at t, U R'd that there is exactly one x and exactly one y such that:

1. x is addressed by U at t.
2. y is a meeting.
3. U referred to x and y in uttering S at t.
4. It is possible for U to drive x to y.
5. x would prefer U's doing so to U's not doing so.
6. At t U intends to drive x to y.
7. By uttering S, U lays on U an obligation to drive x to y.

B. There is exactly one x and exactly one y such that:

1. x is addressed by U at t.
2. y is a meeting.
3. U referred to x and to y in uttering S at t.

Exercitives

X.

R32. 'I nominate Joe Dobson for secretary' may be uttered at t *iff* there is exactly one x and exactly one y such that:

A. x is named 'Joe Dobson'.

B. y is a particular secretarial position.

C. U refers to x and y in uttering 'I nominate Joe Dobson' at t.

D. x is eligible for y.

E. U has the authority to nominate someone for y.

F. Conditions at t are appropriate for the exercise of this authority.

---

[26] For an explanation of construing the IA as *purporting* to promise, rather than just promising, see 4.4.

G. By uttering 'I nominate Joe Dobson' at t, U brings it about that x is placed in nomination for y.

132. *Purporting to nominate Joe Dobson for a certain secretarial position.*[27]
(RS) U purported to nominate a certain person named Joe Dobson for a certain secretarial position in uttering 'I nominate Joe Dobson for secretary' at t *iff* U subjected U's utterance to R32, satisfying at least requirements A., B., and C.
(R) U purported to nominate a certain person named Joe Dobson for a certain secretarial position in uttering S at t *iff*:
A. In uttering S at t, U R'd that there is exactly one x and exactly one y such that:
1. x is named Joe Dobson.
2. y is a secretarial position.
3. U referred to x and to y in uttering S at t.
4. x is eligible for y.
5. U has the authority to nominate x for y.
6. Conditions at t are appropriate for the exercise of this authority.
7. By uttering S at t, U brings it about that x is placed in nomination for y.
B. There is exactly one x and exactly one y such that:
1. x is named Joe Dobson.
2. y is a secretarial position.
3. U referred to x and to y in uttering S at t.

I will append two comments to this list.

1. It will be noted that speakers and addressees were taken account of in the rules and conditions R'd when and only when they entered into the content of the act, as in 27, 28, 29, and 31. When I ask someone to hand me the newspaper or thank someone for recommending me for a job, the identity of the addressee figures in the propositional content. We can't specify precisely what I requested without making explicit who it was I asked to hand me the newspaper; nor can we specify precisely what I am expressing gratitude for without specifying who it was that recommended me for the job. And when I declare the meeting adjourned, what I am saying includes who it is that is so declaring. But where there is no such involvement, no mention is made of speaker and addressee in bringing out the content of the act, even though there is always a speaker, and there typically is an addressee in a particular token of that act type. I may direct to you an assertion that the key is on the table. But even so your identity does not figure in *what* I was saying.

---

[27] For an explanation of construing this IA as purporting to nominate rather than just nominating, see 4.3.

2. Note that only our first two examples are free of referential complexities. All our other cases bear the marks of the semantic underdetermination of singular reference. And this is not just an artifact of our choice of examples. It is rare for someone to make a request, issue an order, make a promise, or perform an exercitive without engaging in singular reference, whether to the speaker or the addressee or to something else. We order or request particular persons to do particular things. We make promises to particular persons or groups in particular circumstances. And what we are requesting or promising someone to do generally involves some particular persons, things, times, places, or situations.

xi. How I-Rules Make Communication Possible

I will take a moment to bring out just how I-rules make successful communication possible. A fluent speaker of a language enjoys the practical mastery of a system that generates an I-rule for any given sentence of the language. This gives him a working knowledge of the I-rule for any sentence of the language he hears or considers uttering. If he wishes to perform a certain illocutionary act, he will be able to pick a sentence governed by an I-rule that makes the sentence usable for performing illocutionary acts of that sort. If he wishes to speak in a literal, first-order manner, he will make use of just such a sentence. If the sentence exhibits multivocality and/or contains the usual kind of singular referring devices, he will have to do more than just pick the right sentence; he will have to make further choices and see to it that there are contextual clues to those choices. But the I-rule will direct him to do this. If he wishes to speak elliptically or figuratively or perform some parasitic IA, he will need to see to it that the audience has some indication of those intentions. The hearer's situation is the mirror image of this. When she hears a sentence, S, her practical mastery of the language enables her to recognize, intuitively, what I-rule governs that sentence. If there are no contextual indications that some nonstandard employment is being made of the sentence, she will take it that the speaker intends to be performing an illocutionary act of the matching type. If the sentence is multivocal, she will be alert for contextual clues as to which of the acts in the potential the speaker means to be performing. If the matching type is referentially unspecific, she will look for clues as to the precise identity of the objects U is referring to. Insofar as she can make a determination about that, she will have identified a referentially specific act being performed. So long as speakers are, for the most part, subjecting their utterances to the relevant rules, except when providing sufficient contextual clues to deviance, and are giving or exploiting sufficient clues to the choices called for by the rules, then if all parties to the transaction have a sufficient mastery of the language, communication should be secured.

xii. Speaker Meaning

Finally a word about the bearing of my theory on "speaker meaning". In terms of the distinction between *what U means by uttering S* and *what U means by E*, where E is some linguistic expression employed by U, it is the former with which we are concerned. It is this concept that is taken as fundamental by the Griceian approach to meaning in terms of perlocutionary intentions. On that account, for a speaker to mean something by uttering S is for that speaker to utter S with a complicated sort of intention to produce a certain kind of effect in the hearer.[28] Sentence meaning is then exhibited as a kind of generalization over speaker meaning. I have already made it explicit that I reject any perlocutionary intention account of speaker meaning, sentence meaning, or illocutionary act performance. I argued in 2.5 that the illocutionary act performed can remain constant while perlocutionary intentions (including those focused on by these theorists) vary widely; and exactly the same arguments apply to attempts to identify speaker meaning with perlocutionary intentions, as I pointed out in 6.5.

My theory makes possible a very simple account of speaker meaning, one that shows how it can remain constant across variations in the perlocutionary intention. We can identify what U meant in uttering S with U's illocutionary intentions; we can specify what U meant just by specifying what illocutionary act he intended to be performing. If he intended to be telling me that Susie is back in town or to be asking me to leave the room or to be declaring the meeting adjourned, then by specifying that, we will have adequately brought out what he meant.

It is true that illocutionary act specifications do not fit smoothly into the *formula* 'He meant . . . . . '. Roughly speaking, that formula seems to be fitted to specify the propositional content rather than the illocutionary force. Thus we would say not 'He meant that he was telling me that Susie is back in town', but rather 'He meant that Susie is back in town'. Not 'He meant that he was declaring the meeting adjourned' but 'He meant that the meeting was to be terminated'.[29] Perlocutionary intention theorists have tended to confine themselves to this formula in specifying speaker meaning and have allowed this constraint to shape their accounts, but I find this tendency unfortunate. Surely the intended concept of speaker meaning is anchored to something more substantive than the appropriate

[28] The formulation by Grice quoted in 2.2 is a simple specification of the kind of intention required. For a much more complicated formulation see Schiffer 1972, 63.

[29] With requests we have a real difficulty in finding any specification that fits neatly into this formula. Schiffer opts for 'He meant that I was to leave the room', but this seems to be appropriate for orders rather than requests. We might try 'He meant that it would be nice of me to leave the room', or 'He meant that he wanted me to leave the room', but it is not clear that I do have to mean either of those when I make a request.

filling for a certain formula in English. In fact, when Schiffer introduces the notion he says:

> (1a) S meant that . . . . . . by (or in) producing (or doing) *x*.
> Utterances of form (1a) are used to report the "message" S was communicating; that is, quite roughly, the "information" S was communicating or the "directive" S was issuing. (1972, 2)

The last restriction to "information" or a "directive" no doubt reflects the constraints of the "He meant . . . . . ." formula. But the initial phrase, "the 'message' S was communicating", suggests that what S meant by uttering *x* was what he was trying to "get across" to the hearer. This suggests as a basic constraint on speaker meaning that it consists of what the hearer would have to realize in order to understand the speaker. And I submit that what I have to grasp in order to understand what you were trying to communicate is simply what illocutionary act you intended to be performing. Granted that he meant that Susie was back in town, did he intend to be reporting this, conceding this, concluding this, conjecturing this, or what? Until I have answered those questions, I have not fully brought out what he meant to be getting across to the hearer. Granted that he meant that the meeting is adjourned, did he mean to be reporting that the meeting is adjourned, complaining that the meeting is adjourned, or declaring the meeting adjourned? Thus an adequate account of speaker meaning will burst the bonds of the 'he meant . . . . . .' formula. Nothing less than a full specification of the illocutionary act U intended to be performing will give us an adequate account.

CHAPTER EIGHT

The Status of Illocutionary Rules

i. Summary of the Foregoing

I have elaborated a suggestion as to the kind of rule that endows a sentence with an IA potential and, thereby, with a certain meaning by governing it. Such rules, I-rules, are *regulative* rules. A regulative rule is one that lays down conditions under which actions of a certain sort are required, permitted, or forbidden. I-rules lay down necessary and sufficient conditions for the utterance of sentences. Like rules of games, and unlike traffic regulations and moral rules, they apply only when the agent is engaged in a certain sphere of activity, which we have roughly adumbrated as the "literal, first-order, communicative use of language". Within limits it is up to the speaker whether she is engaged in activity of that sort. Within limits, because when a speaker is not playing this game it is incumbent on her to see to it that the audience has sufficient indication of that.

An alternative to my account of sentence meaning in terms of I-rule governance, one that also stresses the "conventional" nature of linguistic meaning, is, naturally enough, one in terms of *conventions*, as contrasted with rules. Both in Schiffer 1972 and in Bennett 1976 we find attempts to employ David Lewis's influential account of conventions in Lewis 1969 for this purpose. The upshot of this would be, roughly speaking, that S means that *p iff* there is a convention in the relevant society of using S to mean that *p*. I find Bennett's version of this more formidable than Schiffer's, and

I gave a critical discussion of it in 6.5. In Section iv of this chapter I will give a more general treatment of the distinction.

ii. Regulative and Constitutive Rules

In an influential section of his 1969 John Searle opines that *constitutive* rules bulk large in the semantics of a natural language. Since I maintain that a uniform account of sentence meaning can be given in terms of regulative rules, I would seem to be opposed to that view. But before concluding that, we must get straight about the regulative-constitutive distinction.

Searle makes the distinction as follows.

> . . . regulative rules regulate antecedent or independently existing forms of behavior. . . . But constitutive rules do not merely regulate, they create or define new forms of behavior. (1969, 33)

Thus a rule to the effect that one must stop one's car when the light is red "regulates" behavior, namely, stopping one's car, that is not dependent on that rule for its existence. There could be such activities as driving and stopping automobiles even if there were no such rule. But consider an example of a constitutive rule given by Searle. "A touchdown is scored when a player has possession of the ball in the opponent's end zone while play is in progress" (34). Here the activity in question, namely, scoring a touchdown, could not exist if it were not for this rule, or at least some such rule. The rule "constitutes" this form of behavior, makes it possible for certain doings to "count as" scoring a touchdown.

Are I-rules regulative or constitutive? They are clearly regulative, since they regulate sentence utterance, which is an "independently existing" form of behavior. Consider, for example, R23 from 7.10.

'All lemons are yellow' may be uttered *iff* all lemons are yellow.

Is uttering that sentence made possible, *constituted*, by that rule? Obviously not. People could utter that sentence even if no such rule were in force. That would be the case if the constituent words meant something different, and in that case the sentence would be governed by a different I-rule. Perhaps there could be no such thing as a language, and hence no such thing as sentence utterance, if there were *no* I-rules in force. That would follow from (a) there could be no language if there were no linguistic communication and (b) there could be no linguistic communication without I-rules. But even if this is true, it by no means follows that the practice of uttering 'All lemons are yellow' is dependent on R23 being in force.

On the other hand, I-rules would seem to qualify as constitutive rules since they "create or define new forms of behavior", namely, illocutionary acts. According to our theory, to perform an illocutionary act is, roughly, to utter a sentence as subject to a certain I-rule, "roughly" because of the qualifications summarized in 7.6. If this is what illocutionary act performance *is*, there could be no such activity without appropriate I-rules in force. It appears that I-rules are related to illocutionary acts in just the way Searle says that constitutive rules are related to the "new forms of behavior" they "create".[1]

Thus we are faced with a dilemma. How can the same rule be both regulative and constitutive? But there is an answer to this question. It is possible just because Searle has not defined these terms so as to mark out mutually exclusive types. Whether a certain activity is dependent on, or independent of, a certain rule depends on how that activity is conceptualized. Suppose I say "Please hand me the newspaper", thereby asking you to hand me a certain newspaper. If we conceptualize my action as "uttering the sentence 'Please hand me the newspaper'", then it is *regulated* by the relevant I-rule. I could have been doing something falling under that description even if there were no such rule. But conceptualized as "requesting someone to hand me a certain newspaper", my action is *constituted* by the I-rule, by the fact that my *sentence utterance* was *regulated* by that I-rule. Thus the terms 'regulative' and 'constitutive' do not stand for different types of rules. They stand for different ways in which a rule is related to action concepts. A rule that qualifies as a "regulative" rule lays down conditions under which actions of a certain type are required, permitted, or forbidden. The rule will be related in the "regulative way", "externally", to the action-type instances of which it declares to be required, permitted, or forbidden under certain conditions. But given a rule related in that way to actions of a certain sort, we can use it to define a different action concept, one that is of a higher level than the concept of the kind of action the rule regulates. In some cases this will be the concept of performing an act of the lower-level type as subject to the rule. This is the way I take illocutionary act concepts to be constituted. The same is true of many concepts of moves in games. We can construe *serving* in tennis as throwing up a tennis ball and hitting it with a tennis racket, where the token of that independently existing type is performed as subject to various regulative rules, such as the rule that requires both feet to be behind the baseline prior to striking the ball with the racket. In other cases the higher-level concept will be the concept of an action that *conforms* to a regulative rule governing acts of a lower-level type. Thus, to welcome someone to my home is to conform to the rules of hospitality, rules that can be construed as regulating antecedently existing actions of opening a door, speaking to a person,

---

[1] Of course, the "constitutive rule" for a touchdown cited above is analogous to an analysis of an IA type, rather than to the I-rule underlying that analysis. I will return to this point below when I make an effort to clean up this messy situation.

and so on. In still other cases the higher-level concept can be construed as *violating* a rule that regulates behavior of a lower-level type. Thus to rob someone is to take property that belongs to someone else, in violation of laws that forbid actions of that type. In all these cases the rule is related *constitutively* to action concepts of the higher-level type.

Not all regulative rules enter into higher-level action concepts in this way. That is, we do not always make use of action concepts that are related in this kind of way to regulative rules. But it is always possible to do so. We lack any one word for eating food *as subject to* certain rules of etiquette. The most concise form we have involves an adverbial modifier—'eating politely'. (Cf. 'driving lawfully'.) But clearly we could introduce a single word to express that concept if we felt a need to do so. The possibility always exists of making use of an action concept that is related to a given regulative rule in the way in which the concept of asking someone to hand me a certain newspaper is related to R28.

Thus any regulative rule can also qualify as a constitutive rule (as Searle defines 'constitutive rule') if we take advantage of the possibilities it presents for concept formation. But there are formulations called 'constitutive rules' by Searle that do not in any way qualify as regulative. These are "rules" that specify under what conditions an action, state of affairs, or whatever counts as having a certain conventional status.[2] (See the explanation of "conventional status" in 4.1.) The rule cited earlier concerning scoring a touchdown in football is such a case. Other examples would be a rule that specifies under what conditions a corporation exists, a rule that specifies the conditions under which one is legally liable for damages, a rule that specifies under what conditions a couple is married, a rule that specifies what it is to hold an academic position with tenure, and so on. It is not clear why such principles should be called 'rules' at all.[3] They simply make explicit the conditions under which some state of affairs "counts as" scoring a touchdown or possessing some other conventional status. They are more like a definition of a term, or at least a specification of necessary and sufficient conditions for the application of a term, than like rules in a distinctive sense of the term. They differ from many other specifications of conditions of application in that the term in question denotes a conventional status. On the other hand, they do at least have this in common with regulative rules. Leaving aside moral rules on an objectivist construal, they are socially malleable. (This follows from their being definitions of conventional statuses.) They exist by virtue of social consent, either by members of the society at large or by those who hold power. It is up to duly constituted authorities what are the conditions for being

---

[2]   Searle is careful to indicate that these do not exhaust the category of constitutive rules (34–35). But he does not recognize the kind of regulative-constitutive overlap I have been pointing out.
[3]   Searle acknowledges this reaction, but he puts it down as an unwarranted parochialism.

married, for scoring a touchdown, or for being liable for damages. In any event, despite my reservations about the terminology, to avoid awkwardness I will continue to use the term 'constitutive rule' for these "count as" principles while discussing Searle on semantic rules.

Note that instead of saying that an I-rule like I23 counts as both a regulative and a constitutive rule, we could have left it purely in the former status and replaced its "constitutive" function by a Searle-like "count as" rule—"An utterance counts as *asserting that all lemons are yellow* when it is governed by I23." There is merely a bookkeeping difference between saying this and saying that I23 is itself both a regulative and a constitutive rule. But putting it in the former way can sensitize us to the fact that in many paradigm cases of count-as rules the conventional status thus defined is itself constituted, at least in part, by the holding of regulative rules. The difference between a couple's being married and not being married consists, in part and possibly in whole, in what actions by themselves and others are thereby required, permitted, or forbidden. In getting married one acquires obligations vis-à-vis one's spouse, and certain things are permitted that were otherwise forbidden, and vice versa. Similarly, in becoming chairman of the department I acquire various obligations, and other people acquire obligations to respond to my actions in certain ways. If all social statuses consist in the applicability of regulative rules, we would have shown that regulative rules are the fundamental sort, and that "count as" rules are really metaregulative rules, specifications of the conditions under which regulative rules come into force.

Here is another complexity in this territory. A count-as rule that defines status s as supervening on doing a under conditions c will often presuppose lower-level count-as rules in specifying the a and/or the c. Go back to the touchdown rule. The behavior involved is "being in possession of the ball". But that is not just *physical* possession; it is *de jure* possession, being *entitled* to having the ball. And it is another count-as rule that spells out what that amounts to. One of the conditions involves the opponent's end zone. But a certain part of the field being, at that time, the "opponent's end zone" is itself a conventional status defined by some count-as rule. And so we get the phenomenon of count-as rules piled on top of each other, as well as count-as rules supervening on regulative rules.

To apply all this to the main concern of this book, let's consider the stratification of linguistic behavior in terms of these distinctions. To perform a sentential act one must conform, at least minimally, to regulative grammatical rules governing the concatenation of sequential utterances of morphemes. This can be formulated as a count-as rule defining what it is to utter a token of 'The house is on fire'. To perform an IA one must utter a sentence as subject to a certain I-rule (and in some cases at least partially conform to that rule). This too can be the basis of a count-as rule defining what it is to perform an IA of a certain type. Finally, to perform a certain perlocutionary act, for example, getting one's son to clean his room, is for a certain IA to have a certain causal result. Here the generation of a higher-level act does not involve any additional rules of any sort or any sort of conventional status. Hence Searle would, presumably, not be tempted to suppose that a statement of the necessary and sufficient conditions for getting one's son to clean his room by saying something would be a "constitutive" or any other kind of rule.

Finally, if we want the term 'constitutive' to stand for a type of rule that excludes regulative rules, we had better reserve it for "count as" rules. But if the term 'constitutive' is explained as Searle does, we must recognize that I-rules and many others count as both regulative and constitutive.

iii. Unformulated Rules

It may be doubted that there are any I-rules, as we have described them.

First, formulations of I-rules play no role in the use of language, or in the learning and teaching of first or subsequent languages. There are no rule books for the conduct of illocutionary activity, books to which one could refer in settling disputed points or to which one could appeal when one accuses a speaker of a violation. Indeed, I-rules have never been formulated even in theoretical discourse except my myself and a very few other speech act theorists. This being the case, can we really suppose that I-rules exist, that they are *in force* in language communities, that speech behavior is *subject to* them or *governed by* them? Since speakers do not monitor their speech by reference to such rules, even occasionally or when confronted with a difficult case, can it be supposed that speakers perform illocutionary acts by virtue of laying themselves open to blame in case they knowingly violate I-rules?

Reflections like these give rise to questions concerning the mode of reality of linguistic and other social rules. What is it for such a rule to be "in force" in a social group? And what is it for an agent to guide her behavior by reference to a rule? The doubts just expressed are based on supposing that a necessary condition for all this is that the putative rule be formulated, and that the formulation be available to, and used by, the participants in the sphere of activity in question. And it must be admitted that when formulations of rules are available and invoked, we have a maximally clear case of rule-governed behavior. This is the way it is with "formalized" games for which rules have been drawn up; this is the way it is with traffic regulations, codes of civil and criminal law, and rules of conduct for employees. The present objection assumes that where this ideally perspicuous state of affairs does not obtain, we do not have rule-governed activity.

Perhaps our opponent is challenging us to show how to distinguish rule-governed behavior from "mere regularities" or "mere habits" when rule formulations are not employed. Let's assume that rules in force in a group are generally conformed to.[4] Then how do we distinguish regularities in behavior that are due to the governance of rules from "mere regularities"? How do we identify those cases in which the regularity exists because of the normative force of the rule? Where rule formulations are employed in the ways just mentioned, it is easy to make the discrimination. Where penalties are imposed for rule violations, the diagnosis is even more obvious. There are certain by-and-large regularities in the behavior on a football field while a game is in progress. Offensive linemen usually do not move before the ball is transferred from the center to a back. An offensive player usually does not hold another unless the latter has the ball. It is no mystery why we find these recurrent patterns. The rules of football, as codified in a rule book, forbid one to hold an opposing player unless the latter has the ball. When a player is apprehended holding another player who does not have the ball, a penalty is assessed. When people learn the game, they read the rules or are told what they are. They learn to monitor their own behavior in terms of those rules. It is clear that the regularity exists because the corresponding rule is in force. But none of this applies to the fact that, by and large, people utter 'please pass the salt' in literal, first-order, communicative speech only when they want the addressee to pass them some salt. So why should we suppose that this regularity reflects the guidance and evaluation of behavior in terms of I-rules? Indeed, what does it *mean* to say that such rules are in force?

I will work my way toward answering this question by first considering some other aspects of behavior with respect to which talk of unformulated rules is a going concern. I will look at established practices of explaining regularities in behavior in terms of rules that are not formulated by any of the participants, and practices of taking agents to guide their behavior and criticize the behavior of others in terms of unformulated rules. I will consider what it is about these cases that lead theorists to regard them as involving rules. If we can bring out the basis for doing this, this will provide some content to talk of unformulated rules. Then we can ask whether we have the same kind of basis for supposing that speech is governed by I-rules that are not formulated or even formulable by the participants.

After spending some time in Libya we conclude that people generally stand closer to each other in conversation than in the United States. Let's say that the usual distance in Libya is 1 to 1.5 feet. The question is whether this regularity reflects a rule in force in the society or whether it is a "mere regularity". If Libyans propound a rule of conversational distance in socializing their children, and if the rule is adduced from time to time in jus-

---

[4]   This will not hold of all cases. Speed limits are an obvious exception. Nevertheless I believe that the assumption holds for most rules, and that those rules "more honored in the breach than in the observance" are in a distinct minority.

tification of one's disapproval of the conduct of a conversation, that would settle the matter. But what if Libyans never formulate any such rule and are unaware of shaping their conversational behavior in accordance with such a rule? In that case where can we find evidence to decide between the *rule* and the *mere regularity* interpretations?

I suggest that the crucial data are to be found not in what goes on when speakers are *conforming* to the putative rule, but rather in reactions to *violations*. Here, as elsewhere, a study of pathology can reveal factors that are hidden in the smooth operation of normal cases. If it is a "mere regularity", we can expect exceptions to attract no special notice, except perhaps surprise. If, on the other hand, the regularity reflects a socially accepted rule, we can expect those who observe the violation to recognize it as something incorrect, untoward, not allowed, deviant. Let's call such a reaction an "incorrectness judgment". An incorrectness judgment may be manifested in a variety of ways—by pointing out that "we don't do it that way", by upbraiding the offender, by applying some negative sanction or other, by ridicule, or simply by "acting uncomfortable". Or there may be no overt manifestation at all if there is sufficient reason for inhibition or if the violation is not serious enough to be worth the trouble. Thus my suggestion is that a by-and-large regularity of doing A in circumstances C reflects the sway of a rule if and only if deviations from this regularity will generally evoke incorrectness judgments in members of the society who perceive it.[5] This criterion will serve to distinguish rule-governed regularities from mere regularities whether or not the rules are formulated.

The same criterion will reveal some regularities to be merely that. Suppose that in Libya there is also a regular practice of putting on the left shoe before the right. Again, no such rule in inculcated or invoked. But here, let's say, exceptions do not evoke incorrectness judgments. When someone puts her right shoe on first, no one takes any special notice; she is not upbraided, ostracized, or called to account in any way; witnesses of this event are not rendered uncomfortable. The reason we had for imputing a rule in the social distance case is lacking here.

We can illustrate the same point with aspects of speech that are less hidden than the semantic aspect. A fluent speaker will be capable of recognizing flagrantly ungrammatical constructions like 'The in hit boy' as unacceptable, as being incorrect or not right, without being able to formulate any general rule that is being violated. Even if the speaker does not possess a general concept of grammaticality, he will still recognize a markedly ungrammatical sentence as not okay when he hears it. The same goes for

---

[5] I am not saying that a necessary condition for the holding of a rule is that violations are invariably judged incorrect; people can fail to recognize rule violations, just as they can fail to recognize other facts. Still less am I making it a necessary condition of the holding of a rule that violations evoke overt reactions indicating recognition of inappropriateness. Too many other factors influence the character of overt reactions.

phonology. A fluent speaker of English will recognize 'brnogl' not to be a combination of sounds that "occurs" in English, even if she lacks any capacity to formulate phonological rules. In these cases there is a definite capacity to spot something as wrong without being able to say, in general, what the conditions are for doing it right.

Where a regular practice of incorrectness judgments is associated with a behavioral regularity, we can reasonably suppose that this practice, and its typical behavioral upshots, plays a role in maintaining the regularity. People by and large keep their conversational distances within certain bounds because if they don't they may suffer sanctions—blame, disapproval, punishment, or social ostracization. The strength and frequency of sanctions that are required to maintain a regularity will vary with the frequency of exceptions. If observing the regularity is burdensome or tedious or painful, or if there are strongly motivated alternatives, then more and stronger sanctions are needed than where opposing forces are negligible. But whatever is needed for *maintenance*, sanctions are frequently required to *establish* the regularity in the neophyte. This socialization process provides the clearest indication of the existence of unformulated rules. Where we see a regular practice of rewarding the initiate for refraining from A in C, or punishing him for or discouraging him from doing A in C, we have a particularly clear demonstration of the existence of a rule that forbids doing A in C.

We have been led to the social reality of unformulated rules by way of considering the activity of *critics*, of reactions to rule *violations*. This enables us to answer our first question, what basis we can have for supposing that rules the participants are unable to formulate are in force in a society. And these considerations also provide the answer to the question of what it is for behavior to be *evaluated* by reference to an unformulated rule. However, we have not yet specified what it is for members of the society to *apply* unformulated rules to their first-level activity, determine whether or not to do A in a particular situation *in the light of* or *by reference to* that unformulated rule, *guide* their activity by reference to such rules. What is it for an unformulated rule to play a role in shaping behavior? Does this require that the agent in some sense *know* what the rule is and *make use* of it in monitoring his behavior? And if so, how is this possible in the absence of rule formulation?

Since we got our original purchase onto unformulated rules by concentrating on the second-level activity of noting rule violations, rather than on the agent who is conforming to or violating the rule, we may be well advised to attack the problem of psychological mechanisms by continuing, for the moment, to study the critic. When one recognizes a performance to be incorrect, does one do so, in some sense, *by reference to* the rule? Is one *making use* of the rule? Does the critical reaction presuppose some kind of (perhaps tacit or unconscious) *knowledge* of the rule?

I believe that this question can most usefully be approached by comparing patterns of incorrectness judgments with and without an explicit appeal to a rule. Let's consider two societies, A and B, in which incorrectness judgments with respect to conversational distance are made under the same conditions. In society A the judgers are prepared to back up their judgments by citing a rule and often do so, whereas in society B the judgers are incapable of this. In the two societies the same discriminations are made. And it is not just that in some actual spread of cases there is no discrepancy as to which distances are judged acceptable or unacceptable. It is rather that in both societies people are so constituted (their brains are so programmed) that any distance within, say, 1.5 to 2.5 feet *would be* judged acceptable and any other distance would be judged unacceptable. In both cases we have ample reason to believe that members of the society have acquired a stable disposition to react differently with respect to judgments of correctness or incorrectness to a conversational distance, depending on whether it does or does not fall (roughly) within the 1.5 to 2.5 foot range. The only difference between the cases is that in A, people have also learned how to represent this discriminative capacity in the form of a rule. Thus the difference between A and B can be seen as a special case of the familiar difference between the possession of a cognitive capacity or tendency and the higher-level capacity to conceptualize, describe, or report that capacity. It is like the difference between using a word with a certain meaning and being able to say what the meaning is; or the difference between recognizing another person to be angry whenever presented with certain perceptual cues and being able to specify just what those cues are.

Once we view the matter in this way we are free of the constraint to treat the "formulated rule" case as the basic case, others being intelligible only by derivation or analogy. On the contrary, the basic substance of rule holding lies in what the cases have in common, namely, the pervasiveness in the society of a certain discriminative capacity. It is in the general possession of that capacity that the existence of the rule primarily consists. When the rule gets formulated, that is an added fillip. Society A adds something to the basic case, rather than society B taking something away from it.

But what about whether a "critic" in society B *knows* the rule, *makes use of it* in his criticism, reacts to violations *in the light of the rule*? A proper sense of the diversity of ways of knowing will indicate a positive answer. Think of the analogous cognitive capacities just mentioned. Does the naive judge of the moods of others *know* that, for example, a fixed jaw indicates anger if he has never formulated this generalization? Does the naive speaker of English know that among the meanings of 'run' are (approximately) *operate, force,* and *extend,* assuming that she has never reflected on the matter? Well, as you like it. There is certainly a difference between the reflective and unreflective cases. The former has something the latter doesn't, namely, a capacity to say explicitly that *p*. But does this mean that the un-reflective person doesn't know that *p*? We do frequently talk of knowledge where formulation is not available. We say that the dog knows that he is about to be fed or that someone is at the door. Indeed, we attribute to the dog general knowledge—that rocks are inedible and that steak is edible. With unformulated rule following we have the same basis for imputing knowledge, namely, a stable disposition for making certain kinds of discriminative reactions depending on whether certain conditions are satisfied. In just that way our naive subject knows that a fixed jaw is a sign of anger, that in 'The boundary runs to that tree', 'run' means *extend*, and that only conversational distances between 1 and 1.5 feet are acceptable. This is not a mere knowledge how, such as is involved in being able to drive a nail straight. It involves *cognitive* discriminations, judgments that something is the case or is allowable, discriminations at a more sophisticated level than the perceptual discriminations involved in knowing how to drive a nail straight. For this reason it can claim to be a kind of "knowledge that".

This account enables us to steer a middle course between Chomsky and some of his harsher critics. For it allows us to recognize a genuine *knowledge that* in the no-formulation case, while avoiding the tendency to attribute to the naive speaker an unconscious, "tacit" *representation* of the rules. On this latter view, the only difference between the ideally accomplished grammarian and the typical native speaker is that the former has succeeded in bringing into consciousness a conceptual and propositional structure that exists full-blown in unconscious form in all of us. I am far from maintaining that the notion of unconscious symbolization is absurd or unintelligible, but I fail to see that Chomsky or anyone else has made an adequate case for its postulation in this kind of case. The position advocated here enables us to recognize an important sense in which the naive agent knows that certain rules obtain, while avoiding the supposition that he has formulated the rules on any level.

If this is how matters stand with the "critic", what can we say about the "actor"? Fortunately, in the areas of our present concern the critics are also actors and vice versa. The very same people (all of us) who note incorrectness in conversational distance, themselves engage in conversation at various distances and, by and large, keep those distances within the allowable range. How is this latter regularity in first-level behavior to be explained? Well, the critics, who have the kind of knowledge of the rule we have just been describing, do not lose that knowledge when they assume the role of actor. They carry with them the capacity to discriminate between correct and incorrect distance ranges. This capacity enables them to monitor their own performance, so that when they see themselves veering into the disapproved range they tend to pull back. In this way one may "guide one's behavior" by a rule without being able to formulate it.

It follows from the above that a rule cannot be identified with any particular formulation or set of formulations. This has to be recognized whether or not there can be unformulated rules. We might say "There is no longer a rule in football that limits substitution", but the truth of that statement is compatible with the existence of a formulation of a rule that limits substitution. But then with what is the rule to be identified? Is it the discriminative capacity or tendency, the pattern of formation of incorrectness judgments, the social sanctions that maintain these patterns, or what? I don't propose to answer that question. I will content myself with explicating various larger expressions in which terms for rules appear, such as "R8 (a certain rule) being in force in a society", "one's conforming to or violating R8", "one's guiding one's behavior by R8", "A's evaluating B's behavior in the light of R8", and so on. It would be nice to have an explicit definition of 'rule', rather than just a set of contextual definitions; for an explicit definition would put us in a position to say what a given rule *is* or *consists in*. But I don't know how to do that, and so I will content myself with a piece-by-piece explication of rule talk.

I don't mean to suggest that there are no important differences between cases in which agents work with formulations of the rules and cases in which they don't. As in other matters, when we get things out in the open, the criticism and refinement of discriminations is facilitated. So long as language learning is confined to the way in which a small child picks up her native tongue, things go along well enough without any formulation of phonological and grammatical rules. But when it is a matter of teaching someone a second language in a hurry, explicit formulation of those rules is essential. Again, formulation of the rules will make possible a much more precise system of sanctions, with safeguards against inappropriate application, than when sanction application is a matter of spontaneous reactions to something's seeming not right. My contention is only that formulation is not necessary for rule governance and rule guidance.

iv. Rules and Conventions

This is an appropriate point at which to explain why I treat meaning in terms of *rules* rather than in terms of *conventions*. The latter term is used in very different ways, as we have seen 'rule' to be in 7.3. We need to pin down 'convention', just as I have done for 'rule'. The most prominent contemporary account of convention is the one developed in David Lewis's fascinating book of that title (Lewis 1969). There he specifies conditions under which a behavioral regularity counts as acting in conformity to a convention. Roughly, the regularity must be such that members of a community maintain it because they mutually know that they have maintained it in the past and that it has solved for them a recurring kind of coordination problem. A paradigm example is the convention as to the side of the road one drives on.[6] This analysis has been modified for semantic use in Bennett 1976.[7] The original account was restricted to coordinating *actions* with *actions*. But in communication no (overt) action must be forthcoming from a hearer in order that communication is secured. Hence in order to make the notion of convention applicable to speech, Bennett suggests replacing 'action' with 'doings', where this latter term includes, as well as actions ordinarily so called, belief acquisitions and other responses that, on the Griceian model of communication, the speaker intends to be evoking from the hearer in the typical Griceian way.[8] He then construes the fact that a sentence has a certain meaning in a community as a matter of its utterance being governed by a certain convention.

> In a two-member community, U wants to communicate to A that P, using the Griceian mechanism;[9] and when U utters something, A wants to know what he means by it. In this situation . . . coordination is achieved if U utters something intending to communicate P, and A does think that what U means is P. . . . Now, if U and A mutually believe that in the past whenever U has uttered S he has meant that P, and A has taken him to mean that P, then this mutual belief *both* gives U a reason for again uttering S if he wants to communicate P *and* gives A evidence that when U next utters S he means P. In this way a certain coordination in their *doings* is achieved: their mutual knowledge of a past regularity has led them to maintain it in further instances because it is their best chance of continuing to achieve that coordination in which A takes out of an utterance what U put into it. . . .
>
> So we can smoothly combine Grice with Lewis: conventional meaning involves the use of Lewis-conventions to coordinate the Griceian intentions of speakers with the belief-acquisitions of hearers. (179)

Thus the fact that a sentence, S, means that P consists in there being a convention according to which when one utters S one means that P.[10]

This account of sentence meaning differs in more than one important respect from my rule-based account of sentence meaning. These differ-

---

[6] As this example illustrates, Lewis does not restrict the regularities he is discussing to invariable ones.
[7] Bennett notes (1976, 178) that Lewis has accepted this modification.
[8] See 2.2 for an explanation of this.
[9] For 'Griceian mechanism' see 6.5.
[10] Bennett 1976, 16. Bennett is deliberately ignoring complications deriving from multivocality, figurative uses, and other sources of variety in what one means by a certain sentence. I also note that, as pointed out in 6.5, later in the book Bennett backs away from this account of sentence meaning in terms of convention in favor of one in terms of "non-coincidental regularities", which includes regularities that count as conventions but others as well. However, my present concern is specifically with an account of sentence meaning in terms of Lewis-Bennett style conventions.

ences stem both from the Grice and from the Lewis components. Having already dealt with the Griceian aspect, in 6.5, I would like now to concentrate on the Lewis contribution, but I am unable to cleanly separate them. As the above quotation indicates, the conventions in question are regularities in what a speaker means by an utterance, which is given a (modified) Griceian construal. For U to mean that p is construed as U's intending to produce an activated belief in p in H "by means of the Griceian mechanism", that is, relying on means that are intention dependent in some way. So the speaker meaning that is one pole of the regularity that becomes a convention has already been explicated in terms of perlocutionary intentions. Since on my view speaker meaning is construed in terms of IA performance, which in turn presupposes subjection to I-rules, the order of analysis is quite different. Whereas rules are at the base of my analysis, conventions come into the Bennett position only after speaker meaning has been given an account in terms of perlocutionary intentions. Hence the appeal to Lewis-Bennett conventions instead of rules is not a live option for me. It is ruled out by the structure of my account. A second, perhaps less fundamental difference is that my I-rules, and hence IA's, have to do purely with the speaker end of the transaction. I can say something to my wife, meaning that I will not be home for dinner, even if she doesn't hear me. And, as I argued in 2.4 and 2.5, there is no particular audience reaction I even have to be aiming at in order to mean that by what I say. So the difference between Bennett and myself on sentence meaning goes deeper than the mere difference between rule and convention. It involves differences in the shape of the analyses that prevent me from using Lewisian convention (in Bennett's version) in my construal of sentence meaning.

Nevertheless I can say something about the place to be given such conventions from the perspective of my theory. I don't need to deny that there are conventions à la Lewis, either in general or in communication. I can agree with Bennett that Lewisian conventions of communication hold and make possible the kind of coordination of speaker and hearer that he specifies. What I can't agree with, for reasons given in 2.4, 2.5, and 6.5, is that speaker meaning is to be understood in the Griceian way, and hence that sentence meaning is to understood in terms of his marriage of that account with Lewis's account of convention. As I see it, the conventions are there, but they supervene on meaning, both speaker meaning and linguistic meaning, rather than being constitutive of the latter.

This rule vs. convention discussion has been conducted in terms of Lewis's account of conventions. There are less specific uses of the term in which anything that exists by virtue of social norms that are alterable in principle by social agreement is a "matter of convention". So understood, my rules are "matters of convention".

v. Do I-Rules Exist?

I take it that the considerations of Section iii suffice to show that the nonexistence of I-rules does not follow from the fact that rule formulations typically play no role in IA performance and its assessment. But this only opens up the *possibility* that I-rules have the role I assign them. The question remains as to whether they do so in fact. I will divide the question. (1) Are I-rules in force in linguistic communities? (2) Is it by virtue of being governed by I-rules that sentences have the meanings they have? I will discuss (1) in this section. A large part of the argument of the book is a support for an affirmative answer to (2). In the final chapter I will survey contributions made by previous chapters to that support and add to it by comparing my account of sentence meaning with a variety of alternatives.

Section iii indicates what we should look for to answer (1). When someone issues an utterance that would be in violation of an I-rule if there are such things, is this generally perceived as something wrong, incorrect, amiss, not in order? If that is the case, we should expect negative sanctions of one sort of another, if the social situation makes that appropriate.

As for the evaluative perception side, it seems clear that there are regular patterns of such reactions. When someone promises to do D without intending to do so or without having adequate justification for supposing that he can do so, when someone performs an exercitive without proper authority, when someone asks H to do something without wanting H to do it, we typically recognize that something has gone awry. The speaker shouldn't have said that in those circumstances. But unless we take account of certain complexities, the case for this will seem less strong than it is.

In Chapter 3 I stressed the difference between objective and subjective wrongness and pointed out that in any sort of rule-governed behavior an action can be objectively in violation of a rule without the agent's being properly held to blame for it. This may be because the agent had every reason to suppose that what the rule required was the case, because the violation was justified in this instance through being required to satisfy an overriding obligation, because the agent was forced to do what he did, or for any of a variety of other reasons. Therefore we should not restrict evaluative perceptions to cases of *blaming* the speaker for issuing the utterance.

Here is another problem with the project of flushing out unformulated I-rules by looking for conditions under which speakers are blamed. We assume that every speaker is alive to the importance of linguistic communication and alive, in a know-how sort of way, to the fact that I-rules must be conformed to, by and large, if communication is to be possible. Hence we assume that no one deliberately violates an I-rule except in order to deceive one's audience. But deliberate deception is a violation of a moral rule. It is morally wrong to exploit the rules and conventions of language in the interest of deceit. Hence what is behind the blaming of speakers for what my view counts as violations of I-rules is a *moral* principle that forbids deception, rather than semantic rules.

This plausible-sounding argument suffers from a confusion of levels. The moral rule in question regulates illocutionary act performance. Since such performance is made possible by the external application of I-rules to sentential acts, the moral rule presupposes that latter application. It is deceptive to promise to do D when I do not intend to do D. Thus a moral rule prohibits doing this. But that rule is stated in terms of the illocutionary act of promising, which itself presupposes the regulation of sentential acts by I-rules. Try applying the moral rule directly to sentence utterance. Is it morally impermissible to utter the sentence 'I promise to take you to the meeting this evening' when I have no intention of taking you to the meeting this evening? Only if uttering that sentence in those circumstances would constitute making a promise to take you to the meeting this evening. Otherwise there is nothing morally wrong with the utterance. I didn't do anything morally wrong just now in writing that sentence without intending to take anyone to any meeting this evening. Thus we have two different kinds of rules that attach to two different levels of speech. One is not playing the literal, first-order, linguistic communication game correctly if one utters that sentence in the absence of the conditions specified by the appropriate I-rule. But if one utters the sentence as subject to that rule and thereby is making a certain promise, one thereby becomes liable to moral fault if one does that without the corresponding intention. Hence the moral judgment is not in competition with the judgment of I-rule violation. These are two different faults, the moral one presupposing the possibility of the semantic one.

It may also be felt that some cases of what appear in my system as violations of I-rules are not regarded as "incorrect" or "amiss" in any way that reflects the holding of a regulative rule. Consider false assertions. If I say 'Your son is at my house', succeeding in referring to a son of yours, but that person is not at my house at that time, something is amiss all right, but it may not involve any rule violation. Suppose I have made an honest mistake. What *rule* have I violated? Whether my assertion is true or false is a factual, not a normative, matter. It depends on whether the person referred to is at my house at the time of utterance, not on whether that utterance is in violation of some rule.

This line of argument depends on a level confusion similar to the one just exposed. It is the *assertion* that is true or false, or, if you prefer, it is *what I asserted* that is true or false. The I-rule, on the other hand, regulates the sentential act, and the wrongness that consists in violating that I-rule is something amiss with the utterance of the sentence. If there were no such rule, or if the sentence was not uttered as subject to that rule, there would be no assertion to be true or false. Thus we must distinguish the perception of an out-of-order sentence utterance from the judgment that the assertion, or what is asserted, is false.

Both these confusions arise from the difficulty of peeling off the illocutionary stratum of speech and focusing on the underlying sentential stratum. In acquiring a language we learn to concentrate on the illocutionary level. We often remember what someone said but not exactly what words she used. We focus on the sentential level only when no illocutionary acts are being performed, or when we can't understand them, or when we are not interested in them, or when there is something specially striking about the sentential acts—pronunciation, intonation, or whatever. Hence when it comes to evaluation we naturally tend to concentrate on the illocutionary level. This complicates the task of recovering I-rules from patterns of evaluative perception. The cure for this is to follow up a suggestion made in Section iii and look at what happens when a neophyte is learning the language. There we can't assume that the agent already knows how to perform illocutionary acts and will be doing so successfully most of the time. The speaker is learning how to build an illocutionary stratum on the sentential stratum. Since this is made possible by the mastery of a system of I-rules governing sentential acts, we should be able to ascertain that from a careful analysis of what goes on in this context. And so it is. We seek to get across to the small child that he is not to say 'A rabbit is outside' unless there is a rabbit outside, that he is not, in serious fact-stating discourse, to say 'John's brother is fat' unless John has a brother, that he is not to say 'My foot hurts' unless his foot hurts. I don't mean to suggest that we *formulate* I-rules in the course of the training. We try to get across to him when it is and is not all right for him to utter a certain sentence; this amounts to giving him an implicit grasp of I-rules. And once he has mastered certain sentence patterns, much of the instruction involves teaching him the meaning of words, leaving it up to him to fit them into sentence slots where appropriate. The details of first language learning are enormously complicated. But one thing that is crucially involved is the disposition on the part of the teachers to spot cases in which the learner utters a sentence in violation of an I-rule and apply appropriate correction. Gross sanctions are normally not called for. Mastering a first language is not a laborious or painful task, nor do powerful urges have to be suppressed to attain this goal. But parents do, consciously or unconsciously, reward conformity to I-rules and discourage deviance by their reactions. Second language learning is somewhat similar in these respects except that here the neophyte has already learned to perform and to report illocutionary acts in the first language. As a result, more sophisticated teaching is possible, and illocutionary act concepts can be used in the instruction. ("To ask for a glass of milk in French, you say . . .") Hence the governance of sentential acts by I-rules is not evident here. The empirical case for the existence of I-rules rests to a considerable extent on observations of the way in which social pressure for conformity to I-rules comes into prominence in situations, like those of first language learning, where it is socially important to establish conformity.

Some readers may be worried by the fact that I am committed to an infinite number of I-rules in a language. Since no limit can be placed on the number of meaningful sentences in a language, and since, on my theory, a sentence means what it does by virtue of being governed by an I-rule, we get this result. But how is it possible for an infinite number of rules to be in force in a society made up of persons with finite capacities?

This would indeed be impossible if rules were not distinguished from rule formulations; a rule book of infinite size has not been attained even in our bureaucratic society. But even if we recognize that distinction, we are still liable to fall into thinking of distinguishable rules as existing in separate compartments of the minds of speakers, or as inhabiting separate "strands" or "patterns" of interpersonal transactions. But given the account in Section iii of what it is for a rule to hold in a society, all that is necessary for there to be an infinite number of I-rules in force is that members of the linguistic community should be disposed, with respect to each distinguishable sentence, to see an utterance of the sentence as out of order in case certain conditions are not satisfied. This can be true even if each individual has only a finite capacity, provided these dispositions have a recursive structure. That structure would be provided by an internalized mechanism for generating I-rules from a finite vocabulary and stock of structural principles. And that is the way to think of the matter. We should not think of speakers having a distinct psychological state for each I-rule. Rather, the fluent speaker has acquired a procedure for determining, for any given sentence, the conditions under which an utterance of that sentence would be amiss. It is an enormous, and still unfulfilled, task to give an adequate description of this procedure. But the general lines of the solution to the above difficulty should be clear.[11]

vi. Drawing Boundaries around *I-Act* and *I-Rule*

One task left over by the above is drawing boundaries around the general concepts of *illocutionary act* and *illocutionary rule*. I have provided schemata of analysis for various illocutionary act concepts that have been intuitively identified as such. (They are concepts that are employed to give

[11] Once we appreciate the possibilities of a recursive structure, we should not be disturbed by the fact that an infinite number of the generable sentences in a language are too complex for speakers of the language to handle. That is no problem for the I-rule account because it is a general limitation on any account of sentence meaning. Provided I-rules are generable and usable for any sentences we are capable of dealing with, that is all that can be reasonably required of the I-rule theory.

oratio obliqua reports; they are concepts that we use to make explicit the "content" of an utterance.) Examples of I-rules were developed out of our examples of illocutionary act concepts, and we determined how such rules should be formulated. Can we extract an analysis, definition, or illuminating characterization of the general concepts of an illocutionary act and of an illocutionary rule out of these maneuvers?

Before discussing this I want to point out that the fate of my theories of illocutionary acts and of sentence meaning does not hang on its outcome. If we can say, in more precise and explicit terms than our initial rough criteria, how illocutionary acts differ from all others and how I-rules differ from all other rules, that will be all to the good. But if we fail in that attempt, our theory of sentence meaning will not be devoid of content. So long as we have a workable way of picking out illocutionary act concepts and of correlating them with I-rules, we have a grasp of those concepts that is sufficient to give content to the theory. Nevertheless, I-acts and I-rules do differ in some general way(s) from other acts (rules). And if we had a unified formula for making those discriminations, our understanding of the subject matter would be more complete.

As for illocutionary acts, there is a general characterization that emerges from our schemata. To perform an illocutionary act is to R certain conditions in performing some lower-level act. But this characterization is too general; it covers, for example, moves in games. To serve in tennis is to throw up the ball and hit it toward a certain part of the opposite court, R'ing, for example, that one's feet have not touched the ground inside one's own court before the ball leaves the racket. Indeed, as pointed out in Section ii, wherever we have regulative rules we have the possibility of a concept of performing an action as subject to such a rule. Consider the traffic regulation that forbids a driver from pulling out into the street in the path of oncoming traffic. If I pull out into the street as subject to that rule, I am pulling out, R'ing that the street is clear. But neither here nor in serving in tennis am I performing an illocutionary act. This characterization just gives us a genus of which illocutionary acts constitute a species. What is the differentia?

For one thing, with I-acts, unlike the above cases, the lower-level act is the utterance of a sentence or the production of some substitute for a sentence. At this point I could reopen the controversy in 1.7 as to whether I-acts are restricted to the utterance of sentences or sentence substitutes. But that is not necessary, for we can illustrate nonillocutionary R'ing where the lower-level act is sentential. All we need are some nonsemantic regulative rules that apply to sentence utterance, and such rules are easily found. Consider rules that forbid loud talking in a library or sickroom, and rules that prohibit obscene language in social situations of certain kinds. Since the second example is a bit out of date, I will focus on the first. Suppose I utter 'Where is the card catalog?' in a library with my mind on the rule that one should not speak loudly in that place. It's clear that this R'ing makes no contribution to the illocutionary act performed, namely, asking where the card catalog is. Asking about the card catalog with and without performing the utterance as subject to the rule that requires speaking softly is of the same illocutionary act type. And that's not because the condition R'd has to do with my current utterance. We have included conditions like that among those R'd in exercitives, commissives, and directives, namely, conditions that specify that the speaker by her utterance is producing a certain conventional effect. Indeed, the R'ing that one is speaking softly could go into the constitution of an illocutionary act; it would if the speaker had been making a standard use of the sentence 'I'm speaking softly'. But in the above library case that R'ing did not contribute to any illocutionary act performance. And if I uttered 'Roses are red' in the library, R'ing that I am speaking softly and nothing more (I am practicing conforming to the rule), I didn't perform any illocutionary act at all. Thus not every case of R'ing something in uttering a sentence is a case of illocutionary act performance, and so we can't give a general account of illocutionary acts just by saying that such an act consists in R'ing one or more conditions in uttering a sentence or sentence surrogate.

These same considerations apply to the question of what distinguishes I-rules from other rules. Try the hypothesis that an I-rule is one that lays down conditions for the permissible utterance of a sentence. That would imply that the requirement of speaking softly in the library is an I-rule, and hence that it would always contribute to the constitution of an illocutionary act when a sentence is uttered as subject to it. And it would imply that if we were to add this restriction to one of our I-rules, that would give us a somewhat richer I-rule, subjection to which would generate a richer illocutionary act. But the above library case constitutes a counterexample to these suggestions as well. Hence we must look further to find what distinguishes I-rules from other rules that specify conditions for permissible sentence utterance.

If we go back to illocutionary acts, remembering that they were originally introduced as things done in *communication*, the idea suggest itself that the reason my R'ing that I'm speaking softly in the library case does not contribute to the content of an illocutionary act is that the utterance is not designed to communicate to anyone that I am R'ing that I am speaking softly. This R'ing is not tied to a communicative intent. Recall that I take illocutionary acts performed in interpersonal communication to involve an aim by the speaker, U, to get the addressee to realize that U R's the conditions U is R'ing in performing that illocutionary act. This suggests that we can distinguish the R'ings that are and are not constitutive of illocutionary act performance by the presence or absence of the correlated communicative intention. And illocutionary act concepts are distinguished from other concepts of R'ing that p in uttering a sentence by the fact that they also include the condition that U utters the sentence with the intention of getting the addressee to realize that U is R'ing that *p*.

To be sure, this move will only separate out illocutionary acts in interpersonal communication. It does not distinguish remarking to myself that it's getting warmer by uttering 'It's getting warmer' from uttering that sentence as subject to a rule forbidding the use of obscene language while practicing pronunciation. But the concept of talking to oneself (performing self-directed illocutionary acts) would seem to be conceptually derivative from the concept of talking to others. It would not be surprising if we had to proceed by first explicating interpersonal illocutionary act concepts, and then, at a second stage, construing illocutionary acts in soliloquy by analogy with the former. One might suggest that remarking to myself that it's getting warmer is something like *pretending* that I am remarking to someone else that it's getting warmer, where I play the role of addressee as well as speaker.

It may be thought that by making the demarcation of illocutionary acts depend on communicative intentions we have brought our theory much closer to the Griceian approach than our criticisms of Schiffer in Chapter 2 would suggest. But it is not so. The decisive difference remains. On Schiffer's account of illocutionary acts the *content*, the *constitution*, of an illocutionary act depends on perlocutionary intentions to produce certain effects in addressees. It is differences in the content of these intentions that differentiate one type of illocutionary act from others. Telling A that the car has arrived and telling A that Susie has left differ because of differences in the activated belief the speaker aims to be producing in the hearer. Admitting that the door is open and asking someone to shut off the television differ by virtue of differences in the responses the speaker intends to evoke in the hearer. On my theory, by contrast, all this is done in terms of R'ing. The content of illocutionary act types, what makes one differ from another, depends solely on what is R'd, with the one exception of what makes an act an assertive, and that exception is not at all friendly to Schiffer's account. Intentions to get the addressee to realize something come in only to differentiate illocutionary acts *in general* from other rule subjection acts; and these intentions themselves are to get the addressee to realize *what the speaker has R'd*. Thus they presuppose the concept of R'ing and presuppose that the content of the act has already been determined by the R'ing.

The appeal to communication can also differentiate I-rules from other regulative rules governing sentence utterance. Here the crucial point is the restriction of these rules to a certain sphere of activity, what I termed the "literal, first-order, communicative use of language". Other regulative rules governing speech have no such restriction. If it is forbidden to speak loudly in a library or a sickroom, then loud talking there is out of order whether it is literal or figurative, communicative or just vocalizing. This difference in the scope of the rule reflects the fact that I-rules exist for the sake of making communication possible. Whereas their cousins are enacted and enforced for other reasons. We could distinguish I-rules just by this consideration. An I-rule is a rule laying down necessary and sufficient conditions for sentence utterance, where the social rationale of the rule is the facilitation of communication. If we do it this way, we do not have to explain silent soliloquy as a derivative form of subjection to I-rules. For even though soliloquy does not involve interpersonal communication, it remains true that the basic rationale for the existence of I-rules is that they make interpersonal communication possible.

Now that we have shown how to separate I-rules from other rules, it only remains to point out that the demarcation of illocutionary acts could have been done in terms of the kind of rules one utters one's sentence as subject to. Proceeding in this way, we would say that an illocutionary act is an act performed in uttering a sentence as subject to a rule that satisfies the above condition for an I-rule. However, I feel that the previous demarcation in terms of R'ing plus communicative intention keeps things closer to the way illocutionary acts are viewed by their agents.

vii. The Meaning of Subsentential Units

I have now presented my IA potential theory of sentence meaning, which is at the same time an I-rule theory. To round it out I must say a bit by way of going beyond the restriction to *sentences*. But only a bit. I can promise nothing substantial in this book along that line. This is obviously a limitation, but perhaps the reader will agree that the book is long enough with this limitation and will agree that a descent into the semantic structure of sentences is well left to another occasion.

Nevertheless it would be remiss of me not to give some idea of the direction in which the present account points us when we tackle the problem of word meaning. That direction has already been hinted at. It derives from one of the basic commitments of my theory, namely, that the starting point for understanding the nature of linguistic meaning is the sentence.[12] This is crucial for any view that takes linguistic meaning to be derived from what speakers do with language in communication. For the sentence is the smallest unit that can be used (without ellipsis) to perform an act of communication. A theory of meaning along those lines will have to begin by showing how the meaning of a sentence is what makes it usable for an act of communication.

But then how is such a view to explicate the notion of a sentential con-

---

[12] As was pointed out in 6.3, the priority of the sentence for understanding the nature of meaning is compatible with the priority of subsentential units in understanding the fact that a particular sentence means what it does.

stituent's having a certain meaning? If sentence meaning is conceptually basic, then we must understand a word's having a certain meaning as its capacity to make a distinctive contribution to the meaning of sentences in which it occurs. And if sentence meaning is IA potential, then the meaning of the word 'biscuit' will be a matter of its having a potential to make a certain distinctive contribution to the IA potential of sentences in which it occurs. We might think of this as a second-order IA potential. Given first-order IA potentials for sentences, a word has the potential to affect those IA potentials in a certain way.

But how are we to specify these second-order IA potentials? As I pointed out in 6.3, we can, sometimes by straining a bit, find terms for what one is doing with a given part of the sentence when performing an illocutionary act. Thus, when I say to you "What is the title of the book you have in your hand?", one can say that I was using 'book' to *denote* published linguistic productions, rather than, for example, the actions of charging someone with a crime. Again, if I say "Please bring me the book with the red cover", I might be said to use 'with the red cover' to *specify* the kind of book an instance of which I was asking someone to bring me. And if the utterance were declarative instead of imperative ('That book has a red cover'), we could say that 'has a red cover' is used to *predicate* a property of the book. And, turning to referring expressions, we can say that the last speaker was using 'the book with the red cover' to *refer* to a certain book. These examples make it appear that we can specify the meanings of subsentential units in terms of what speakers do with them in communication. But the trouble with this from the standpoint of a use approach to meaning is that the semantic terms used here—'denote', 'specify', 'predicate', 'refer'— are used without any explication in terms of what speakers do. The supposed explanation in behavioral terms consists in saying, in each case, that the speaker is using the expression with a certain *semantic* status. And that semantic status remains unexplicated in terms of use.

But there is a more direct way than this of exploiting the notion that a word's having a certain meaning consists in its making a certain distinctive contribution to the meaning of sentences in which it occurs. This way features the IA potential account of the meaning of sentences. Keeping a firm grip on that, we can exhibit the meaning of a word by indicating how it contributes to the IA potential of various sentences in which it occurs, that is, how it contributes to the I-rules that govern the sentences. To keep this demonstration within bounds I will concentrate on assertions, the rules for which are maximally simple, and I will restrict myself to what is R'd in making these assertions. I will further simplify matters by ignoring multivocality, figurative speech, underdetermination of reference by meaning, and other such complications.

With these restrictions, let's consider how the I-rule for a given sentence is varied by putting different words into a given slot, for example, the slot in the sentence frame 'That's a _____'. Inserting 'cemetery', we get an I-rule that requires for correct utterance that the item referred to is *a place for the burial of the dead*. Whereas inserting 'knife', we get an I-rule that requires that the item referred to is *a utensil for cutting things*. We will get an analogous difference if 'cemetery' and 'knife' are successively inserted in the slot in other sentence frames such as 'We own a _____' or 'There is no _____ in this place'. I would suggest that by running through examples like this, we can make clear the way in which the meaning of a word enables it to make a certain distinctive contribution to the meanings of sentences in which it occurs.

Let me be explicit as to what these exhibitions are and are not designed to do. Starting with the negative side, they are not put forward as a way of specifying word meanings in the semantic description of a language (the lexical component thereof). They would be hopeless in that role. We could never run through all the sentence slots in which the lexical item in question could occur. The impossibility of a semantic description of a language's including an enumeration of I-rules for sentences one by one would be multiplied by this procedure. It is no part of my program in this book to develop a procedure for giving the semantic description of a language; but it is clear that the lexicon would have to use some more concise way of specifying word (morpheme) meaning than this, whether by synonyms, a theoretical characterization of properties signified, or whatever. My suggested exhibition is designed to get across the ontology of word meaning—*what it is* for a word to mean what it does. The basic idea is that this is for the word to make a distinctive contribution to the meanings of sentences in which it occurs. The above examples serve to *illustrate* that idea.

If we have an adequate grammar of the language to work with, we could do something more systematic along this line. Suppose we have a transformational grammar in which there is a finite number of sentential forms in the base. If one of those is 'X [something referred to] is a ø', we can work with that in exhibiting the meaning of 'knife', rather than the more specific 'That's a _____'. If we may assume that the semantics of the language attaches solely to the base constructions, with transformations leaving that unaffected, we can give the complete semantics in the base. I am not proposing any such linguistic hypothesis. I mention it only as an example of how we might exhibit word meaning in a more systematic fashion.

CHAPTER NINE

The IA Potential Theory of Meaning and Its Alternatives

i. Preview

I have now completed the exposition of my IA potential theory of sentence meaning. It is time to turn to a more extended defense of the theory than I have presented thus far. I may as well admit that I have no knock-down argument. Such defense as I can offer will consist of the following. (1) Its initial plausibility. (2) Demonstrations of its efficacy when put to work. (3) Answers to various objections. (4) Defects of its alternatives from which it is free. Bits of all these tasks have been accomplished, or at least indicated, in previous chapters. As for (4), for example, I said in Chapter 6 why I take my view to be superior to a perlocutionary act potential account, but most of (4) remains to be done.

I will take these four headings in the order listed. For each I will briefly review the relevant earlier remarks and then fill out the discussion. (4) will take up most of the space.

ii. Initial Plausibility of the Theory

Early on in Chapter 6 I introduced what I called the "Use Principle".

IV. An expression's having a certain meaning _consists_ its being usable to play a certain role in communication.

IV. was arrived at by an inversion of one of my axioms of meaning.

A2. The fact that an expression has a certain meaning is what enables it to play a distinctive role in communication.

The suggestion was that if playing a distinctive role in communication is what its meaning enables an expression to be used for, why not say that its having a meaning simply consists in its usability to do something of that sort? But the inversion cannot be taken for granted. Even if holding a professorship enables me to attend departmental meetings, we can't infer that being a professor *consists* in being able to attend departmental meetings! I need to justify this transition.

A full consideration requires looking at several principles in the neighborhood of IV. First I will distinguish a more generic and a more specific principle. The former, in turn, can be divided into a weaker and a stronger version. The weaker generic version is:

IVGA. The fact that an expression has a certain meaning supervenes on (is determined by, is a function of) what users of the language do with it. (The semantics of a *language* supervenes on facts about *speech*.)[1]

This is not the strongest generic version because it stops short of *identifying* having a meaning with facts about what it is used (or usable) to do. But it is the commitment on which all further developments of use theories are based. The fundamental insight here is that semantic (and other) facts about the structure of a language do not float freely in the void. They do not constitute an autonomous realm. Apart from what members of a community do with the language there are no phonological, syntactical, or se-

---

[1] John Hawthorne has pointed out to me that this principle might seem to rule out "external" influences on meaning such as those stressed by Putnam in his famous fantasy in which people whose paradigms of 'water' have some chemical constitution different from H_2O do not, according to Putnam, mean exactly the same as we do by 'water'. But, as I understand IVGA and its successors they do not rule out such external contributors to meaning. They do not imply that meanings are (wholly) "in the head". The account of "what users of the language do with it" can include their interactions with the environment as well as purely self-enclosed goings on.

Another problem, also called to my attention by Hawthorne, concerns the fact that a language is usually thought of as indefinitely extendable by such devices as conjunction. This has the consequence that there are sentences in the language far too long and complex to be usable by anyone. Hence speakers don't "do anything" with such sentences. Hence their meanings do not supervene on, or consist in, what speakers do with it or what it is usable by speakers to do. This complication can be handled in several ways. Among the simplest are (1) construe these principles in terms of an ideal speaker who is not subject to ordinary human limitations and (2) replace 'do' with 'would do' and 'usable' with 'would be usable', where the latter formulations are understood as something like 'would if a speaker were able to handle the sentence'. I will assume that one or the other interpretation is tacitly understood.

mantic facts about it. A language is an abstraction from what language users do. There is no other ontological foothold for it.[2] When I come to compare the IA potential theory with rivals, I will have quite a bit to say about approaches ("hypostatic" theories) that violate IVGA., in spirit if not in letter, by taking semantic concepts and semantic facts to be primitive, not anchored in facts about what language users do.

As just intimated, IVGA. is weaker than the full generic aspect of IV., which would read:

IVGB. An expression's having a certain meaning *consists* in its being usable by speakers to do certain things.

Here is what I take to be the rationale for the move from "supervenes on" to "consists in". The former is the reasonable way to think of the matter only if there is something to meaning over and above usability. But what could that be? Answers to this question are proffered by theories of meaning opposed to mine. These include inter alia *referential* theories (having a meaning amounts to *standing for* something (referring to, designating, denoting, naming . . . something); *truth condition* theories; *ideational* theories (having a meaning is expressing, or being a sign of, ideas in the mind). Versions of such theories will be criticized in this chapter. The point here is that the preference for IVGB. over IVGA. depends on the inadequacy of all attempts to find something other than usability that constitutes linguistic meaning. I will not be able to show that all such theories fail, but I will undertake to do so for the most prominent ones.

Now for the more specific version of the Use Principle, which consists in its choice of *communication* as the use of language that is crucial for meaning, the version that was formulated above as 'IV.'. What alternatives are there? There is at least one that deserves attention—the use of language as a vehicle of thought. This certainly bulks large in the total picture. Whatever the possibilities for thought that is not linguistically expressed, it is clear that much of our conscious thought is linguistically encoded. The dictum "Thought is the conversation of the soul with itself" rings true. Even if we can engage in rudimentary thought without mastery of any language, it is inconceivable that with that limitation we could think about abstract subjects. Try thinking about literature, politics, or human emo-

---

[2] At least this is true for "natural languages", i.e., languages that are actually used in communities. We can, of course, think of *possible* languages apart from any such involvement. But my concern here is with what it is for expressions to mean something in languages that are used for communication. So-called formal languages devised by logicians are also exempt from the Use Principle. The "meanings" of "expressions" in such "languages" are stipulated by their creators. But these have the status of *possible* languages (or fragments of such), not *actual* languages.

tions, not to mention philosophy, without expressing any of it in language. Moreover, there is just as close a tie between what a sentence means and what thought it can be used to express as there is between what a sentence means and what illocutionary act it is fitted to perform. Just as it would be futile, in the absence of a special code, to invite someone to dinner by saying 'The Middle East peace process has bogged down', so a like impossibility attaches to using that sentence as a vehicle of the thought that nothing can travel faster than light. So we have to take seriously the idea that *the expression of thought* is the use of language in terms of which to develop a use theory of linguistic meaning.

To be sure, there need be no rivalry here. Why can't we be evenhanded and recognize that a sentence's meaning what it does is a matter of both its usability to perform illocutionary acts of a certain type and its usability as a vehicle of a certain thought? There are two ways of avoiding undue partiality. First, there is the point that illocutionary act performance always carries with it expression of thought. In admitting that I locked my keys in the car, I also express the thought that I locked my keys in the car. This suggests that we may have already accommodated the *vehicle of thought* use of language in the IA potential theory. But one who is tempted to put thought *rather than* communication center stage in a use theory of meaning would presumably be thinking of "silent thought", thought that does not involve (interpersonal) communication. And that suggests another possibility for evenhandedness. Why shouldn't we think that a sentence's meaning what it does consists in its usability both for performing illocutionary acts and as a vehicle for silent thought? Why must it be one or the other?

But despite these considerations, I believe that there are strong reasons for giving preference to interpersonal communication in an account of linguistic meaning. I will list several (possible) reasons for this, in ascending order of importance.

1. One might try to argue that communication is the most basic and distinctive use of language, in that it is an activity that is most inescapably dependent on language for its success. Perhaps we could scrape by in our private thoughts without language much more than we do. But without language our communicative resources would be drastically restricted. This has been a frequent theme in treatments of language. It was vividly put by Locke at the beginning of Chapter 2 of Book III of his *Essay*.

> Man, though he have great variety of Thoughts, and such, from which others, as well as himself, might receive Profit and Delight; yet they are all within his own Breast, invisible, and hidden from others, nor can of themselves be made appear. The Comfort and Advantage of Society, not being to be had without Communication of Thoughts, it was necessary, that Man should find

out some external sensible Signs, whereby those invisible Ideas, which his thoughts are made up of, might be made known to others. For this purpose, nothing was so fit, either for Plenty or Quickness as those articulate Sounds, which with so much Ease and Variety, he found himself able to make.[3]

But despite the honorable lineage of this way of thinking, it suffers both from underestimating the need of language for thought and from overestimating its indispensability for communication. I will not rest my case on it, even in part.

2. Granted that the meanings of sentences are intimately connected with both thought and communication, there is a methodological advantage to focusing on the latter. Overt, communicative speech, being publicly observable, provides a more accessible object of study than private thought. Early modern philosophy, with its stress on privileged access to conscious states, thought otherwise. But the vicissitudes of pre-twentieth-century attempts to develop theories of consciousness have made us more skeptical of its usefulness. What people do with words in overt speech has proved a more fruitful subject of investigation. I fancy that the exploration of IA's and IA potential in this book illustrates that point. Had I set out to follow the trail of the use of language in private thought, I doubt that I would have uncovered such riches.

3. Another reason for focusing on communication is that private thought, when linguistically structured, can be viewed as a special case of communication, but not vice versa. Much silent thought can be construed as communication with oneself—asking oneself questions and suggesting answers, for example. This encourages us to apply a communication-based account of language to the understanding of the use of language in thought, treating the latter as a limiting case of the former.

4. Still, by far the most important reason for employing a communicative form of the Use Principle is that only it will cover the semantic waterfront. The discussion in this book shows that some of the semantic contents of sentences come into play only in interpersonal communication. This is most obvious for the semantic resources used in Exercitives. Any semantic components that give a sentence the usability to adjourn a meeting, christen a child, or the like will have no application to solitary thought. Even if what carries propositional content can always figure as a vehicle of inner thought, the same cannot be said for what carries illocutionary force. To be sure, one can think about adjourning meetings, firing employees, and the like. But then the sentences that serve as vehicles for such thoughts would not be the ones that have the special function of doing those things. We must be careful to get this point straight. As we saw in

[3] Edition of the *Essay* by Peter N. Nidditch, 1975, 404–405.

our treatment of exercitives, they can often be carried out by uttering sentences like 'You're fired' that also can be used for assertive illocutionary acts. The present point concerns certain semantic components of sentences that are specially designed for exercitive performance—'*I declare* the meeting adjourned', rather than 'The meeting is adjourned', or 'Your employment is *hereby* terminated', rather than 'You are no longer an employee of the company'. Since there are aspects of sentence meaning that can be handled by an IA potential account but are left out by a thought-vehicle potential account, whereas there are no semantic resources that can be used for thought but not for communication, that is a decisive reason for favoring a communicative version of the Use Principle.

The above takes us as far as the full content of the Use Principle:

IV. An expression's having a certain meaning *consists* its being usable to play a certain role in communication.

but not as far as the IA potential principle, which focuses on IA performance as the communicative use that is crucial for meaning.

V. A sentence's having a certain meaning consists in its being usable to perform illocutionary acts of a certain type.

Here I need only advert to what I have already laid out in this book. Since illocutionary act reports were demarcated as those speech act reports that make explicit "what the speaker said" (in a sense of that in which it involves the *content* of the utterance), what the utterance was designed to communicate, it is clear that if sentence meaning is to be construed as usability to perform communicative acts of a certain kind, the illocutionary act kind is tailor-made for the purpose. What could be closer to sentence meaning than a usability to perform utterances with a certain *content?* Content is what linguistic meaning is all about. This point is what was behind the argument in Chapter 6 to the effect that even if sentence meaning is extensionally equivalent to perlocutionary act potential, a sentence has that latter potential only because it has a certain illocutionary act potential. The sentence 'Please pass the salt' has the standard potential of getting someone to pass the salt only because it is usable to request someone to pass the salt. It would be absurd to try to move in the other direction and suppose that it is usable to request someone to pass the salt only because it is usable to get someone to pass the salt. The plausibility of taking IA potential to be more deeply embedded in the semantics of the sentence than perlocutionary act potential reflects the fact that the IA potential is in terms of the *content* of the utterance for which the sentence is fitted while the PA potential is not. Sentences with quite different contents could share the potential of getting the auditor to pass the salt, for example, the peremptory 'If you don't pass the salt, I'll send you to your room'.

Another earlier passage that can be used to support the IA version of the Use Principle is the development of the concept of a matching IA potential in 6.8. The point is this. For any meaning of a sentence we can identify an IA type such that an addressee, just by knowing that the speaker intended to be directly exploiting that meaning, can thereby tell that the speaker intended to be performing an IA of that type. The meaning of 'I admit that the door is open' is such that if I know that you intend to be exploiting that meaning in the most direct way, I will thereby know that you intend to admit that a certain particular door is open. The meaning of 'Please close the door' is such that if I know that you intend to exploit that meaning in the most direct way, I thereby know that you intend to be asking someone to close a certain particular door. Just by virtue of having a certain meaning a sentence is rendered standardly usable to perform illocutionary acts of a certain matching type. Furthermore, it seems clear on reflection that if the meaning of 'I admit that the door is open' were quite different from what it is, it would no longer be usable, in literal, first-order, communicative speech, to assert that a certain particular door is open. Given this tie between sentence meaning and IA potential, we are warranted in taking IA performance to be the kind of use a potential for which is constitutive of sentence meaning, and thereby to develop the Use Principle in terms of IA potential, the final statement of which is:

VII. A sentence's having a certain meaning consists in its being usable to perform illocutionary acts of the matching type (that is, to have the matching illocutionary act potential).

There is one other feature of these principles for which we have not yet made explicit the justification. Why should we identify sentence meaning with *usability* to do so-and-so, rather than with *being used* to do so-and-so? Why is it IA *potential* rather than IA *performance* that is constitutive of meaning? The shortest and best answer to this question is found in the generative force of language. No limit can be put on the number or complexity of sentences in a language. No matter how large a set we construct, we can enlarge it by combining members of the set into more complex sentences. Therefore, there will be many sentences of a language that are never employed to perform illocutionary acts. Hence meaning must be construed as something potential rather than as something actual. Moreover, even with sentences that are put to use, their meaning is not exhausted by their actual track record. By virtue of meaning what they do, they retain a potential to be used an indefinite number of further times to perform matching IA's. Meaning cannot be tied down to a set of actual speech episodes.

iii. Efficacy of the Theory in Application

In Chapter 6 I said that an adequate account of linguistic meaning will throw light on the following questions.

A. How does an expression's meaning fit it to play its distinctive role in communication?
B. What is it to know (learn) the meaning of an expression?
C. How is an expression's having a certain meaning related to what a speaker means by the expression on a certain occasion?
D. What is it to understand what a speaker has said?
E. What is the relation of meaning and reference?

Narrowing this down to our specific concern in this book, sentence meaning, we can see that the IA potential account provides satisfactory answers to these questions.

A. A meaning of a sentence fits it to play a distinctive role in communication just because that meaning consists in the sentence's being usable to perform illocutionary acts of a certain type.
B. To know (learn) a meaning of a sentence is to know (learn) what kind of illocutionary acts that meaning fits it to be used in performing. It is both necessary and sufficient for knowing what a sentence means that one should be able to tell when it is being used correctly in illocutionary act performance.
C. If sentence meaning is illocutionary act potential, we have a built-in way of relating sentence meaning and speaker meaning. What a speaker means by uttering a sentence (assuming a literal, straightforward, direct use of the sentence) can be read off the specification of the illocutionary act the speaker is performing, which is of the type a potential for performing which constitutes the meaning of the sentence.
D. To understand what a speaker said is to know what illocutionary act she was performing, which, in the literal, straightforward, direct use of language, constitutes an actualization of the potential that constitutes the sentence's meaning what it does.
E. The IA potential theory makes less of a distinctive contribution to the relation of meaning and reference than to the above four issues. Nevertheless I believe that the discussion of the place of reference in illocutionary rules in Chapter 7, to which we were led by the IA potential account of sentence meaning, does shed genuine illumination on this thorny issue.

There are other problems in the philosophy of language to which we could apply the IA potential theory, but most of them would require a detailed extension of the theory into the semantics of subsentential units, something that lies beyond the bounds of this book. The above five applications give some idea of the power of the theory to deal with issues in the philosophy of language. But how much of a case this makes for the IA potential theory partly depends on how it fares in competition with its alternatives. Other accounts of meaning have something to say about these issues as well. The question remains as to whether the IA potential theory's treatment of them is superior to that of its rivals. Though in this chapter I will be making objections to other views, I will not have the space to make systematic comparisons of their treatments of each of the above problems with the way my theory deals with them. Some bits of this, however, will come out in the criticism of the other theories.

iv. Replies to Objections

Almost all the objections I consider worth discussing have already been considered. In 6.4 I responded to the claim that IA potential is too close to sentence meaning to provide an illuminating account thereof. In the same chapter I argued that the fact that my account makes use of unreduced intentional concepts is not to be held against it. In Chapter 7 I confronted and, I believe, defused charges of vicious circularity. But there are two further objections to which I will respond here and now.

First, it may be held against my theory of sentence meaning that it fails to make fruitful contact with linguistics. There has of late been a great deal of interaction between philosophy of language and linguistics, sparked but not restricted to the Chomskian revolution in linguistics. Some philosophers of language intend their work to be relevant to the ongoing development of ways of describing languages, particularly the semantics thereof. Some may dismiss Part II of this book just because it is not in that camp.

My reply to this is twofold. First, I plead guilty to lacking a primary concern with the methodology of linguistics. That is, indeed, an honorable enterprise and I wish it well. But there are many issues concerning language to which philosophers can properly address themselves, and this is not one to which this book is devoted. My interest here is in the *ontology* of linguistic meaning, *what it is* for a unit of language—in this book a sentence—to have a certain meaning. One can make progress on this issue without getting into questions about the form a description of a language would best take; and I believe I have done just that. But second, although I have not entered into detailed issues in linguistics, I do not admit that my results are completely irrelevant to that discipline. After all, linguistics is necessarily concerned with linguistic meaning and, more specifically, with the meanings of sentences. It is commonly recognized that a crucial test for a given semantic description of a language is that it yield as output a correct assignment of meaning to any given sentence of the language. And so linguists cannot avoid being concerned with what it is for a sentence to have a given meaning. If they tried to dissociate themselves for that issue, they would be abandoning their own subject matter. Hence it should be of importance to linguistics to have a correct account of what sentence meaning amounts to. I have not sought to draw specific implications from my theory of sentence meaning for the conduct of linguistics. But it is far from clear that there are no such implications to be drawn.

The second objection I will consider here is this. It may be contended that even if one approaches meaning through the illocutionary act version of the Use Theory, one should wind up identifying sentence meaning not with a sentence's IA potential, but with what gives the sentence that potential, the basis of the potential. I agree with the positive part of the objection. I agree that a sentence meaning is to be identified with what *gives* the sentence an IA potential. That is why I have identified a sentence's having a certain meaning with its being governed by an I-rule, which, on my view, is the basis of its IA potential. But I don't take that to exclude identifying the meaning with an IA potential. Where a power or potential has a basis, as it does here, it can be identified with that basis. The fragility of a piece of glass can be identified with the molecular structure by virtue of which the glass will break if struck in a certain way. No doubt, the *concept* of fragility is different from the *concept* of a certain molecular structure, and the term 'fragile' does not have the same meaning as 'has . . . . molecular structure'. But it doesn't follow that the *state* of the glass picked out by 'fragile' is any different from the state picked out by 'has . . . . molecular structure'. A state, like anything else, can be identified in different, nonequivalent ways. The ultimate justification for the identification of a disposition (power, potential) and its basis is this. If we were to take fragility as a state of the glass over and above the molecular structure by virtue of which the glass is fragile, we would be hypostatizing states without any empirical or theoretical warrant. No examination of the glass itself will disclose any state it is in, vis-à-vis fragility, over and above the physical constitution by virtue of which it will shatter when struck with a certain force.[4] Note that this is a particular example of the difference between the concept of P and the nature of P, a difference that has become familiar to philosophers in recent years.

v. Mapping Alternative Theories

I now turn to the fourth of my tasks in this chapter, the one to which most of the chapter will be devoted, namely, a comparison of my theory of sentence meaning with its alternatives. As a prelude to this it will help to

---

[4] For further defenses of this position see Armstrong 1968, chap. 6, sec. 6, and Alston 1971b.

distinguish the aim of the present theory and of those I consider to be on the same playing field, from the aims of other segments of the philosophy of language that are pursued under the terms 'meaning' and 'semantics'. First, I am trying to understand the ontology of linguistic meaning, the nature of the semantic aspect of natural languages that are used in human communities. This is quite different from the task of constructing artificial "languages", or fragments thereof, for one or another purpose, usually logical or grammatical. This latter enterprise makes use of semantic terms like 'denote', 'extension', 'intension', 'sense', and so on. But it typically takes them for granted and does not delve beneath that terminology to the realities they indicate. To be sure, one engaged in the construction of artificial languages may also be interested in the ontological issue. But the point remains that artificial language construction itself is to be distinguished from an attempt to solve my problem.

The term 'theory of meaning' is also applied to the semantic description of a natural language. Thus people speak of developing a "theory of meaning" for English or Kwakiutl or Swahili. This too is an enterprise that involves using semantic notions for descriptive purposes, rather than delving into the ontology of what these terms signify. It is related to the present enterprise somewhat as the ethnological description of a culture is related to a philosophical account of the kind of status a culture has.

I find it useful to organize alternatives to my view around the commitments made by IA potential theory. We can think of different alternatives as directing their opposition to IA potential theory at different levels of basicness. The more basic (and generic) the commitment that is denied, the more radical the opposition. We can distinguish the following points of opposition, moving from the more to the less basic.

1. Focus on sentence meaning as the initial point of entry into the nature of linguistic meaning.[5]
2. The thesis that sentence meaning is, or supervenes on, or is a function of, what users of the language use it for.
3. The focus on communication as the crucial aspect of the use of sentences for understanding the meaning of sentences.
4. The identification of illocutionary act performance as the crucial aspect of communicative use for understanding the nature of sentence meaning.
5. The concentration on illocutionary act *potential* as the way in which illocutionary act performance bears on meaning.
6. The rule subjection account of what gives a sentence a certain illocutionary act potential.

[5] Remember the point made in 6.3 that this is compatible with another respect in which word meaning is prior to sentence meaning.

Most of the important oppositions to my account can be identified by what items from this list they deny. But they are by no means equally represented in the literature. It is views that deny 1., 2., and/or 4. that have dominated the scene. So although it would be instructive to consider views that are distinctive in denying 3., 5., or 6., I will not indulge myself to that extent. In any event, I have already said a bit in support of 3. and 5. in Section ii of this chapter. And 6. was defended at length in Chapters 7 and 8. With respect to the other three, I have said my say about the most prominent alternative to 4. in 6.5, where I indicated why I thought that a perlocutionary act potential account of sentence meaning is inferior to an IA potential account. That leaves us with 1. and 2., to which I shall devote most of the rest of my attention. The only important feature of opposed theories I will discuss that falls outside this structure is the inability of certain theories that do embrace 2. to handle the full range of IA's. This problem will dominate Sections x and xi.

My choice of particular theories to discuss is heavily influenced by my overriding aim to point up issues on which alternatives to my theory are inferior and by a need to keep the discussion within manageable bounds. Therefore I have sought theories that (a) present significant contrasts to mine, (b) are simple enough to permit these contrasts to be set out concisely, and (c) are of sufficient interest to be worth discussing. I am unable, within the confines of this book, to discuss all important theories of meaning. If you don't find your favorite theory here, remember the reasons for the selectivity.

vi. Words or Sentences as Fundamental

Thesis 1. has become something of a commonplace in philosophical treatments of linguistic meaning. It seems to have been Frege who started the ball rolling in that direction, though for different reasons from those of use theorists. The tendency can be traced back to Kant, with his emphasis on "forms of judgment" as the key to fundamental concepts. Previously the usual practice was to begin by trying to understand the meaning of minimal meaningful units and then to understand sentence meaning in terms of composition out of the former. The meaning of subsentential units, in this tradition, was usually understood in terms of their "standing for" or "symbolizing" ideas, concepts, thoughts, or other mental carriers of "content". Thus Aristotle's *On Interpretation* begins:

First we must define the terms 'noun' and 'verb', then the terms 'denial' and 'affirmation', then 'proposition' and 'sentence'.

Spoken words are the symbols of mental experience and written words are the symbols of spoken words. Just as all men have not the same writing, so all men have not the same speech sounds, but the mental experiences, which these directly symbolize, are the same for all, as also are those things of which our experiences are the images. . . .

As there are in the mind thoughts which do not involve truth or falsity, and also those which must be either true or false, so it is in speech. For truth and falsity imply combination and separation. Nouns and verbs, provided nothing is added, are like thoughts without combination or separation; 'man' and 'white', as isolated terms, are not yet either true or false. In proof of this, consider the word 'goat-stag'. It has significance, but there is no truth or falsity about it, unless 'is' or 'is not' is added; either in the present or in some other tense.[6]

Two millennia later Locke was still beginning his semantics with words, construing them as "signs" of ideas. Here is a continuation of the passage quoted above from Book III, Chapter 2 of the *Essay*.

The use then of Words, is to be sensible Marks of *Ideas*; and the *Ideas* they stand for, are their proper and immediate Signification.

The use Men have of these Marks, being either to record their own Thoughts for the Assistance of their own Memory; or as it were, to bring out their *Ideas*, and lay them before the view of others: *Words in their primary or immediate Signification, stand for nothing, but the Ideas in the Mind of him that uses them*, how imperfectly soever or carelessly those *Ideas* are collected from the Things, which they are supposed to represent. When a Man speaks to another, it is, that he may be understood; and the end of Speech is, that those Sounds, as Marks, may make known his *Ideas* to the hearer.[7]

It is clear from this that, whatever may be the case with Aristotle and others, Locke has a communicative use theory of meaning. In terms of my theses listed above, although he rejects 1., he accepts 2. and 3. (and, presumably, has no conception of 3.–6.). The communicative use that he takes to be the key to meaning is "making known the speaker's ideas to the hearer". That is how Locke thinks of communication. The words one utters are produced as signs of the ideas in one's mind; and if things go well the hearer will take the words as signs of the ideas they were produced to signify.

So far this is an account of speaker meaning. It tells us what it is for a particular speaker to mean so-and-so by a certain word. Linguistic meaning, what the word 'cat' means in English, Locke, like Grice, thinks of as a generalization from what speakers mean by 'cat' on particular occasions: ". . . so far as Words are of Use and Signification, so far is there a constant connection between the Sound and the *Idea*; and a Designation, that the

---

[6]   16a. The translation by E. M. Edghill. The passage quoted is found on p. 40 of McKeon, ed., 1941.
[7]   Nidditch, ed., 1975, 405.

one stand for the other: without which Application of them, they are nothing but so much insignificant Noise" (*Essay*, III, 2.7).[8]

There are many difficulties in Locke's semantic theory. Because of the central role played by *ideas*, any difficulties in his account of ideas will carry over here. His view of communication as making known to the hearer what ideas are in the mind of the speaker does not seem true to what actually goes on in speech. There are also epistemological problems as to how one speaker is supposed to be able to tell what idea other speakers regularly use a given word as a sign of. But my main concern here is with the emphasis on word meaning. That feature of the view contributes to the inadequacy of his construal of communication, since it introduces a sort of atomism that falsifies what typically goes on. Interestingly enough, there is a recent version of a Lockean view of meaning and communication in Armstrong 1971 that corrects Locke on just this point. Armstrong expresses very well the considerations that have led many communication theorists of meaning, including myself, to start with sentence meaning:

> . . . if we want to develop a theory of meaning in terms of communication, must we not concentrate on the meanings of *sentences* rather than words? If somebody utters a mere part of a sentence, as a word usually is, what does that communicate? In general, very little. Suppose I just say, "Horse". Has anything much been communicated? In general, a complete sentence is needed to get something across. . . . And so a theory of meaning that is based on the communicative function of language must treat the sentence as in some way semantically fundamental. (428)

My present purpose does not require going into the details of Armstrong's account. He opts for semi-Griceian intentions (he says 'objectives') to produce beliefs in hearers as to what sentences are used as signs of. And, like Locke, he moves from speaker meaning to sentence meaning via a regularity in a community as to what a given sentence is used as a sign of.

vii. Naive Referential Theories

Many of the alternatives to my view are found in those thinkers who oppose 2., the idea that the meaning of linguistic units is a matter of, or supervenes on, facts about what speakers do with those units, the idea, as we might say, that semantics is based on pragmatics (Alston 1980b; Brandom 1994). Before getting into particular views, I will paint a broad picture of what they have in common. They all take some semantic terms to be primitive. Even if they do not explicitly espouse this, they accept it in practice.

---

[8] Nidditch, ed., 1975, 408.

They typically speak of *denotation, connotation, intension, extension, reference,* and the like as if it is clear what these amount to, apart from any explanation in terms of what speakers do in using the language. They, in effect, treat the semantic side of language as if it were floating freely in a void, an autonomous realm that is not tied down to any flesh-and-blood realities on earth. I will use a deliberately derogatory term and speak of *hypostatic* semantics.

The crudest form of hypostatic semantics is found in what we may term *referential* theories. Here are a few quotations that give the flavor of the most naive version.

> Words all have meaning in the simple sense that they are symbols which stand for something other than themselves. (Russell 1903, 47)

> . . . The components of the fact which makes a proposition true or false, as the case may be, are the meanings of the symbols which we must understand in order to understand the proposition. (Russell, "The Philosophy of Logical Atomism", in Russell 1956, 196)

> To say that words have meaning is to say that they refer to something other than themselves. (Ruby 1950, 17)

These passages take it that there is some one sort of relation that words have to what, speaking as neutrally as possible, they are usable to talk about. This relation is variously termed 'stand for', 'refer', 'designate', 'signify', 'denote', and 'name'. Names are often taken as the model for all meaningful linguistic units. Hence the view has been satirized by Ryle as the "'Fido'-Fido" theory of meaning. But whatever candidate we pick for the all-purpose relation, we cannot sustain the thesis that all meaningful words stand in that relation to anything. Take *reference.* That is a relation in which "referring expressions" stand to their referents.[9] These include proper names, pronouns, and "definite descriptions" like 'the prime minister of Great Britain'. But it takes little reflection to realize that this relationship is distinctive of expressions that can occupy the subject position in subject-predicate statements and have the function of making explicit what the statement is about. That is not a function carried out by common nouns, adjectives, verbs, or adverbs, not to mention prepositions or conjunctions. I can't refer to anything, pick it out as a subject of discourse, with 'pencil', 'small', or 'runs'. What would 'small' refer to? Smallness? Well,

[9]   This is on the assumption that it is proper to think of a linguistic "referring expression" as referring to something. I do not accept that. I take it that referring is something speakers do with such expressions. But since the accounts of meaning under discussion make this assumption, I will go along with this for the sake of argument.

'smallness' refers to smallness, but 'small' doesn't. 'Small is a property' is ungrammatical, as is 'Runs is an activity' (unlike 'Running is an activity'). Some words can be used to refer, and many others can't.

But this is a relatively superficial defect. It shows only that the "referential" theorist must complicate things by recognizing a variety of ways in which words are related to the extralinguistic. Russell at a later stage wrote:

> It is obvious to begin with, that if we take some such word as 'Socrates' or 'dog', the meaning of the word consists in some relation to an object or set of objects. (Russell, "On Propositions", in 1956, 290)

This marks two advances over the previous formulations. First, Russell merely says the meaning of each word consists in *some* relation to an object or set of objects, not necessarily the same relation in each case. And second, he locates the meaning not in the object to which it is related but in the relation. The latter modification saves us from the absurdity of implying that everything in the world is a meaning. Since anything whatever can be referred to, if the meaning of a word is *what* is referred to, everything turns out to be a meaning!

Another fatal difficulty in a referential theory that takes the meaning to be the referent is the fact that meaning and referent do not march in lockstep. Expressions with different meanings can have the same referent. Frege's famous example concerned 'the morning star' and 'the evening star', phrases that refer to the same planet but have different meanings. The obverse of this gap, same meaning but different referents, is also common. One can use an "indexical" like 'I' with the same meaning to refer to many different items, as many as there are users of the pronoun.

Going back to the first difference in the last quotation from Russell, we see that loosening things up in this way makes it possible to treat reference, properly speaking, as a special case and recognize other word-world relations for other sorts of expressions. Common nouns, adjectives, and verbs can be said to have *extensions*. In each case the extension is the class of things to which the word can be truly applied. The extension of 'pencil' is the class of pencils, the extension of 'runs' is the class of things that run, and so on. And if we move away from the extensional, predicate terms can be said to have *intensions* or *connotations*, which we make take for the moment to consist of the property or set of properties the possession of which makes something a member of the extension.

viii. More Sophisticated Referential Theories

One interesting attempt to move beyond naive referential theories is made by C. I. Lewis (1946). Lewis distinguishes four "modes of meaning". He briefly explains them as follows.

(1) The *denotation* of a term is the classification of all actual things to which the term would be correctly applicable.

(2) The *comprehension* of a term is the classification of all possible or consistently thinkable things to which the term would be correctly applicable.

(3) The *signification* of a term is that property in things the presence of which indicates that the term correctly applies, and the absence of which indicates that it does not apply.

(4) Formally considered, the *intension* of a term is to be identified with the conjunction of all other terms each of which must be applicable to anything to which the given term would be correctly applicable. (39)

Elsewhere this purely intralinguistic conception of (4) is called *linguistic meaning*, and it is contrasted with intension as *sense meaning*, "constituted by the criterion in mind by which what is meant is to be recognized" (37).

Although Lewis speaks of all these as "modes of meaning" he makes it clear that he thinks of *intension* as being the meaning of a term, par excellence. And it is "sense meaning" that he takes to be basic. "Linguistic *expression* of what is meant and what is apprehended, is the dependent and derivative phenomenon" (37).

Lewis holds that all terms have meaning in all these modes. Hence his pluralism does not save him from the trap into which more naive referential theories fall by seeking to fit all meaningful linguistic expressions onto a Procrustean bed.

> . . . all words have significance in the sense of signifying something essential for the use of them in a truthful statement. And . . . their having meaning in all four modes follows from that. (82)

In supporting this dictum, he says that an adverb like "'quickly' applies to instances of walking, boiling, being seen, etc., and signifies that property of them which might be called quickliness—the property common to all things that take place quickly—just as red applies to all things which are red" (81). And a preposition like 'in' "applies to any case of being in something, or of something being in something else" (81). But if 'apply' means here what it ordinarily means (and no indication to the contrary is given), then the above could be true only if it were accurate to say things like 'Those Chinese boxes are in' (not meaning, of course, that they are fashionable) and 'Your walking is quickly'. *That* is what it would take to *apply* an adverb or a preposition to something. But these utterances are nonsense.

But how about singular referring expressions, common nouns, and adjectives? Do they have all these modes of meaning in just the same sense?

Lewis recognizes a distinction between singular referring expressions (which he repeatedly lumps together under the rubric 'names') and predicates. Thus he defines a term as "a linguistic expression which names or applies to a thing or things, of some kind, actual or thought of ", giving us a disjunction. Names *name* (naturally), while predicates *apply*. But his discussion systematically blurs even this distinction. His canonical characterization of the four modes of meaning, quoted above, speaks indifferently of terms "applying" to things. And in other contexts he talks as if all terms were names. Thus Lewis is by no means free of the massive conflations to which referential theories are liable.

Another distinction we have been discussing has to do with whether sentences or sentence constituents are taken as semantically primary. Lewis, like the simpler accounts illustrated at the beginning of this section, falls in the latter group. He does deal with the meaning of sentences, or at least of what he calls propositions. By 'proposition' he means "a term capable of signifying a state of affairs" (48). His example is 'that Mary is making pies' or 'Mary making pies'. He takes such terms to have meaning in all his modes. The extension of all true propositions he takes to be the actual world, while all false propositions have a null extension.[10] The signification of a proposition (the property the actual world would have to have to be its extension) is a "state of affairs", construed as a complex property, such as the state of affairs that consists in Mary making pies. The linguistic intension of a proposition is the set of all propositions it entails. And so on. That something has gone seriously amiss here becomes apparent when Lewis draws the conclusion that when we assert a proposition what we are doing is attributing the property it signifies to the actual world. Instead of this throwing light on what it is to make an ordinary assertion, for example, that Mary is making pies, it simply declares that assertion to be equivalent to some more complicated assertion, that the actual world is characterized by Mary's making pies. This either leaves us without any account of what it is to make the latter assertion or generates an infinite regress. For corresponding to the more complicated assertion is the proposition 'the actual world being characterized by Mary's making pies', and to assert that is to attribute it to the actual world; and . . . .

But to get back to the main theme of this section, Lewis is a good example of a "referential" theorist surreptitiously explicating semantic terms by reference to their use but not making any theoretical point of this. Look back at his initial characterization of the "modes of meaning". The denotation is the class of actual things to which the term *applies*. That notion of applying figures in the explication of all the modes. Even linguistic intension is explained in terms of the terms that must be *applicable* to anything

---

[10] This is substantially equivalent to Frege's view that the extension ("Bedeutung") of a true sentence is *The True*, and of a false sentence *The False*.

to which the given term is applicable. And to *apply* a term to something is to perform a certain kind of illocutionary act. In setting things up in this way Lewis is (perhaps unconsciously) bowing to necessity. If we are going to explain the meaning of basic semantic terms, there is no real alternative to explaining them in terms of what people are doing in speech.[11] Otherwise the terms are left dangling without any intelligible connection with the semantic aspect of language.

The tendency to ignore this conceptual dependence of the semantic on the pragmatic is encouraged and reinforced (I won't say "wholly due to") the procedures of formal semantics. There semantic status is bestowed on linguistic units by stipulation. Since any formal "language" is created de novo by the logician, she is free to lay it down that 'a' refers to Chicago and 'P' designates the property of being crowded. There is no tendency to root these semantic statuses in the use of language, for the "language" is not used as natural languages are. And such use as it has must honor the dictates of its creator. Immersion in this kind of activity can make one comfortable with speaking of what words in natural languages refer to, denote, and so on without any attempt to ground this talk in a consideration of what members of the linguistic community do with those words.

I look next at a work that appeared just one year later than Lewis 1946, namely, Carnap 1947. As an attempt to throw light on the nature of meaning it has many similarities to Lewis, but with Carnap this occurs in the context of setting up, or at least sketching, certain formal languages and using them for developments in logic. Nevertheless Carnap announces as "the main purpose of this book" "the development of a new method for the semantical analysis of meaning, that is, a new method for analyzing and describing the meanings of linguistic expressions" (v). Hence we can take him as addressing himself to the problems of Part II of this book.

In outline the most fundamental part of Carnap 1947 goes as follows. There are specifications of the meanings of various singular and general terms by what Carnap calls "semantical rules", some of which were quoted in 7.3. Here they are again.

A. Rules of designation for individual constants:
    1. 's' is a symbolic translation of 'Walter Scott'.
    2. 'w'—(the book) Waverley.
B. Rules of designation for predicates:
    'Hx'—'x is human (a human being)'
    'RAx'—'x is a rational animal'
    'Fx'—'x is (naturally) featherless'

---

[11] This last claim will, no doubt, be met by the protest that extension and intension can be explained in terms of the truth value of sentences, which is independent of considerations of use. Below I shall provide reasons for supposing this independence not to hold.

'Bx'—'x is a biped'
'Axy'—'x is an author of y' (4)

The "rules" are said to "translate" these symbols into English, which is used as the metalanguage. We can then formulate a "rule of truth" for the simplest atomic sentences.

> An atomic sentence in S_1 consisting of a predicate followed by an individual constant is true if and only if the individual to which the individual constant refers possesses the property to which the predicate refers. (5)

Thus the sentence 'Bs' is true if and only if Scott is a biped. Rules of truth for truth-functionally compound sentences are then given in the usual way.[12]

Carnap then introduces the notion of 'L-truth' for a sentence, S, in a language, L. This amounts to its being possible for the truth of S to be established on the basis of the semantical rules of L alone, without any reference to extralinguistic facts. And he extends the equivalence relation (*iff*) to "designators"—predicates and singular referring expressions—from its primary use with sentences. So, for predicates, A:

A_1 *iff* A_2 just in case (x) (A_1x *iff* A_2x).

And for singular terms, B:

B_1 *iff* B_2 just in case $B_1 = B_2$.[13]

He then introduces *extension* and *intension* as follows.

> Two designators have the same extensions *iff* they are equivalent (D_1 *iff* D_2)
> Two designators have the same intensions *iff* they are L-equivalent (it is L-true that D_1 *iff* D_2).

He then assigns extensions and intensions by looking for entities that are the same for equivalent or L-equivalent designators respectively. He finds a suitable extension for predicates in what he calls the "corresponding" class, the one the predicator is "for", as he says. He does not explain these terms explicitly, but the course of the discussion makes clear that the "corresponding class" for 'human' is the class of humans, that is, the class of items to which 'human' can be truly applied. The intension is identified

---

[12] All this is a simplified version of Tarski's procedure for giving a definition of 'true in L' for a particular (formal) language. I will touch on Tarski and his epigones below.
[13] I have modified Carnap's notation in various ways in order to streamline the exposition.

with the "corresponding" property, the one the possession of which makes the possessor a member of the class that is the extension. So the intension of 'human' is the property of being human (18–19).[14] Turning to singular expressions he takes the extension to be "the individual to which it refers" (40) and the intension to be "the individual concept expressed by it" (41). Finally, following Frege, he takes the extension of a sentence to be its truth value (26), and its intension to be the proposition expressed by it (27).

It is crystal clear from this that in Carnap's "semantical analysis of meaning", he is up to his ears in semantic terms that are not explicitly explained in terms of the use of language or in any other way. These include pretty much the ones we found in C. I. Lewis—'apply' (at least implicitly), 'refer', 'express', and the unspecific 'corresponding'. Last but not least, there is the term 'translation'—implying synonymy, equivalence of meaning—in terms of which the semantic rules of designators are explained. So this is a prime example of hypostatic semantics, without even as much of a (largely implicit) pass at grounding in use that we have in C. I. Lewis. What gives the enterprise such value as it has lies not in a radical account of how to understand meaning, but in its contribution to logic, especially modal logic. More generally, my criticisms of hypostatic semanticists must be tempered by the consideration that many of them may well have been intending not to produce a fundamental account of the nature of meaning, but rather to trace out the semantic structures of various linguistic complexes. But though that motivation is primary for many, it is also true that many, including Lewis and Carnap, do also aim at laying bare the nature of linguistic meaning.

One significant difference of Carnap from Lewis concerns the relative priority of word and sentence. On the one hand, Carnap's rule of truth for atomic sentences presupposes the semantic status of subsentential units, and in that way word semantics is prior. Moreover, like Lewis and like Frege and his numerous followers, he treats the meaning of sentences in terms (intension and extension) that have their basic application to subsentential units. And however useful this may be for semantical foundations of logic, it distorts the understanding of the kind of semantic status that is distinctive of sentences in natural languages, something that is brought out by the IA potential theory. But, on the other hand, extension and intension, taken by Carnap to be his main semantic concepts, are introduced on the basis of the truth, or L-truth, of certain sentences. So in

---

[14] Carnap indicates that other choices would be possible (19). Later in the book he explores the reduction of extensions to intensions. Moreover he is careful to disavow any serious ontological commitment to classes and properties in a robust metaphysical sense of these terms. All this would have to be gone into if I were seriously engaged in Carnapian exegesis. But for present purposes I will concentrate on the initial presentation I have been summarizing. I might add that whatever happens later in the book, it is not without significance that this is the way Carnap introduces his enterprise.

one way we have priority in one direction and in another way priority in the other direction.

ix. Truth-Conditional Approaches

Perhaps the most prominent current approach to meaning takes the truth conditions of sentences as the most basic semantic concept, and seeks to explain other semantic concepts in terms of that. If this could be done, it would answer some of the objections brought above to the likes of Carnap and C. I. Lewis. In particular, it would unambiguously put sentence meaning in the center of the picture. Furthermore, in the eyes of many of its advocates, it would provide a way of grounding semantic statuses that is an alternative to the Use Principle. For, it would seem, truth can be understood apart from a consideration of what speakers *do* with language. What makes a truth-value bearer true is its relation to what it is "about", not anything users of the language do with it. My critical examination will uncover reasons for abandoning this claim of independence of use, as well as reveal other shortcomings of this approach.

This approach to sentence meaning has had many partisans. Here is a small sample.

> ... A knowledge of the truth conditions of a sentence is identical with an understanding of its meaning. (Carnap 1958, 15)
> ... A man understands a sentence insofar as he knows its truth conditions. (Quine 1975, 88)
> ... To give truth conditions is a way of giving the meaning of a sentence. (Davidson 1967, 310).

Much of the recent discussion of truth-condition semantics has centered on Davidson's proposal to employ a Tarski-style definition of truth-in-a-language as a semantic description of a language.[15] If I were to embark on a critical examination of Davidson's theory, along with the exposition of Tarski needed as a background, I would expand the chapter beyond what my publisher will bear. Hence I am going to touch lightly on those features of any truth-condition theory that seem to me to render it ineffective as a general theory of sentence meaning.

An obvious implementation of the above quotations would equate each sentence meaning with a set of conditions for the truth of the sentence "on a reading", the one that gives it that meaning. But this approach is doomed from the start. It faces the crashing difficulty that, in general, a sentence

---

[15] Cf. the definition of 'Davidsonic boom' in *The Philosopher's Lexicon*, a collection of definitions of philosophers' names turned into common nouns, verbs, and adjectives. "Davidsonic boom—the sound made by a research program when it hits Oxford."

as a bearer of meaning in a language (a sentence type) has no particular truth value and so is governed by no conditions for such. What is the truth value of 'She's coming around the mountain'? We can't begin to discuss truth value until we know to whom 'she' refers, which mountain is in question, and at what time this is said to be happening. But the meaning of the sentence in the language doesn't settle these matters. What I just said reflects the phenomenon of the underdetermination of reference by meaning that by now will be all too familiar to readers of this book. This sentence can be used with one and the same meaning to say of any one of innumerable females that she is, at any one of innumerable times, coming around any one of innumerable mountains. And depending on how this all this is rendered determinate in a particular case, we get one or another truth value for the statement thereby made by an utterance of the sentence. Since the sentence itself lacks a truth value while retaining a constant meaning, that meaning cannot be identified with any set of truth conditions.

Philosophers of language managed to ignore this seemingly obvious fact for so long because the logical and mathematical origin of twentieth-century philosophy of language focused their attention on what Quine has called "eternal sentences", those that are not (standardly) used to make different statements in different contexts, like 'A triangle is a three-sided plane rectilinear figure'. For those are the kinds of sentences that are prominent in mathematics. When the developments in the logico-mathematical sphere began to be applied to natural languages, various maneuvers were made to avoid giving up the whole project of truth-conditional semantics. These include (a) taking a sentence to change its truth value, (b) switching from sentence type to sentence token, and (c) Davidson's ploy of construing meaning as a relation between a sentence, a speaker, and a time. But all these moves simply change the subject. The sentence meaning we seek to understand is what a sentence (type) has by virtue of its meaningful constituents and its grammatical structure. It is what is assigned to the sentence by an adequate semantic description of the language. Such a description could not possibly deal with the staggering number of individual sentence tokens or the equally numerous relations between sentences, speakers, and times. And if sentence meaning is to be equated with truth conditions, these cannot be allowed to change while the meaning remains constant. The fact is that it is sentence types whose meaning is dealt with in semantics, while truth value and truth conditions apply to one of the things that sentences are used to issue in speech, namely, statements (assertions).

Then what is the relation of sentence meaning to truth conditions? It is simply that the meaning of a sentence, together with various contextual factors, determines the truth conditions of a statement made by uttering the sentence in a certain context. Something like this approach to the matter has been taken up by various theorists. A good example is David Lewis's "General Semantics" (1972). I will briefly bring out some highlights of this essay both for its way of dealing with truth and sentence meaning and as a further development of some themes in C. I. Lewis and Carnap.

At the base of Lewis's semantical system are three basic grammatical categories—sentence, name, and common noun—and a fundamental, undefined semantic term, 'extension'. He follows Frege in taking the extension of a sentence to be its truth value, the extension of a name to be the thing named, and the extension of a common noun to be the set of things to which it applies. He recognizes that the extension of a meaningful unit depends on the meaning and on other things as well—facts about the world (what cats there are), time and place of utterance, identity of the speaker, the surrounding discourse, and so on. He treats meaning or "intension" as a *function* from the other factors as arguments (called collectively an *index*) to an extension.[16] Thus the intension of a name is a function from an index to things; the intension of a common noun is a function from an index to sets of things; and the intension of a sentence is a function from an index to a truth value, or alternatively, to a set of possible worlds, the set of those in which the sentence is true at that index. And so Lewis, like Davidson, ascribes truth values to sentence types in relation to something(s), but with a wider variety of "somethings". For both, the uniqueness of truth value is sacrificed for the ability to apply it to the same entities as meanings.

Though extension is the more basic notion, it is intension that is the prime candidate for *meaning*. But Lewis recognizes that although it is plausible to regard intension as *being* the meaning of simple units, when it comes to complex units like sentences, this does not cut things finely enough. Most bothersome is the fact that all necessarily true sentences have the same intension; for any such sentence the function yields truth as extension from any index whatever. Hence he follows the lead of C. I. Lewis and Carnap in identifying the meaning of a complex with what he calls "semantically interpreted phrase markers", which are analyses of the complex into its meaningful components with the intension of each component specified.[17]

Another novel feature of the system is how Lewis handles intensions of derived categories in such a way as to increase the centrality of sentences to semantics. These intensions are also treated as functions, but functions from intensions to intensions of larger units to which they contribute, not

[16] Kaplan (1989) effectively criticizes the procedure of lumping all these things together in a single "index" when dealing with indexicals. But his refinements do not affect my discussion of Lewis.

[17] More exactly, since he recognizes that for some purposes this cuts meaning too finely, he offers us a choice between this and intension, one being better for some purposes and another better for other purposes.

from indices to extensions. The process of agglutination continues until we reach sentence intensions. Here is an illustration of the simplest kind. An intransitive verb can be construed as a function from name intension to sentence intension. Thus, as Lewis says, 'grunts' takes a name, for example, 'Porky', and makes a sentence, 'Porky grunts'. That is, the meaning of 'grunts' determines what sentence intension results from combining it with the intension of 'Porky'. Here is a longer route to the sentential terminus. An adjective takes a common noun, for example, 'rose', and makes a noun phrase, 'yellow rose'. The meaning of 'yellow' is such as to take the intension of 'rose' as argument and yield the intension of 'yellow rose'. The meaning of 'the' in turn is a function that takes a noun phrase like 'yellow rose' as argument and yields the intension of a singular referring expression 'the yellow rose'. That intension in turn is a function that takes the intension of a predicative expression like 'is lovely' and yields the intension of a sentence, 'The yellow rose is lovely'. (I forbear building up 'is lovely' from its simple components.) Thus the meanings of nonbasic units are anchored at one end by names and common nouns and at the other end by sentences. Names and common nouns still have a semantic status that is not specified in terms of their contributions to sentence meaning; and it would seem impossible to make a scheme like this work without recognizing some such units. But all other sentential constituents have their meaning specified in terms of the way in which they contribute, through one or more steps, to the meaning of sentences.

In extracting some lessons from this material from D. Lewis for the present discussion, I will first consider to what extent it is subject to the same objections as the positions of C. I. Lewis and Carnap, and then go on to consider it as a version of truth-conditional semantics. As for the former, whereas C. I. Lewis and Carnap introduce the intension and extension of terms by talking of what speakers of the language do with those terms, apparently without being aware that they are doing so, David Lewis brings these matters in quite explicitly. The companion piece to "General Semantics" is entitled "Languages and Language" (1975). There he sets out to explain what it is for a language of the sort described in "General Semantics" to be the language *of a community*. To put it shortly, this is explained as amounting to a convention of truthfulness and trust in the use of the language in question. This is somewhat closer to an account of linguistic meaning in terms of facts about the use of language in a community than we have with C. I. Lewis, Carnap et al., but only somewhat. It does not involve explaining in terms of use what it is for linguistic units *to have meaning*. On the contrary, the account in "General Semantics" is supposed to do that. Any abstract system that conforms to the description given there counts as a (possible) language, that is, a system that is possibly a language spoken in a community. And to lay out the semantics of any language (actual or possible) is to describe it in the terms provided by "General Semantics". That account does not so much as mention what speakers would be doing if they used the language, except insofar as this is implied by talk of what expressions "name" or "apply to".

Hence, in the end, I have to say the same thing about D. Lewis as I did about C. I. Lewis and Carnap. They all leave semantic statuses dangling in the void. They fail to acknowledge any need to explicate them in terms of use, without suggesting any alternative. The way this works out in D. Lewis is that he uses, in "General Semantics", a totally unexplicated concept of extension, and hangs all the rest on that peg, by a series of ingenious moves. Anything that fits the formal structure in the right way constitutes what he calls 'extensions', 'intensions', and so on. But there is nothing in the explanation that ties this down to language, ordinarily so called, much less the semantic side thereof. The formal structure Lewis sets up can be exemplified by an enormous variety of relationships other than those involved in language. Let's say that the "extension" of a married person is that person's in-laws. Then we can think of that person's marital status as a function from mate to extension (i.e., in-laws). This is obviously far from what Lewis had in mind, but in order to explain why it isn't he has to rely on a semantic notion of extension he has done nothing to pin down.

As for truth-conditional semantics, though Lewis does not explicitly present his theory in terms of truth conditions, he clearly construes sentence meaning in terms of truth value, but in a more complex way than the views of the sort I condemned at the beginning of this section. Though a sentence type is assigned a truth value, it has a certain value only relative to an "index", not *überhaupt*. In this way Lewis sticks fairly closely to the tradition of taking sentence types to be true or false, but at the same time recognizes that what truth value a sentence bears (and what the conditions are for this) will vary with various contextual factors. Furthermore, and this is the saving grace, the *meaning* of the sentence is identified not with some particular conditions for truth of the sentence, but rather with a constant function from indices to truth values (and then with the "semantically interpreted phrase structure" that is a refinement of that function). What we have, surprisingly enough, is a close relative of my view that the meaning of a sentence with assertive potential is a determinable illocutionary act potential, each determinate form of which results from a particular one of Lewis's "indices".

x. Attempts to Get Beyond Assertion I

Now I come to what should be the most obvious limitation of truth-value–based theories of sentence meaning—the fact that not all meaningful sentences are susceptible of truth values, even in the derivative way we have found some sentences to be. Sentences usable for making statements can be said to have a truth value relative to what D. Lewis calls an "index". But obviously not all sentences are used (standardly) to make statements; and hence not all of them can be given just this treatment. Consider the following utterances (supply an appropriate index in each case where needed).

1. "Where is the library?"
2. "Please pass the salt."
3. "Let's go to the movies."
4. "Thanks for the lift."
5. "You are acquitted of this charge."
6. "Let me congratulate you on your appointment."

It would make no sense to ask of any of these sentences, even given a context of utterance, whether it is true or false. This being the case, how can anyone suppose that a *general* account of sentence meaning can be given in terms of truth conditions? The answer undoubtedly lies in the kind of occupational bias we have seen to be responsible for many serious errors in the philosophy of language. One who is preoccupied with logic, the logical regimentation of language, or the use of language in theorizing and other intellectual activities, is naturally led to think of language as a device for such pursuits. And so illocutionary acts of the kind I call "assertives" crowd others out of the field of view.

D. Lewis is not unaware of this problem and in his 1972 he bites the bullet by roundly denying that the meanings of sentences fit them for any illocutionary use other than assertion. Here is his way of defending this strongly counterintuitive position.

> A meaning for a sentence, we said initially, was at least that which determines the conditions under which the sentence is true or false. But it is only declarative sentences that can be called true or false in any straightforward way. What of non-declarative sentences: commands, questions, and so on? If these do not have truth-values, as they are commonly supposed not to, we cannot very well say that their meanings determine their truth conditions. (205)

Lewis proposes to cut the Gordian knot in one decisive stroke. Each non-assertive sentence is taken to be a paraphrase of the corresponding "explicit performative", which is then taken as standardly used to make a statement. 'Please close the door' is taken as a paraphrase of 'I request you to close the door', 'Is the door closed?' as a paraphrase of 'I ask you whether the door is closed', and 'The meeting is hereby adjourned' as a paraphrase of 'I declare the meeting adjourned'. The explicit performatives are then taken, contra Austin, as standardly usable to assert that the illocutionary act in question is being performed by the speaker. When I say 'I request you to close the door', I assert that I am requesting you to close the door. These explicit performatives are then given the "General Semantics" treatment in terms of intensions that are functions from indices to truth values. Lewis takes the explicit performative in each case to "underlie" the nondeclarative sentence as deep structure and thereby give the semantics of the "surface" nondeclarative transformation. Thus all sentences are, semantically, assertive in character.

Without minimizing the ingenuity of this approach, I am convinced that it will not wash. (1) I do not agree that explicit performatives are standardly used to assert that a certain illocutionary act is currently being performed by the speaker. Even if I should have occasion to claim that I am now requesting you to close the door, I would do so by saying *that*, that is, by uttering some sentence like 'I am now requesting you to open the door'. To use the explicit performative 'I request you to open the door' to make that assertion is deviant. The usability of the one sentence to make the assertion and the other to make a request exactly mirrors the semantic difference between them. And so the truth conditions of 'I am now requesting you to open the door' do not suffice to bring out the meaning of 'I request you to open the door'.

(2) Explicit performatives are not available for all illocutionary acts and, so, not all nonassertive sentences have corresponding explicit performatives. What is the corresponding explicit performative for 'How disgusting!'? Saying 'I express disgust at that' is not a way of expressing disgust or of asserting that I am doing so. The view does not cover the whole territory.

(3) But the most crucial flaw is this. Lewis acknowledges that 'I order you to close the door', as well as 'Close the door', is usable to order someone to close the door as well as to assert that one is issuing that order. But it follows from his theory that the former potential, unlike the latter one, is extrasemantic; that it is not by virtue of meaning what it does that the sentence is usable to issue that order. But sentence meaning is not so constricted. It is as much a part of knowing the language to be able to tell what kind of *order* 'Close the door' is standardly used to issue as it is to be able to tell what kind of *statement* 'The door is closed' is standardly used to make. Nor does this knowledge have to do with nonsemantic aspects of language. The fact that 'Close the door' is usable to issue an order with a certain content is as much a resultant of the meanings of its constituents and the way they are put together as is the fact that 'The door is closed' is usable to make a statement with a certain content.

Lewis tries to neutralize the implausibility of his position by analogizing it to cases in which the usability of a sentence to do something is clearly nonsemantic in its provenance.

> I agree that there are two alternative uses of this and other performative sentences: the genuinely performative use and the non-performative self-

descriptive use. . . . It still does not follow that there are two meanings. Compare the case of these two sentences.

I am talking in trochaic hexameter.

In hexameter trochaic am I talking.

The latter can be used to talk in trochaic hexameter and is true on any occasion of its correctly accented utterance. The former cannot be so used and is false on any occasion of its correctly accented utterance. Yet the two sentences are obviously paraphrases. Whether a sentence can be used to talk in trochaic hexameter is not a matter of its meaning. (211)

Lewis clearly has the right diagnosis of this case. But the fact that there are differences in use that are not semantic has no tendency to show that the one in question is of that sort. With disarming candor, Lewis admits this.

The distinction between using a sentence to talk in trochaic hexameter or not so using it is one sort of distinction; the distinction between using a performative sentence performatively and using it self-descriptively is quite another sort. Still I think the parallel is instructive. A distinction in uses need not involve a distinction in meanings of the sentences used. (211)

True enough; it need not. But with 'Close the door' and 'I am ordering you to close to door", I would say, it clearly does. Lewis ends this paragraph by saying: "I see no decisive reason to insist that there is any distinction in meanings associated with the difference between performative and self-descriptive uses of performative sentences, if the contrary assumption is theoretically convenient." But, as I see it, there is such a decisive reason: the strong linguistic intuition of a difference in meaning. To be sure, as I said above, I don't even agree that there is a self-descriptive use of explicit performatives. But even if I did, I would need far stronger reasons than Lewis has advanced to give up the seemingly obvious fact that the semantic structure of 'Close the door' renders it usable to issue an order with a certain content.

Many other theorists, while recognizing that not all sentences can be treated in terms of truth values, restrict themselves to sentences with assertive potential, giving only a passing reference to the further task of extending the treatment to other sentences (Dummett 1991, 114–121; Barwise and Perry 1983, 118–119). There are also less Procrustean ways of starting with some kind of truth-conditions account of assertions and moving from that to other IA types, less Procrustean because they do not deny that these other IA potentials are provided by meaning. These attempts use the treatment of assertive sentences as a model for analyzing the meaning of all others. But even here the assertoric bias is evident.

The most obvious way of generalizing the account of assertive sentences exploits the point that all sentences can be said to express propositions.

(In my approach this is derivative from the fact that all sentences have illocutionary act potentials, and illocutionary acts involve both propositional content and illocutionary force.) Thus an utterance of 'Please close the door' may be said to express the proposition that a certain door is closed. An utterance of 'I promise to read your paper by tomorrow' may be said to express the proposition that a certain paper is read by a certain person by the day after the utterance. These propositions are as much expressed by these sentences as the proposition that arsenic is poisonous is expressed by the sentence 'Arsenic is poisonous', even though only the latter "explicitly presents" the proposition. This suggests switching the truth-conditions account from the sentence (or statement it can be used to make) to the proposition expressed. Since all sentences express propositions, truth conditions can be associated with every sentence in this way. The meaning of 'Please close the door' can then be given by the truth conditions of the proposition that the door in question is closed.

The inadequacy of this treatment is obvious on the face of it. If we take several sentences that express the same proposition but have different illocutionary act potentials, it can be seen that, contrary to the present account, they have significantly different meanings. Thus consider:

1. 'The door is closed.'
2. 'Is the door closed?'
3. 'Please close the door.'
4. 'I promise to close the door.'
5. 'Would that the door is closed!'
(Assume the same context of utterance in each case.)

These sentences are by no means synonymous. One who sought to ask whether the door is closed by saying 'The door is closed' or 'Please close the door' would rightly be taken to be deficient in her grasp of (the semantics of) English. From the standpoint of my theory, the trouble here is that the meaning of the sentence has been identified with the propositional content expressed, leaving out the illocutionary force.

A number of theorists, recognizing this complexity but still starting with an account of the propositional content aspect of sentence meaning in terms of truth values, have proposed to add to that an account of illocutionary force. This is often done in terms of rules for the correct utterance of sentences, and in that respect these views are similar to my own. I will briefly consider two such treatments.

In Stenius 1967 he treats what he calls 'sentence radicals' such as 'that John lives here now' in terms of truth value in the spirit of Carnap. The above sentence radical is true just in case what 'John' denotes has the property denoted by 'lives here now'. He then recognizes that the same sentence radical can occur in indicative, imperative, and interrogative sentences:

1. John lives here now.
2. John, live here now!
3. Does John live here now?

Since these sentences are not wholly equivalent in meaning, there must be more to their meaning than the meaning of the sentence radical. The difference comes in what Stenius calls 'mood' and what I have been calling 'illocutionary force'. His treatment of this is in terms of rules for permissible utterance, developed in terms of a Wittgensteinian language game. If we adapt his formulation to natural language sentences, here is a "report rule" for 1. and a "command rule" for 2.

Report rule. (for speaker) Utter 1. or not depending on whether what 'John' denotes has the property that 'lives here now' denotes.

Command rule. (for addressee, John) Make it the case that you have the property denoted by 'lives here now'.

The report rule requires the truth of what is asserted as a necessary condition of permissible utterance. Thus it is equivalent to one aspect of my I-rule governing an assertion that p, namely, the requirement that p. The command rule, on the other hand, amounts to a rule of compliance on the part of the addressee, something that is absent from my purely speaker-oriented account.[18]

I find two major defects in this account. First, it shares with hypostatic theories a treatment of the propositional content aspect of a sentence in terms of unexplicated, dangling semantic terms like 'denote'. Second, it is severely restricted in the range of illocutionary forces it covers. In the article under discussion only assertions and commands are dealt with. And the sketchy suggestions for extension do not sound promising. For example, at the end of the essay he indicates that he thinks that "performatives" could be treated like utterances in a play, as "feigned" illocutionary acts of some other sort!

In Pollock 1982 we find a view similar to Stenius in broad outline, but considerably more elaborated. The account of propositional content is similar to Lewis 1972, taking that aspect of the meaning of a sentence

---

[18] In sec. xxiii Stenius considers the possibility of a command rule for speakers but declines to bring it into the account.

to be a function from what he calls "pragmatic parameters" (Lewis's "index") to a proposition, instead of Lewis's truth value (7).[19] This function Pollock calls an "S-intension". Through most of the book Pollock talks as if the meaning of a sentence is just its S-intension. But in Chapter 12 he recognizes that sentences like Stenius's triad mentioned above can have the same S-intension (propositional content) but not exactly the same meaning. Thus he winds up taking sentence meaning to be a conjunction of S-intension and illocutionary force, the latter of which Pollock calls "speech act potential" (254).

Like Stenius, Pollock takes different kinds of speech acts to be defined by rules for sentence utterance. To *state* is to utter a sentence with a prima facie obligation to conform to the rules for stating (242). These include a rule of sincerity (roughly, do not utter the sentence unless you justifiably believe the proposition expressed) and a "Gricean" rule (do not utter a sentence unless you are trying to bring the members of your audience to believe the proposition expressed if they do not already) (244–245).[20] Other types of speech acts are distinguished by being governed by other sets of rules. To request is to utter an appropriate sentence with a prima facie obligation to conform to "rogative" rules (260). Rogative rules makes sentences usable to make requests subject to a requirement that one not utter the sentence unless (1) one wants the proposition expressed by the sentence to be true and (2) one is trying to bring it about that the hearer, H, bring it about that the proposition is true (261). These rules parallel the rules for stating: the rule of sincerity and the "Gricean" rule.

As far as the second objection to Stenius (insufficient coverage) is concerned, Pollock does better. He provides different analyses for requests, commands, yes-no questions, and wh-questions as well as for statements. And yet this merely scratches the surface. We are still without any account of commissives, expressives, or exercitives. And only a few types of directives have been distinguished, while the territory of assertives remains completely unexplored.

Thus views like that of Stenius and Pollock are subject to two main objections. First, in their non-speech-act–based account of propositional content they are in the same boat as hypostatic theories in leaving basic semantic terms dangling in the air, rather than rooting them in facts about the use of language. Second, they fail to provide resources for all the distinctions between illocutionary act types and all the distinctions between sentence meaning that constitute potentials for different illocutionary act types. Whereas my IA potential theory of sentence meaning is free of both defects. I take the first objection to be ineluctable for any view that tries to

[19] Pollock's view is complicated by a distinction between propositions and statements (in the sense of what is stated). I will not be able to go into that here.
[20] Note that what is required for stating is not that one have such an intention but only that one put oneself under an obligation to have it.

handle the propositional content aspect of sentence meaning apart from IA potential. But all we can say against Stenius and Pollock with respect to the second objection is that they have failed to provide resources sufficient for making all the needed distinctions. That would be a weak argument for the conclusion that this can't be done by any such theory. And there is a treatment in the field that does avoid the second objection, while still being subject to the first. That is the one developed in Vanderveken 1990.

xi. Attempts to Get Beyond Assertion II

Vanderveken's overall conception of sentence meaning is similar to mine: ". . . the meaning of an elementary sentence in a semantic interpretation will be that function which gives as value for each possible context of utterance, the elementary speech act which consists of the illocutionary force and the propositional content expressed respectively in that context by the marker and the clause of that sentence" (47). Thus he takes sentence meaning to be illocutionary act potential. The difference at this point is that whereas I identify each sentence meaning with a single illocutionary act type, often very generic, which then gets realized in many more specific forms, Vanderveken identifies the meaning with a function from utterance contexts to maximally specific illocutionary act types. There is a simple translation from one of these formulations to the other.

Vanderveken handles propositional content in terms of truth conditions in a roughly Fregean way. Thus he too is guilty of leaving many basic semantic concepts without any explication. But he develops resources for making indefinitely many distinctions between illocutionary act types. He does this by using six of the twelve dimensions of variation spelled out by Searle in 1979.

1. Illocutionary point (including direction of fit)
2. Mode of achievement of 1.
3. Propositional content conditions
4. Preparatory conditions
5. Sincerity conditions
6. Degree of strength. (105–121)

Dimensions 4. and 5. are familiar from the discussion of Searle's 1969 analysis of promising in Chapter 3. Preparatory conditions are the ones I take to be presupposed in an illocutionary act (such as the capacity of an addressee to do what he is requested to do). Sincerity conditions have to do with what psychological states are expressed by an act, such as belief for an assertion and interest in H's doing A for a request. Dimension 3. has to do with what sort of proposition is expressed (for example, a proposition attributing a future act to the speaker in a promise). Dimension 6. primarily has to do with the strength of psychological states expressed in 5. (for example, the firmness of belief expressed). But 1. and 2. deserve further explanation.

Here is Vanderveken's explanation of 1.

In the performance of an elementary speech act, the speaker always relates in a certain way the propositional content to the world of the utterance so as to determine a direction of fit between language and the world. If . . . the speaker makes an assertion or a report, the point of his utterance is to represent how things are, and the propositional content of the speech act is supposed to match a state of affairs . . . in the world. Such utterances have the words-to-world direction of fit. If, on the other hand, a speaker makes a request or gives advice, the point of his utterance is not to say how things are, but to try to get the hearer to act in such a way that his behavior in the world matches the propositional content of the speech act. Such utterances have the world-to-words direction of fit.

The illocutionary point is the principal component of illocutionary force because it determines the *direction of fit* of utterances with that force. A speaker who performs an illocutionary act may have all sorts of other intentions and perlocutionary purposes. . . . But he always has at least the intention to achieve the illocutionary point on the propositional content, because that point is the purpose which is essential to the type of speech act that he performs.

. . . There are five and only five basic illocutionary points of utterances. These are:

the *assertive point* which consists in representing as actual a state of affairs;

the *commissive point* which consists in committing the speaker to a future course of action;

the *directive point* which consists in making an attempt to get the hearer to do something;

the *declarative point* which consists in performing an action which brings into existence a state of affairs by representing oneself as performing that action;[21] and the *expressive point* which consists of expressing propositional attitudes of the speaker about a state of affairs. (104–105)

Vanderveken also, following Searle 1983, distinguishes *conditions of success* and *conditions of satisfaction* (129–134). The former simply consists in succeeding in performing an illocutionary act of the type in question. The latter is tied to the notion of direction of fit. Those with the words-to-world direction, assertives, are satisfied *iff* the propositional content is true

---

[21] This covers the same territory as my *exercitives*.

(133). Of those with world-to-words direction, commissives are satisfied *iff* the speaker does what he thereby commits himself to do, and directives are satisfied *iff* the addressee does what he is "directed" to do. Declaratives (exercitives) are said to have a double direction of fit. They are satisfied *iff* the speaker produces the conventional effect in question (world-to-words) by way of representing himself as producing that effect (words-to-world) (133).[22] Strangely enough Vanderveken and Searle take expressives to have an "empty" direction of fit (134). If I were using this scheme I would say that the direction is words-to-world, and that an expressive is satisfied *iff* the speaker actually has the attitude expressed.

It is clear that this scheme differs in important respects from mine, particularly concerning the illocutionary point and conditions of success. Most saliently, whereas I take the actual production of a conventional effect in commissives and, especially, in exercitives to be over and above the illocutionary act performance, which simply consists in "purporting" to do so, these theorists build this production into the conditions of success for such illocutionary acts. (See the discussion of this issue in 4.3–4.5.) Another important difference consists in the perlocutionary attempt that is said to be the essential condition for directives. For reasons given in the discussion of Schiffer in Chapter 2, I do not agree that one cannot succeed in performing a directive without making an attempt to get the hearer to do something. My "hopeless" cases in 2.5 illustrate this. When I order my son to do his homework without having any hope whatsoever that he will do it, I could not be said to be attempting to get him to do anything, but I issued an order nonetheless. Finally, for assertives the "point" is simply the IA, the whole package, rather than some feature in terms it can be best understood. To "represent as actual the state of affairs of Jim's being tall" is just a long-winded way of saying "asserting that Jim is tall".

Thus Vanderveken's theory, although it avoids many of the defects of its predecessors in this chapter, is still subject to two major objections. (1) The account of illocutionary force is subject to various difficulties in detail, such as those just enumerated. (2) The account of propositional content makes use of semantic concepts unanchored in the use of language.

xii. Conclusion

I have surveyed a number of theories of sentence meaning that are different from mine. And I have pointed out in each case defects that are absent from my IA potential theory. Insofar as my selection is representative of the most important alternatives, I take it that this provides strong confirmation of my approach to sentence meaning.

---

[22] Unlike the words-to-world condition of satisfaction for assertives, it is not required that this representation be true.

Appendix

In listing these items I will indicate in each case the section of the book in which each first occurs.

Definitions and Other Explanations of the Meanings of Terms

D1. *Sentential act concept*—a concept the application of which to a person makes explicit what sentence he uttered. (1.7)

D2. *Illocutionary act concept*—a concept the application of which to a person makes explicit the "content" of her utterance. Alternatively, it is a concept the application of which to a person constitutes an *oratio obliqua* report. (1.7)

D3. *Perlocutionary act concept*—a concept the application of which to a person makes explicit some effect his utterance had on his audience. (1.7)

D4. *Sentential act concept*—a concept the application of which to a person makes explicit what sentence he uttered, or what subsentential unit he uttered as elliptical for a sentence, or what sentence surrogate he produced. (1.7)

D5. In uttering S, U R'd that p—In uttering S, U knowingly took on a liability to (lay herself open to) blame (censure, reproach, being taken to task, being called to account), in case of not-p. (3.2)

D6. In uttering S, U R'd that p—In uttering S, U recognized herself to be rightfully subject to blame, etc., in case of not-p. (3.2)

D7. In uttering S, U R'd that p—In uttering S, U knowingly took on a liability to being incorrect (wrong, out of order) in case of not-p. (3.4)

D8. In uttering S, U R'd that p—In uttering S, U subjected his utterance to a rule that implies in application to this case that it is permissible for U to utter S only if p. (3.5)

D9. In uttering S, U R's that p—In uttering S, U represents p as being the case. (3.5)

D10. In uttering S, U R's that p—In uttering S, U purports to know that p. (3.5)

D11. I is the matching illocutionary act type for sentence meaning M *iff* I is the most inclusive type such that a sentence with meaning M can be used to perform tokens of I just by virtue of having that meaning. (6.8)

D12. I is the matching illocutionary act type for sentence meaning M *iff* I is the most inclusive type such that an addressee, just by knowing that U is uttering a sentence with meaning M and intends to be communicating, can thereby know that U intends to be performing a token of I. (6.8)

D13. I is the matching illocutionary act type for sentence meaning M *iff* I is the most inclusive type such that an addressee, just by knowing that U is uttering a sentence with meaning M and intends to be making a straightforward, direct use of that sentence, can thereby know that U intends to be performing a token of I. (6.8)

Principles

I. Illocutionary acts presuppose sentential acts, but not vice versa. (1.7)

II. Perlocutionary acts presuppose sentential acts, but not vice versa. (1.8)

III. Perlocutionary acts *may* be based on illocutionary acts, but not vice versa. (1.8)

IV. An expression's having a certain meaning consists in its being usable to play a certain role (to do certain things) in communication. (6.2)

IVGA. The fact that an expression has a certain meaning *supervenes* on (is determined by, is a function of) what users of the language do with it. (The semantics of a *language* supervenes on facts about *speech*.) (9.2)

IVGB. An expression's having a certain meaning *consists* in its being usable by speakers to do certain things. (9.2)

V. A sentence's having a certain meaning consists in its being usable to perform illocutionary acts of a certain type. (6.4)

VI. Sentence meaning is illocutionary act potential. (6.4)

VII. What it is for a sentence to have a certain meaning is for it to be usable to perform illocutionary acts of the matching type (that is, to have the matching illocutionary act potential). (6.8)

VIII. For any illocutionary act type there is a certain sentence meaning (the matching sentence meaning for that illocutionary act type) such that a sentence's being usable to perform an illocutionary act of that type is its having that meaning. (6.8)

IX. A sentence's having a certain illocutionary act potential consists in its being subject to a certain illocutionary rule. (7.1)

X. A sentence's having a certain meaning consists in its being subject to a certain illocutionary rule. (7.1)

XI. A sentence's having a certain meaning consists in its being subject to a certain rule or convention. (7.2)

Axioms of Meaning

A1. A fluent speaker of a language ipso facto knows the meanings of many of the expressions of that language. (6.1)

A2. The fact that an expression has a certain meaning is what enables it to play a distinctive role (enables it to be used in a distinctive way) in communication. (6.1)

A3. Knowledge of the meaning of the sentence uttered is the linguistic knowledge a hearer needs in order to understand what is being said. (6.1)

A4. The meaning of a sentence is a function of the meanings of its constituents plus relevant facts about its structure. (6.1)

A5. Reference is, usually, only partly determined by meaning. (6.1)

A6. The truth conditions of a statement are at least partly determined by the meaning(s) of the sentence used to make that statement. (6.1)

A7. A linguistic expression means what it does by virtue of being governed by a rule or convention. (7.2)

Schemata of Analysis for Illocutionary Act Types

Exercitives

U O'd in uttering S (where 'O' is a term for purporting to be producing a particular conventional effect, E) *iff* in uttering S, U R'd that:

1. Conceptually necessary conditions for E are satisfied.
2. U has the authority to produce E.
3. Conditions are appropriate for the exercise of that authority.
4. By uttering S, U is bringing about E. (4.3)

Commissives

U C'd in uttering T (where 'C' is a term for a commissive illocutionary act type, a purporting to produce an obligation on U to do D) *iff* in uttering S, U R'd that:

1. Conceptually necessary conditions for U's being obliged to do D are satisfied.
2. H has some interest in U's doing D.
3. U intends to do D.
4. By uttering S, U places herself under an obligation to do D. (4.4)

Directives

U D'd in uttering S (where 'D' is a term for some directive illocutionary act type, a purporting to be producing a certain kind of obligation on H to do D) *iff* in uttering S, U R'd that:

1. Conceptually necessary conditions for the existence of the obligation are satisfied. (These include such things as that it is possible for H to do D, that D has not already been done, etc.)
2. Circumstances of the utterance of S are appropriate for the production of the obligation in question. (This includes the appropriate authority for orders, the right kind of interpersonal relationship for requests, etc.)
3. By uttering S, U lays on H a (stronger or weaker) obligation to do D.
4. U utters S in order to get H to do D. (4.5)

Expressives

U expressed a P (some psychological state) in uttering S *iff* in uttering S, U R'd that U has a P. (4.6)

Assertives

U E's that p (where 'E' is a term for a mode of asserting that p) in uttering S *iff*
A. U R's that:
1. p
2. One or more further conditions as indicated above, these conditions differing for different E's.
B. S explicitly presents the proposition that p, or S is uttered as elliptical for a sentence that does explicitly present the proposition that p. (5.5)

Bibliography

Alston, William P. 1963a. "Meaning and Use." *Philosophical Quarterly* 13: 107–124.
———. 1963b. "The Quest for Meanings." *Mind* 72: 79–87.
———. 1964a. *Philosophy of Language.* Englewood Cliffs, N.J.: Prentice-Hall.
———. 1964b. "Linguistic Acts." *American Philosophical Quarterly* 1: 1–9.
———. 1965. "Expressing." In *Philosophy in America*, edited by Max Black, 15–34. Ithaca: Cornell University Press.
———. 1971a. "How Does One Tell Whether a Word Has One, Several, or Many Senses?" In *Semantics: An Interdisciplinary Reader in Philosophy, Linguistics, and Psychology*, edited by Danny D. Steinberg and Leon A. Jakobovits, 269–284. Cambridge: Cambridge University Press.
———. 1971b. "Dispositions and Occurrences." *Canadian Journal of Philosophy* 1: 125–154.
———. 1974. "Semantic Rules." In *Semantics and Philosophy*, edited by Milton K. Munitz and Peter K. Unger, 17–48. New York: New York University Press.
———. 1977. "Sentence Meaning and Illocutionary Act Potential." *Philosophical Exchange* 2: 17–35.
———. 1980a. "Level Confusions in Epistemology." *Midwest Studies in Philosophy* 5: 135–150.
———. 1980b. "The Bridge between Semantics and Pragmatics." In *The Signifying Animal*, edited by Irmengard Rauch and Gerald Carr, 123–134. Bloomington: Indiana University Press.
———. 1980c. "Irreducible Metaphors in Theology." In *Experience, Reason, and God*, edited by Eugene T. Long, 129–148. Washington, D.C.: Catholic University Press.
———. 1987. "Matching Illocutionary Act Types." In *On Being and Saying*, edited by Judith Jarvis Thomson, 151–163. Cambridge: MIT Press.

———. 1991. "Searle on Illocutionary Acts." In *John Searle and His Critics*, edited by Ernest Lepore and Robert Van Gulick, 57–80. Oxford: Basil Blackwell.

———. 1994. "Illocutionary Acts and Linguistic Meaning." In *Foundations of Speech Act Theory: Philosophical and Linguistic Perspectives*, edited by Savas L. Tsohatzidis, 29–49. London: Routledge.

———. 1996a. *A Realist Conception of Truth*. Ithaca: Cornell University Press.

———. 1996b. "Truth and Sentence Meaning." In *Man, Meaning, and Morality*, edited by R. Balasubramanian and Ramashanker Misra, 91–110. New Delhi: Indian Council of Philosophical Research.

Armstrong, David M. 1968. *A Materialist Theory of the Mind*. London: Routledge & Kegan Paul.

———. 1971. "Meaning and Communication." *Philosophical Review* 80: 427–447.

Austin, J. L. 1962. *How to Do Things with Words*. Oxford: Clarendon Press.

Bach, Kent. 1994. "Semantic Slack: What Is Said and More." In Tsohatzidis 1994.

Barwise, John, and John Perry. 1983. *Situations and Attitudes*. Cambridge: MIT Press.

Bealer, George. 1982. *Quality and Concept*. Oxford: Clarendon Press.

Bennett, Jonathan. 1976. *Linguistic Behaviour*. Cambridge: Cambridge University Press.

Black, Max. 1962. *Models and Metaphors*. Ithaca: Cornell University Press.

Brandom, Robert. 1994. *Making It Explicit*. Cambridge: Harvard University Press.

Carnap, Rudolf. 1935. *Philosophy and Logical Syntax*. London: Kegan, Paul, Trench, Trubner.

———. 1942. *Introduction to Semantics*. Cambridge: Harvard University Press.

———. 1947. *Meaning and Necessity*. Chicago: University of Chicago Press.

———. 1958. *Introduction to Symbolic Logic and Its Applications*. New York: Dover.

Cohen, L. Jonathan. 1964. "Do Illocutionary Forces Exist?" *Philosophical Quarterly* 14: 118–137.

Davidson, Donald. 1967. "Truth and Meaning." *Synthese* 17: 304–323.

———. 1980. *Essays on Actions and Events*. Oxford: Clarendon Press.

Dennett, Daniel C. 1982. "Beyond Belief." In *Thought and Object*, edited by Andrew Woodfield, 1–95. Oxford: Clarendon Press.

———, ed. 1987. *The Philosophical Lexicon*. Newark, Delaware: American Philosophical Association.

Donnellan, Keith. 1966. "Reference and Definite Descriptions." *Philosophical Review* 75: 281–304.

Dummett, Michael. 1973. *Frege: Philosophy of Language*. London: Duckworth.

———. 1991. *The Logical Basis of Metaphysics*. Cambridge: Harvard University Press.

Goldman, Alvin. 1970. *A Theory of Human Action*. Englewood Cliffs, N.J.: Prentice-Hall.

Grice, Paul. 1957. "Meaning." *Philosophical Review* 66: 377–388. Reprinted in Grice 1989.

———. 1968. "Utterer's Meaning, Sentence-Meaning, and Word-Meaning." *Foundations of Language* 4: 225–248. Reprinted in Grice 1989.

———. 1969. "Utterer's Meaning and Intentions." *Philosophical Review* 78: 144–177. Reprinted in Grice 1989.

———. 1989. *Studies in the Way of Words*. Cambridge: Harvard University Press.

Kaplan, David. 1989. "Demonstratives." In *Themes from Kaplan*, edited by Joseph Almong, John Perry, and Howard Wettstein, 481–563. New York: Oxford University Press.

Katz, J. J. 1966. *Philosophy of Language*. New York: Harper & Row.

Katz, J. J., and Jerry A. Fodor. 1963. "The Structure of a Semantic Theory." *Language* 39: 170–210.

Koestler, Arthur. 1968. *The Ghost in the Machine.* New York: Macmillan.

Lewis, C. I. 1946. *An Analysis of Knowledge and Valuation.* La Salle, Ill.: Open Court.

Lewis, David. 1969. *Convention.* Cambridge: Harvard University Press.

——. 1972. "General Semantics." In *Semantics of Natural Language*, edited by Donald Davidson and Gilbert Harman, 169–218. Dordrecht: Reidel. Reprinted in Lewis 1983.

——. 1975. "Languages and Language." In *Language, Mind, and Knowledge*, edited by Keith Gunderson, 3–35. Minneapolis: University of Minnesota Press. Reprinted in Lewis 1983.

——. 1983. *Philosophical Papers*, vol. 1. New York: Oxford University Press.

Loar, Brian. 1981. *Mind and Meaning.* Cambridge: Cambridge University Press.

Locke, John. 1975. *An Essay Concerning Human Understanding*, edited by Peter H. Nidditch. Oxford: Clarendon Press.

McKeon, Richard, editor. 1941. *The Basic Works of Aristotle.* New York: Random House.

Moore, G. E. 1962. *The Commonplace Book.* London: George Allen & Unwin.

Pollock, John. 1982. *Language and Thought.* Princeton: Princeton University Press.

Quine, Willard Van Orman. 1975. "Mind and Verbal Dispositions." In *Mind and Language*, edited by Samuel Guttenplan, 83–95. Oxford: Clarendon Press.

Ruby, Lionel. 1950. *Logic: An Introduction.* Chicago: Lippincott.

Russell, Bertrand. 1903. *The Principles of Mathematics.* Cambridge: Cambridge University Press.

——. 1919. *Introduction to Mathematical Philosophy.* London: George Allen & Unwin.

——. 1956. *Logic and Knowledge*, edited by Robert Charles Marsh. London: George Allen & Unwin.

Ryle, Gilbert. 1957. "The Theory of Meaning." In *British Philosophy in the Mid-Century*, edited by C. A. Mace, 239–264. New York: Macmillan.

——. 1961. "Use, Usage, and Meaning." *Proceedings of the Aristotelian Society*, Supplement 35: 223–230.

Schiffer, Stephen R. 1972. *Meaning.* Oxford: Clarendon Press.

——. 1987. *Remnants of Meaning.* Cambridge: MIT Press.

Schlick, Moritz. 1936. "Meaning and Verification." *Philosophical Review* 45: 339–369.

Searle, John. 1968. "Austin on Locutionary and Illocutionary Acts." *Philosophical Review* 77: 405–424.

——. 1969. *Speech Acts.* Cambridge: Cambridge University Press.

——. 1979. *Expression and Meaning.* Cambridge: Cambridge University Press.

——. 1983. *Intentionality.* Cambridge: Cambridge University Press.

Stampe, Dennis W. 1968. "Toward a Grammar of Meaning." *Philosophical Review* 77: 137–174.

Stenius, Erik. 1967. "Mood and Language Game." *Synthese* 17: 254–280.

Strawson, P. F. 1950. "On Referring." *Mind* 59: 320–344. Reprinted in Strawson 1971.

——. 1971. *Logico-Linguistic Papers.* London: Methuen.

Tormey, Alan. 1971. *The Concept of Expression.* Princeton: Princeton University Press.

Tsohatzidis, Savas L., editor. 1994. *Foundations of Speech Act Theory.* London: Routledge.

Vanderveken, Daniel. 1990. *Meaning and Speech Acts*. Cambridge: Cambridge University Press.

von Wright, Georg Henrik. 1971. *Explanation and Understanding*. Ithaca: Cornell University Press.

Wolterstorff, Nicholas. 1980. *Works and Worlds of Art*. Oxford: Clarendon Press.

Index

Kant, Immanuel, 286
Kaplan, David, 221–22, 298
Katz, Jerrold, 193, 196–97, 199–200
Knowledge, 56
  of meaning, 149, 152–53
  purported, 63
Koestler, Arthur, 197
Kripke, Saul, 215

Language, 28
  artificial, 285, 293
  formal, 293, 297, 301
  learning, 267–68
  private, 156
  recursive structure of, 268, 281
  requirements for, 155–56
  semantic description of, 148
  used in communication, 155
  as vehicle of thought, 277
Laws, 83
Lewis, C. I., 290–93, 295–96,
    298–300
Lewis, David, 124, 165–66, 195, 197,
    251, 262–64, 298–303
Literal speech, 203, 223, 238, 251,
    266. *See also* Figurative speech
Linguistic output, 51–53
Linguistics, 283–84
Linguistic type, 148
Linguistic token, 148
Loar, Brian, 163
Locke, John, 163, 278–79, 287–88
Locutionary acts, 17, 25. *See also*
    Phatic acts; Phonetic acts;
    Rhetic acts; Sentential acts
Logically proper names, 209, 225

Meaning
  axioms of, 149–51
  and communication, 152, 157
  concept of, 147–52
  entitative treatment of, 154
  knowledge of, 282
  modes of, 291

ontology of, 147, 152, 162, 283,
    285
  ordinary meaning of, 153
  and reference, 152, 282, 290
  referential theory of, 289–96
  sense ___, 291
  senses of, 148
  speaker ___, 37–40, 43, 148,
      249–50, 282, 287–88
  supervenes on speech, 276
  of words, 272–74
  See also Semantics; Sentence mean-
      ing; Theories of meaning
Metalanguage, 294
Metaphor, 185, 233–24
  involves definite illocutionary act or
      not, 233
  literal paraphrase of, 233
Method of discovery, 153
Monologue, 44–45
Mood, 305
Moore, G. E., 116
Morris, Charles, 197
Multivocality, 80, 148, 151, 164, 175,
    188–89, 202, 204–7, 213, 238

Names, 289, 292, 298. *See also* Proper
    names
Natural facts, 83
Non-illocutionary act uses of sen-
    tences, 80, 137, 186, 201–2
Normativity, 59, 71, 84, 100, 105, 142
Normative distinctions, 194
Normative effects, 81. *See also* Con-
    ventional effects; Conventional
    facts
Normative stance, 71
Normative state of affairs, 55, 58, 62
Norms, 58

Objections, 55
Obligations, 84, 96–97
  disjunctive, 100–101
  objective, 60